Gutenberg

The Master Printer

ALSO BY MARY E. GEKLER

Johannes Gutenberg:
Father of Printing

Gutenberg

The Master Printer

Mary E. Gekler

MG Publications

Oak Park, Illinois

Printed in United States of America

TO THEA

Types to they that
be of the Craft are
as thing that be
Alive, and he is
an ill worker who
handleth them
not gently and
with Reverence.

Cover Design by Egon Ungar
Illustrations by Paul Brinkman Klein

TABLE OF CONTENTS

ACKNOWLEDGEMENTS

So many people have given their help and encouragement to me over the years, it is difficult to single out those who have helped me the most with this long and involved Gutenberg project. Some have died since the work began but continue to shower blessings which have finally resulted in the publication of this book.

The late Fr. Irenaeus Herscher, O.F.M. librarian emeritus of St. Bonaventure University, New York, was my most faithful correspondent, advisor and friend. We met in 1968 when Professor Aloys Ruppel of Mainz was given an honorary degree by the University during the Fifth Centenary of Gutenberg's death. Father introduced me to Franciscans in Strasbourg who showed me the city. In Rome, I met the late Fr. Robert Prentice, O.F.M. professor of history, Pontificio Ateneo Antoniano. Fr. Robert later read my various research papers and offered valuable assistance in many areas.

At Rosary College, River Forest, Illinois, much closer to home, I was privileged to have the late Sr. Winifred Mary Carmody, O.P., as a consultant. Sister was professor of paleography and incunabula, could read Vulgate Latin as easily as English, and shared many of the hours I spent in this library.

In all, I visited eleven libraries in the United States and Europe, including the Library of Congress, Washington, D.C.; Newberry Library, Chicago; Gutenberg-Museum, Mainz; Archives et Bibliothèque, Strasbourg; the Vatican Library, Rome; and the Bibliothèque Nationale, Paris. In Munich I was able to examine the Constance Missal, which was at the Haus der Kulturinstitute at that time.

I am greatly indebted to F. Joseph Fuchs, archiviste de la Ville de Strasbourg, for his generous giving of time and talent. His knowledge of source material and where to find it was invaluable.

To the late Professor-Dr. Ruppel of Johannes-Gutenberg University and founder of the Gutenberg-Museum, Ich gebe meine Herzlichen Grüsse und vielen Dänk for his inspiration and kindness. His wife and daughter have become my dear friends.

My editor, Irene Sunny Jepson, deserves special thanks for her many trips to Chicago and excellent help with presentation of material. And I am most grateful to Max Plaut for his scholarly input of historical material which strengthened the research underlying the story.

To Anne M. Johnston and Marjorie Blazek, my typists, my deepest appreciation for giving their own time to copying the manuscript on a word processor and printer, and making the discs from which type was set by computer for this book. It is particularly fitting that Gutenberg's story should be the beneficiary of the newest 20th century printing technology.

Lastly, to the late Leland J. Arms of San Francisco, whose interest in the enigmatic Master Gutenberg led me to what has become a lifetime avocation, I hope he would be pleased with the results of my study and this book, representing as it does a dream fulfilled for both of us.

Deo gratias!

EXPLANATION OF PRINTING TERMS 1450/1991

Books today are divided into signatures for publication purposes, each signature containing 16 pages, comprised of four 4-page forms nested and folded once through the center. A book of 136 pages, for example, would contain eight 16-page signatures and two-4 page forms. All books must have total pages numbering in multiples of four, or which can be divided by four.

In Gutenberg's time, signatures were called "quires" composed of four sheets, a "quaier" or "quaterna" meaning four. A sheet was half a calfskin. One sheet was two "folios;" one folio was two pages. A single page was indicated as folio a or folio b. Folios were also called "leaves".

16 pp...quire	signature
4 pp...sheet	form
2 pp...folio	sheet
1 p ...ff a&b	page
500 sheets...ream	ream (or 20 quires
10 reams...bale of	of 25 sheets
5000 sheets	each)

The page numbering systems compare like this:

la	lb ...	1 folio
front	back	
right	left	
p.1	p.2 ...	2 pages

Folios were not identified as "Recto" - right of fold, or "Verso" - left of fold until much later. Quires of eight folios were marked with Roman numerals - QIV or QXII, etc., with a key word at the bottom of the last page of each quire. Gutenberg's quires were numbered in multiples of eight folios; our signatures are numbered in multiples of 16 pages.

In this book, I use Gutenberg's terminology - quires, sheets, folios, and pages, for convenience in counting.

The Gutenberg Bibles contain 80 quires in both volumes, actually 40-1/2 quires (648 pages) in Volume I, and 39-1/2 quires (636 pages) in Volume II, with the last folio 318 (2 pages) blank. Total number of text pages is 1282.

To find the page numbers of a given folio, double the folio number, which becomes a left page (even number) and the page preceding it, right page (odd number). Example: folio 317 becomes pages 633-634.

Book sizes or page sizes compare this way:

octavo	5-1/2 x 8-1/2"
quarto	8-1/2 x 11"
folio	11 x 17"
sheet	17 x 22"
calfskin	22 x 34"

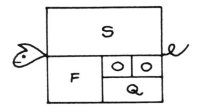

Heliogravure N. E. Kupferstich V. Hans Kohl.
Courtesy of the Gutenberg-Museum, Mainz, Germany.

PROLOGUE

Johannes Gensfleisch zum Gutenberg, a fifteenth century patrician and master goldsmith, was dedicated to an idea which culminated in two of the most important contributions to our world - individual, movable metal type and the printing press.

In his hands printing became an art, and the "Gutenberg Bibles," the first Bibles printed from metal letters on a printing press, are masterpieces in the world of art. Yet the Father of Printing, the man of flesh and blood, has been forgotten and overshadowed by the beautiful books and magnificent inventions he gave to the world. He stands today in the shadows of obscurity, in a maze of little-known facts, an unknown man even to many within the tremendous printing industry he founded.

No collection of books has been written about him. Biographical information is painfully incomplete and inconsistent, sometimes erroneous and maligning of the truth. None of his printed works - The Weltgericht or World Judgment, the Donatus Latin grammars, Missals, Indulgences, Bibles - bear his name, the date or place of publication. No personal mementos are to be found. No portrait was painted during his lifetime. No trace of his family home, the Hof zum Gutenberg in Mainz, remains today. The Franciscan church where he was buried has been destroyed. Gutenberg never married, although descendants of his family may still be living in Germany.

If Gutenberg had lived in Italy, he would have designed Roman letters instead of Gothic. If he had lived in Greece, he would have used the Greek alphabet and may have printed the Iliad. Italy, however, did not possess the large quantities of metal and paper needed for his work; and in Greece the opportunity was lacking because of the Turkish occupation: all artists and scholars were fleeing to Venice and Rome, initiators of the Italian renaissance.

It is ironic that Nicholas V, who was Pope at this time, (1447-1455), an avid book lover and the builder of the Vatican library, should have had his interest in literature sharply diverted by the conquest and fall of Constantinople. This catastrophe consumed his whole attention, though it must have been a consolation for him to know that printing of the Holy Scriptures was being accomplished in Europe at the same time other men were fighting to free the Eastern Church from the Infidels.

It is ironic that Gutenberg's first printed works were for the Church, when his invention of the printing press figured so largely in the Great Schism and wave of Humanist and secular literature to sweep over Europe in the sixteenth century.

It seems providential that the Holy Bible was the first book brought to America by Franciscan friars - to the country discovered only 24 years after Gutenberg's death.

The importance of printing upon modern life cannot be overstated, and the chapter in history when modern printing began has a part to play in bridging understanding.

The fruits of Gutenberg's invention have not always been blessings to society. Some men have condemned printing as an instrument of the Devil. Disraeli once lamented "books are fatal, the curse of the human race..the greatest misfortune that ever befell man was the invention of printing." Yet other men believe that "books are the food of the spirit"-Nutrimentum Spiritus-as inscribed on the Berlin Royal Library, and cannot live without them.

Gutenberg could not know how far or in how many directions printing would be developed, but he knew great potentialities existed and may have understood better than anyone else that printing would capture the minds of men and be used by men for good and ill purpose.

As a young man, Gutenberg bypassed the traditional life open to him as the educated son of a patrician family in favor of learning the manual art of goldsmithing. As an adult, he passed over the opportunities for publishing success in other areas by choosing to print books and to perfect and complete the single monumental task of printing the Bible.

If Gutenberg had printed a dictionary, a volume of law or the classics as his first large book, his name would have been perpetuated with that work. If he had concentrated on volume printing of Donatus, calendars and catechisms, he would have become a wealthy man because of the popular demand for these small books.

Gutenberg could print nothing, however, on his own authority. Only by request and with consent of members of religious orders, monastery abbots or the church hierarchy was it possible for anyone in the fifteenth century to copy and publish books used in schools, by the church or by the laity. Gutenberg was no exception. Had he been able to print the Bibles without full cooperation from the hierarchy in Mainz and Rome, this would have been a greater accomplishment of subterfuge than of typography. The first printing of the Bible was a secret, but one kept by the Church, not from her. The Bibles were not condemned or confiscated when they appeared. No one was excommunicated from the Church for printing them. One day, perhaps, when the archives in Rome, Constance, Basel and Avignon are examined, correspondence will provide the evidence linking Gutenberg and his work to the men who initiated the Bible project.

Gutenberg had demonstrated that Donatus and Missals could be printed successfully and in a short time. Why then did Gutenberg print the Bible? Was it for prestige, money, a personal ambition? All of these things?

Not only was the Bible the largest book in the world, over 1000 manuscript pages, it was also the most valued and most difficult text to copy in metal letters and to print without error. The tremendous quantity of almost 200 Bibles required more metal, more paper and vellum, more presses, more men, money and time than most men would be willing to give, regardless of the rewards and prestige attached. By consenting to publish the Bible, Gutenberg took on a long, tedious job. He also went heavily into debt to equip the large printing office he needed for the work. The Bibles required five years to complete.

Having made the commitment, however, Gutenberg was determined to see the project through to the best of his ability, and his first concern was to print the most beautiful and perfect edition possible. Publishing the Bible was a matter of personal and professional pride, but it was not an opportunity he deliberately sought. Gutenberg's consent testifies to his largeness of vision, his generosity of spirit.

The key to Gutenberg's personality lies in his works: a

testament to the excellence of his craftsmanship, his keenness of mind and perseverance of heart. Yet his achievement was not of works only, but the giving of self with patience, industry, dedication and surrender of any hopes he may have had for personal or financial reward.

The story of modern printing begins with Gutenberg, and at a time and place in history when it was possible for his ideas and his work to be developed, take root and grow.

The master goldsmith and master printer were the same man; the inventor and publisher were the same man. Gutenberg was a technician, teacher, a creative genius, and the story of the man eclipses even his great achievements.

M.E.G.

Oak Park, Illinois.

PREFACE

Gutenberg is honored in his home city of Mainz, Germany, in many ways. As Mainz' most famous citizen, a statue of Gutenberg stands in Gutenbergplatz in the center of town. A university is named for him, and a printing museum. The Franciscan church where he was buried is gone and a wide street now covers the area. But a visitor can see the ruins of St. Christoph's church where Gutenberg was baptized, Algesheimer Hof where he died, and the site of his printing shop on Schustergasse. The World Typography Museum is a handsome, modern building housing two of the original printed Bibles and a replica of Gutenberg's workshop. Here visitors can see how metal letters are cast by hand and purchase a souvenir Latin page printed on a press like the one Gutenberg used.

Gutenberg is honored also in Strasbourg, France, where he cast his first letters, built his first press, and made his first prints. A statue has been erected here, too, in Place Gutenberg near the cathedral and an old hotel bears his name. The suburb of St. Arbogast where Gutenberg lived has been replaced by a large highway intersection, but the home of Konrad Sahspach who built Gutenberg's first press may be seen at No.6 Place de la Grande Boucherie. The old city, in fact, remains much as it was in Gutenberg's time. The great cathedral spire was completed and dedicated while Gutenberg lived in Strasbourg.

The Strasbourg statue shows Gutenberg standing and holding a sheet of paper in his hand. On the page are the words "Et la lumière fût" which mean "And the light was made." The words are from Genesis and refer to the creation of the world when God separated the light from the darkness. They are appropriate words because printing brought the Dark Ages to an end and marked the beginning of the Renaissance and modern history in the West.

How precisely did Gutenberg's work begin? Where did the idea come from to cast letters of the alphabet from metal and to print from them? Was there a need for more books and for a faster, cheaper method of producing books in volume?

For centuries books were written by hand, copied and recopied primarily for use in the monasteries, schools and universities. All books were scarce. Only the nobility, the wealthy, could afford to buy them, and few people could read. Wood block books became popular in the Middle Ages and were available in small editions only, but it was not possible to print hundreds of copies from each block,and much time was spent re-carving pages and correcting mistakes.

Gutenberg was familiar with wood block books, but knew nothing about the copper or bronze "tontypes" which had been made in Korea in the early fifteenth century, nor about Pi Sheng's method of casting individual clay characters in the eleventh century, Korea. Gutenberg may have known of Koster's work in Haarlem with individual letters cut from wood, although Koster died in 1440 and his was not a commercial enterprise. It is more likely that the two men worked simultaneously, and independently, unaware that they pursued the same idea in principle of printing from single letters, used repeatedly and interchangeably in different combinations.

The idea of casting individual letters from metal originated with Gutenberg, a goldsmith, who was entirely familiar with the processes used to cast and mint coins. He knew metal was durable, that it could stand tremendous pressure, and that hundreds of successive printing impressions could be made without damaging the letters.

Gutenberg didn't know which metals, molds or casting techniques would work until he had made many experiments. He began with the punches and matrices as a goldsmith would. He designed a new adjustable and reusable mold - and redesigned it when he discovered that uniform height of the letters was critical to getting legible prints. Filing the letters was not the answer. Gutenberg changed his metal formula for the letter castings countless times. He needed a special ink and made his own. His first press was a small, portable letter press, adapted from the block press used by wood block printers. Later Gutenberg designed and built the large printing press, with attached sliding table top and tympan, which was used, basically unchanged, for 300 years. With this equipment, printing became an efficient operation, and books of any size and quantity could be published in days instead of years.

Gutenberg discovered, however, that printing with metal letters presented several problems and limitations which manuscript did not. Mistakes in manuscript could be erased with pumice and the words written over again. Gutenberg's letters were cast in reverse, and spelling words correctly from look-alike letters was difficult. It was a skill that could be mastered, but Gutenberg never imagined how frustrating or how expensive making corrections could be.

The size of a manuscript book varied with the size of the monk's handwriting. Gutenberg's letters were one size only, comparable to 18- or 24 point type as we know type sizes today and "set solid" with little space between each line. They had to be big enough for the compositor to grasp, yet small enough to get many lines on a page.

Gutenberg had to devise ways to make his metal lines of text the same width, and he did so by adjusting space between words and using abbreviations, as the monks did. Margins could be changed, but the number of metal letters in a line and the number of metal lines on a page were not the same as with letters written by hand.

Also, the monks wrote their pages in succession, in 8-folio (16-page) quires, which was not difficult when making only one copy. Printing many copies of each page with the four sheets in each quire flat, not nested together, meant keeping the pages and sheets in order - not an easy task, then as now, when printing both sides.

In short, before Gutenberg could produce a clear, readable printed page and achieve an efficient typesetting and printing operation, he had to find answers to many problems he never knew existed. Casting the letters was only the beginning.

The men working with Gutenberg were not all goldsmiths like himself. Some were members of the guild of St. John and St. Luke, which included bookbinders and woodcarvers. His compositors (typesetters) and printers were learning skills similar to those acquired by the wood block printers but in new ways and applications which demanded specialized knowledge and ability. In effect, if not in fact, Gutenberg established the first printer's guild, and the men who were apprentices and journeymen in his shop in turn became master printers.

To the people of Gutenberg's day, even block printing looked like magic. The sight of a blank sheet of paper suddenly filled with words was as amazing to them as the instantaneous computer screen print-out or electronic word processor are to people of our decade. Gutenberg's contemporaries were very superstitious, and the mysterious printing process was labeled a "black art" long after books were commonplace.

If the statue in Strasbourg or in Mainz could speak, Gutenberg might say how grateful he was to his family, friends, and the men who worked with him for their encouragement, good advice, friendship, love, loyalty and hard work which had made the printing and the books possible. His answers to questions would be candid.

Why did he go to Strasbourg? Gutenberg might be asked. "Because my brother and I were exiled from Mainz!" How did the work begin? "It began with the alphabet. But printing from metal letters is not as simple as A-B-C!"

Many people in Mainz knew how work on the Bibles began, but only Gutenberg himself could remember how the idea of metal letters originated almost 40 years before...and to him, 1428 seemed like yesterday.

Gutenberg's story begins in Strasbourg, where Johannes and Friele Gensfleisch arrived as young men and when printing and books and Bibles were as far from their minds as they were from home.

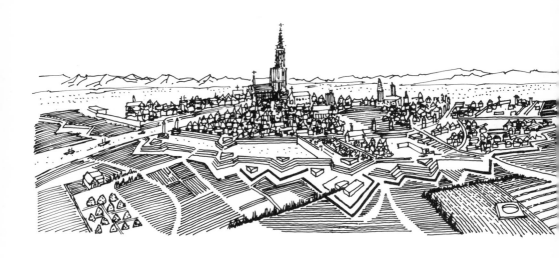

STRASBOURG
1428-1446
The Metal Letters and the Printing Press

I. THE BROTHERS
CHAPTER I

Johannes Gensfleisch and his brother, Friele, stood at the rail of the small barge as it nosed its way from the main course of the Rhein into the L'Ill river at Strasbourg. On either side were flat, green farmlands, still wet and muddy in patches, and in the distance they could see the roof-tops of the city and its cathedral, barely visible through the morning haze. It had stopped raining and the sky was grey and overcast, though soon the sun would come out, burn off the haze and a warm, autumn day begin.

Coming ever closer to the city, the young men could see the grand sweep of the L'Ill and four canals separating from it. Johannes wondered which was the river and which the canals, the waterways looking like fingers of a glove, surrounding and dissecting this island city. Mainz was built right down to the edge of the Rhein, he thought. Strasbourg was protected on all sides by a natural moat! Four watch towers stood on the points of land between the channels. The barge kept to the right, its bell ringing as the two tow horses on the bank pulled them past the covered bridges. Children had already crowded the embankment to wave and call greetings to the passengers.

They could see the famed cathedral clearly now. It was an immense structure. The single tower rose meters above the other buildings, and there was scaffolding on the tower.

"That must be for the spire the captain told us about," Johannes said. "Look, Friele. One high tower! Isn't that odd?"

Friele was checking their entry papers and was annoyed at the slow progress coming into the quai. The week's trip south from Mainz had been tiring, and he was anxious to disembark.

"Look at those red headdreses!" Johannes exclaimed. "Did you ever see anything like that, Friele?"

Johannes smiled and tipped his hat to a pretty girl looking down at them. She wore a white waist and dark blue dirndl, and her cap was crimson with huge wings on either side.

Friele looked up off-handedly. "You don't have to wave, Henne," he scolded. "Remember who you are!"

"We are strangers here." Johannes answered good naturedly. "We should be friendly."

"I hope Count von Ramstein is here to meet us," Friele replied. "He will have a carriage. Watch for him!"

The barge was easing into the quai now, at St. Thomas, the sign said, and a throng of people had gathered to welcome the new arrivals. The dialect, Johannes noted, was quite different from the speech they were used to. Now and then he caught a familiar word as the captain shouted instructions to the men. It would take time to become accustomed to the language, but he liked the new sounds and sights which greeted them.

Like Mainz, Strasbourg was a free city of the Empire, and the same size, with 5000 inhabitants. It was a cathedral city, a port city, and the center of trade in Alsace, attracting merchants and artisans of every kind. Strasbourg was also famous as the place where the three grandsons of Charlemagne had sworn their oaths dividing the empire between them in 862. St. Bernard had preached the Second Crusade in 1145 from the cathedral of Notre-Dame.

From a Franciscan friar traveling with them, Johannes learned that Roman legions had named the city "Argentoratum." The Diocese was established in the fourth century and was originally part of the large Mainz diocese. The first bishop was St. Amand. The name "Strateburgus" or "Strasbourg" came into use in the fifth century.

The Strasbourg cathedral was dedicated in 550 by Bishop St. Arbogast, the friar said, but fire destroyed the first and second basilicas. Construction of the present edifice was begun in 1190, and the spire, now being erected, was the work of Master Johann Hultz of Cologne.

As they turned in from the Rhein, the friar had pointed out the small communities that had grown up beyond the L'Ill around Strasbourg. The newest settlement was near the canal Zurich and the church of St. Guillaume to the east.

The two brothers from Mainz were among the many citizens who had been exiled from the city by Archbishop Conrad von Daun in a dispute between guild and patrician council members. They would be given permission to reside in Strasbourg until the edict was revoked, but when this would be, Johannes did not know. He was 30 years of age and not married, but Friele, the older, had left his wife and two children behind. The prospect of being away from them for an indefinite time was the reason he was so disagreeable. For his brother's sake, Johannes hoped the exile would be short. He did not view their journey as a hardship but as an opportunity. Johannes had not been to Alsace before. Living in Strasbourg would be an adventure!

While Friele presented their papers to the customs official, Johannes waited on the quai with the trunk and other baggage. He looked in vain for Count von Ramstein. No carriage arrived. Then Friele returned with a message saying that the Count had had to go to Savern and would not be back until Friday. He had made arrangements for them to enter the city, however, and to conduct business at the bank, leaving his personal vouchers for their credentials.

"Count Luthold has reserved rooms for us at the Kammersell Inn, wherever that is," Friele said irritably.

"Oh, Friele, we'll manage." Johannes answered. "I think the Count has been very efficient. I'm sure these boys know where the Kammersell is. They have a cart and can carry the baggage for us."

Johannes repeated the name, Kammersell, to three boys who quickly loaded their cart and started off down the street. Johannes and Friele followed them, keeping an eye on their round blue caps as they turned the corner. There were familiar hallmarks above the doorways, interesting shops and houses with red and white Alsace banners flying from the rooftops. Suddenly the cathedral was directly in front of them, still two blocks away, but looming skyward at the end of the street. Johannes and Friele paused to look up.

"What a magnificent building!" Johannes exclaimed.

"Yes, it is," Friele had to agree.

"Notre-Dame," one of the boys volunteered with pride, and crossed himself. As they arrived at the square, bells began to chime the hour of None and a double line of black-robed monks entered one of the giant portals. The boys trundled the cart to a handsome, half-timbered house just to the left of the cathedral high tower.

"Le Kammersell," a boy announced.

The five-story Inn was dwarfed by the huge church, its roof no higher than the flying buttresses, Johannes noted. The Dom of St. Martin in Mainz was large but only half the height of Notre-Dame. Gothic in design and built of large rosestone blocks, the Strasbourg cathedral had three main doors beneath a gigantic rose window. Above it, the two towers were connected by stonework, and from the north tower rose the octagon and spire.

"Imagine the view from up there," Johannes said.

"Pay the boys, will you," Friele answered, and went directly into the Inn.

Smiling and holding their caps in their hands, the boys thanked Johannes for the generous coin he gave to each of them.

"Speyer? Cologne? Basel?" the oldest asked.

"Mainz," Johannes answered. "We come from Mainz."

"Ahhh," the boys replied, much impressed, and chattered among themselves.

"What is your name?" Johannes asked. Pointing to himself, he said "Johannes," then pointed to each boy.

"Pierre," the oldest answered, and introduced the others. "Georges.. Henri."

Johannes bowed slightly and smiled. "I am Johannes Gensfleisch," he told them.

"Gensfleisch?" the youngest lad repeated. "Gensfleisch from Mainz!"

All the boys laughed at this, then hurried away, pulling the cart after them, leaving Johannes amused and puzzled by their behavior.

Inside the Inn, Johannes and Friele sat down at a long table and ordered wine. They were both weary and hungry now, and the food smelled good.

They were served a dry white wine from a green bottle.

"This is excellent," Friele said, noting the light, fruity taste.

"As good as the Rheingau, I'd say," Johannes agreed and poured another glass.

The meal began with thick onion soup and a loaf of crusty white bread as long as a man's arm. This was followed by a platter of roast pork, potatoes and sauerkraut, then large wedges of cheese and a bowl of stewed fruit were put on the table with another bottle of wine.

Johannes had not eaten so much in a long time. His brother too was relaxed and in better humor. Friele stretched his legs. It was good to be on level ground again. The atmosphere in the Inn was noisy but friendly, and most of the patrons, Johannes noticed, were patricians and merchants. Some were passengers from the barge.

"Tomorrow we shall deposit our annuities at the bank." Friele said. "Will you go with me?"

"I want to explore the city," Johannes answered. "I would like to see the spire and meet the master mason."

"Plenty of time for that," Friele said, "I'm going to our room. I want to write Friele-Else and tell her we arrived safely."

As they left the dining hall, Johannes noticed that the innkeeper smiled when Friele paid for their meal and wrote his name on the bill.

"Gensfleisch?" the man asked.

"That's right," Friele replied.

"Friele and Johannes Gensfleisch..from Mainz," the man repeated. "Good afternoon, gentlemen!"

Johannes strolled outside to walk around the cathedral and look at the buildings on the square. Most of the men on the scaffolding were coming down as it was getting near dusk. Johannes stood and watched as the men descended the staired turret from the tower and disappeared into the streets. He saw the barge captain talking with a tall blond man who handed him a piece of paper, then left. Seeing Johannes, the captain came over to speak with him.

"That was Master Hultz," the captain said. "We delivered some rope for him. The men have to be tied on the scaffolding so they won't fall off in a strong wind."

Johannes nodded understandingly. "I'd like to meet him!" he said.

"You will, and he'll be glad to meet someone from Mainz," the captain answered. "I told him we had several exiles from the Rheingau this trip."

"There will be more, I'm afraid," Johannes told him. "Have a safe voyage the rest of the way, Captain."

They said goodbye and the captain walked back to the quai, leaving Johannes watching the last sunlight touch the great stones of the cathedral over his head.

Strasbourg was different, he thought, from the other cities they had visited. It was busy, interesting, colorful, and already he felt completely at home. Crossing the square to the Kammersell, Johannes passed in front of the massive church and crossed himself. They had arrived safely, thank God. He would sleep well tonight.

CHAPTER 2

The next day the brothers breakfasted early, then set off for the bank on Place Broglie. "Broglieplatz," as Johannes called it, was the largest square in Strasbourg and they were able to identify it by the large clock on the City Hall. The people looked clean and prosperous, Friele noted, and the bright red-winged caps were everywhere, bobbing and blowing like sails. I must send a little one home to the baby, Friele thought.

Handsome houses of timbers and masonry like those in Mainz and Eltville fronted the narrow streets, though the walkways were wide and cobbled. There were numerous wells and fountains at almost every corner. Pugent smells drew attention to the abattoir where cattle were slaughtered, but as if to compensate for this, fragrant, colorful flowers bloomed from every window ledge. The canals were lined with fishermen, sitting on the bank, on the bridges, or in flat-bottomed boats. Johannes would buy line and bait, he thought, anxious to see what the catch might be.

Thursday was market day in the cathedral square, and Friele and Johannes found themselves in the center of activity. They visited all the stalls, sampled the fruit and nuts, meringues and tarts, and some wonderful, layered, puffed pastry called "brioches," which they had never seen or tasted before. A soft, spready sausage called "paté" was made from goose liver, Friele learned. The food in Alsace, he decided, was delicious.

Count Luthold von Ramstein arrived at the Kammersell as promised the following day. A pleasant, distinguished man around 50 years old, he apologized for being unable to meet them earlier, but was glad to know that their papers had been accepted without difficulty.

"Your father and I were good friends," the Count said. "I am proud to know and to be of service to his sons. How is your dear mother? You must meet my family and my friends. You will come to my home for dinner on Sunday!"

Did they like Strasbourg, the Count asked? They would meet people from many cities here. They must tell him about the quarrel between the Mainz council members, he went on.

Even Friele was amused by the Count's rapid questions and remarks that tumbled out like beans from a bag. Their mother was well, Friele told him. She still lived at Hof zum Gutenberg with their sister, Else, her husband, Claus Vitzthum, and daughter, Little Else. Their older half-sister, Patze, was married to Peter Blashof, a former mayor of Mainz, whom the Count also remembered. Friele's wife and two children were in Mainz, he said. The children were small. Odilgen, the little girl, was three years old and Orte, his son, only a year. It had been hard to leave them.

The Mainz Council, Friele explained, was composed of both patricians and members of the various guilds, with the patricians in the majority. In an effort to weaken the patrician faction and to gain for themselves a stronger voice in civic affairs, the guilds had proposed that only patricians who were also guild members could serve on the Council. They were able to force the archbishop to agree with them, and patricians must comply or be exiled from the city.

He was a member of the goldsmith guild, Johannes said, and eligible to serve on the Council, yet his brother, who had served as a patrician member as their father had done, was now ineligible because he was not a guild member.

"I am eligible to serve," Johannes said, "but Friele is not. It's a ridiculous situation. The guilds are wrong!"

Guild members who had expected the younger Gensfleisch to side with them in the dispute were angered by Johannes' sentiments and his decision to leave Mainz with him, Friele said. Some had even wanted Johannes expelled from the guild.

" 'My loyalty is to my family,' Johannes told them, 'not to the guilds, not in this case.' To my brother, it was a matter of principle," Friele said. "He felt that guild membership should not be a requisite for patricians who served on the Council any more than it should be necessary for guild members to be patricians in order to serve."

Friele had been embroiled in the political fight for some time, he went on, and had no choice but to accept the archbishop's ruling and seek asylum in another city.

"Johannes had a choice and chose to go with me," Friele said with admiration.

"I didn't want the Gensfleisch name associated with the new guild leadership and policies that are unfair," Johannes added. "It's that simple." He did not mention that he also had personal reasons for leaving Mainz at this time. Grete might have become his wife had he stayed in Mainz, but that marriage presented problems. The memory of Lisl would always remain in his heart. Ten years before, they were to have been married, and Lisl had died.

Johannes had been apprenticed then, like Friele, as an accountant but he hated the work. After their father's death, the same year, both brothers received an annuity and Johannes promptly used his to pay for an apprenticeship in the goldsmith guild. The work at the mint he found completely satisfying, and after seven years he had become a master. Yet continuing at the mint did not interest Johannes any longer, and he welcomed the chance to go with Friele to Strasbourg. The trouble between the Council members had come at an opportune time. Johannes' reasons for supporting his brother were sincere, and he was ready for change in his life, wherever it might lead.

Sympathetic to the unending and universal problems between guild and patrician members of a city council, Count von Ramstein was pleased by Johannes' spirit and independence and by the brothers' respect for each other.

"Your father would be pleased," he told them. "Friele looks like his father, I think. You resemble your mother," the Count said to Johannes, indicating his red hair. "Now tell me what your plans are. What do you want to do while you are here?"

Friele was an accountant for the city of Mainz, he said, as their father had been. Johannes was a master goldsmith at the episcopal mint. Custodians of the mint were relatives from the Sorgenloch branch of the family. and Johannes and cousin Rudi had served their apprenticeship together.

The Count could arrange for a position at the bank for Friele, he said, and if Johannes wished to join the goldsmith guild in Strasbourg, he would introduce him to Master Claude Lebert.

"Lebert is very pompous," the Count confided. "He will be impressed that you are related to the mintmasters at Sorgenloch, but he will not favor your action against the guild council members. Still, he can be of service to you."

They would meet Lebert and other members of the Strasbourg guilds at his home, von Ramstein said.

CHAPTER 3

Friele and Johannes Gensfleisch zur Laden zum Gutenberg were the guests of honor at the von Ramstein home. Greeted formally by the Countess, they met each of the guests and their wives and were soon drawn into friendly conversation.

Johann Riffe, the sheriff from Lichtenau, was a likeable gentleman who had a large stable, and he offered to lend Johannes a horse during his stay in Strasbourg. Nicholas Heilmann, who owned a paper mill, was interested in hearing about new business in Mainz. His brother, Fr. Anthony Heilmann, was deacon at the church of St. Pierre le Vieux.

The Iserin Tur family were relatives of the von Ramsteins and thought privately that the Count's hospitality to exiled citizens was in poor taste. Their daughter, Ennelin, however, a beautiful child of 12 or 13 years, was enchanted with Johannes. She reminded him of his niece, Else Vitzthum. Had Little Else also grown up so fast, Johannes wondered, and was she wearing her hair so becomingly?

It pleased Johannes most of all to be introduced to Master Johann Hultz, master of works of the cathedral spire, whom he had seen briefly the night of their arrival. Hultz and his wife were warm, ingenuous people who made Johannes feel that he had known them a long time.

"Of course, you must come to see the spire," Hultz said in answer to Johannes' question. "Though I may bore you with a recital of our long and beautiful work," he added with quiet humor.

Johannes accepted the invitation with enthusiasm. "I'll come as soon as I can!" he said.

Master Lebert was as the Count described, a man of self-importance who said openly that he thought guild members should form a majority on the city council. "This is the case in Strasbourg," he told Friele.

Equal representation was fair, Friele answered. "Most guild members serving on the council are patricians, but not all patricians belong to the guilds. It is unfair that the council make guild membership the primary requirement for serving the city."

Lebert eyed Friele suspiciously, "I understand your brother is a goldsmith?" he asked.

"Yes, and Johannes thinks as I do," Friele replied.

"Well, I hope you are able to return to Mainz soon," Lebert said stiffly.

The days and weeks passed quickly, and Friele was glad to be busy. In his frequent letters to his wife, he told her of the von Ramstein reception, his position at the bank preparing accounts, and his own concern that they still had received no official word from Mainz that the archbishop's ruling had been revoked.

"Try not to worry," Friele wrote. "I know it is hard for you with your sister away. Ask Sophie if she can stay with the children. I hope Orte's fever is gone. Tell Odilgen to be a good girl. I am sending you the money you wanted for the candle holders. Must they be silver? We were sorry to hear that Herr Meier died."

He and Johannes were fine, Friele went on. They had decided to stay at the Kammersell. People had been very kind to them.

"Only one thing has been difficult and embarrassing for us," Friele continued. "Gensfleisch means goose flesh. In Strasbourg, in all Alsace, I think, one of the favorite dishes is a paté made from goose liver. It is much tastier than our own liver sausage, I must say. But it is hard enough being strangers here without having a name people laugh at. Count von Ramstein suggested we use the name Gutenberg instead. We think that's a good idea, and I am sure Mama will understand. I am sending you some lace and ribbon and toys for the children. Kiss the little ones for me. I count the days until I see you again. My heart is full of love for you, my dearest wife."

By contrast, Johannes' letter to his sister, Else, was short and cheerful. "I have a horse," he began, "and am seeing everything! The countryside is flat and the Vosges mountains to the west look just like the Taunus at home - thick woods, high and misty. The villages are quiet, a cluster of poor cottages and barns surrounding a church. The peasants grow potatoes and cabbages, but the farms are small. The vineyards have been harvested and will produce more wine than last year, some people say. I have not climbed the cathedral spire because of bad weather and am so anxious to see it. Master Hultz is from Colgne and has become a good friend. Tomorrow I go to St. Arbogast, a small abbey close by the city. Fr.

Sebastian has invited me to visit their library and scriptorium. Tell Mama we go to Mass on Sunday and Holy Days and have received the Sacrament. We are both well and happy. A kiss for you, Mama, and Little Else. My best to Claus and tell Rudi to write. Your devoted brother, J.G. Gutenberg."

Friele is lonesome, Johannes thought, but I am not lonesome! He was glad Friele had work to occupy his time, but hoped they would stay in Strasbourg until spring, or possibly summer. He had not been to see M. Lebert and had made no inquiries as yet at the mint or at the guild. After the holidays perhaps. Now he must take advantage of the clear weather to travel where he wanted. Fewer men were on the spire and he was sure their work would be suspended over winter.

It would soon be Christmas, and the approaching holy days filled Friele with sadness and longing. Surely next year his family would be together. He should have insisted Friele-Else join him for Christmas, he said.

They would decorate a tree for the Hultz and von Ramstein children, Johannes told him. Sharing their customs with new friends and enjoying the customs of Alsace with them would be a new experience for everyone. "Christmas is Christmas wherever you are, Friele," Johannes said. "You must not be unhappy!"

Friele's spirits rose when a large package arrived from Mainz. Among the gifts were two miniature portraits of the children and locks of their hair.

CHAPTER 4

Spring came unofficially to Alsace when the storks arrived in March. Just as in Mainz, people heralded the event as a sure sign that winter was past and the warm days of spring not far away. Everyone considered the storks as good luck and put out bundles of sticks or built nesting platforms on roofs and chimneys to lure the tall white birds to stay. If they landed and nested on a housetop, lightning would not strike that house. New babies in the household would be strong and healthy. If a stork walked toward a young girl, she was certain to be married soon.

The male birds were the first to come. They chose the nests, then the females arrived, and the loud clattering of bills in courtship could be heard all over the city. Usually three or four eggs were laid, one at a time, and at the end of April the first fuzzy heads appeared. Unfortunately, some offspring died during the spring storms when they were blown off the high nests or succumbed to chill and wetness. The death of a stork was a bad omen, and people feared a death in their own families as a consequence.

For weeks after hatching, the parent birds were busy keeping their fledglings fed. Peasants cultivating the fields were sure to be accompanied by storks walking behind them, snatching up frogs and mice. And on hot summer days, some chicks were even seen to drink water that their parents brought in their mouths. As the young birds grew and exercised their wings, they too clattered bills with their nestmates.

The storks usually stayed until late August or September. By then the youngsters were in full plumage, snow white with black tips on their wings but without the red legs and bills of the adults. One day, suddenly, hundreds of storks rose in the air, circled the city, and headed south. It was a spectacle Gutenberg had never tired of watching.

Customarily, storks nested on the dome of the cathedral. Even during the years of building the spire, the storks had returned. The bells and work activity never seemed to bother them. This year, however, the cathedral nest was empty, and everyone in Strasbourg was apprehensive about what this foretold. It did not matter that 217 nests had been counted in the city, the most important one was not occupied. Workmen refused to mount the spire. Someone would surely fall and be killed, they believed, unless storks took the nest on Notre-Dame. The storks were a sign of God's blessing, people said, and their absence was a sign of God's displeasure.

"The Lord is testing your faith," the priests told the people. And prayers increased. Lenten fasting and penance took on added significance.

"I think more people are praying for the storks to come than are praying for their immortal souls this Lent," Fr. Anthony said.

"You are very likely right," Johannes agreed. Still, it was strange, he thought, that the cathedral did not have a single nest.

Palm Sunday came. By now the city was in mourning, and sadness and fear gripped everyone. It was difficult to relive the Lord's Passion and Death and to accept the Will of God, if storks did not nest on the cathedral that year.

"The empty tomb is proof of God's love for us," Fr. Anthony said from the pulpit of St. Pierre. "The empty nest proves only that storks are unpredictable creatures! We are fools if we put our trust in them instead of in God!"

Finally, on Easter Thursday, a pair of storks was seen on the cathedral nest. The people were overjoyed. It was a miracle, they said, and strengthened their faith that the greater miracle of Christ's Resurrection from the dead had truly happened.

Six weeks later, four eggs began to hatch, and the nestlings were promptly named for the four disciples, Pierre, Andre, Jacques and Jean - or Jeanne, though no one was concerned about such details.

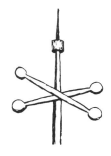

Shortly after Whitsunday, on a tender, new spring day, Johann Hultz showed Gutenberg the work in progress on the cathedral spire. They met on the high platform above the rose window and flying buttresses where the men kept their tools, ate, and rested during bad weather. It was 330 steps to the platform, and another 170 steps to the top of the graceful octagon tower supporting the spire. The octagon had four tiered turrets containing four spiral staircases flanking the slender bays. One day, Hultz said, bells would be hung in the vault of the octagon.

Standing at the foot of the spire, Hultz described his design of delicate openwork construction as each tier of the spire narrowed toward the peak. There would be eight tiers—four of which had been completed. Six turrets with stairways went to the sixth tier, where the design became square. Four turrets would rise to the shaft supporting the lantern. The canopy stretching out from the lantern was to disappear into a flower and cross, and at the very top would be a statue of the Blessed Mother. The cross would have four arms instead of two, so it could be seen from all directions. When complete, Hultz said, the spire and the point would rise 42 meters above the octagon, another 136 steps. In all, the spire would be 636 steps or 142 meters from the ground.

To the east, Gutenberg could see the Rhein and the Black Forest. To the west were the Vosges and Mount Ste. Odile. The view on this clear day was breathtaking. It seemed to Gutenberg that he was standing on a cloud with a toy village at his feet.

Watching the men as they walked along the top tier, setting the stone for the tier above, Gutenberg marveled at their apparent disregard for the dangers of stepping or reaching too far. He could hear them talking and laughing as they steadily received and set the heavy stone in place. It was unbelievable that men could work so high, Gutenberg remarked.

"The men appear to work casually," Hultz said, "but they do not take risks. They are experienced workmen and can set stone as fast up here as they would on the ground. And they are prayerful men who rely on the saints - and the storks - to keep them safe."

The scaffolding, ropes and canopy also protected the men, Hultz said, though nine fatal falls had occurred.

"It's dangerous in a strong wind or if we're caught in a storm. The tower and spire attract lightning, you see. And when it gets hot, the stone becomes too hot to handle. The men perspire and chisels fall out of their hands. Even the drinking water is warm."

"Can you work in the winter at all?" Gutenberg asked.

"Not past the middle of November," Hultz answered. "It's usually too cold and icy even with sand on the steps of the turrets. Most of the men go home for Advent and Christmas, so we begin again in February or March."

By working the men in two shifts in summer, Hultz explained, he avoided the worst heat in mid-afternoon. The first crew began at sunrise and worked until early afternoon. The second crew worked from Vespers until the sun went down. It was a 12-hour workday, and the crews alternated shifts every two weeks.

Hultz introduced Gutenberg to the foreman, a short, stocky man named Karl, and told him to permit Gutenberg to climb to the platform any time he wished.

"We never permit strangers or townspeople to come up," Hultz said. "I cannot be responsible for them. Only the archbishop - and yourself - have this privilege!"

Returning to the platform and then to ground level, Hultz and Gutenberg continued their conversation in the Kammersell, where they each enjoyed a stein of beer.

"His Eminence," Hultz confided, "wants the spire completed in his lifetime. But he complains because the early work hours disrupt his meditation. Too much noise, he says. And he doesn't like the men working after Vespers for the same reason. VonDiest would like the spire assembled on the ground, I think, then lifted into position!"

Gutenberg laughed, and was pleased that Hultz felt he could speak so frankly.

"Archbishops can be a problem," Gutenberg agreed. "I know!"

Was the design complicated? Was that why the work had taken so long, he wondered.

"No, the design is basically simple," Hultz replied. "It is not the design or changes in the design that hold up progress. In the beginning, I revised Master Ulrichs's plans and raised the staircase turrets just to the foot of the steeple. The spire plans are my own, and these have not been changed. I am grateful for that. But you just can't believe the delays and time lost since we started."

Hultz looked at Gutenberg wearily. "I wish the work could go faster. But workmen get sick or hurt. We don't have enough materials or the shipment orders are not signed properly. The weather! Money! Arguments between the men. The spire and point will be 42 meters. Ulrich built the entire octagon, 34 meters, in twenty years. It's taken us ten years and we're only a third finished!"

"The spire gets smaller as you reach the top," Gutenberg smiled. "But I know how you feel. It's discouraging. At least when you are finished, the spire will be a masterpiece. It is one of a kind and will last forever."

Half serious, half joking, Gutenberg asked about the possibility of erecting a twin spire.

Hultz glared and put down his stein. "Never!" he said. "A second spire would destroy the proportions! The magistrate has abandoned such plans. "Not urgent" he says. I entirely agree with him. Two towers of this height would be a terrible mistake!"

"I think so too," Gutenberg answered thoughtfully. "The symmetry is perfect as it is, though at first the single tower seemed strange to me."

Had there ever been a fire, Gutenberg wanted to know.

"The last fire was in 1298," Hultz exclaimed, and quickly crossed himself. "May all the saints save us from a fire in this cathedral."

As they continued to drink and talk, Gutenberg noticed that Hultz wore a scapular and wondered which one it was. He had been told that Hultz went to Mass every Monday in the cathedral chapel and prayed for his men.

Hultz belonged to the brotherhood of St. Francis - the St. Thomas chapter in Strasbourg, he said, and invited Gutenberg to come to one of their meetings.

Had Gutenberg been to St. Arbogast, Hultz inquired. The monastery had a fine library which he thought was well worth seeing.

Gutenberg had visited St. Arbogast several times, he told his friend. "And you think building the spire goes slowly!" he laughed. "The monks sometimes work years on one book! Several monks might each copy a different book. Or to make more than one copy at one time, the monks take turns reading the text aloud while other scribes write down the words! I never knew how many monks were needed to copy manuscripts or how very much time it takes!"

"Why don't you visit one of the wood block printers?" Hultz suggested. "They can print as many as 25 or 50 copies of a book in a few months. Words and even pictures are carved onto wooden blocks which are inked and then printed by laying paper on top of the blocks. The pages aren't as perfect as manuscripts but block books are much cheaper to buy."

"I'd like to see that," Gutenberg said with interest.

"Let me know what you think," Hultz replied, and got up to leave. "Tomorrow is another holy day," he added, shaking his head. "Sometimes I think there are too many holy days and not enough work days. No wonder it takes us and the monks so long to accomplish anything!"

II. THE IDEA
CHAPTER 5

Watching the monks in the monastery scriptorium and bindery had been a fascinating experience for Gutenberg. The entire process of book production was meticulous and amazingly efficient, although time consuming. It was no wonder, Gutenberg thought, that books were so expensive.

Each monk wrote a quire at a time, a quire consisting of 8 leaves or 16 pages, nested and folded once through the center. Pages could be three sizes - folio(one sheet folded), quarto(one folio folded), or octavo(one quarto folded). This meant that from one sheet, the monks got two folio size pages, four quarto size, or eight octavo size. And if the book was on vellum, it was possible to get two sheets from one calfskin though the sheet sizes would vary with the size of the animal.

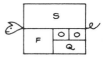

The size and style of handwriting of each monk was different and this affected the number of pages in a book. Some books, Fr. Sebastian explained, had very small letters and many lines on a page, while others, like a Psalter, had large letters and few lines on each page. The bigger the handwriting, the more pages were necessary, and vice versa. Bibles were usually folio size, Fr. Sebastian said. Missals were quarto size, and the books of the Canonical Hours were octavo size to be held comfortably in one hand. Psalters were always folio size because this made it easier for several monks to see the words and notes of chant from one book placed in front of the choir.

As each manuscript was completed, any errors in the text were erased with pumice and corrected. If the books were to be illustrated, then the quires were sent to the artist, who designed decorative page headings or initial letters at the beginning of chapters. Using many colors and sometimes gold leaf, the artists added small pictures of saints, birds, flowers and scroll work to beautify the text.

In the bindery, the quires were gathered together in order and each one carefully stitched through the center and through a cloth backing glued to the folded edges. The covers were wood boards often covered with tooled or jeweled leather and closed with bosses or metal clasps to keep the pages flat. It was customary to stamp the title and author on the cover and spine of each book with single letter punches, Gutenberg learned.

Would Gutenberg be able to cast some bosses for them, Fr. Sebastian asked. Of course, Gutenberg told him, and he would make a new set of punches, if they liked, using a different letter style for stamping the covers. Gutenberg was glad to be of service.

"Paper and vellum are costly to begin with, and so much care is given to making each book a work of art," Gutenberg told his brother. "But only one copy! The block printed books may be inferior in quality, but at least several copies can be made in a short time."

"You're used to minting coins," Friele replied. "One punch, one mold, and you can cast hundreds of coins. Producing books isn't that simple."

"The block books aren't simple to make either," Gutenberg answered. "In fact, the work is even more tedious than manuscript, if that's possible." Gutenberg's visit to the block printing shop had wearied him in the same way the the work at the scriptorium had wearied him.

"All the wood letters must be carved in reverse, for one thing," Gutenberg said: "They use a mirror, and carve three or four lines of text on to one block, usually under a picture. But the letters break after so many impressions. Wood soaks up the ink. The prints are not clear.

"The men are skilled carvers, and the small letters most carefully made," he went on. "Suppose it's a 24-page book. They carve 24 blocks, one for each page, and then keep recarving and replacing them as needed. If there's a mistake in spelling, a letter or word left out, they must carve the entire block over again, or find themselves with fifty prints with the same mistake on each one! Rather than waste the paper, they're inclined to let a mistake remain until the block wears out. Wood is the wrong material, that's certain. The letters should be made of metal - and single letters, not lines of words Then mistakes would be easy to fix - just change the letter!"

"Why don't you make some reverse letters and see if you can print from them," Friele suggested.

"Metal wouldn't break," Gutenberg said. "And with the proper mold, each letter would be exactly alike."

"Like coins," Friele said.

"What would you do, Johannes?" Hultz asked Gutenberg, when he told him about the block printing method. "Cast lines or blocks of metal?"

"Neither," Gutenberg answered, "I'd cast each letter by itself. Single letters of the alphabet could be cast as easily as coins, but the mold would have to be different."

"In what way?" Hultz wanted to know.

"Well, I'll try to explain," Gutenberg said. "In the first place, the pattern for a coin isn't mirror copied. The matrix or mold is face up and the coin comes out face up. But if you were to make prints from these coins, the prints would be reverse, backwards. To make prints you can read, you must have a reverse casting from a reverse matrix. The punch to make a reverse matrix is cut right side up."

"I'm not sure I understand," Hultz said.

"Look at this punch - one for stamping the book covers," Gutenberg replied. "Pressed into the leather, the letter is face up. You see?"

"Yes. Like a butter mold."

"Or a letter seal pressed into wax," Gutenberg said. "But prints must be made from reverse images. In this, the block printers are absolutely correct."

"Would ink stick to metal?" Hultz wondered.

"Oh, yes, if it was tacky," Gutenberg told him. "It's the mold that would present the problem. You'd have to cast letters with a face and body— and the matrix would have to fit inside the mold."

It was a problem that could be solved, Gutenberg felt, when he had the time to work on it. The idea was intriguing. Printing from metal letters was possible, he was sure.

"The little blocks with letters on them that children play with," Hultz said, "help them learn how to spell. If you had enough letters, Johannes, you could copy a whole page and print a whole book!"

"And the words could be taken apart and the letters rearranged and used over again," Gutenberg answered, "just like the childrens's letter blocks."

As he reflected on the two methods he had seen for producing books, Gutenberg believed both methods were unsatisfactory. The block printers achieved quantity but with mediocre results. The monks got beautiful results, but each book was one of a kind. The wood carvers were artist craftsmen in their way just like the calligraphers and illustrators were artists with pen and brush.

Gutenberg pondered other difficulties with manuscript work - ink blots and candle wax sometimes ruined a whole quire. In block printing, when the small wood letters broke off under repeated pressure, the printers sometimes made corrections by hand, on fifty copies of ten or more pages, while new blocks were carved. Such misuse of time was abhorrent to Gutenberg, who respected patience and skill and work well done, but who

B Punch

E Matrix

E Casting

B Print

also knew there were fast and efficient ways of doing most jobs. There was surely a way of achieving both fine quality books and enough copies to make the time and work worthwhile.

Metal letters are the answer, Gutenberg thought. But it might take longer to construct the mold and cast the letters than it does to write a book by hand. I'll see what I can do when we return from Ribeauville, he promised himself.

CHAPTER 6

A day's journey south of Strasbourg, Ribeauville was the headquarters of the musicians guild where every September the Feast of the Pipers or Pfeiffertag was celebrated. It was one of the most colorful fetes in Alsace, Count von Ramstein said, and he insisted that Johannes and Friele attend with him and his family.

The event coincided with the birthday of the Blessed Virgin Mary, honoring her and the lord of Chateau Ribeaupierre who was protector of all musicians and minstrels in the area. The lord's ancestor had brought a statue of the Virgin home from the Crusades and it was carried in a joyous procession, surrounded with music makers of every kind. Numbering close to 100, the participants included marshals of the Empire and men at arms who played flutes and trumpets, fiddlers, bagpipers, men with brass horns and trombones, jugglers and dancers. The King of the Pipers was traditionally Lord Ribeaupierre, who led the procession dressed in royal velvet and carrying an ancient viole shaped like a guitar.

People came from everywhere for Pfeiffertag—merchants with painted wagons, peasants in holiday dress, chevaliers on horseback. It promised to be three days which Gutenberg and Friele would enjoy immensely.

"Even in the Rheingau, there is nothing quite like this," Friele said, watching the festivities. He purchased toy horns and drums to send home to his children, and later, with a little urging from Johannes, joined in the street dancing.

The musicians played tirelessly all day and most of the night. Barrels of wine and beer were drunk, and huge amounts of food eaten. Pfeiffertag was undoubtedly one of the happiest and noisiest fetes the brothers from Mainz had ever experienced.

Michaelmas or St. Michael's day was celebrated at the end of September, and then, after the vineyards were harvested, a succession of grape festivals began. On both sides of the Rhein from Cologne to Basel, cities and villages would be crowded with visitors, sampling the new wine and comparing it to wine of the previous year. When good weather and rainfall promised a large harvest and the sweetest, full-flavored grapes, it would be a "morgen" year.

On their return to Strasbourg, Count von Ramstein accepted an invitation to visit Haut Koenigsbourg castle, near Selestat. Situated on a high hill, the chateau could be seen from all directions and afforded a magnificent view of the countryside. Riding up the mountain road, however, Gutenberg injured his knee when his horse reared and threw him against a tree. The sprain was painful and forced them to remain at the castle until Gutenberg felt better. The delay was no hardship. The spacious surroundings, and the hospitality of their gracious host made the week's stay extremely pleasant.

Koenigsbourg was walled and fortified but a more graceful structure than those on the Rhein near Mainz, Gutenberg thought. The chapel was two stories high and the windows made of stained glass. There were kennels and falcon enclosures, herb and flower gardens. A blacksmith, baker, bootmaker, weaver and tailor were on hand to satisfy every need of the castle residents.

Their tower rooms were comfortable, and the landgrave's two daughters taught Gutenberg and Friele the game of chess. After meals in the great hall, Friele noted that large squares of fine linen were used to wipe one's face and hands. He would tell his wife to order similar squares made for them.

"We have tasted wine from both cups, Friele," Gutenberg said. "Country wine from earthen cups, and now noble wine from silver goblets." It was easy to forget his injury and a temptation to prolong his recovery.

But Friele was anxious to get back to Strasbourg where they still awaited word from the Mainz Archbishop that they could return home. They had been away from Mainz more than a year.

Back at the Kammersell, Gutenberg limped around with a cane. He felt restricted and irritated because he couldn't work at the scriptorium or walk very far. Sitting outside in the cathedral square, he watched the work on the spire and visited with the men. Taking pen and paper with him, he began to make drawings of letters, punches and a casting mold.

The punches should be brass, Gutenberg decided, and the matrices lead. Both of these metals could be purchased easily from the guild. But how big should the letters be, he wondered. What should they look like? Some letters, like M and W, were wide; others. like L and I, were thin. Some dipped below the lines on a page, like g and p.

Gutenberg wrote his name and held the paper up to the sunlight. To print right side up, the letters had to be backwards, going right to left. Or they could be upside down, going left to right. He decided it was much easier to read them in reverse.

Gutenberg soon had a group of school children around him, watching shyly as he continued to write out letters of the alphabet. They were puzzled, however. The letters didn't look right.

"You made the letters backwards, Master," one of the boys said.

"So I did," Gutenberg answered. "What is your name?"

"Joseph," the boy replied.

"All right, Joseph, I'll show you a trick." Gutenberg lettered the name with the letters reversed.

Gutenburg

ᕹᴉudꞁɐꓕꞁꞁꓱ

"I can't read that!" the boy said indignantly.

Gutenberg flipped the paper over and held it to the light.

"Joseph!" the boy said excitedly. "It spells Joseph!"

"If you write the letters backwards," Gutenberg confided, "you can read them in a mirror. It's secret writing."

"It's magic!" Joseph exclaimed. "It's magic!"

It only looks like magic, Gutenberg smiled, but he nodded. He wouldn't spoil their fun.

The casting mold would be vastly different from the molds used to mint coins, Gutenberg discovered. It must be constructed so that the letter and the body of the letter were cast in one piece. The metal letters must have a body to hold on to. They couldn't be flat.

The sides of the mold had to adjust to accommodate both wide and narrow letters. And the mold had to made of iron, so it could be used repeatedly to make many castings of the same letter.

"We cannot use a sand mold," Gutenberg told Hultz. "We must use an iron mold. Sand molds are destroyed after the casting is made and are useless. The mold I make can be used again. The matrix should slide in and out of the bottom somehow. The casting metal is poured in from the top. Then by changing the matrix for each letter, one casting mold can be used to make all the letters. A different mold is not needed for each letter."

"The way silversmiths work, you mean," Hultz said.

"And goldsmiths, too!" Gutenberg answered.

How did Gutenberg propose to make the sides adjustable, Hultz wanted to know.

Had he ever watched artists frame pictures? Gutenberg asked. They used the double L principle, he explained. Two L-shaped pieces of wood were adjusted wider, narrower, longer, shorter, to provide the desired size opening in the center. Gutenberg would do the same thing, he said.

The drawing Gutenberg made of the casting mold indicated that it could be held in one hand so the operator could pour hot metal into it with the other hand. Two screws were enough to hold the four moveable parts in place. The two L sides could be locked in position and then unlocked to release the casting.

"Do you know someone who could make this mold for me?" Gutenberg asked Hultz.

"Yes, I do," Hultz said. "The locksmith Colonjard."

"The man can be trusted not to show the plans to anyone?"

"Yes," Hultz assured him. "What metal will you use for the letter castings, Johannes?"

"I don't know," Gutenberg answered. "I don't know. An alloy of lead, I suppose. That comes later. One step at a time!"

Experimenting with casting metals must be postponed until he could stand on his feet and move about better, Gutenberg said. In the meantime, he would work sitting down and begin to carve the punches and make a set of matrices. This was the beginning.

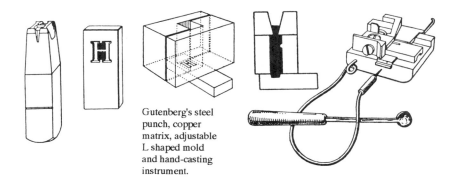

Gutenberg's steel punch, copper matrix, adjustable L shaped mold and hand-casting instrument.

III. THE WORK
CHAPTER 7

Von Ramstein became interested in Gutenberg's project and offered to give him workspace in the shed next to the stable on his estate. Gutenberg was delighted. He could work in private yet had access to the charcoal he needed for heating metal and could keep his horse with him. The blacksmith, Jacques, could help him when necessary.

"This idea of yours," the Count said one evening at dinner, "is so new, so different. I think it best if we keep it to ourselves for awhile, until you have cast some letters and printed from them."

Gutenberg agreed. "The results might be disappointing," he said.

"If you are successful, that will be the time," the Count believed, "to demonstrate how printing from metal letters can be accomplished."

"The casting mold must remain a puzzle to others," Gutenberg told him. "When the screws are removed, no one must be able to guess how the pieces fit together or even what the mold is used for. I don't know yet what the metal alloy for the letters will be, but that, too, will be my secret."

Working with punches and matrices, however, the tools used by all goldsmiths, would not evoke any curiosity, Gutenberg thought.

When Colonjard delivered the casting mold, Gutenberg was very pleased. The L sides opened and closed smoothly, moving on a track that could be locked into place. The handle was well balanced. The matrix fit snugly beneath the opening made by the L sides. The only adjustment needed was a minor one - to make the pin holding the pieces together a little longer.

"You are a fine craftsman," Gutenberg told the locksmith.

Colonjard was glad his work earned approval and smiled broadly. "The mold is different from any I have ever seen," he said. "What will you cast from it, Master?"

"Horseshoe nails, perhaps," Gutenberg answered off-handedly. "I am experimenting." He was unoffended by the question but made it clear that the locksmith must not be curious.

"Will you address the Guild sometime?" Colonjard asked.

"I will," Gutenberg assured him. "In time. I must be satisfied with the results before I show the work to anyone. You have shown the mold to no one?"

"No one, Master," Colonjard said. "I am proud to have served you."

Gutenberg wondered if membership in the guild would be an advantage. He must not offend Master Lebert and he would be purchasing a lot of metal for the letter castings. Cooperation was necessary. A lot depended upon how long they would remain in Strasbourg, and how well the work progressed.

Gutenberg was anxious to try out the mold with the matrices he had completed, but he discovered immediately that the matrices had been punched in the wrong place. The letter should be at the top, not in the center of the matrix. The matrices must be rectangular, he decided, so the letter positioned exactly under the opening made by the L sides.

Gutenberg noted also that the depth of the letter impression in the matrix was important, and that the relief letters on the punches must be carved a certain height. Otherwise the matrix was too shallow and the letter cast from it did not show sufficient detail. The corners and hairline strokes must be sharp or the letter wouldn't print legibly.

Gutenberg remelted the lead and made another set of matrices, hopeful now that the new letter castings would be entirely satisfactory. Testing each punch, each matrix, and each letter as it was cast was tedious work. Gutenberg was not satisfied with the combination of lead and tin he was using for the castings, but would postpone working on that problem until after the Easter holidays. The preparation took a long time, he discovered, though he had to admit the winter had passed quickly.

Two incidents occurred which strengthened Gutenberg's resolve to continue. The first was a disastrous fire in the St. Arbogast scriptorium. A nearly completed copy of Eusebius was destroyed when a candle blew over and burned through a set of quires. Working alone, the old monk had answered the bell and left the room, forgetting to snuff the candle and close the window. When he returned an hour later, it was too late to save anything.

"The quires will be rewritten," Fr. Sebastian said, "but poor Fr. Mark is sick with remorse. He had worked on the book almost a year."

Such accidents rarely happened, he said, but the danger was always present. Unfortunately, also, the monastery rarely had several copies of any volume. Books were chained to the library shelves to prevent them from being stolen and even then some disappeared or were stripped of their bindings by unscrupulous visitors.

"The Eusebius is one of our most precious volumes," Fr. Sebastian told Gutenberg sadly. "If only it had been one of the schoolbooks, the Donatus, instead!"

The second incident which increased Gutenberg's incentive came unexpectedly from the blacksmith, Jacques. The big man with the strong hands who worked in the stable near Gutenberg's workshop had forged the runners of a sled for von Ramstein's son. The Count had given Jacques a new leather apron in appreciation and pinned to it was a written note of thanks from the boy. Jacques treasured the paper more than the apron, it seemed, keeping the note on a nail on the wall of the stable. Gutenberg asked Jacques about it.

"I know my name is on it," the blacksmith answered proudly, "even though I can't read the words."

"I will read the paper for you," Gutenberg said.

"Oh, the Count told me what it says. I know the words by heart, but I wish I could read!" Jacques said. "I would like to know what the letters are. Then I could spell my name! Then I could read the prayers under the pictures in Notre-Dame."

Gutenberg was moved by the earnestness and longing of this humble man. He told Count von Ramstein of Jacques' desire, and the Count was shocked.

"Why should a blacksmith learn to read?" the Count asked bluntly. "All the peasants know the responses at Mass from memory. Many of the nobility have prayer books but cannot read them!" The idea of Jacques learning his letters and writing his name was preposterous.

Gutenberg did not think Jacques' desire strange, however. The man was sincere, and he was intelligent.

"Even slaves have been taught to read," Gutenberg answered quietly. Some peasants were able to draw and could copy letters and pictures better than himself, he said.

Being able to recognize letters and to understand the words made from them was important, even for a blacksmith, Gutenberg thought. Not only to read prayers, either. Many peasants were cheated by masters and merchants who knew they could not read the receipts or papers they signed, and an "X" could be made by anyone. When his first prints were made, Gutenberg promised to give one to Jacques and would help him to read it for himself.

CHAPTER 8

On a cold March day, Gutenberg was alone in the stable, stirring the hot metal in the crucible with a shaking hand. If the castings are perfect today, I will show Friele and the others, he thought. If they aren't, I shall keep another failure to myself.

Very carefully Gutenberg dipped the small ladling spoon into the yellow metal and poured the metal into the casting mold. Then he plunged the mold into a pail of cold water. Steam rose, and when he thought the metal had cooled sufficiently, he unlocked the mold over his work bench and the casting fell out. He did not remove the excess metal, or jet, which clung to the body of the casting, but quickly turned it upside down to see the letter on the other end. The crossbar and hairline strokes were sharp and true. It was a perfect capital A.

"In solid gold!" he said. "Praise God!"

Just as carefully, Gutenberg made a second casting. The letter was perfect. Then tapping the casting gently with a hammer, Gutenberg removed the jet. "I'll file this second one," he said to himself.

Back and forth went the file, until the end felt smooth to the touch. He stood the letter face up on the worktable. It gleamed in the light of the fire.

"Beautiful!" Gutenberg exclaimed. "It's beautiful!"

Taking the matrix out of the mold, Gutenberg put in another matrix and repeated the process. He was working in his shirt sleeves with an apron tied around his neck. His hands were red and his hair wet with perspiration.

"Just like coins," he laughed.

Gutenberg changed the matrix several times until he had used up all the gold melted in the crucible. He compared each letter. He was especially pleased by how well the locking and release lever of the mold worked. The brass punches laying on the table were almost as shiny as the letter castings, he thought.

"It works," Gutenberg said with deep satisfaction. "It really works!"

There was no one to share this excitement with, however, and Gutenberg hastily put out the fire and put on his coat. He must show Friele and Hultz the castings and how words and prints could be made. Wrapping the gold letters carefully in a soft cloth, Gutenberg slipped them into his belt. He took the mold apart and put its four pieces in the cuff of his boot. The punches and matrices he hid under the window ledge.

It was dark and cold outside now, but Gutenberg didn't notice as he got on his horse and galloped full speed into town. He wore no gloves and forgot his hat. The many long weeks of work had culminated in one afternoon of exhilarating and positive success, and Gutenberg was elated. The gold he was carrying was more valuable than money.

Viewing the letter castings spread out on a table in their room at the Kammersell, Friele and Hultz were also excited by what they saw. There were ten letters, neatly filed, plus one with the jet intact.

"Gold, Johannes?" Friele said.

"May I touch them?" Hultz asked.

"The letters are reversed," Gutenberg told them. "But in a mirror you can see how the prints will look." Gutenberg quickly arranged the letters to form a word. Holding the letters between his fingers, he held them before the mirror.

"Oh, I have them backwards," he said, and quickly changed the order. "Now look."

ΑΙUͺƎͺͺΑ

ΑͺͺƎͺUͺΑ

A · 2
L · 3
I · 1
E · 1
U · 1
M · 1
N · 1

Friele and Hultz stared in disbelief. The word was Alleluia.

"Alleluia!" Friele exclaimed.

"It's magic!" Hultz said.

"How many other words can you spell from these ten letters?" Gutenberg asked his brother.

Friele studied the castings and slowly rearranged them. "The n's and u's look the same," he remarked, and after a pause, "I can make two words, I think."

"What are they?" Hultz asked, looking over Friele's shoulder.

"Amen! and Lumen!"

"Three words from ten letters!" Gutenberg said.

"Amazing. It's amazing!" Hultz kept repeating.

Friele was ecstatic. "You said it could be done, Henne. Here is the proof! I am so proud of you!"

Gutenberg also wanted to demonstrate how the casting mold worked, but Friele was more interested in the letters and the words that could be formed so easily. Hultz was most impressed by the fact that reverse letters could be read in a mirror, and that Gutenberg had cast his first letters in gold.

"You are truly a master craftsman, Johannes," Hultz said with admiration.

"I shall have to remelt the gold into coins again," Gutenberg said. "But I shall keep the two A's. The next letters will be cast in lead, and then I'll be anxious to make a first print."

"You should scratch the date on the casting." Friele told him. "9 March 1430."

Gutenberg showed the mold and the gold letters to Count von Ramstein, Fr. Anthony and Johann Riffe. They all agreed that printing success was assured and swore to keep Gutenberg's activities a shared secret between them. Riffe was concerned that the wood block printers would try to prevent another method of printing from being introduced.

"The goldsmith guild would forbid Johannes from printing anything whatsoever!" von Ramstein said.

"The Count is right," Riffe agreed. "Casting metal letters for printing is entirely new, and anything new is looked upon with great suspicion."

Metal for the letters would be expensive, Gutenberg told them. They would be cast from an alloy of lead, tin and antimony, and he would need paper.

"My brother can get paper for you," Fr. Anthony said. "The guild will allow you to buy metal at low rates, I'm sure, but let them think it is for something else. Brass for door handles and book clasps. Lead for the molds."

It would be some time before he had enough letters to print anything, Gutenberg said, but he knew it was wise to keep the work private. He had made significant progress, and his friends were encouraging.

CHAPTER 9

In April the Alsace countryside was adorned with white and pink blossoms as orchards of peach, pear, cherry and apple trees came into flower. Crocus from which bright yellow saffron was obtained, bell flowers and snowdrops spread their blanket of beauty everywhere. Spring was Gutenberg's favorite time of the year.

The air smelled different, the brown fields were tinged with green and soon would be plowed. Chestnut buds swelled to the size of small fists then opened into giant leaves and tall candle-like flowers. On the first of May, Our Lady's Day, muguettes or lilies of the valley were in bloom, and peasants carried baskets of them from the country to sell in the cathedral square. Everyone wanted a bouquet to place before the statue or picture of his favorite saint. The huge nave of Notre-Dame, as well as every church in Strasbourg, was perfumed with these dainty, white, sweet-smelling flowers.

Gutenberg and his brother placed their bouquets beside the others at a side altar of the cathedral and said a prayer for the family in Mainz. Mary's Day was a holiday there too.

The first week in May, news came that all exiled patricians now could return to Mainz. A copy of the official announcement was posted at the Guild Hall and read from the church pulpit. Signed by Archbishop Conrad, and dated 28 March 1430, the document stated that "citizens of the old families and heirs were not bound to become guild members unless they wished of their own free will."

Friele was overjoyed. Claus and Friele-Else had written also and he read their letters over and over again.

"At last we can go home!" Friele exclaimed. "It's not a rumor!" He and Gutenberg sat on a bench outside the Kammersell where the other exiles had gathered to celebrate their good fortune.

"It is wonderful news," Gutenberg agreed.

"After almost two years, think of it!" Friele said. "We can be home for Whitsun, Henne! We can leave on Saturday!"

"I'm very happy for you," Gutenberg answered.

"Is that all you have to say?" Friele asked, expecting his brother to share the excitement. "What's the matter?"

"I don't think I shall go with you," Gutenberg said.

"Not go home?" Friele was stunned.

"No," Gutenberg said. "There are too many things to be done here. I wouldn't be able to work on the letters in Mainz."

"Of course you could work in Mainz," Friele argued. "You can get all the metal you want from Uncle Otto. Don't you want to go home?"

"Not just yet."

Friele could see that his brother meant what he said. "I don't understand you, Johannes," Friele said angrily. "Why is working in Strasbourg better than working in Mainz? I'd like to know because people will ask me! What do I tell Mama and Else?"

"Let's not argue, Friele," Gutenberg answered as he got up and walked alone across the square.

Friele followed him toward the quai, but neither spoke.

"I'm sure you think I'm crazy." Gutenberg said finally. "Until the news came, I never really thought about staying in Strasbourg. I could get metal in Mainz, yes. But I don't want to go home until I have accomplished something. I'm 32 years old, Friele. I have to prove to myself that the idea of printing from metal letters is possible. I have yet to find the right formula for the metal castings. How long that will take I don't know. And in Strasbourg I don't have to answer any questions, if I don't want to."

"Do you intend to become a citizen of Strasbourg?" Friele asked pointedly.

"Oh, no," Gutenberg answered. "Never. I won't ever change my citizenship, Friele. I like Strasbourg and the friends we've made, and I will go home one day. I just want to stay here a little longer, that's all."

Friele was surprised but satisfied with his brother's explanation. He was no longer angry. "Write to Mama" he said.

"You can take the letter with you," Gutenberg replied. "I hope she will understand."

Gutenberg friends found his decision unexpected also. That he took the new work so seriously and wanted to pursue it was commendable, they thought. Friele was sincerely pleased by Gutenberg's ambition and determination to continue working. He had a goal, a dream perhaps - and wanted to achieve it. That was good.

Johannes could have stayed in Mainz instead of becoming an exile with me, Friele reflected. If he wanted now to stay in Strasbourg, that too was his choice to make. Friele knew that going back to the Sorgenloch mint would not bring lifetime satisfaction to his brother. Johannes has talent and imagination. He's more intelligent, more creative than I am, Friele thought. The casting mold was a brilliant and original piece of work. If anyone could cast metal letters and print from them, it was Johannes Gensfleisch!

"I do understand," Friele told Gutenberg as the two of them packed Friele's trunk. "You are right to want to stay and finish the work. I wish you every success."

Gutenberg was glad for his brother's acceptance of his decision and for the encouragement.

"I'm sorry I got angry, Friele said. "I shall miss you very much, you know."

"Perhaps I can come home next year," Gutenberg answered.

Friele sensed a touch of wistfulness in the remark. It would be lonesome for Johannes, despite the work which lay ahead.

"Henne, will you tell me if you need money?" Friele asked. "The work will be expensive. The only way I can help is to make sure you have enough money for the things you need."

This generous gesture was so typical of his brother, Gutenberg thought. Never selfish, intensely loyal, that was the way Friele had always been, and these two years together had cemented their friendship and love for each other. Friele's approval of his decision was not necessary, but it pleased Gutenberg to know that Friele thought the work was worthwhile and wanted him to see it through.

"Just tell the family," Gutenberg said, "that I am working as a goldsmith. If the printing isn't successful..."

"But it will be!" Friele told him. "Send me your first print. Promise."

"That I will," Gutenberg smiled, "Whatever it is. Whatever it is!"

Friele's departure from Strasbourg was much more festive than their arrival had been. Exiles from Basel and other cities were already aboard the barge and would have many stories to tell. Loaded down with packages and gifts, Friele said he felt like a peddler.

"Did you forget anything?" Gutenberg asked, depositing a large basket of cheese on the quai next to Friele's belongings. "The paté, the silk for Friele- Else?"

"I have them," Friele said.

Embracing his brother and those who had come to see him off, Friele got on the barge happy and smiling.

"Write to me!" Gutenberg reminded him.

"Remember what I told you!" Friele called.

The boat slipped away, and Gutenberg stood waving for a long time until it turned into the canal Zurich and was out of sight.

Filled with a sudden longing to see Mainz again, Gutenberg headed back to the Kammersell low in spirit. Friele was returning to a life he knew and loved, to a future which was secure. He would be reunited with his family and watch his children grow up. He would be successful and contented. Why can't my life be like that? Gutenberg wondered. The idea of printing from metal letters was intriguing, but was it worth all the time and effort it would take? Gutenberg didn't know the answers. He didn't regret his decision, but he was sad to see his brother leave.

Sensing this, Fr. Anthony had waited at the Inn with an invitation for Gutenberg to join him for supper. "We have a prayer that helps in times like these," the prelate said. "The Lord is guiding me and nothing shall be wanting to me. He has set me down where there is good pasture," Strasbourg will be good pasture for you, Johannes, you'll see. You'll never regret taking the second step."

"Second step?" Gutenberg was puzzled.

"Yes, the first was coming here in the first place. Your future, your work for the moment are here, not in Mainz."

"I'm not ready to go home yet," Gutenberg admitted. "It's just hard to say goodbye to Friele."

"Then think of how good it will be when you see him again, when you go back to Mainz," Father smiled.

Gutenberg's good humor returned with the realization that he, too, could go home now whenever he wished. He was an exile no longer!

CHAPTER 10

True to his word and intention, Gutenberg began his experiments with metal for the letter castings after Friele left. His friends saw little of him. The von Ramsteins invited him to stay with them, and Gutenberg accepted their offer when he began to begrudge the time wasted in travelling back and forth from Strasbourg. He appreciated the convenience, not only of living so close to the shop but also the warm hospitality and home-like atmosphere of the estate.

Gutenberg purchased quantities of brass, lead, tin and antimony. Brass for the punches, lead for the matrices, and he would use a mixture of lead, tin and antimony for the letter castings. The small foundry consisted of a charcoal bed, large melting pot, mortars and pestles. He covered the dirt floor with reeds and planks to make it warmer in winter. A row of shelves and bowls to hold the finished castings lined one wall.

Gutenberg first completed the full set of punches and matrices, making one for each small and capital letter, number and punctuation mark. This took weeks of uninterrupted work. The casting of the letters, however, went rapidly, although filing off the overflow jet of surplus metal was tedious work. Holding each letter in a vise helped somewhat. Casting coins was far easier, Gutenberg thought. At least they were bigger and not so easy to lose.

Weeks quickly passed into months. Gutenberg grew a beard and when he made one of his rare visits to town, Johann Hultz hardly recognized him.

"You are a recluse," he said. "And so much thinner."

Fr. Sebastian was also concerned about Gutenberg's health as blisters and burns on his hands continued to look red and sore. When Gutenberg's arm became stiff and he had trouble holding things, the monk insisted he stay at St. Arbogast until the condition improved.

"You are risking blood poisoning or even lead poisoning, Johannes," he said. "The letters are not worth that!"

By this time, Gutenberg had cast hundreds of letters, but he was satisfied with none of them. Either they shrank after cooling or the hairline strokes did not hold up. Sometimes the letters broke when he removed the jet. It was very disheartening.

"I feel more like an alchemist than a goldsmith," Gutenberg told Hultz. "I'm using the right metals, I know, but I don't know how much tin or how much antimony to add. The alloy must be very hard. It's trial and error."

"Have you made any prints yet?" Hultz asked.

"No. I can see if a letter is sharp or not without making a print," Gutenberg told him. "If the spaces within a letter fill in, or a cross stroke disappears, I recheck the punch, I recheck the matrix. It's endless repetition. The mold works perfectly. But I still haven't found the right combination of metals for the castings."

Gutenberg reluctantly consented to take a few days rest at the monastery, which lengthened to a week and then into three months. The paralysis had spread up his left arm, his appetite was poor, and he knew it was useless to keep on working. Under the patient nursing care of the monks, Gutenberg gradually recovered. His hands and fingers became limber again by constantly squeezing the woolen ball Brother Paulo, a weaver, had made for him.

Gutenberg's confinement was irritating, however, and he grumbled about working in the mint for seven years without getting sick. He fretted about leaving the mold, the valuable metal and all his equipment at von Ramstein's. The Count assured Gutenberg that Jacques would take good care of everything. Nevertheless, Gutenberg insisted that Jacques bring him the mold and bury the bulk metal, letters, punches and matrices in the stable where no one could find them. He couldn't risk any losses.

Late fall Gutenberg and Paulo rode out to von Ramstein's to make sure the shop was closed up properly. Retrieving the letters and satisfying himself that the metal and other equipment were safely hidden, Gutenberg was resigned to postponing the work until spring. He would stay at the Kammersell during the winter and spend his time filing the letters.

"Perhaps you can help me, Paulo," Gutenberg told him. And if Fr. Sebastian gave permission, Paulo might assist him in the shop later on. The cheerful monk was good company and Gutenberg needed someone with him.

"Would you like to work for me?" Gutenberg asked. "I will teach you myself, and can give you a small stipend besides."

"I'd like that very much," Paulo answered enthusiastically. The metal letters the Master had showed him could be made into lines of words and pages just like the strands of wool could be woven into a blanket.

"I'd like to make words and print pages," Paulo said. "And I can read," he added proudly.

When Gutenberg returned to the shop, Paulo was allowed to assist him and the work went much faster. While Gutenberg mixed the metals, Paulo made the castings. The monk learned quickly and enjoyed seeing the little letters come out of the mold one after another. He learned to lop off the jet metal with one quick stroke of the hammer and to file the ends smooth.

To test the castings for hardness, Gutenberg stood them in rows, placed tightly together in a tray, then put the tray under a small cheese press filled with sand. By repeatedly raising and lowering the lever to bring the weight of the press down on the letters, he checked for breakage under pressure.

The exercise strengthened his arm, Gutenberg said, and if the letters didn't break, then he thought they might have the combination of metals he was looking for.

To check the printing impression of a letter, Gutenberg inked each casting on an ink ball before it was filed and then stamped it on a piece of paper. Imperfections not visible to the naked eye stood out clearly on the paper print. He checked the punches the same way.

"If the punch makes a sharp print, then the casting should make a sharp print," Gutenberg explained to Paulo. Punches and letters were remade if the test prints weren't perfect. Sometimes a new matrix was necessary.

When the punch was stamped too lightly or too deeply into the matrix, the casting would not print clearly either.

"Why don't we ink a whole tray of letters?" Paulo suggested. "Then we can see right away which ones are sharp and which are not. Paulo's suggestion meant checking for sharpness after the letters had been filed. It might save time, Gutenberg thought, and he agreed to try.

An assortment of letter castings were placed in the tray and inked with the ink ball. Gutenberg then rolled a sheet of paper over the letters. All the letters appeared to be sharp, but when Gutenberg and Paulo saw the print, they were dismayed. Some letters didn't print at all. Some broke through the paper. The ink on the print was not uniform but light in places and heavy in others.

"The table must not be level," Paulo said. He adjusted the table, and made a second print, with the same unsatisfactory result.

"A good idea, Paulo," Gutenberg said, "But it doesn't work. We'll have to check each letter by itself."

Paulo was greatly disappointed. "But I don't understand it," he said. "Most of the letters have been stamped already. The test prints were perfectly clear. Why aren't the letters as sharp and clear when we ink a whole tray?"

This was puzzling to Gutenberg also. "I don't know," he said. "I don't know—unless we aren't filing them evenly."

If the letters were sharp but didn't print, he reasoned, they must be too short. They had been filed too much. And if the print was smudgy and blurred, the castings must be too tall. They weren't filed enough.

"We'll just have to be more careful when we dislodge the jet," he said, "and not file the castings so much."

Paulo was comforted by Gutenberg's assessment of the problem. It was easier to make a print of an entire tray of letters, Gutenberg agreed. He thought they should continue to stamp the individual letters before the jet was removed, however, but after the letters had been filed, they would print a tray.

"We will remelt the short letters we can't use," he said, "and refile the tall ones. I think we learned something today, Paulo."

The letters must be the same height to print evenly, of course, Gutenberg thought. This was as important as perfectly cast letters, perfect punches and perfect matrices. Filing the letters was still drudgery, however, and Gutenberg wanted a hundred castings of each letter.

To relieve the monotony of making test prints from a jumble of letters, Paulo began assembling letters into words - starting with names, dates, and days of the week. But when the tray print was made, all the letters were backwards. Rearranging them, Paulo managed to get a second print with the letters in proper order.

Paulo also discovered that he could copy a handwritten page by placing it in a window, facing the pane and the light. It was easier, than using a mirror, he said. Either way, the words were reversed and could be copied in reverse, and it was easier for Paulo to read letters from right to left than upside down.

Even so, some letters looked so much alike it was hard to tell which were d's and which were p's and b's. And if these letters, were inverted, they printed upside down!

Composing words and sentences facinated Paulo, and Gutenberg smiled at the seriousness of his young assistant. He was pleased to see how much Paulo had learned so quickly and how skillful he had become.

IV. THE FIRST PRINTS
CHAPTER 11

"When are we going to print something, Master?" Paulo asked, as they prepared to close the shop for the night.

The question had been in his mind for days, now that the supply of letters was almost complete. The routine of casting, stamping, filing and test-printing would soon come to an end, and still Gutenberg had not said anything about what he wanted his first printed page to be.

"What would you like to print?" Gutenberg asked.

"Oh, that choice should be yours, Master," Paulo replied. "but something in Latin. Something from the Holy Scriptures, I think."

Gutenberg knew Paulo was anxious to use his skill with the letters to compose and print an entire page, but what page? Gutenberg had not thought much about it.

"I'll ask Fr. Sebastian," Gutenberg said. "And yes, we have enough letters now for at least a page."

The feast of St. Arbogast was next week, Paulo said. The monks would be pleased to have Gutenberg make his first print on that day.

Gutenberg wiped his hands on his apron and sniffed his fingers. "Printing is messy, dirty work," he said. "But I like the smell of ink! It is a good smell!" Then he washed his hands in pine oil to remove the black ink which still covered his palms and fingers, and took off his apron. "I'll get some fine paper," he said.

The ink was made from a combination of linseed oil and lampblack, the same ingredients used by the block printers and painters. Gutenberg used less oil, however, so the ink was tacky and thick enough to stick to the metal without running off or filling in between the letters. He also added a little varnish so the ink would dry more quickly on paper. Gutenberg had tested different combinations of the ink ingredients just as he had for the casting metal. It was like making bread or cake, he thought - the same ingredients in different proportions made the difference in texture. The knack of applying the ink evenly from a small sheepskin bag Gutenberg learned from the wood block printers.

The small press Gutenberg used was similar to a block press. Block printers had adapted a cheese press to their use by removing the round bottom board and making the top board attached to the screw square instead of round to cover a square wood block. The design was satisfactory for printing a page of metal letters also, though Gutenberg padded the board with cloth which smoothed the paper and gave a more even printing impression. And he changed the lever on screw to move back and forth instead of up and down. The push and pull movement was not as tiring and made it easier to control the pressure applied to the paper.

Fr. Sebastian was delighted to know Gutenberg was ready to print and was pleased to be asked to select what would be printed.

"Something from Scripture, you think," he said. "One of the Psalms perhaps. Part of Genesis. The Beatitudes. No." Fr. Sebastian thought a moment. "Why don't you print the Pater Noster, Johannes. This prayer to Our Father is familiar to all."

"An excellent choice, Father," Gutenberg answered. "It's not too long either."

"I'll make the handwritten copy for you myself," Fr. Sebastian said. "May I come and watch you work?"

Paulo composed the letters as Gutenberg looked on and explained to the priest exactly what was being done. "Composing is the most difficult part," he said. "Each letter must look like the letter in the window. It must face the same way. Paulo knows the Pater by heart, but still it's easy to make mistakes. Actually, someone who couldn't read could still copy the letters correctly, if he was careful."

Paulo worked slowly and said the words aloud as he worked. Gutenberg and Fr. Sebastian watched in silence so as not to distract him.

"That's the first line!" Paulo announced." 'Pater Noster, qui es in caelis.' How does it look?"

"Fine," Gutenberg said. "When you finish, we'll make a test print and check for mistakes. Don't worry if some letters are upside down."

"Shall I begin the second sentence by itself or continue in the same line?" Paulo inquired.

"It would be nice to separate the lines, I think," Fr. Sebastian said. Gutenberg agreed.

"All right," Paulo said. "Sanc-ti-fi-ce-tur...n-o-m-e-n space t-u-u-m," he continued, repeating each letter and syllable. The work took time.

Gutenberg saw Jacques the blacksmith standing in the doorway, and motioned to him. "Would you ask the Count to come here," he said. "Tell him it's important."

When the Count arrived, Gutenberg explained what Paulo was doing.

Jacques did not intrude, but from his part of the stable he could hear the monk singing. What was he singing? It sounded like the prayer in church!

" 'Panem nostrum quotidianum da nobis hodie,' " Paulo sang.

Jacques was bewildered. He could hear conversation, followed by silence, then the prayer began again. Jacques fell to his knees and waited. Finally he heard "Et ne nos inducas in tentationem" and the last word was repeated "ten-ta-ti-o-nem."

"Sed libera nos a malo," came from Paulo's lips. "Amen."

"Amen," Jacques repeated and crossed himself.

Gutenberg, Fr. Sebastian and Count von Ramstein also repeated the Amen and looked reverently at the tray of letters Paulo placed on the table.

Gutenberg jammed little pieces of wood in the corners of the tray to keep the letters snug, and applied the ink ball. He lay a quarto size sheet of paper on top of the letters, placed the tray under the press and lowered the screw. Then he raised the screw and removed the tray. Lifting two corners of the paper very carefully, he withdrew it and held it up for all to see.

"The ink is not dry. We must wait a moment," he said. Laying the page gently on the table, Gutenberg stood back so the others could get a closer look. "Remember this is a test print. We must see if there are any mistakes.

"It's beautiful," was all Fr. Sebastian could say. "Beautiful."

"You read it first, Paulo," Gutenberg said. "Then each of us will read it."

"I don't know what to say, Johannes," von Ramstein said. "I've never seen anything like this before!"

"I left out a u here," Paulo said. "An i is missing too. Ne nos is two words. The s is backwards. Oh, Master!"

"Don't be upset," Gutenberg told him. "It's fifty words and 247 letters. There are bound to be mistakes the first time."

"You counted the letters?" von Ramstein asked with surprise.

"Of course," Gutenberg answered. "We had to be sure we had enough i's an t's!"

Reading the prayer in turn, Fr. Sebastian noticed one word spelled wrong but the Count saw no mistakes. One of the capitals wasn't clear, Gutenberg thought, and he thought the first two words and the last word should be in capital letters.

After Paulo made the corrections, Gutenberg made second print. It was blurred and the last line wasn't straight. The margins were not right either,.

"Everything should be more or less centered on the page," he said, "with a little more space at the bottom." He lay the paper more carefully on top of the letters and made another print.

Five test prints were necessary before Gutenberg was satisfied and took out the watermark paper he had purchased.

When the first print on fine paper was made, everyone looked to Gutenberg for his approval. "Fine work, Paulo," Gutenberg said. "Fine work!"

Then Fr. Sebastian blessed the page, and the Count sent Jacques to the house to bring them a bottle of cognac.

Paulo was a little embarrassed by the compliments everyone gave him but smiled proudly. "It is a beautiful page, isn't it," he said. "And only took about three hour's time."

"You could have written the Pater much faster than that, Johannes," the Count laughed.

"But only three or four copies," Gutenberg responded. "Tomorrow we shall print fifty copies in less than three hours!"

CHAPTER 12

The following day Gutenberg and Paulo worked until late afternoon making fifty prints of the Pater Noster. They averaged about ten prints an hour, spoiling only six with thumb smudges of ink. The ink dried fairly quickly, but Gutenberg did not want to lay the sheets on top of each other. Finding a place to dry them became a problem. Paulo suggested hanging them over a wire the way monks did after pages had been illuminated. Folio sheets were folded over a wire, but the Pater quarto sheets could be attached with dab of wax in the middle of each page, he said. This was a good idea, Gutenberg thought, and he asked Jacques to string the wire for them.

"The pages look like laundry up there," Gutenberg laughed.

"They will look like manuscript," Paulo answered, "when I put a stroke of red ink on the capital letters."

The printing took time but had gone better than Gutenberg expected. The block press had worked well for them and he was pleased. But we don't print from wood blocks, he thought. This is a letter press. A letter press, because we print from metal letters!

Fr. Sebastian would keep his copy of the Pater Noster in the Missal he said, "to always remember this July 21 feast of St. Arbogast." Johann Hultz, Count von Ramstein and Fr. Anthony treasured their prints because Gutenberg had made them. But to Jacques the blacksmith, the Pater itself was the treasure. Now he could see the words the monk had been singing. Now the holy words were on paper he could hold in his hand.

Gutenberg read the prayer aloud for Jacques, moving his finger slowly along each line of letters. Jacques didn't speak and his eyes filled with tears.

"You can read the Pater for yourself now," Gutenberg said gently.

Jacques kissed the paper and put it inside his shirt. "God bless you Master," he said, "as long as you live."

Gutenberg's satisfaction with the initial success of the Paters was dampened by the tiresome task of refiling letters that were too tall and recasting those that were too short. The test prints always revealed letters of irregular height, and it was a time-consuming process to accumulate a quantity that did print evenly. It would take weeks to get enough good letters for the other prints they hoped to make.

"We can't add metal on!" Gutenberg told Johann Hultz. "I wish I knew what to do."

The two friends often discussed each other's work at the Kammersell and while Hultz was sympathetic, he could offer no solution.

"If filing isn't the answer, there should be a way of casting the letters the same height so they don't have to be filed. You'll find a way, Johannes," Hultz told him. "You always have."

But Gutenberg was discouraged.

When winter came, work on the spire was suspended until the snow and ice melted and it was safe to climb the turrets. Strasbourg winters weren't as severe as those in Mainz, though the canals froze and men fished through the ice. Children enjoyed sliding down the canal embankments and playing games on the ice which reminded Gutenberg of his own boyhood. A favorite sport was kicking a piece of wood from one bridge to another.

When it was too cold to work with wet mortar, many of the cathedral masons from other cities went home to be with their families and would not return until spring. Those who stayed, some of the wardens and stone cutters, often found work at the abbeys and monasteries where they received food and clothing in exchange for labor. Still, winter was a time of hardship. Homes were damp, dark and crowded, and even a mild sickness could be fatal. In March, after a thaw, the streets and roads were muddy, but a welcome sign too that warmer weather was on the way and planting could begin.

While Gutenberg struggled with his problems with the letters and prints, Paulo remained busy in the shop at von Ramsteins, often working alone when Gutenberg was in Strasbourg. Eager to compose and print other prayers, he was delighted when Gutenberg purchased a ream of paper from Nicholas Heilmann.

"Print whatever you like," Gutenberg told him, "But only ten copies. We'll keep fifty sheets for test prints and save the rest. We can't print a book until we have more letters and until I find a way to make the columns straight on both sides."

Gutenberg wanted the lines of letters to be as even on the right as on the left. He had experimented with the Pater lines and saw that when sentences followed each other as continuous text, the right edge was uneven, ending a word short or a few letters long. Words could be abbreviated and divided, but metal letters could not be squeezed together the way handwriting often was.

The width of the lines was not Gutenberg's most immediate problem however. He had to find a way to make the letters the same height. What good were the punches, the matrices, the mold, the metal formula, if perfect letters did not produce perfect prints! Perhaps Hultz was right, Gutenberg thought. Change the mold somehow and cast the letters in such a way that filing would not be necessary. But studying the mold and taking it apart gave him no clue about how this could be done.

At St. Arbogast, the monks marveled at the Paters and Fr. Sebastian's description of how they had been made. But some were envious because so many copies could be printed faster than the monks could write them.

"Does it matter so much that some letters print light or dark?" Fr. Sebastian asked Gutenberg.

"Yes," Gutenberg answered. "Each one should be as sharp as pen and ink! Every letter and every page should print clearly. Otherwise, they are no better than wood block letters and prints! And I'd like to print something in columns. When the letters are even and the columns are even, then I can print anything. But I'm not ready yet. Maybe never."

"Be satisfied with what you have accomplished," the monk told Gutenberg. "And ask God's help to overcome these other obstacles. If they can be overcome."

"I am positive there is a way of casting the letters so they can be perfect the first time," Gutenberg replied. "I can't be satisfied until I know how to do it."

An unforeseen difficulty developed when Gutenberg requested metal from guildmaster Lebert and was refused. Lebert knew about the new mold, he said, and was angry because Gutenberg had not told him about it. An adjustable mold, very well made, that opened and closed like a lock? Why hadn't Gutenberg shown it to the guild? What was the mold to be used for? If Gutenberg wished to buy metal, he should demonstrate the mold as soon as possible. Lebert was a person of authority and resented the man from Mainz acting so independently.

"Monsieur Lebert," Gutenberg answered, "I am not a member of the Strasbourg guild. I am not obliged to show you anything! But I will, at the proper time." He needed metal for a second mold because the first one did not work properly. The mold could be used to cast bolts and screws possibly, one mold for any size bolt, and the mold could be used over again.

Lebert scoffed at this. They had molds for bolts and screws. Still, he was interested. Perhaps the mold could be used for other things. "We would like to see it," Lebert repeated.

"And I need metal to make it!" Gutenberg replied. "I will demonstrate it as soon as I can."

Lebert's anger subsided. "We would like you to become a member of the guild, Master," he said, "but we must examine your work first. Until then, I will see that you get the metal you need."

Hultz was not surprised that Lebert knew about the mold. Colonjard had been proud of his part in the work, Hultz told Gutenberg, and he had kept it a secret until the mold was finished. Then he couldn't help bragging.

"Colonjard promised he would tell no one," Gutenberg said. "He broke his promise to me."

"The man meant no harm, Johannes," Hultz answered, "and he is a fine craftsman. Let him make the second mold for you."

But how could the mold be used to cast bolts and screws, Hultz wanted to know. The letters were square. Bolts were round. It would be no problem, Gutenberg assured him, and he had to tell Lebert something.

"If I solve the problem with the letters, then I will demonstrate the mold," Gutenberg said. "But I didn't say when this might be possible."

"Lebert will like the mold," Hultz replied. "He may not like the idea of casting letters from it. Will you become a member of the guild in Strasbourg?"

"Perhaps," Gutenberg answered. "Perhaps. But I want to be able to bargain. The mold for metal, and membership in the guild for freedom to pursue my own work. The guild is welcome to the mold design."

Tired and frustrated with what seemed insurmountable problems, Gutenberg received news that his mother was dying in Mainz. Anxious and upset, he made plans to go home immediately. He was also relieved in a way to transfer his anxieties to family matters.

Gutenberg would take only the casting mold, some punches and matrices, and a bag of letters with him. The quantities of bulk metal and paper, the foundry equipment and letter press, he would leave in Strasbourg with Count von Ramstein. They would be safe with him.

Perhaps he would remain in Mainz, Gutenberg told the Count. If so, the paper and metal, everything could be sold. Or he would send for it later. "I don't know what I will do," he said.

"Where you work doesn't matter," the Count replied. "But you must not abandon the work, Johannes, or everything you have accomplished so far will be lost."

"I have accomplished so little," Gutenberg answered wearily. "Finish the work, I keep telling myself. But nothing gets finished!"

Hultz and Fr. Anthony also tried to dispel his sense of failure.

"The work is incomplete, that's all," Hultz reminded him. "Like the spire. You haven't failed in your purpose, Johannes. Nor have I. If we stop now, then we admit failure."

Fr. Anthony knew that seeing Gutenberg again was more important to his family than the letters, the prints, any work he has done. "You're going home because your family needs you, and you're a good son." he said. "The work is important to you, but you are important to them. We hope you will come back soon, but don't make any decisions for a while. Let God show you the way."

Standing on the quai where Friele had left in such high spirits three years before, Gutenberg and his friends, by contrast, were a quiet little group. No one spoke very much as they shook hands and said goodbye. It was difficult, not knowing if Gutenberg would return or if any of them would meet again.

"Johannes is like a son to me," von Ramstein said, as the barge pulled away.

"And a brother to me," Hultz said.

"Johannes will be back," Fr. Anthony assured them. "He will want to see the finished spire and recover his equipment. We must hope that he sees his mother before she dies."

Gutenberg had mixed feelings as the barge entered the Rhein. He was glad to be going home, yet he would miss Strasbourg and the people who had become dear to him. They care about me and my work, he thought. I hope they know I am grateful. Had he really been in Strasbourg five years?

It became warmer, and the barge moved slowly. Gutenberg wondered if he should have traveled overland to shorten the journey. Then he remembered the farewell gifts he had received and opened them.

Fr. Anthony had given a wheel of his favorite cheese. Fr. Sebastian, a large paté and six blessed candles. From Count von Ramstein, there were twelve bottles of wine. Johann Hultz had sent a stone from the spire, and chiseled his mark on it. Jacques had forged a cross from two horseshoe nails. Paulo's package looked like a book.

Gutenberg unwrapped the sheepskin packet. In it was a set of ten half quires, eight pages each, octavo size. He turned the pages and saw that there were prints on every page! The Ten Commandments, the Sanctus, the Agnus Dei..the chants Da Pacem, O Salutaris, Tantum Ergo..the Laudate Psalm, the Regina Caeli. Gutenberg couldn't believe his eyes.

These weren't single pages like the Pater Noster. Paulo had used quarto leaves and printed two pages on each side of each leaf, then nested and folded them to octavo size, the way manuscript books were assembled.

The letters were surprisingly sharp and uniform. The ink had covered well. The titles and margins were nicely placed. Paulo had even left space for a two line initial on each page. Only four of them were painted in, but the effect was startling - black text highlighted with red and blue initials.

Gutenberg had taken several of the Pater Nosters with him, but Paulo's collection was extraordinary. How had he ever managed to compose so many lines and to print them so beautifully, Gutenberg wondered. How long and patiently he must have worked! Gutenberg replaced the prints and sealed the packet.

"The work is important to Paulo," Gutenberg said aloud. "I hope it is as important to me."

CHAPTER 13

Gutenberg left the barge at Speyer and obtained a horse to carry him the remaining 20 leagues into Mainz. North of Strasbourg travel by land would have been slow because of the thick woods and hills, but from Speyer north the countryside was flat. Gutenberg rode fast and without fear along the well- traveled road. He would be home easily in two or three days.

Everything was familiar this last lap of the journey. The road overlooked the Rhein now and vineyards rose endlessly on the gentle slopes to the left. Beyond Worms and Oppenheim, the small villages of Nierstein, Nakenheim, Laubenheim and Weisenau had changed little, and Gutenberg was filled with excitement and apprehension as he approached Mainz' south gate. He could see the six towers of St. Martin's cathedral clearly through the near-dusk.

Hof zum Gutenberg was on Christophstrasse not far from the Dom, and Gutenberg hoped and prayed there would be no black drape on the door. He urged his horse to a slow trot. Thinking of the house brought the family history to mind. The house was one hundred years old, built by Gutenberg's great-great- grandfather, Pederman zum Eselweck. His daughter, Nesa, had inherited it when she married Peterman zum Gensfleisch, and six generations of the family had lived in it. Gutenberg's mother, his sister Else, her husband Claus Vitzthum, and little Else lived there now. Did they still have a cat, he wondered. How old was Little Else? Surely a young lady by now after five years. Friele's daughter, Odilgen, was nine and Orte, her brother, a busy six-year old, Friele had written proudly. Gutenberg wondered if the children would remember him.

Gutenberg rode down the Rheinstrasse to turn left at the Fischtor. The large Domplatz looked just the same - the well, the shops, closed now because it was dark. I should light a candle in the Dom, he thought. Tomorrow I'll come with Else. Dear Else. And Claus. What a blessing he has been since Friele and I left Mainz together. He looked after Mama and Friele-Else, too, before her sister came to stay with her. Friele and his family lived in Eltville now, in a grand new house, Else wrote.

Gutenberg was hot and tired as he approached Hof zum Gutenberg. He could see the black iron gate and the Gensfleisch hatchment over the door-the man with a cape and carrying a bowl. There was no black drape.

"Oh, thank God," he breathed.

With a lighter heart, Gutenberg whistled loudly and pounded on the knocker. He dismounted and waited impatiently for someone to open the door.

At age 59, Frau Gensfleisch was still a pretty woman. Much thinner and frailer than Gutenberg remembered, she was nevertheless alert and attentive to everything around her. To see her three children together again before she died had been her constant prayer.

"Now I can go to God in peace, Henne," she told Gutenberg, her eyes smiling. "Both of my sons are home!"

Sitting by her bed each day, Gutenberg told his mother about Strasbourg and the metal letters. He showed her the Paters and prayers Paulo had printed. He told her about Hultz and the spire. He even described for his sister how to make the little cherry tarts he was so fond of. Being with everyone again was wonderful, and Gutenberg wondered why he had stayed away so long.

Aside from Claus and Friele, Gutenberg did not discuss his work with anyone. When Friele urged him to go to Sorgenloch and talk with cousin Rudi about the problems bothering him, Gutenberg was not interested. He refused to think about any future plans. "Not yet," he said. "I'm here, that's enough. There's no hurry."

Gutenberg especially enjoyed his nieces and nephew, and while his mother continued to be well, he took them to Mittelheim to see the old church of St. Aegidius.

Not far from Eltville and on the shore of the Rhein, the church was famous because of the anchorite who had lived under the altar and for the legend of St. Urban and the well.

St. Urban was known throughout the Rheingau as the foreteller of a good or poor grape harvest, Gutenberg told the children. In the spring, his statue was carried from the church and stood in the vineyard. If the sun shone on that particular day, it meant a fine fall harvest and Urban was rewarded with wreathes of flowers round his neck. But if it rained, a poor harvest was expected and Urban was punished by being lowered into the well where he must either drink the water or drown in it. The plucky old saint, and a pope at that, had suffered the indignity of immersion many times. The past spring he had been spared, Odilgen said, and Gutenberg was glad.

The story of the anchorite at St. Aegidius was a true one, and visitors to the church could see the niche under the altar where a nun once lived and prayed. Wishing to be as close to the Blessed Sacrament of the Lord as possible, her self-imposed imprisonment and solitude brought both fame and blessings to the people of Mittelheim who regarded her as saint.

"Your mother and father and I used to play anchorite," Gutenberg told the children. "One time Friele and I made a little box for Else to live in and brought her a candle and piece of bread to eat. Then she said her prayers. Only your father and I went off and forgot all about Else! When we came home, our Papa asked 'where's your sister?' and we remembered we had left her alone in the box. Well, Else came home by herself, crying, and we were punished. Your mother used to say she might have become a nun if we hadn't been so mean!"

"Papa never told us that," Orte said.

"Mama did," Little Else said. "But I know she's glad she got married instead."

Odilgen thought she might like to be a nun, but said she'd rather live in a convent.

Gutenberg's mother died quietly on August 2, 1433, less than a month after his arrival. Her funeral was large, attended by many relatives from the Wirich and Furstenburg, Gensfleisch and Gelthuss sides of the family, and by Patze Blashof, the only child of her husband's first marriage. Else Wirich Gensfleisch was buried beside her husband in the nave of St. Francis church.

At home, after the De Profundis was recited, the will was read. Friele, Else and Gutenberg each received an annuity, and Gutenberg inherited the family home.

"Mama hopes you will marry," Else told her brother.

"Perhaps I shall one day," Gutenberg answered, "but until then, this is your home, too, as long as you and Claus wish to stay."

He was going to Sorgenloch now, Gutenberg told Friele, to visit Rudi and Uncle Otto, hoping they would be able to help him solve the aggravating problem with the height of the metal letters. Whether he remained in Mainz or not depended on many things.

CHAPTER 14

Gutenberg and his cousin Rudi had been apprentices together at the episcopal mint in Sorgenloch, where Uncle Otto and his brothers were the custodians. Everything Gutenberg knew about metal, he had learned from the master goldsmiths at Sorgenloch. If Rudi couldn't solve the height problem, Gutenberg knew it would be useless to continue his work. And if they did solve the problem, then he needed the cooperation of the Mainz goldsmith guild to buy metal and train men to work with him. Would the guild be willing to help, Gutenberg wondered.

"Master Gering has never forgiven you, Johannes, for not supporting the guild five years ago," Rudi said, when they sat down to talk. "You not only stood by the patricians, you went into exile and have been away a long time. I don't think you would be reinstated in the guild. I know you couldn't buy metal, except from us."

"I wouldn't be allowed to work in Mainz, you mean," Gutenberg answered. "Even if I show the guild my new mold?"

Rudi and Uncle Otto shook their heads. Neither thought Gutenberg would be able to get support from the guild.

"You could work privately, yes, but I don't think you could open a shop, if that's what you'd like to do," Rudi said.

"What new mold have you made?" Uncle otto asked. "Did you bring it with you?"

"Yes," Gutenberg told them. "And I need your help."

Gutenberg unwrapped a leather package and removed the four pieces of the casting mold and laid them on the table. Then he took out a handful of punches and matrices and a bag of metal letters. Beside them, he placed two prints of the Pater Noster.

"The mold is used to cast letters - like these," he said. "For printing pages like this. The Pater was printed from metal letters."

Rudi and Uncle Otto were dumbfounded. "The prints look like manuscript!" Rudi said.

"I hope so!" Gutenberg laughed. "My idea is to cast letters of the alphabet, make them into words and then print the words on paper. I'll show you how it's done."

"I can't believe these aren't written by hand," Uncle Otto said.

Gutenberg assured him they were not, and stood several of the castings face up so he could see them better.

"The letters are in reverse, of course, to print right side up. Watch." Gutenberg quickly arranged the letters to spell their names and smiled to see their looks of astonishment.

"Why do you want to print from these letters?" Uncle Otto asked.

"Because, Uncle, from single letters you can make as many words as you want and as many lines and pages as you want. Because metal is hard, it lasts longer and prints better than wood," Gutenberg explained, "so you can make as many copies as you want. We printed fifty Paters, just like these. And I could print fifty different pages and make fifty prints of each page in less time than it takes to write fifty pages, one copy, by hand. I can print books this way!"

"You want to print books - from metal letters?" Uncle Otto asked in amazement.

"It's possible," Gutenberg answered. "It is possible."

"How do you cast the letters?" Rudi wanted to know.

"I'll show you," Gutenberg said. He assembled the mold, inserted a matrix, and pretended to pour in the metal. He unlocked the mold and held up a letter casting. "There you are."

"Casting is simple," Gutenberg continued, "but composing the lines of letters takes time. And filing the letters after they are cast. The problem is I can't file them the same height. The letters don't print evenly."

"The mold is ingenious, Johannes," Uncle Otto said. "I've never seen anything like it. It's adjustable, and you can use it over again. The same mold makes castings any size you want, as many as you want!"

"The guild would be very interested in the mold," Rudi said.

"But not for letters, not to print books," Uncle Otto said. "You're a dreamer, Johannes!"

"The Paters prove it can be done, Uncle," Rudi said. "You take the letters apart and use them over again. Metal doesn't break. I've seen wood block books, Johannes. The quality is poor. What kind of metal do you use for the casting?"

Gutenberg told them about the many experiments and changes he had made in the metal formula before getting the alloy he wanted. "The hairlines are sharp, you see. There's no shrinkage. But I can't control the height. We've filed hundreds of castings and recast hundreds more, just to get enough to print clearly."

"A lot of work, Henne," Uncle Otto remarked. "You're right about one thing - filing isn't the answer. If you want letters the same height, they have to be cast that way, in the mold."

"Do you know how it could be done?" Gutenberg asked.

"We can work on it," Rudi answered.

The next day, watching Gutenberg pour metal and make a few castings, Rudi was struck by the ease and quickness of the work. Removing the jet and then filing each letter afterwards was time-consuming, however, and not precise.

"What you need, Johannes, are feet for the castings to stand on," Rudi said. "You must change the funnel to make an overlap at the base. You want three flat feet, that's all."

"Show me what you mean," Gutenberg replied.

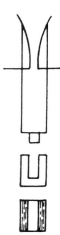

"The jet must not come straight up from the base," Rudi went on. "Make it come up on one side only. Overlap the funnel on three sides so you have a lip. The lip becomes the feet, you see. You can change the funnel or put a U-shaped piece around it. Either way. Then the base will stand level, on the feet, and the height is always the same. I'll make a wood model for you."

Taking a small square peg, the size of a casting with jet attached, Rudi scored it at a mid point on three sides, then cut an angular notch tapering in from the top to that point on each side.

"The flat side of the angles, at the bottom, are the feet," he said. "This is the jet. And so when you knock it off, it should leave a depression between the feet. All you do is file out a little deeper between the feet, if necessary. I think it will work."

"So do I, Rudi!" Gutenberg answered excitedly. "Flat feet! Why couldn't I see that before!"

"The castings are too small," Uncle Otto observed. "Why don't you make the base or shank longer so you can hold on to them?"

"Well, the two L sides could be higher, I suppose," Gutenberg said. "What do you think, Rudi?"

"A good idea," Rudi agreed. "The castings will be a little heavier too and that might help. Maybe as wide as your thumb, Uncle?"

Changing the mold took some time. New L sides were cast, and Rudi designed and cast the new funnel piece that would rest on top.

"I think compressing the metal will help," Rudi said. "The extra height and weight should make a difference."

"I concentrated on the shrinkage and hardness for the face of the letters," Gutenberg said, "and never realized that height of the castings would be so important. The base and feet are as important as the face!"

The new mold still consisted of four pieces of metal locked together, plus the U-shaped funnel, and handle. The size overall had not changed perceptively. When it was completed, Gutenberg asked his cousin if he would like to make the first casting.

"Leave the jet on," Gutenberg told him, "so we can see if the feet are wide enough. The overlap must be wide enough."

Rudi made the casting and they both examined it. Satisfied, Rudi made a second casting and handed to Gutenberg. "You strike the jet, Henne," he said.

Gutenberg put the casting in a vise and tapped the jet firmly with a hammer. The metal did not come off cleanly but the feet were there. "Let's try it again." Gutenberg said. "Use less metal, Rudi, so the jet isn't so high."

The third time all of the jet came off but there was no depression between the feet. "Make another." Gutenberg said.

It took practice to strike off the jet just right. Sometimes the depression was good, other times it was not, though the feet remained flat and smooth. They repeated the process over and over, taking turns casting and removing the jet. By late afternoon, Gutenberg thought they had enough useable castings to make a test print.

"Shall we make the print tonight or wait till tomorrow?" Gutenberg asked.

"Do it now," Rudi answered wearily. "Let's see the proof that the letters are the same height. We'll both sleep better."

Putting the new letters in a tray the way he and Paulo had done, Gutenberg inked them and made a test print. It was perfect. Each letter was sharp and clear, and the lines had printed uniformly, without leaving any light or dark spots on the paper. The work had taken all day, but the results were what they had hoped for.

"We've done it!" Gutenberg said. "We've finally done it! Letters with flat feet and big enough for Uncle Otto to hold!"

"I'm glad," Rudi replied. "I'm glad for you, Henne. Now let's go home. I'm hungry! We can tell Uncle Otto tomorrow."

"I couldn't have done it without you, Rudi," Gutenberg said. "The new funnel and lip made all the difference."

Uncle Otto was impressed by his nephews' accomplishment and pleased to have had a small part in it. He insisted his brothers come to see the finished work, though it was the mold rather than the letters which interested them the most. Before leaving Sorgenloch, Gutenberg gave Rudi and Otto the letters of their names cast in silver to keep as a remembrance.

Finding a solution to the letter height problem meant that from now on all the prints would be perfect, and Gutenberg returned to Mainz thinking seriously about the printing he wanted to do. Despite what Rudi and Otto had said about the guild masters, Gutenberg was confident he could gain their support by showing them the Paters and prints Paulo had made and by offering to demonstrate the mold and his method of printing from metal letters on a letter press. A small book was possible now and would be impressive.

Gutenberg let his horse walk at a leisurely pace, and as he turned north onto the Alzey road, every view was familiar to him. Now in early fall,the woods were dark red and the black bark of the maples would soon be hidden behind a mass of orange and yellow leaves. He passed a towering pine, a landmark that had survived some hundred years. Its topmost branches were weighted with pine cones and the lower branches dipped to the ground in a wide, lacy green circle. Birds were congregating, and Gutenberg saw a pheasant fly away and hide.

The country was peaceful. Some fields had been cut leaving a toasted, dry scent in the air. Gutenberg remembered that his father used to say 'Mainz is only as prosperous as the land beyond her walls'. That was true, he thought. Cities changed, but the land changed little, as long as the lords of the castles were not fighting each other. There had been terrible days when the fields and vineyards were destroyed by soldiers and horses running through them. This year Gutenberg hoped rain would not spoil the harvest before all of the grain was safely stored for the winter.

Gutenberg decided to discuss his future printing plans with friends at a dinner at his home. "Would you mind being my hostess?" he asked his sister.

"Oh, I'd like that very much!" Else said.

"It's not too soon after the funeral?"

"To go out perhaps, but not to have company," Else told him. "Who would you like to invite, Henne?"

Gutenberg wanted Friele and Claus, he said, Rudi, Uncle Otto, if he would come, cousin Arnold Gelthuss, and Claus' friend, Dr. Conrad Humery. "I'd also like to ask Karl Mueller from the guild, and the deacon

54

from Eltville who Friele knows well."

Clause agreed that both Mueller and the deacon should be included. "The guild might refuse you an apprentice," Claus said, "but the monastery might cooperate by loaning you someone like Brother Paulo. You need an assistant."

"That's eight for dinner," Else said, "plus you and me and the wives."

"It is not necessary for the wives to come," Gutenberg replied.

"Friele-Else will be hurt," Claus observed, and thought they must ask her.

"This is not a social evening." Gutenberg said, "but Claus is right, and Friele-Else is family. If only she wasn't so disagreeable."

"I'll tell her you and Claus insisted that she come," Else teased. "That's eleven, and Little Else makes twelve. An even number is better."

Else, Claus, Friele and Gutenberg had always been close, but Friele's wife, called 'Friele-Else' because there were so many Else's in the family, was a selfish and self-righteous person. Her family, Hirtz, were patricians of Mainz also but had never held positions in the civil government as the Gensfleisch had done. Friele-Else was sensitive to this and very proud of the social status her marriage had given her. Friele indulged her extravagances. Their home in Eltville was a mansion. Yet Friele-Else was jealous and resentful of Else and Claus living at Hof zum Gutenberg.

Family relationships had often been strained, and Claus tried to ease the strain, although Friele-Else made it difficult. Gutenberg knew that his sister had been hurt many times.

"I don't let Friele-Else upset me anymore," Else told her brother. "She will expect to be asked, and for Friele's sake, we must not offend her."

"She will bring flowers," Claus said, "and we must be appreciative!"

"She will criticize the food but eat everything," Else laughed. "What would you like me to serve, Master Gensfleisch?"

After enjoying a delicious meal of fish, venison with white asparagas and cherry tarts for dessert, the guests were interested in what Gutenberg had to say about his work.

"You want to print a book?" the deacon from Eltville asked incredulously. "Which book?"

"A Donatus, perhaps. Or a book of the Canonical Hours," Gutenberg answered. "Anything else would be too ambitious right now. Do you think the abbot would give me permission to print 25 Donatus, Father?" The

Donatus was a Latin schoolbook, and Gutenberg knew the monks never had enough copies for their students.

The Benedictine cleric was a scholarly, middle-aged man who listened intently as Gutenberg described his metal letters and the ability to print from them. He was impressed with the Paters and said so. But he was not prepared for anything like the request he had just heard.

"You are not a member of the clergy, Master!" he said. "Print Donatus? The abbot could not give you permission. The Archbishop would have to consent, and Archbishop Conrad is very ill." The Benedictine shook his head. "I also doubt that scriptorium monks will appreciate your method of duplicating manuscript, or your offer to print Donatus for them."

"But the Paters show what can be done," Gutenberg answered stubbornly. "I didn't need the archbishop's permission to print in Strasbourg! A Benedictine monk was my assistant! Let me show you what he has printed!"

Gutenberg showed the deacon Paulo's collection of prayers. They were very nice, the deacon admitted, but made no further comment.

"Books in Mainz are published by the monasteries, Master," the cleric went on. "I suggest you print other things. A list of fast days, for example. Copies of the tax lists would be useful."

"I'm not interested in tax lists!" Gutenberg retorted angrily.

"Public announcements then," Arnold Gelthuss suggested. "Books could come later."

"We printed fifty Paters!" Gutenberg replied. "We could have printed a hundred! I could copy a Donatus just as easily!"

"But not without approval," the cleric repeated. "You are a goldsmith, Master Gensfleisch. Printing from metal letters as you describe would have to be sanctioned by the guild and by the clergy. You cannot proceed independently in either case. Perhaps if you printed something for the guild first."

"You will be reinstated in the guild, I'm sure," Karl Mueller said. "Master Gering may not be friendly, but he could not deny you membership. The trouble would come in getting apprentices to work with you. You can't work alone. You have to train people to help - not monks, but goldsmiths."

"Could I open my own shop?" Gutenberg asked Mueller. "The guild is welcome to the mold, but I want to work as I please. I have no objection to training guild apprentices, but printing for the guild does not interest me. If I allow the guild to use the mold, I don't want Master Gering telling me what I can use it for!"

"Which is more important," queried Claus, "the mold and the letters or what you can print from them?"

"What I print now is most important," Gutenberg answered. "I haven't worked so hard and for so long to print tax notices. Or a list of fasting regulations!"

"However, you need metal and paper," Mueller reminded him, "and the guild could get them for you."

"You have been away from Mainz a long time, Master," Dr. Humery said. "Whatever you propose to do will be criticized. If the clergy would help, then I'm sure the guild would also. But you can't rely on Gering or the guild to give you everything you want. Gering might not want to use the mold, and he might even forbid you from using it. I think there are too many problems for you here, Master. My advice would be to return to Strasbourg. Print books there, if you can, and then come back to Mainz when Gering and Archbishop Conrad are gone."

This blunt summation of the situation, Gutenberg found difficult to accept. He could not understand the opposition and restrictions he faced in Mainz, yet there was truth in what his friends had said. Working without help from the guild and the clergy would be as difficult as working with their help. Gutenberg's enthusiasm and impatience to begin work with the new letters changed abruptly by realities made painfully clear.

Even Friele had not anticipated the deacon's lack of encouragement, yet it seemed to him that his brother was also uncompromising about printing books and maintaining independence from the guild.

CHAPTER 15

"Why must you print a book, Johannes?" Friele asked as he and Gutenberg rode together to Ingelheim, once a palace of Charlemagne not far from Mainz. "Why can't you work at home? You don't need a shop."

"Gering would never give me a minute's peace, wherever I worked," Gutenberg answered. "And unless I print an entire book, with an abbot's blessing, no one will believe it can be done. I had thought of printing something else, but changed my mind. I want to print something important. And a book, even a Donatus, would be important."

Dr. Humery was right, Gutenberg said. In Strasbourg he had good friends in and out of the clergy. He could buy metal and paper easily. Lebert would be honored to have him join the guild.

"I risk nothing if I work in Strasbourg," Gutenberg told his brother. "But here I could jeopardize everything I've accomplished so far. I'm going back, Friele, and if I don't succeed, it's better to be a failure in Strasbourg than in Mainz."

The day was crisp and a light snow had fallen, sparkling in the sun and giving life to the ruins of the imperial palace. Gutenberg always liked the view from this hill overlooking the big islands of the Rhein and Johannisberg monastery on the far side. They would return home by the Finthen road, a route Gutenberg and Friele had often taken as boys together. Neither said much as they sat and rested their horses. Friele accepted his brother's decision, and they did not discuss it further.

"You have Mama's annuity now," Friele said, "That will help you establish a shop in Strasbourg. You must give my regards to Count von Ramstein and all the others."

"I don't know how long I'll be gone," Gutenberg said. "But Mainz is my home and I will come home again. When I do, I'll have my books with me."

"And then I shall say 'Johannes Gensfleisch - Johannes Gutenberg' - that famous man is my brother!" Friele answered proudly.

Gutenberg was glad for this time with Friele. It would be more difficult leaving Mainz now than it had been before, and Gutenberg still felt the loss of his mother. Renewing his ties with the family, however, had been very satisfying. They reined their horses at a small inn near the caretaker's house.

"Shall we have a glass of wine, Friele?" Gutenberg asked.

"Cognac, I think. I'm cold!" Friele said.

"Cognac, of course!" Gutenberg agreed. "We must drink to the emperor and to each other!"

Else was saddened most by the thought of Gutenberg's departure. He had been home such a short time, it seemed. She knew he was excited about the future, but that didn't lessen her own sense of loss. Making a visit to St. Francis church where their mother was buried, Gutenberg and Else left flowers at her grave and then sat in the churchyard to talk.

"I won't leave until after Epiphany," Gutenberg told his sister, "but

I must go before ice freezes on the river, or I may have to stay until spring."

"I wish you could," Else answered.

"Mama said I was to buy metal," Gutenberg said, "and I think I will rent a house in Strasbourg. Then you and Claus can visit me."

"That would be nice," Else replied. "Would you marry a girl from Strasbourg, Henne?" she added.

Gutenberg was surprised by the question. The Alsacian girls were pretty and charming, he said, but he had really been too busy to think of marrying anyone. Else didn't mind who he married, she told him, if they came back to live in Mainz.

"I will be back," Gutenberg promised. "I shan't die in Strasbourg."

Else's eyes filled with tears. "We'll miss you so much, Henne," she said.

Gutenberg squeezed his sister's hand and kissed her. "I'll miss you," he said. "My dear Else."

The bells for the Angelus sounded, and Gutenberg and Else walked out of the churchyard arm in arm. "You must promise to write more often," Else scolded, but she was smiling now. "We will visit you soon!"

It was late February when Gutenberg again found himself at a barge railing, going slowly up the Rhein to Strasbourg. All the family had been at the Fischtor to see him off, and everyone had brought a present. Else and Claus gave him a mirror. Little Else knitted the scarf he wore. Orte and Odilgen gave him a cake to eat on the way. Friele and Friele-Else had given him a large statue of St. Christopher, protector of travelers. Gutenberg didn't know where he would put it, but was glad it was made of wood instead of stone. The warmest memory was of the three children standing on the shore and singing "Wiedersehn" as the barge pulled away. Their clear voices carried sweetly across the water, and the captain had rung the bell.

Rudi and Uncle Otto met the barge at Oppenheim to say goodbye. Gutenberg wished Rudi were able to go to Strasbourg with him. If he was successful with the printing, perhaps they might work in Mainz one day, Gutenberg told his cousin. Rudi sincerely hoped that would be possible.

Sitting on the deck as the barge moved slowly up river, Gutenberg had time to think. The block printers and monks might resist my work, but not all. Guild members might be unwilling to learn something new, but not all. I will find someone in Strasbourg who will print books with me! And if pages can be written in quires, they can be printed in quires, with 25 copies of each page instead of only one. I must have many more letters. I must have a larger press too, one that is big enough to print folio size sheets.

Gutenberg thought also of what Claus had said. 'The idea of printing books in many copies, as you describe, is frightening, Johannes. Not because it's impossible, but because it might be possible!' And what had he told his nephew? 'There is only one Orte Gensfleisch and one Johannes Gensfleisch. We have to make our names mean something. Something good and a credit to the family.'

Gutenberg continued his journey, mulling over the many things to be done when he got to Strasbourg. He was confident that with the new mold the work would progress rapidly. He would apply for membership in the Strasbourg guild and show Lebert the casting mold. Then he was assured of getting the metal he needed. Lebert would be privy to the work with the letters, and while he might not understand or approve, he would not interfere.

V. THE ROMANCE
CHAPTER 16

Gutenberg received a warm welcome from his friends in Strasbourg. They were happy to learn that his major problem with the letters had been solved and that he planned to work in Strasbourg once again.

Gutenberg had received an annuity from his mother, he said, which enabled him to purchase the metal and other materials he needed. He wanted to rent a house so he could have guests and entertain properly, and he also would like to rent a small shop in town where he could work.

"I must not impose on Count von Ramstein any longer," Gutenberg told Fr. Sebastian. The monk suggested that he consider leasing their guest house near the abbey at St. Arbogast and Gutenberg went to see it.

Situated less than a league south of the city, the property included an orchard, stable and barn. The house was partially furnished and had a fine reception hall and large kitchen wing for servants. Gutenberg would stay, he said. The house was perfect for him.

Within a fortnight he hired Lorenz Beildeck and his wife as caretaker, cook and housekeeper. He bought a horse and wagon, geese, a sow with a litter of pigs and a calf. The von Ramsteins gave him a half-grown Bernese puppy, named Madchen, who they said would become an excellent cart dog. Gutenberg then found a shop in town not far from the Kammersell that was large enough for the foundry and other printing equipment.

Within three months of his arrival, Gutenberg was able to write his brother, "I am living like a country gentleman and have my own workshop!"

Gutenberg was exhilarated by the opportunities and comfort which his new life at St. Arbogast offered him. He liked the country and its privacy, the smell of the woods and fields. He enjoyed watching the crows fly back and forth in the late afternoon, always in pairs and cawing at each other. The chapel bells were a welcome sound at night.

The monks were good neighbors, and Mme. Beildeck often found cheese and fresh eggs left at the door which she repaid with baskets of fruit or crocks of jam. Beildeck tended the garden and the animals and made regular trips to market to buy and sell. In exchange for Beildeck's help in their vineyard, the monks promised Gutenberg a share of the wine at harvest time.

Gutenberg had never been happier, and work on the printing was set aside as he occupied himself with the pleasures of his small estate.

Furnishing the house had cost quite a bit of money, and the bulk metal which Gutenberg had ordered so he could begin casting was expensive. Unexpectedly, Gutenberg found himself in an embarrassing situation, Although the bank of Strasbourg had honored his letters of credit, his annuities from Mainz had not arrived. Gutenberg promptly filed a claim against the city of Mainz for 300 gulden. When clerk Nicholas von der Haft arrived in Strasbourg to investigate the claim, but without authorization to pay it, Gutenberg had Nicholas jailed as surety until the funds were released. The unfortunate clerk spent two months in jail until Gutenberg received the money due him.

With this matter settled, Gutenberg began to enlarge his social activities and accepted Nicholas Heilmann's invitation to attend a costume ball on the Tuesday before Lent. Mardi Gras, it was called.

Standing in the courtyard of Heilmann's home, enjoying the revelers and the cool night air, Gutenberg was approached by a beautiful brunette wearing a bright green silk dress and a gold mask. She seemed to know him and gaily asked questions about Mainz and Friele. Gutenberg was intrigued.

"You don't remember me, do you?" the girl asked mischieviously.

Gutenberg admitted that he did not.

"I am Ennelin zur Iserin Tur. We met five years ago at Count von Ramstein's when you and your brother first came to Strasbourg."

Gutenberg vaguely remembered a pretty child with black curls who had reminded him of his niece, Little Else.

"I have not forgotten you, Master Johannes Gensfleisch zum Gutenberg!" Ennelin said.

"And I will be delighted to see you again," Gutenberg answered, "when you take off your mask!"

From that evening on, Gutenberg saw more and more of Ennelin zur Iserin Tur. He enjoyed her company. The girl was vivacious, and she was artistic. Ennelin, he discovered, like to copy the pictures in the initial letters of her prayer book, and the small colored figures were nicely done. She could not read Latin well, however, and Gutenberg found himself helping her and her brother, Raoul, with his lessons from the Donatus and Doctrinale grammars. Raoul, about eleven, was not interested in books or Latin but was rewarded for his efforts by being allowed to ride Gutenberg's horse.

For Ennelin's birthday in July, Gutenberg gave her a cross made from amber stones set in gold. He had cut and polished the stones himself and made the setting. Raoul gave his sister the gold chain for around her neck. It was a handsome gift, fashioned with love and accepted with love.

CHAPTER 17

When it became obvious that Gutenberg and Ennelin were deeply attracted to each other, Ennelin's parents did not object to the romance. Of an old and proud patrician family, they were flattered that a patrician from Mainz wished to marry their daughter. Ennelin was sixteen, and finding a husband for her had been ill-fated twice before. The first young man died and the second had entered the Dominican Order. The Iserin Turs hoped their daughter would marry although their son's marriage in a few years was more important because it meant an heir and would bring money into the family.

That Gutenberg was not from Strasbourg and twenty years older than Ennelin, the Iserin Turs considered unimportant. He had a substantial income, judging from the recent annuity settlement, and one day Ennelin would be mistress of the Hof zum Gutenberg in Mainz. Personally, Gutenberg was charming. He was talented. He knew important people in Strasbourg and was well regarded by them. Altogether, it was a good match, and Gutenberg's suit for Ennelin's hand was approved. An elaborate wedding, with a sizeable dowry, was planned for late fall at the church of St. Pierre le Vieux.

Gutenberg wrote his family the happy news and waited impatiently for Friele to send the necessary papers. When they arrived, it only remained for the Archbishop of Strasbourg to give his consent.

As a citizen and patrician of Mainz, Gutenberg was free to live where he chose and to marry whom he chose. In Strasbourg, his status as a resident, no longer in exile, required only that he swear allegiance to the city, pay taxes and serve in the militia, if necessary.

The summer passed quickly as Gutenberg and Ennelin made plans for the wedding. Friele and his wife, Else and Claus would come to Strasbourg, they said, and bring the children. Friele's family were invited to stay with Count von Ramstein at his home, and Else, Claus and Little Else would be guests of the monks at St. Arbogast. Gutenberg's own house was made ready for Ennelin's arrival. New furniture, linens and tapestries were ordered, and everything cleaned and polished to Mme. Beildeck's satifaction.

Mme. Beildeck liked Ennelin. A bit spoiled perhaps and young, she thought, but sensible also and with a happy disposition. They would get along well. Gutenberg's friends were happy for him. Count von Ramstein thought the Iserin Turs might be meddlesome, but he too liked Ennelin and believed she would make Gutenberg a good wife. Johann Hultz and his wife were glad that Gutenberg would share his life and have other interests besides his work. He had become so attentive to Ennelin, in fact, that Hultz rarely saw him.

Everyday Ennelin received a note or a poem from Gutenberg. On Sunday, when they took walks together, he always wore a different coat which surprised and delighted her. He brought unexpected gifts of chocolate, perfume or silk ribbon. Once Gutenberg had gone all the way to Haguenau to get Ennelin a lute and gold braid for her cape.

As the weeks passed, however, Gutenberg became impatient, then annoyed, when the marriage permission papers from Strasbourg authorities did not come. He made repeated inquiries at the cathedral chancery but got no response. Fr. Anthony tried to find a reason for the delay, but also without success. Finally. the answer came. Residents of Strasbourg who wished to marry citizens of Strasbourg must themselves become citizens within one year.

Gutenberg was outraged. Why hadn't someone told him this before! But neither Fr. Anthony nor Fr. Sebastian was aware of such a requirement.

"I will never renounce my rights and privileges as a citizen of Mainz!" Gutenberg told Fr. Anthony. "I will not disgrace myself or my family! Becoming a citizen of Strasbourg means I deliberately become an exile for the rest of my life! I can never return to Mainz honorably! And if I forfeit my annuities and title to my property, how can I live here and support a wife?"

Nor could Gutenberg plan on returning to Mainz inside of a year. He could not work in Mainz now, he explained to Fr. Anthony. That's why he had returned to Strasbourg! How long he would stay was uncertain. The new work was just beginning. He couldn't abandon it!

"The abbot could intercede," Fr. Anthony said, "but it would take months and be expensive, with no guarantee of success. Guillaume von Diest makes a few exceptions."

"I'd have to bribe everyone from the deacon to the Archbishop, you mean," Gutenberg replied angrily. "The archbishop of Mainz has given his consent, that should be enough. He is grand elector of the Holy Empire! Von Diest is not even an elector."

"Then it is useless, Johannes," Fr. Anthony said sadly. "You must release Ennelin from her promise. There is nothing else you can do. Unless you wish to be married secretly."

"I do not wish to be married secretly!" Gutenberg answered. "That would be unfair to Ennelin."

"Then it seems you have no choice," Fr. Anthony told him. "I'm sorry, Johannes."

Sick at heart, Gutenberg told Ennelin what had happened and that their betrothal must be broken. No marriage was possible for him as long as he remained in Strasbourg.

"I understand why you cannot become a citizen of Strasbourg," Ennelin said, "but I can become a citizen of Mainz! We can still be married and live in Mainz."

But Gutenberg could not promise that they would be able to leave Strasbourg within a year. His work might not be finished.

Was this work so important, Ennelin asked. More important than their life together? "You never talk about your work," she said. "I don't even know what it is!"

Ennelin was deeply hurt, and her shock and bewilderment gave way to anger and tears. "You are cruel, Johannes!" she cried. "You don't love me! Or you never could be so cruel! You don't want to marry me!"

Nothing Gutenberg could say would ease the pain they both felt. He would speak to her parents and hoped they might understand what he had to do.

The Iserin Turs were humiliated. They had no sympathy for Gutenberg, and saw him now as a stranger who had misled and embarrassed them. They had been too hasty, they believed, in giving their consent. Gutenberg must have known there were impediments. He should not have proposed marriage. He was not free to marry! Why had he returned to Strasbourg? Was he forbidden to work in Mainz? Perhaps he didn't own Hof zum Gutenberg after all. What were the experiments and mysterious work that took so much time and money? And if Gutenberg lost his Mainz citizenship and his annuities, he had no income! Their daughter would not be allowed to marry an impoverished goldsmith and live in a cottage at St. Arbogast! The marriage contract would be annulled and Ennelin sent at once to a convent to spare her further disgrace.

The whole affair which had begun so happily six months before was ending in unhappiness and bitterness, Gutenberg wrote to his brother. He blamed himself. He should have found out what the marriage requirements of Strasbourg were before proposing to Ennelin.

"I love her with all my heart," he wrote, "but I cannot marry and continue to live here. I cannot ask her to wait until the work is finished and then come to Mainz. The Iserin Turs have entered a suit against me in the ecclesiastical court for breach of promise."

Fr. Sebastian thought Gutenberg had done the honorable thing by breaking the engagement. "You leave Ennelin free to marry someone else," he said. "She is young. I am sure she will want to marry one day. But her parents are seeking revenge because their pride has been hurt. The citizen of Mainz must pay for dishonoring citizens of Strasbourg!"

By filing suit, in Fr. Sebastian's opinion, the Iserin Turs were only thinking of themselves. They weren't thinking of Ennelin. "A breach of promise suit ruins her chances now for marriage to anyone," he told Gutenberg. "Any man she chooses will be frowned upon, and anyone they choose for her will feel threatened by similar action and will avoid association with her family. It is tragic, for both of you."

During the hearing of the case in court, a man named Schott gave testimony which so angered Gutenberg that he called Schott a perjurer. The outburst cost him fifteen florin personal damages.

The ecclesiastical court waited on its answer, hoping that a reconciliation might come about, that either the Iserin Turs or Gutenberg would reconsider. Neither changed their position. Nine months later, on August 30, 1437, the case was settled, but the terms of settlement were never known.

Gutenberg's friends speculated about whether he had paid the court costs or made a settlement of some kind to Ennelin's parents, but this Gutenberg never confirmed or denied. Gutenberg hoped that some day Ennelin might forgive him. He vowed never to marry.

VI. THE PARTNERSHIP
CHAPTER 18

The break with Ennelin and the public attention given to his private affairs was a terrible experience for Gutenberg. The disappointments, aggravation and litigation of the past year had drained away much of his time and energy and left little incentive to begin his own work again. With the lawsuit ended, however, Gutenberg reassessed his position. He now received an additional annuity which had previously been paid to his brother and which Friele turned over to him, but Gutenberg's funds were desperately low.

In the shop, the new casting mold was working well, but Brother Paulo had been sent to another monastery and Gutenberg had no one to help him. He needed money to replenish his supplies of metal and paper. When Andreas Dritzehn, a young goldsmith, wanted to learn the art of polishing precious stones and offered to pay for instructions, Gutenberg agreed to teach him.

Gutenberg liked Andreas. He was a bright, talented young man who learned quickly, and whose ambition and dedication reminded Gutenberg of himself. In a few months Andreas was able to earn considerable money on his own cutting and polishing gem stones. He also became a frequent guest at St. Arbogast. It pleased Mme. Beildeck when he brought them gifts of wine and pears, and he always had news from Strasbourg.

Early in 1438, Andreas learned that the pilgrimage to Aachen would take place the following year. Local pilgrimages to the shrine of St. Odile near Strasbourg were made every year, but the great pilgrimage to Aachen took place every seven years. Thousands of pilgrims made the journey to this imperial city near Cologne which had been the favorite residence of Charlemagne - where he was born and was buried, and where emperors for seven centuries had been crowned. Its magnificent palaces, bridges, baths, cathedral and school were renowned throughout the Empire.

The pilgrimage presented an opportunity for Gutenberg to make money when he needed it.

One of the most popular items which pilgrims took with them were small hand mirrors of polished metal mounted in jeweled holders. By holding the mirrors above the crowds, pilgrims could capture the image and magical powers of the holy relics and statues carried in procession. Highly prized, these souvenirs of pilgrimage were often nailed to doors or affixed to church bells. Gutenberg had seen such mirrors many times and knew how they were made.

"We could make these mirrors and sell them at a handsome profit." he told Nicholas Heilmann and his friend Hans Riffe. "Should we consider it?"

"Pilgrimages are profitable," Riffe answered candidly, and both men agreed that making mirrors for the Aachen pilgrimage would be a very worthwhile venture. Riffe was willing to pledge part of the cost, he said, and if Gutenberg would instruct Andreas and Nicholas' younger brother in the art, all of them could share the profits.

Gutenberg and Riffe, it was decided, would each contribute 160 florin to purchase glass, stones and metal. Andreas Dritzehn and Andreas Heilmann would pay 80 florin each for two year's instructions. When the mirrors were sold. Gutenberg would receive half the profits, Riffe one quarter, and the two Andreas' each one-eighth.

Two kinds of mirrors would be made. Some were fashioned by pouring molten tin over hot glass plate. When cooled, the tin formed the reflecting surface behind the glass. Others, called bullseye mirrors, were made by blowing small globes of glass and passing into them a mixture of air, antimony and resin. The mirrors were mounted in metal holders studded with polished stones.

In six months, Gutenberg and the two Andreas had completed nearly 5,000 mirrors. It was a prodigious feat, and Gutenberg was tremendously proud of the young men. Fr. Anthony and Fr. Sebastian planned to go to Aachen with pilgrims from Strasbourg and would take many of the mirrors with them to sell along the way.

Then an announcement came which changed all their plans. The pilgrimage was to be postponed until 1440 to celebrate the Pope's return to Rome.

Nine years before, Fr. Sebastian explained, Pope Eugene IV had fled from Rome disguised as a monk and had been living in exile in Florence, under the protection of Cosimo de Medici. Those prelates opposing the Pope continued to meet in council at Basel, where they had dared to proclaim a new pope. This audacious act and the prospect of another antipope contesting the papal throne so enraged emperor Sigismund and other sovereigns that they withdrew their support of the Council and urged the pontiff to return to Rome. The pilgrimage to Aachen would take place

1431
1440

when this had been accomplished.

The pilgrimage would be larger than ever, Fr. Sebastian predicted, but to Gutenberg and his friends, the year's delay was a bitter disappointment.

"It is bad luck, the worst luck," Gutenberg said. "There's nothing we can do except wait until next year." The mirrors would be sold eventually.

"But what do we do until then!" Dritzehn wanted to know.

Dritzehn's brother, Georg, was not sympathetic. "I don't think you will ever sell the mirrors," he jibed. "And don't expect me to loan you money until you do!"

Georg had belittled the scheme to make mirrors from the beginning and resented his brother's association with Gutenberg. The postponement only confirmed his belief that Andreas was wasting his time.

The materials purchased for the mirrors must be used, however, and it was with half-hearted effort that the two Andreas finished the mirrors and stored them away in boxes. Gutenberg, they noticed, spent more time working by himself, often at night after they had gone home. He never offered any explanation and the young men were curious about what the work might be. Gutenberg was casting metal, they were sure, because the foundry was still warm in the morning. And he needed paper for something, because Heilmann's brother, Nicholas, had delivered a sizeable supply of paper.

Finally they ventured to ask Gutenberg what he was doing. "Could we help you, Master?" Heilmann asked.

Gutenberg did need help, he said, with work he had begun some years before. "I must tell you nothing or everything about it. But yes, I will tell you, and I will show you something you've never seen before."

When Dritzehn and Heilmann saw the metal letters, the press and the prints that had been made, they were astounded.

"This work is much more important than the mirrors, Master!" Dritzehn exclaimed. "We could print books!"

Heilmann was intrigued with the perfect prints of the Pater Noster and couldn't believe they weren't written by hand. "Would you teach us this art, also?" he said. "I'm sure we could learn."

"Please teach us," Dritzehn asked eagerly. "No other master in Strasbourg can teach us as much as you!"

Gutenberg would like the three of them to work together, he said. But there were many things to consider. Paper and metal were expensive and the mirrors hadn't been sold.

"We would pay for instructions," Heilmann told him.

"I can mortgage property I've inherited from my father," Dritzehn said.

"Let me think about this a few days," Gutenberg answered. "I shall talk with Herr Riffe and will let you know what can be done." Until then, he cautioned, they must not speak about the work to anyone.

Dritzehn would say nothing to his brothers. "Your brothers are different," he said to Heilmann, "but mine would only cause trouble. I don't want them to know anything about printing. Not yet!"

"Do you really think we could print books?" Heilmann asked.

"Oh, yes!" Dritzehn assured him. "And this time we will be rich!"

In their excitement and anticipation of learning to print with metal letters, the mirrors and the pilgrimage were forgotten.

CHAPTER 19

"Certainly teach the young men," Riffe told Gutenberg. "With their help, you can at last make real progress!"

Count von Ramstein was pleased also, but thought they should become partners. An instruction agreement, in his opinion, did not protect Gutenberg. "What if you gave two year's instructions again and no books were printed in that time, or nothing sold, like the mirrors?" he asked. "The young men might not be so loyal to you then. They might leave and begin printing on their own. You would have nothing."

Von Ramstein advised sharing ownership of the equipment, the finished work, the risk, the responsibility, and the profits, if there were any. "Invest equally and share equally in everything," he said.

Riffe agreed that a partnership this time would be best. Gutenberg was reluctant, however, to share the equipment. He had made most of it himself, he said, and he had purchased all the materials himself. That was true, Riffe told him, but when Gutenberg died, what became of the equipment?

"Should the equipment belong to your heirs or to the men who have worked with you?" Riffe argued. "If you form a partnership, Johannes, and one of you dies, the others will keep title to the equipment and be able to continue the work."

When they made the mirrors, Riffe pointed out, no permanent

equipment was needed, just the few hand tools belonging to each of them and the assorted stones and metal they used. Printing, on the other hand, required a press, the letters, a foundry, which was permanent equipment of value. This property would be protected if owned mutually in a partnership.

In the mirror agreement, von Ramstein reminded them, the heirs received the profits if Gutenberg, Riffe, Dritzehn or Heilmann died. "I think only partners should share the profits." he said. "You can make other provisions for the heirs, but keep the printing profits for yourselves."

Gutenberg thought this suggestion was wise. He could see the importance of keeping the work and the profits in the hands of his associates.

"How long should the partnership be for," Riffe asked, "three years?"

Gutenberg thought five years. Dritzehn and Heilmann had already received two year's instructions, he said. After seven years, they would qualify as master goldsmiths, and he was assured of their services until then.

"How much money will you need, Johannes?" Riffe wanted to know.

Gutenberg estimated 500 florin. If Riffe became a partner, the four of them could invest 125 florin each. "For Dritzehn and Heilmann, that's 25 florin a year for five year's expenses and instructions. Do you think that's reasonable?" Gutenberg asked.

"Very reasonable," Riffe said. "The instructions are virtually for nothing."

"And they can pay in installments," Gutenberg added. "50-40-35 florin between now and next spring. The investment should not be a burden for them, but we will need money at the start for paper and additional equipment." In five years, he thought they would have printed and sold enough books to repay the entire investment and give each partner a nice profit besides.

"Well, then" von Ramstein said, "I suggest that the heirs receive 100 florin at the end of five years, should one of you die. And specify that heirs cannot become partners. Heirs should not benefit two ways!" At the end of five years, the partnership could be dissolved, renewed, changed, whatever Gutenberg and his partners wished to do, the Count said.

"The inheritance is guaranteed, but our profits are not," Riffe added with a smile.

It was a good plan, however, they all agreed. His friends had offered good advice, and Gutenberg was grateful. Von Ramstein declined to become a partner himself, but he would loan money to the partnership, he said, if it was needed later on. And if the two Andreas learned quickly enough,

Gutenberg thought it might even be possible for them to print a small prayer-book for the pilgrims going to Aachen. They would start work immediately, he said.

Dritzehn and Heilmann were tremendously proud to become partners with Gutenberg and knew the five years would pass quickly. They would work independently at first, Gutenberg explained, until the press and other equipment were properly installed. Casting the letters, composition and printing must be done at the shop, but the punches and matrices could be finished at home, he said. Nicholas Heilmann would supply the paper. Konrad Sahspach would build another press. Gutenberg would make all purchases for materials and keep the accounts.

By early December, the partnership agreement was drawn up and signed by Gutenberg, Riffe and Heilmann. Dritzehn, who had made plans to go hunting, said he would sign the agreement when he returned.

"I shall bring home a boar's head!" Dritzehn promised.

Everyone was in high spirits when Gutenberg closed the shop for the holidays and looked forward to the new year.

CHAPTER 20

At St. Arbogast, the Beildecks were busy with preparations for the guests Gutenberg had invited during the Christmas octave. Hearths were cleaned, firewood cut, plates and goblets washed and polished. The house was decorated with sweet smelling pine boughs and holly. The silver bells Friele had sent from Mainz were hung outside the front door.

Hultz and his family were expected Christmas Eve when Mme. Beildeck would serve the traditional fish and spice bread. On Christmas **1438** Day, they would feast on roast pork and jellied veal, a specialty of Alsace. There would be apples, nuts and raisins for the children, plum tarts and hot cider.

In the yard outside the monastery chapel, the monks erected a creche of the Nativity, following the custom started by St. Francis of Assisi 200 years before. Recreating the scene of Jesus' birth with carved and painted wood figures of the Holy Family, shepherds and angels, and with live sheep, goats and a donkey tethered nearby, the events of that Holy Night became real and wonderful. Scores of peasants and villagers came to pray before the manger crib and to leave candles which would burn, through the night.

Christmas in the great Strasbourg cathedral was awesome and beautiful, Gutenberg knew, but for him and Hultz too, the quiet and peace of St. Arbogast seemed more like Bethlehem and the shepherds' field described in the Gospels.

Gutenberg and the Hultz family attended Vigil Mass at the monastery together. As they walked to the chapel they could hear the bells of the city, echoing over the rooftops and carried on the chill air into the countryside. They could see the dark high tower of Notre-Dame in the distance with torches blazing from the tiers. They paused to kneel before the creche.

"We have much to celebrate and to thank God for," Hultz said quietly. "Your work begins again, Johannes, and soon mine will end. Next Christmas the spire will be finished." Only the cross and point remained to be put in place, he said.

Early Christmas morning, Gutenberg was surprised when Meinhard Stocker, the father of one of Dritzehn's friends, appeared at the door. A heavy man, Stocker was breathing hard and his wide, red face was solemn. He came in but declined the brandy Gutenberg offered him.

"I have sad news, Master." he said. "Very sad news."

"What happened?" Gutenberg asked anxiously.

"Andreas is dead, Master..Andreas Dritzehn is dead."

Gutenberg stared at Stocker in disbelief. "Dead? Andreas?"

"I came as soon as I could, Master," Stocker said, wiping his eyes. "He died last night at my home."

So shocked he could hardly stand, Gutenberg sat down and asked Stocker again to tell him what happened.

His son and Andreas came back from Brumath only two days ago, Stocker related. Andreas was sick with chills and a fever.

"He knew he was ill, Master," Stocker said. " 'I am deathly ill' he said."

Tears ran down Gutenberg's cheeks. "Go on," he murmured.

"He told us about the agreement you had made. He had read it, but he didn't sign it. He was too weak to sign it. 'My brothers will never agree with Master Gutenberg' he said."

Gutenberg didn't seem to hear. "Holy Mother of God," he cried and crossed himself. "I can't believe it. I can't believe it."

"There was nothing we could do for him," Stocker said.

Andreas Dritzehn was buried two days later. It was one of the saddest days Gutenberg had ever known and a personal loss he and Andreas Heilmann felt most deeply. In just the past few months, the young man had mastered the art of cutting punches and matrices. He had cast letters and could read them backwards. He had composed lines of words and hoped to begin printing as soon as the shop reopened. He had no doubts that this time they would succeed.

"I cannot replace Andreas," Gutenberg told Riffe sadly. "I shall not try to replace him. Heilmann and I must carry on the work." But he knew it would be difficult.

Andreas' death was a great loss to the new partnership. It also created two immediate problems which Gutenberg had to resolve as soon as possible. Andreas still owed 85 florin to the partnership, a debt his brothers were now responsible for. And he had borrowed one of the casting molds to check the fit of his matrices. The mold was still at his home, and Georg Dritzehn had promised to return it when the mourning period was over.

Gutenberg was concerned, however, that the many mourners would see the mold, examine it, and perhaps even steal it. He must recover it himself or render it useless to anyone else. Gutenberg decided to send Beildeck to the Dritzehn home with instructions to remove the two screws from the mold so its four pieces came apart. Then the mold became an object no one could identify, use, or put together. Beildeck was also to tell Georg Dritzehn that Gutenberg would see him soon to settle Andreas' outstanding account.

Andreas' brothers were entitled to his share of the profits from the mirrors when they were sold and to the polished stones he still had in his possession. They would not receive Andreas' share of the printing profits, however.

"They will expect to share these profits also," Riffe told Gutenberg, "and if they don't, I doubt that they will pay Andreas' debt, even though it is their obligation to do so. Andreas was right when he said his brothers would never agree with you." If Georg paid anything, Riffe believed, he would want something in return.

"They get an inheritance of 100 florin," Gutenberg said.

"But not for five years," Riffe answered. "I think you should settle the inheritance now instead of five years from now. They don't inherit Andreas' profits, but their inheritance pays Andreas' debt. End the matter, Johannes. Consider the debt paid and offer them fifteen florin immediately."

Gutenberg had to agree it was best to end Andreas' interest in the partership as soon as possible.

"It's to your benefit as well as theirs," Riffe said. "And if Georg is sensible, he'll accept your offer. If he doesn't, you aren't obliged to pay the inheritance."

"If Andreas had lived," Gutenberg replied, "his brothers wouldn't get anything. I'll remind Georg Dritzehn of that!"

Georg Dritzehn's had neglected to return the casting mold, and the prospect of doing any business with him was distasteful to Gutenberg. He had never liked Georg always telling Andreas what to do and was glad Andreas had had a mind of his own. Nicholas Dritzehn followed his brother like a sheep. Andreas had more talent and sense than either of them, Gutenberg thought.

Riffe did not trust Georg Dritzehn, knowing better than Gutenberg his unsavory reputation as a minor city official and tax collector. The man was overbearing, had a violent temper, and had been involved in many civil disputes. He took pleasure in asserting his authority. Even if there was no debt, Riffe knew Georg Dritzehn would never wait five years to collect 100 florin.

CHAPTER 21

A month after Epiphany, Georg and Nicholas Dritzehn called at Gutenberg's shop. They came unannounced, and Gutenberg was not there. They lingered and talked with Andreas Heilmann, asking him about the mirrors and the new work their brother had told them about. Heilmann had nothing to show them, he said. They would have to come back and speak with Master Gutenberg.

"I think they were snooping, Master," Heilmann said. "They didn't see any of the letters or the prints. But I didn't like it. I told them to come back tomorrow, before Vespers."

"Good," Gutenberg replied. I'll be here."

"I had Andreas' tools and the stones in a box ready for them." Heilmann said, "but Georg wanted a receipt from you."

"He shall have it!" Gutenberg frowned. "He shall have it."

When the Dritzehns returned, they were sullen and unsmiling. They looked rather like bears in their heavy fur coats which they opened but did not remove. Andreas never owned a coat so fine, Gutenberg thought.

"I am a man of my word, Master," Georg began, and produced the four pieces of the mold from his pocket. "Everyone wondered what it was," he said. "I think it's broken."

"We can fix it," Gutenberg replied. "Thank you, Georg!" He accepted the mold, then turned over the box of Andreas' belongings and a copy of the receipt. "We shall miss Andreas very much," Gutenberg said. "He was a fine craftsman."

"He left a lot of debts," Georg answered disagreeably. "We can't pay them all. Perhaps when the mirrors are sold. But we are prepared to repay his debt to you, Master." Georg changed his tone as he said this and smiled. "Andreas believed the printing would be successful and for once I agreed with him."

Nicholas Dritzehn had nothing to say, Gutenberg noticed, and sat uncomfortably on a chair which all but disappeared under his huge frame.

Andreas had paid him forty florin, Gutenberg said, but still owed 85 florin. It was a large sum, he admitted, and he was glad to know Georg intended to pay.

"The inheritance you will receive is large also," Gutenberg said. "By the terms of our partnership agreement, the heirs receive 100 florin at the end of five years. But because you are willing to pay Andreas' debt, I am willing to settle the inheritance now. I will consider the debt paid and give you fifteen florin within a fortnight."

Georg was surprised at this proposal. "I thought we inherited Andreas' share of the profits," he said, "like the mirror profits."

"No," Gutenberg answered. "Because the printing agreement is a partnership, only partners share in the profits."

"Well, then," Georg countered," I propose that we forfeit our claim as heirs and become partners in Andreas' place. Eighty-five florin is twice what he paid to you. If we pay it, we are entitled to partnership, I'd say. Surely Andreas' quarter share of profits will be more than fifteen florin, or 85 florin!"

"Perhaps," Gutenberg answered," but heirs cannot become partners. That, too, is part of the partnership agreement."

"You mean even if we pay the remainder of his investment in the partnership, we still cannot become partners?" Georg asked.

"The heirs receive 100 florin," Gutenberg repeated. "You also inherit Andreas debt, but your inheritance pays this debt. You pay nothing and

still receive fifteen florin."

Nicholas looked at his brother expectantly. "And we needn't wait five years," he said.

Georg ignored the remark. "What becomes of Andreas' share of the profits?" he demanded.

"The remaining partners will divide his share," Gutenberg answered.

"Then you should refund to us the 40 florin Andreas has already paid!" Georg replied angrily. "I question your partnership agreement, Master! It is unfair! You cannot exclude the heirs so easily!" Andreas had not received five years's instructions, Georg said. He didn't see any prints or paper in the shop. What had the money been used for?

"If we pay Andreas' debt, we should inherit his profits or be allowed to become partners," Georg insisted. "I shall make our claim in court and the magistrate shall decide! You'll have to answer many things, Master!"

"If I have to, I will," Gutenberg answered, "but my offer is fair. You know that an inheritance with a debt against it need not be paid. Our partnership agreement is clear. You cannot force us to change it. And no refund is in order. You forget that there may be little printing and no profits with only two working partners. You have no case, Georg."

"You may be mistaken, Master! Fifteen florin doesn't end the matter. Come, Claus!" Georg shouted and stalked to the door.

The two Dritzehns walked several paces without speaking to each other. "I thought you read the agreement!" Nicholas chided his brother. "Heirs don't inherit profits but partners do, you said. We'll pay the debt and become partners, you said."

"Forget what I said!" Georg answered.

"You didn't expect the Master to settle the inheritance now, that's all," Nicholas replied. "You knew the inheritance paid the debt. And if we get fifteen florin, that may be more than the profits!"

"You are a fool Claus," Georg told him.

"And I think you're a fool to take your claim to court. Gutenberg has a written agreement."

"But Andreas didn't sign it!" Georg answered. "And if we give up our claim as heirs and put 85 florin into the partnership, we should become partners!"

At the shop, Gutenberg poured himself a brandy. He couldn't believe the Dritzehns wanted to become partners with him. Georg's sudden interest in printing and confidence in their success were surprising and suspicious. 'For once I agree with Andreas,' Georg had said. But Andreas did not tell his brothers about the new work or the partnership, I'm sure of that, Gutenberg thought. I expected Georg to refuse to pay the debt and then demand return of the 40 florin when he learned that heirs didn't inherit profits. But Georg was willing to pay the debt before I told him about the inheritance. Then he offered to relinquish any claim as heirs in favor of becoming partners, in order to receive Andreas' share of the profits!

Was it possible, Gutenberg wondered, that the Dritzehns had read Andreas' copy of the agreement and knew about the provisions concerning heirs, partners and the 100 florin inheritance? They must have known, he decided. Georg didn't want to wait five years to collect the inheritance. He expected partners would realize profits much sooner and that the profits would be more than 85 or 100 florin.

The man cannot be trusted, Gutenberg thought. Heilmann suspected the Dritzehns of snooping. I suspect they are capable of stealing!

Looking about the room, Gutenberg made a quick decision. He would move the printing equipment out of the shop that night. At St. Arbogast it would be safe.

Gutenberg left hurriedly and went first to Riffe's home, then Heilmann's and told them what he planned to do. Riffe would ride to St. Arbogast, he said, and fetch Beildeck and the wagon while Gutenberg and Heilmann packed the printing equipment.

"Tell Beildeck we'll need another barrel, and as many bags, bottles and pots as he can find," Gutenberg said. "And hurry! We must be out of the city before curfew!"

Gutenberg and Heilmann emptied the water barrel and began packing it with the ingots of bulk metal, jars of linseed oil, ink and sacks of charcoal. These they set carefully between layers of straw. Heilmann wrapped the punches, matrices and casting molds in leather aprons and rolled the clean sheets of paper in sheepskin. There was no time to dismantle the letter press. They would have to take it and the foundry equipment the way it was, as best they could, Gutenberg said.

Packing the letter castings presented the biggest problem. Gutenberg had put the letters in shallow bowls which sat in rows on shelves in the workroom. Because fifty or so castings of each letter couldn't be mixed up, the contents of each bowl had to be packed separately.

"We never had so many letters before," Gutenberg said, "and we have nothing here to put them in!"

"Could we seal the bowls with wax, Master?" Heilmann asked.

"We don't have enough candles," Gutenberg answered. "We can put the capitals and small letters for each letter together. That will cut the work by half!"

"What about this?" Heilmann said, producing a faded Alsacian banner from behind the wood box. "We can tear it into squares and tie the letters inside."

"A good idea," Gutenberg told him.

When Riffe and Beildeck arrived, they brought a barrel and an assortment of containers. Gutenberg began at once to pack the mirrors while Heilmann put the letters in bottles. But the bottles got heavy and not all of them had corks. In his haste, Heilmann dropped one which broke, scattering letters and glass on the dirt floor.

Exasperated and knowing it was getting late, Gutenberg decided it was useless to try and take all the letters with them. "We'll take what we can and melt down the rest," he said. "There's no other way."

"Melt down the letters!" Heilmann exclaimed. Even Riffe was shocked.

"What else can we do?" Gutenberg demanded. "We can't leave them here!"

The melting pot was still in the firepit, and Gutenberg gathered up the rest of the bowls and dumped the letters into the pot. Heilmann and Riffe watched in horror as they disappeared and sank to the bottom.

"All our work!" Heilmann gasped. "Gone, without a trace!"

"We'll cast more letters," Gutenberg answered. "We must leave nothing of value behind!"

No one spoke as the three men helped Beildeck load the wagon and got ready to leave. The heavy melting pot was hung on a hook over the end of the wagon, steam still rising from it. But in lifting the letter press, it slipped and fell to the ground, breaking apart.

"Leave it!" Gutenberg said. "No, don't leave it. We'll fix it or build another!"

Beildeck held the reins as Gutenberg and Heilmann climbed up on the wagon.

"We'll be back for the table and chairs tomorrow," Gutenberg told Riffe. "Tell Hultz and Heilmann's brothers what we've done and why."

"I will, Johannes," Riffe answered. "Good luck."

Standing by his horse, Riffe watched as the wagon lumbered down the dark, quiet street. Curfew sounded just as they turned onto the St.

Arbogast road.

Riffe was still stunned by the events of the past few hours. Everything had happened so fast! Gutenberg was right to move the equipment because the Dritzehns might steal or even destroy it. St. Arbogast was the safest place for them to work from now on. Yet Gutenberg himself had destroyed his finished castings - letters which had taken months to accumulate! Drastic but prudent, Riffe thought. Gutenberg couldn't take any chances. And they would cast new letters!

The possibility of a lawsuit hadn't disturbed Gutenberg, nor was Riffe concerned. The Dritzehns could not force the remaining partners to accept them, and the present partnership could be dissolved, if necessary. St. Arbogast was a new beginning, Riffe believed, and he hoped that his friend would be able to work at last without interference, without further set-backs. Gutenberg deserved to succeed!

Early the following morning, Georg and Nicholas Dritzehn went back to the printing shop. No one answered their knock, and peering through the small window, they could see the room was dark. The fire was out. No smoke rose from the chimney. Georg tried the door, and to his surprise found it unbolted. They stepped inside.

The room was bare except for a table and the chairs they had sat on the night before. Marks on the floor showed where the boxes of mirrors had stood and where something heavy had been rolled or dragged out the door.

'The fox!'' Georg exclaimed. ''The old fox!''

Angrily he walked to the back room. It was empty too. Near a firebed in the middle of the floor, he saw where metal had been spilled.

"There's nothing here," he shouted. "Gutenberg has taken everything!"

Following behind, Nicholas spied a crumpled piece of paper on the floor and picked it up. "Look at this, Georg," he said. "There's writing on it!"

"Let me see!" Georg answered. He examined the paper and was puzzled. The same letters appeared over and over in lines, like pages from a school copy book.

"What does it say?" Nicholas asked.

"Nothing!" Georg replied. "These aren't words, just letters. It looks like handwriting to me. What kind of printing is that?"

"Here's something else," Nicholas said. He held up a small piece of metal near the firebed. "There's a circle, carved on one end. Here's another. A half moon, it looks like."

Nicholas showed the castings to his brother. "What are they?"

"I don't know!" Georg replied irritably.

Nicholas fingered the castings then tossed them aside.

"Is there anything hidden under the table?" Georg asked.

Nicholas turned it over and found nothing, and in doing so got a black, sticky smear on his hand. It smelled oily and wouldn't come off. "Paint!" he said with disgust.

"That's ink," Georg told him. "You write with ink! Come, Claus! I don't see any mirrors. We could have sold the mirrors. And there's no metal worth anything. What was the money used for, I wonder!"

"They even took the wine," Nicholas said peevishly.

"Well, we shall make our complaint to the court and force Master Gutenberg tell us what he has been doing," Georg said defiantly. "I want to know what cost Andreas so much money!"

CHAPTER 22

The Dritzehns filed their complaint a month later. The first hearing, before two councilmen, was scheduled in early spring. At that time the Dritzehns called 24 witnesses, and testimony became so lengthy that a second hearing was held. Gutenberg called 14 witnesses, some of whom were the same persons who had testified earlier.

1439

The witnesses included Meidhard Stocker, in whose home Andreas Dritzehn had died; John Dritzehn, his uncle; Annie, his cousin, and her husband, Johann Schultheiss; John Niger who said Andreas had instructed his tenant farmers to sell grain because he needed money to purchase metal; and Hans Friedel of Seckingen who had acted as surety for a loan Andreas had made for 101 florin.

Also testifying were Johann Riffe; Andreas Heilmann and his brothers, Fr. Anthony and Nicholas whose mill supplied paper to Gutenberg; Lorenz Beildeck who Georg Dritzehn accused of perjury; Konrad Sahspach, a wood turner, who built Gutenberg's press; Johann Hultz; and John Dunnius, a goldsmith. who said he had received 100 florin from Gutenberg in the last three years for metal used "for work related to printing."

Although Andreas Dritzehn had not signed the partnership agreement, Gutenberg and Riffe swore to the provisions it contained. The partners possessed the equipment jointly, Gutenberg said. They were to share equally, to have no secrets from one another, and were not obliged to teach the art to others. Gutenberg knew that Andreas had mortgaged property inherited from his father and had had to raise money from tenant farmers in order to go into business with him. This had no bearing on the lawsuit, however, he said, and he was not liable for Andreas' debts. Freddy of Seckingen later testified that at the Easter Fair Gutenberg had paid him part of Andreas' debt himself.

Gutenberg's forthright statements made a favorable impression on the councilmen. It was evident also that Gutenberg's friends, associates and members of his household held him in high regard. They referred to him as 'Junker' or young gentleman and described him as a fair and generous man, energetic, foresighted, versed in many crafts. Gutenberg's dedication to his work and his desire to protect it and his partners from unjust claims were admired. The councilmen could find no fault with the printing agreement and Gutenberg's enforcement of it. The council would give its verdict later in the summer.

All activity in Strasbourg now was focused on preparations for the grand ceremonies that would take place June 24, 1439, the feast of St. John the Baptist. On that day, also known as the Summer Christmas, the cathedral spire would be dedicated.

Rising to a height of 142 meters, the spire of Notre-Dame became the tallest ever built, and Hultz was proclaimed the greatest master in the Empire. His work of twenty years was at last gloriously complete. Bishops, lords and nobles, master craftsmen, architects and guild officials from every province were expected to come to Strasbourg for the month-long celebration.

In a long letter to his brother, Friele, Gutenberg described the festivities. "The city overflows with distinguished visitors," he wrote. "Every day another dignitary arrives and his colors are raised in the cathedral square. Every house, bridge and boat on the canals displays the red and white Alsacian colors. The streets are festooned with flags from every city on the Rhein.

"The scaffolding around the spire and lantern has been removed, and the eight tiered turrets are beautiful to see. But the cross is still hidden from view by a long silk drape which will be loosed from the platform after the dedication Mass. Hultz says the cross can be seen from every direction because it has two cross beams and is ten meters above the canopy of the lantern. At the very top is a gold statue of Our Lady. I am honored to sit with other masters during the Mass and shall carry the banner for the city of Mainz.

"Many people remember the dedication of the octagon in 1419," Gutenberg went on. "Others remember when the belfry above the rose window, joining the two bell towers, was completed in 1399. One old man told me his father was the first to climb to the platform in 1365 when the third stories of the towers were built. I venture to say no one here tomorrow will forget when the spire was finished.

"There were three Masses because of the feast day and five thousand people in the cathedral," Gutenberg continued later. "Then at three o'clock in the afternoon Hultz led the procession up the staired turrets to the platform where the most honored guests would watch the unveiling of the cross. We watched from the roof of the Kammersell. Everyone wanted to be a high as possible, and people sat like birds on the chimneys, windows and even on the masts of barges, waiting for the final moment. Because the archbishop could not climb the 330 steps to the platform, he was seated in the inspector's chair and lifted by pulleys to the top of the south tower. It was a long ascent, 66 meters, and there was much suspense until he reached the top safely. Everyone cheered as he stepped onto the platform. I'm sure he was dizzy, but he waved his hand. The many years of soliciting funds to build the octagon and spire have not endeared Archbishop Guillaume to the people of Strasbourg, but they had to admire the old man's courage this day.

"Just before Vespers, the great moment came. Trumpets blared, drums rolled, and then all was quiet as the archbishop lifted a saber and cut the rope holding the drape. As it fell away, bright sunlight beamed on the cross and on Our Lady. Thousands of rose petals floated down from the lantern. Five hundred white doves were released from the platform. The great bell of the cathedral tolled, churchbells rang, and cheer upon cheer rose in waves across the city. It was the most tremendous spectacle I've ever seen.

"The extension of the cross above the spire and lantern is in perfect proportion. It seems to reach out and just touch the sky, like a flower opening its petals. The visiting masters are at a loss to describe the grace and symmetry of the tiers and stonework.

"Then, at night, the spire was lighted for the first time. Torches were lit the full height of the four octagon turrets, in each of the eight tiered turrets of the spire, and in the lantern. You can't imagine a more dazzling sight - the huge single tower and the pyramid spire ablaze with light! Only once in a lifetime, only once in the history of Strasbourg, has there been such a glorious day!"

With completion of the spire on Notre-Dame, Hultz joined the illustrious group of masters whose names were written with the saints in the annuals of the cathedral - Rudolph le Vieux, Erwin and his son John, Gerlach, Michel of Fribourg, Claus de Lore, and Ulrich of Ensingen. Hultz' prestige was enormous. He was honored by bishops and magistrates and offered commissions from many cities. All of these were refused, however. Hultz would never build another spire, he said, and he would never leave Strasbourg.

"Strasbourg is my home," he told Gutenberg. "This cathedral is my home. And I shall stay, to begin the repairs to the nave." He would be working inside, he said, and the weather wouldn't matter any more. "No rain, no wind." Hultz smiled, but there was a touch of sadness in his voice, Gutenberg thought. "I shall miss the view from the spire," Hultz said. "Sunrise from way up there is magnificent."

The archbishop also received praise for his legacy to the city of Strasbourg. The octagon and spire had been his dream for forty years, and although the cost in lives and in money was great, he had lived to see the dream fulfilled.

Then, less than four months later, on October 6, 1439, Archbishop Guillaume II died. He had been archbishop of Strasbourg forty-five years. Now black banners flew from the cathedral tower and draped the portals as he was laid to rest in the crypt beneath the altar. After a month of mourning, Conrad IV was installed as the new, eleventh bishop of Strasbourg.

The final hearing in the Gutenberg-Dritzehn dispute took place in September, with the verdict promised within a fortnight. The archbishop's death had postponed this decision, but Gutenberg expected an answer before Christmas. Further delay was not possible, he knew, because the case must be resolved within a year of Andreas' death. On December 12, the council announced its decision. Gutenberg's partnership agreement and the settlement clause concerning heirs were upheld. The Dritzehns had to pay the 85 florin their brother owed to Gutenberg, and if Gutenberg so wished, the debt could be subtracted from the inheritance, in which case, the

Dritzehns would receive fifteen florin. They could not become partners. Gutenberg had won handsomely.

Curiously, the testimony which defined Gutenberg's work generally, was sufficient to change Georg Dritzehn's desire to share in the work. Gutenberg was a dreamer, he said. The printing, however he did it, would never be profitable. Ridicule was Georg's answer in defeat.

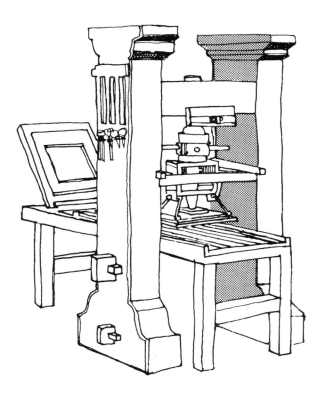

VII. THE FIRST BOOKS
CHAPTER 23

During the hot summer months of the on-going Dritzehn hearings, Gutenberg and Heilmann managed to recast the letters needed to replace those that had been melted down. They should be working in cooler weather, Heilmann said good naturedly, but he liked the privacy of St. Arbogast and was glad Gutenberg had moved the shop.

Two rooms off the kitchen became the foundry, storeroom and workshop. There was more space than they had had in town, and the partners could work as early or late as they chose without closing the shop at curfew. Gutenberg could receive visitors conveniently and leave when he had to, knowing the Beildecks were on hand to look after the equipment. Mme. Beildeck made sure meals were on time and liked having the Master and Andreas at home to cook for. Her husband was always available for making repairs and doing errands in Strasbourg. It was an agreeable arrangement for everyone.

Gutenberg ordered a new press from Konrad Sahspach. The letter press had been repaired, but Gutenberg wanted it secured in a frame that could be anchored to the floor. He also wanted a long table attached to the frame with a sliding tray on top to hold the heavy page form of letters. Then the form could be moved easily under the press and back again after a print was made.

Nicholas Heilmann suggested that a tympan be used to position the paper when he saw how difficult it was for his brother, Andreas, to do this properly by hand. A similar rack was used in the paper mill to pick up sheets and dry them. The same principle could be used to drop a sheet of paper on the letters, Nicholas said. By placing each sheet in the same place each time, the margins were always the same and less paper would be wasted getting a perfect print.

Gutenberg was extremely pleased with the tympan and new press frame which stood higher than his head. Made of large square beams, it held the press securely and kept the table and press bed level.

The original cheese press which had become a block press and then a letter press, was now a real printing press.

Andreas Heilmann became adept a placing the paper, inking the letters and making prints. The big, husky lad could handle the press screw with ease, yet had the light, sure touch needed to make clean prints one after the other. He developed a rhythm to his work by repeating a short prayer each time - "Gloria tibi"(page under the press), "Domine"(press down), "Jesu Christi"(press up).

Brother Gerard became a good compositor. Using a Donatus to copy from, he had learned to compose words and lines and discovered he could read Latin backwards as easily as forwards. He enjoyed the work and took the same pride in it that Paulo had earlier. Every mistake in spelling was carefully corrected until the test prints were perfect.

As the supply of letters grew, it became necessary to keep the many castings of each letter in something other than the saucers Gutenberg had used. The letters should be placed in front of the compositor, Gerard thought, in the same way paints were kept on a palette.

Beildeck would build a box for them, he said, with partitions in it so all of the different small letters, capitals, numbers and punctuation marks had their own cubbyholes. This letter box, as they called it, stood on an easel. Now with the letters within arm's reach and in one place, Gerard could work much faster.

A major flaw, however, was revealed suddenly one night as Gutenberg was eating dinner. There was a loud crash in the workroom. Madchen, the dog, yelped as in pain, the cat screamed, and both animals ran through the kitchen and out the door terrified with fright.

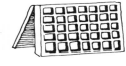

Rushing in to see what happened, Gutenberg found the easel and letter box on the floor. Castings were everywhere. It was the worst mess he had ever seen. The letters weren't broken, but he knew it would take a week or more to sort them out and repair the damage.

Someone had left the door open, but the real fault lay with the easel itself, Gutenberg decided. It was unbalanced and must be constructed differently.

"Perhaps two letter boxes, one on each side of the easel would be better," Beildeck said. "Then two compsitors could work at one time."

"That's for another day, Renz," Gutenberg told him. "The letter box isn't damaged. We'll put it on the counter and make another easel another time."

"We learned something," Gutenberg told Fr. Sebastian philosophically. "And poor Madchen did, too. She hasn't been near the workshop since!"

The year 1439 had been eventful in many ways, Gutenberg reflected. But now with the Dritzehn suit behind him, the new press completed and

Heilmann and Gerard able to work together so well, he was impatient to begin printing in earnest. Their first book, he announced, would be a small edition of the Donatus. It was good choice, Fr. Anthony thought, because this standard Latin text was used in all monastery schools.

Remembering his own days as a student, Gutenberg could sympathize with the boys who spent so much time copying the book or reciting their lessons from one book passed around the classroom. Texts were never alike because the boys were careless, and different mistakes, corrections and omissions appeared in every copy. Even the teachers' copies were seldom perfect. Using printed Donatus, both teachers and students would have identical books. The books would still have to be shared, but with more copies to share, it would not be necessary to recopy the Donatus continually by hand year after year.

Soon after the late snows melted, the first group of pilgrims began to arrive in Strasbourg on their way to Aachen. The mirrors could finally be sold, and Heilmann and Fr. Anthony quickly set up booths at St. Arbogast and at St. Pierre. Gutenberg planned to buy paper for the Donatus with his share of the proceeds and was pleased to see that the mirrors sold exceptionally well.

The monks at St. Arbogast were hosts to a group of Dominican pilgrims who planned to stay until Lent. Their interest was not in mirrors, however, but in obtaining 25 copies of the Weltgericht or World Judgment to take with them. Unfortunately, only three scriptorium monks could be spared for the task. Fr. Sebastian did not want to refuse the prior's request, still how could he be of assistance? Then he remembered the Pater Nosters and the the collection of prayers made by Brother Paulo.

Astonished and impressed by what he saw, the prior asked to meet Master Gutenberg.

"I will introduce you to him," Fr. Sebastian said. "He will show you himself how the work is done."

The next morning Fr. Sebastian and the prior walked across the monastery yard to Gutenberg's home.

Gutenberg was proud to show his visitors the workshop, the new press and the Donatus pages that Gerard was working on. He asked Heilmann to make a print of the first page and gave it to the prior. After seeing Gutenberg's letters and how they were used, and convinced that there was nothing mysterious about the work, the prior repeated his request for copies of the World Judgment.

"I will be honored to print the Judgment for you, Your Grace,"

Gutenberg said. "How many pages is it?"

"About 30 leaves, 60 pages, I think," Fr. Sebastian said. "Quarto size."

"That would be 15 folio sheets in one copy," Gutenberg answered. "I will print 50 copies, if I can get enough paper."

"I will purchase the paper," the prior said, "if you can print 50 copies of the Judgment as perfectly as the Paters. But there must be no mistakes!"

"We will read and correct the pages for you, Master," Fr. Sebastian offered. "We will help as much as we can."

The prior would leave for Aachen on Ash Wednesday. "Will you be able to complete the books by then?" he asked.

"We shall do our best, Your Grace," Gutenberg promised. "We will start work at once!"

Gutenberg's heart was pounding as he thanked his guests and said goodbye. Their first book! The World Judgment, and the mirrors, were going to Aachen! He couldn't believe it. And to think that the Paters were printed seven years ago!

"Saddle the horse!" he called to Beildeck. "Andreas and I are going to town. We must tell Hultz and Fr. Anthony the good news!"

But Heilmann was not enthusiastic. "Brother Gerard will be disappointed," he said. "The Judgment is in German, not Latin. And it's for the Dominicans, not the Benedictines. Our first book should be in Latin and for the monks at St. Arbogast!"

"We will print the Donatus later," Gutenberg answered. "The prior needs the Judgment now! It doesn't matter what language it's in! We must celebrate, Andreas!"

Nothing could dampen Gutenberg's spirits and he laughed aloud as they galloped down the road to Strasbourg. Though, perhaps, I should not have suggested 50 copies, he reflected. Lent is only two months away! I hope we have enough letters. If not, we'll cast more! And Fr. Sebastian will help us. What a good man he is.

Leaving Heilmann at St. Pierre, Gutenberg reined his horse in front of Hultz's door and took a bottle of cognac from his coat.

Gutenberg's euphoria was sustained by the wine, and Hultz listened intently as Gutenberg repeated what had happened. The Dominican prior was his first customer! The book was in German, but what difference did that make. True, they didn't have much time and printing 50 copies would take longer. There might be more than 60 pages. He hadn't seen the Judgment!

It was a fine opportunity, Hultz agreed. The prior could have taken the book to another scriptorium. "Whether he would have been so willing for you to print the Judgment if it was in Latin, I don't know," Hultz smiled. "Are you sure you can print 50 copies, Johannes?"

"We can do it, if we don't make too many mistakes," Gutenberg answered. "There is less risk if we print 25 copies because we use less paper, but less satisfaction also! Three scriptoriums could produce 25 books. I want to show that 50 books can be printed in the same time or less time than it takes to write them by hand!"

The number of pages would make a difference, Gutenberg admitted. When he knew how long it took to compose one page and to make 25 prints then he could decide whether 50 copies should be attempted.

"If it is not possible in the time we have, I will say so. We won't print 50 copies of half a book!"

Hultz was pensive. He knew Fr. Sebastian was deeply interested in Gutenberg's work and wanted to help him as well as the Dominicans. The prior's interest was limited to finding a solution to his present problem. If Gutenberg failed, the prior had not solved his problem. And would he blame Gutenberg or himself, Hultz wondered.

"You are committed to printing the Judgment," he said. "The prior is committed to you printing it for him. That is sufficient for now. You both acted impulsively, I think. The prior may not really expect you to print 50 books, and he will be satisfied with 25. I think the monks will still make some handwritten copies for him."

"Well," Gutenberg answered, "if the prior changes his mind and I see that 50 copies are possible, I shall buy paper from Nicholas Heilmann myself and print 25 Judgments for St. Arbogast! If it can be done, I want to prove it can be done!"

When Hultz and Gutenberg walked out to the courtyard, they were startled to see the sun coming up. "The work won't be easy, I know," Gutenberg said, washing his face at the well. "You must pray for us, Johann."

"Everyone in St. Thomas brotherhood will pray for you," Hultz replied. "And I will help any way I can."

On his way home, Gutenberg thought about what Hultz had said. Was he being over-confident? Would the prior have second thoughts? Count von Ramstein would say that printing 50 books was foolhardy.

Meeting again at the monastery, Gutenberg and the prior agreed to a new plan. The prior would order 25 books, he said, and the monks would supply ten handwritten copies. "If you print 50 books, Master, that is your decision. And if you do, I will gladly purchase ten more. Having 35 or 45 Judgments to take to Aachen, I never dreamed might be possible. I think you should keep the rest of the books for yourself and your friends in Strasbourg.

The Dominican smiled and shook Gutenberg's hand. "Your new art of printing is a wonderful thing, Master," he added, "a truly wonderful thing. I hope work on the Judgments will go well."

CHAPTER 24

Fifty copies of the Weltgericht were printed and bound before the Dominicans departed for Aachen. The books consisted of 38 leaves quarto size, 19 folio sheets in each book, with text on 74 pages, and required 1,000 folio sheets of paper. By taking turns at the press, Gutenberg, Heilmann and Hultz managed to make up to 100 prints a day and been able to finish in the time allowed.

The prior was tremendously pleased with the results. He paid Gutenberg generously and also ordered 25 Donatus for the Dominican school in Colmar when these books were printed. Fr. Sebastian knew that Gutenberg had earned the respect of an important and influential friend.

The work had been more difficult than Gutenberg imagined, and he learned many things from the experience. Composing and correcting the pages had gone well, but took a lot of time. It took almost as much time to disassemble the pages and put letters back in the letter box. Despite what seemed to be a large supply of letters, Gutenberg felt even more letters were needed so that four pages instead of only two or three could be in forms at once. The lines of text were even on the left but uneven on the right. And because the metal letters were larger than the handwritten letters they copied, manuscript could not be duplicated in the same space, line on line, on a page. This was the reason there were more pages in the printed Judgments than in the manuscript copy.

It became clear to Gutenberg also that some procedures must be changed to make the entire composing and printing operation more efficient. Before he began the Donatus, more letters and more men - compositors and printers, were necessary. And he needed more shelf space for the reams of blank paper and the finished sheets after they were printed.

Gutenberg's greatest concern, however, was printing the four pages on each sheet and the four sheets in each quire in sequence. If this wasn't done, the loss in paper, money and time could be disastrous.

Prints must be on the proper sheet and on the proper side of the sheet. Any mistake meant that all misprinted sheets must be thrown away, replaced, composed again if necessary, and printed a second time. Sharp letters, perfect text, clear prints meant nothing, if a page was printed in the wrong place.

Fr. Sebastian did not understand why printing pages in sequence should be a problem until he saw how Gutenberg must work. The monks assembled their quires first, nesting and folding the four blank sheets together, and then writing the pages, one at a time, one quire at a time. The printers, however, made multiple copies of each page before going on to the next. The sheets of their quires had to be kept flat to lay on the press, and quires were not assembled until the four pages on each sheet had been printed.

Each quire in the Judgment had been separated into four piles of 50 sheets each, and only after 50 prints of each page on each sheet had been made, were the sheets put together to make 50 quires. When sheets 1-2-3-4 were nested and folded, the pages were in order 1a through 8b.

But while the printer was working and the sheets were separated and unfolded, Father saw that pages 1a and 1b and 8a and 8b were on the same sheet, sheet 1 - with 8b and 1a on the front, 1b and 8a on the back! Pages 2a and 2b and 7a and 7b were on sheet 2. Pages 3a and 3b and 6a and 6b were on sheet 3. Pages 4a and 4b and 5a and 5b were on sheet 4. The printers made 50 prints of the first two pages of each sheet, 1a-b, 2a-b, 3a-b, 4a-b on sheets 1-2-3-4, then 50 prints of pages 5a-b, 6a-b, 7a-b, 8a-b, with the sheets in reverse order 4-3-2-1.

Fr. Sebastian and Gutenberg had watched closely as each sheet of the Judgment was printed, but it had been difficult. The printed pages looked so much alike, it was easy to mistake one for another. They could be printed upside down, on the wrong sheet, on the right instead of the left, on the front instead of the back, unless the printer paid strict attention to the order of pages and sheets before making 50 prints.

Once ten sheets were printed before it was discovered that the second page was upside down. Another time, 20 sheets had to be replaced and three pages were composed twice. Such expensive mistakes made it clear to everyone that printing in order was the most important procedure of all.

Each Judgment contained five quires, and gathering the printed sheets together one by one to make fifty sets of each quire was a very satisfying task, but it required careful attention also or pages would be out of order. Likewise, the five quires in each book had to be in order, so the quires were numbered.

The monks of St. Arbogast, who were familiar with gathering sheets and quires together for one book, were amazed by how quickly 50 books could be assembled - in a matter of minutes!

By the middle of summer, Gutenberg was able to resume work on the Donatus and had managed to solve most of the technical problems. To make the lines of letters as straight on the right as on the left, he adjusted the space between words, used abbreviations and hyphenated words. He cast two letters on one matrix. Letters which tended to be uneven across the bottom were recast so the lines would be straight.

Gutenberg needed almost a thousand letters for one page of the Donatus and hired an apprentice goldsmith to help with the casting. With additional letters and two compositors, he was able to have four pages composed and in forms at one time. As a result, reading and correcting the pages progressed more rapidly and printing could begin without delays. Another apprentice helped Heilmann ink the pages so he could work faster.

Fr. Sebastian thought guide quires were needed to keep all of the pages in order. The test print or corrected print of each page could be pinned in a quire of four blank sheets, with each sheet and each page numbered. Then the guide quire sheets could be separated, allowing the printer to match his sheets and pages to them, and begin each new page where it belonged. He would see too when the top of his page forms must be inverted to print right side up. And with a complete quire of test prints for reference, Gutenberg would be able to see what a finished quire looked like before it was printed.

The guide proved to be an excellent solution to the sequence problems and indispensible to following the progress of pages and quires until they were completed.

Disassembling the Donatus pages so the letters could be used again still took a great deal of time for Gerard and the other compositor. Then assistance came in an unexpected way when two students from St. Pierre appeared one day at Gutenberg's shop. Fr. Anthony had sent them, they said, to help take page forms apart. They had lost a book and the task was intended as punishment.

Not certain if the boys could read Latin well, Gutenberg was reluctant to entrust them with this work, but he let them try. To his surprise, the boys had no difficulty whatever. The words were familiar and they could recognize the letters quickly, even in reverse. They were able to replace the letters in the letter box with astonishing speed and accuracy. And the boys enjoyed the work.

"This is fun, Master," they said. "May we come again and help?"

Gutenberg consented, and the next day five boys appeared. It soon became an honor to work for Master Gutenberg a few hours each week. The boys took turns, and Gutenberg repaid them with a stipend for paper and ink. One of the oldest wanted to learn how to compose letters instead of taking them apart, and Gerard agreed to teach him.

Continual practice with the Latin words resulted in a remarkable improvement in the boy's reading and spelling ability at school.

"Your shop is a better classroom than ours," Fr. Anthony told Gutenberg, noting their progress.

"We have all learned something," Gutenberg said. "With the boy's help, we will finish the Donatus much sooner!"

The boys, too, were proud of themselves. Gutenberg promised to give each boy his own copy of the book when the Donatus were published and to print his name on a nameplate, glued inside the front cover.

CHAPTER 25

The first edition of the Donatus appeared in the fall of 1440. Gutenberg printed 50 copies, 35 for the Dominican prior and 15 for St. Pierre, St. Arbogast and himself. Each book was 36 pages of text, on 18 leaves quarto size, and bound into two quires of 8 leaves each plus one sheet of two leaves. Including the test prints and waste paper, a full ream of 500 folio sheets had been used. Heilmann and his assistant produced an average of 75 prints a day by themselves and had completed the 1800 page prints inside of a month. It was an outstanding achievement.

There was a noticeable improvement in the letters and lines and few mistakes in composition. Most important, printing in sequence had been accomplished with none of the serious difficulties and misprints encountered with the Judgment. There had been no pressure to finish before a certain date, and the flow of work had moved smoothly as each man became more familiar with his specific task. Gutenberg was especially pleased because the Donatus was in Latin and so many of the books would be used locally.

Gutenberg sent copies of the Judgment and the Donatus to his brother and sister in Mainz. To his surprise, Friele responded with a request for 20 Donatus from the pastor at St. Stephans. Soon after, another request for 15 books came from an abbey in Freiburg. Gutenberg decided to publish a second edition of 50 Donatus immediately, certain that the remaining copies would be sold in Strasbourg. Using the set of test prints in the quire guide, Gutenberg marked some changes in style, adding larger capital letters and chapter headings, and making corrections in the text that had been missed the first time.

"I wish I dared print 75 to 100 books," Gutenberg thought. "Composition time is the same whether we print 10, 50 or 100 books. In fact, it sometimes takes longer to compose and correct one page then it does to make 50 prints. It makes sense to print as many copies as possible." But Gutenberg knew he couldn't afford to buy more than 500 sheets of paper in advance, and he could not risk a sequence mistake and perhaps losing 100 sheets. The men needed more experience.

Before attempting a more ambitious project, Gutenberg would analyze the cost in time and materials for the Judgment and the Donatus. Then he would know better what might be planned in the future.

The prior had reimbursed Gutenberg for the Judgment paper and included an additional 25 florin, which Gutenberg shared with Riffe and Heilmann. He had not figured his other expenses for this book. The expenses for the Donatus, paper and wages for the three new apprentices, Gutenberg had borne himself. After the Donatus were sold, however, the two partners repaid part of this cost from their share of the profits and also agreed that money should be set aside for wages and paper before profits were divided.

Paper cost about 10-12 florin a ream. Wages were based on the number of men employed and the time required to complete composition and printing of 50 books. Gutenberg's other expenses included the ink, metal and equipment used, but he wasn't sure how much of this cost should be considered part of his total cost.

The price of a handwritten book was based on the amount of paper or vellum used. Customers paid separately for illustration and binding. The monks' time was not a factor because they received no wages, but for Gutenberg time was an important factor. The more pages in a book, the longer it took to compose and print them, and Gutenberg's printing equipment was much more expensive than quill pens and ink.

The big difference between manuscript book cost and printed book cost, Gutenberg explained to his partners, lay in the fact that the monks' costs were based on a single copy, while their costs were based on 50 copies.

"Suppose one manuscript book costs one florin," he said, "and 50 books cost 50 florin. As far as I can determine, our total cost for 50 Donatus was about 30 florin, or a little more than half what 50 manuscript books would cost! Donatus usually sell for one florin each. We charge the same price but could charge less and still make a profit after expenses are paid."

Moreover, should they ever print 100 books, Gutenberg added, their costs would not double. Paper cost and printing time would double, but expenses for composition time and the amount of ink, metal and equipment used would remain about the same. Their profits could double!

Gutenberg compared the amount of materials used for the Donatus and Judgment. The Judgment was 76 pages quarto size - 38 leaves, 19 folio sheets for one book, 950 folio sheets for 50 books. Another 50 sheets had been used because of the mistakes and reprinting necessary. The Judgment had 74 pages of text. The last two pages were blank.

It was better to have blank pages left over than lines left over, Fr. Sebastian had said, but Gutenberg was disturbed. He had not known exactly how many pages the Judgment would be and began printing the fifth quire before realizing that the text would end on p. 74. He had used four full quires and 12 pages in the last quire for 10 pages of text. Had the Judgment been 72 pages, there would have been no blank pages and they could have printed 55 books from 1000 sheets.

Each Donatus was 36 pages quarto size - 18 leaves, 9 folio sheets, and 450 sheets required for 50 books. As they neared the end of composition here, it became evident that the text would be longer than anticipated. Gutenberg had added one sheet of four pages, or 50 sheets in 50 books. If the Donatus had been 32 pages as expected, he could have printed 56 books from 450 sheets. He could have printed 62 books from 500 sheets.

Gutenberg had allowed 50 sheets for test prints and waste paper, or 10 percent of a ream. This was excessive, he thought. Test prints must be made on cheap paper, and only five percent of the total sheets used should be allowed for waste.

Somehow, Gutenberg thought, I must be able to calculate correctly the number of pages in a book and the number of sheets needed in a book before we begin. I must know how many books can be printed from 500 sheets, or how many sheets I will need for x number of books before the pages are composed and paper ordered. And the number of pages in a book depends on the number of lines on each page.

The Donatus had 26 line pages. Would adding two lines make enough of a difference, Gutenberg wondered. Could a Donatus be printed on 32 pages? If so, he would seriously consider printing a third edition of 100 copies.

Gutenberg reviewed what he had learned from Fr. Sebastian about sheets, leaves, pages and quires. Full size sheets folded once made two folio size leaves or four folio size pages. Folio sheets folded once made two quarto size leaves or four quarto pages. Quarto sheets folded once made two octavo size leaves or four octavo pages.

Most books like the Donatus, Judgment and Missal were quarto size with single columns of text and required folio size sheets. A Book of Hours could be octavo or quarto size, depending on the size of the illustrations. Only Psalters and Bibles had folio size pages, two columns of text, and required full size sheets of paper or vellum.

Quires consisted of four sheets folded together to make 8 leaves, 16 pages, and were stitched through at the fold when bound. Short quires of three or two sheets were possible. Even single sheets could be folded and bound. But it was impossible to bind a half sheet or a single leaf of two pages.

The number of pages in a book, Fr. Sebastian had said, must always be in multiples of four or a number that could be divided by four because any size sheet, folded, became four pages. Likewise, the number of leaves must be in multiples of two because each sheet folded became two leaves. A book could have 32 or 36 pages, but not 30. It could have 16 or 18 leaves, but not an odd number 15 or 17.

If the Donatus were to be 32 pages, how many lines must be on each page? Or if the pages had 28 lines each, how many pages would be in each book? Gutenberg used arithmetic to find the answers.

The 36 Donatus pages he had printed were 26 lines each, for a total of 936 lines. If the Donatus was 32 pages, Gutenberg found he would need 30 lines on each page, actually 30 lines on 31 pages and six lines on p. 32. He had to add four lines to each page to reduce the book by four pages! If the pages were 28 lines each, he would need 33 pages plus 12 lines on p. 34. But a book of 34 pages could not be bound!

An easier way to estimate lines and pages was to apply the reverse principle: 30 lines on 32 pages was the same as 32 lines on 30 pages...28

lines on 34 pages was the same as 34 lines on 28 pages. But a book of 30 pages could not be bound, and 34 lines on a page left no margin whatever.

Gutenberg noted also that by adding one line to a page, he picked up one page of 26 lines on 26 pages. Adding two lines to a page, he picked up 26 lines every 13 pages.

Estimating the cost and amount of materials needed to print books in quantity was more work and more difficult, Gutenberg thought, than casting the letters and printing in quires.

"I have done so much arithmetic," Gutenberg told Hultz, "my head is dizzy! I was a goldsmith before I became a printer. Now I must be a mathematician before I can become a publisher!"

The table where Gutenberg sat was strewn with waste sheets he had covered with numbers and equations. "I've been comparing the Donatus and Judgement," he explained. "The Donatus should have been 32 pages, not 36, and we had two blank pages in the Judgment, if you remember. And I want to get the most number of books from the fewest number of sheets. The size of a book is important when we print 50 copies."

Hultz looked at the many notations Gutenberg had made. "Why do you want the Donatus to be 32 pages?" he asked.

"Reducing each Donatus by one sheet, or four pages, would save 50 sheets in 50 books," Gutenberg answered. "Enough to print six more books! In order to print a 32-page Donatus, I can either add four lines to each page, which saves four pages, or the monks can take out four pages. A 28 page Donatus would be better still."

"Why couldn't you do both?" Hultz asked. "So many of the prayers are repeated, the monks might be willing to take out four pages. And if you added four lines to each page, the Donatus would be 28 pages."

"Pages, sheets and lines! Pages, sheets and lines! The words go through my head like a litany," Gutenberg said wearily. "But you're probably right. I'd need only seven sheets in each book, or 350 sheets for 50 books."

"You would need 700 sheets then for 100 books," Hultz said.

"And 1050 sheets for 150 books," Gutenberg answered. "The 36-page Donatus had nine sheets in each book, and 50 copies required 450 sheets. Do you see what this means, Johann!"

Gutenberg was suddenly so excited, he broke off the tip of his quill. "That's three times the number of books from twice the number of sheets! Look! 50 books, 36 pages, 450 sheets...150 books, 28 pages, 1050 sheets,"

Gutenberg repeated. "A little more than double the number of sheets."

"The next Donatus should be 28 pages then!" Hultz replied.

Gutenberg saw that he could get the answers he wanted two ways: Multiplying the number of sheets in one book by 50 or 100 books, gave him the total number of sheets he would need for that many books; or dividing the number of sheets in one book into 500 or 1000 sheets, told him how many books he could print from that number of sheets.

This information showed the savings he could expect and other comparisons which were important in planning the size and number of books to be printed in the future.

PER BOOK	NO. BOOKS				NO. SHEETS	
	50	100	150	200	500	1000
28 PP—7 Sheets	350 Shs	700 Shs	1050 Shs	1400 Shs	71 Bks	142 Bks
32 PP—8 Sheets	400 Shs	800 Shs	1200 Shs	1600 Shs	62 Bks	125 Bks
36 PP—9 Sheets	450 Shs	900 Shs	1350 Shs	1800 Shs	55 Bks	111 Bks

"Printing 50 copies of a book at one time," Gutenberg wrote to his brother, "is like baking 50 loaves of bread at one time. We must think in large quantities of paper, just as the baker thinks in large quantities of flour. This involves risk, of course. If we make a mistake, we might have 50 copies of it and lose 50 sheets. The baker might burn half his loaves. But careful planning and workmanship will result in the quantities and quality of printing we want to achieve.

"Like the monks, we know that the number of lines on a page determines the number of pages and sheets in one book. But we must know the number of sheets needed for 50 books a certain size, or the number of book possible from 500 sheets before we begin. We know how to print books, now I'm learning how to do it efficiently.

"The faster we are able to compose pages and print them," Gutenberg went on, "the lower our cost in time. And total costs become less, not more, the more copies we print at one time. The more books we print, of course, the larger our profits when the books are sold. Profits so far from the Donatus and Judgment have given us a small return on our investment, but I expect future profits to be much greater. "We are reprinting 50 Donatus exactly like the first edition. It is not economical to print less than 50 copies, but next time, I'd like to print 100 copies. We will keep as many pages in forms, as we can. Then we can adjust the number of lines on a page much faster, and reprinting will be faster when pages don't have to be composed a second time.

"Hultz and the Beildecks want me to go with them to the shrine of St. Odile," Gutenberg concluded. "She is patroness of Alsace, you know, and has healing powers over the eyes. My eyes burn from reading numbers and letters so long! Perhaps the waters of the holy spring will make them better. I did not forget Orte's birthday and am sending him a present. Please give everyone my love. Write to me soon. This is a copy of the chart I made. Brother J."

Gutenberg did not have to wait long for news from Mainz. A letter from his sister Else arrived on the next boat and was full of family news. Little Else and Henne were expecting a baby in the fall, and had just moved into a house in Frankfurt that Grandma Humbrecht had given them. Orte was 15 and would become a soldier in Diether von Isenburg's personal guard.

"Most of his friends are in the archbishop's guard," Else wrote, "but Friele wouldn't permit it. 'The exiled Gensfleisch do not serve Erbach' he said. Von Isenburg is only 30 years old and very handsome. He has just been named provost of the cathedral churches of St. Victor and St. John. Odilgen is a sweet girl, as always, but not well. Her mother worries about her and Friele, too. Dr. Humery and his wife have a son, after all these years. He is so happy! Uncle Otto had a fall and can hardly walk. Rudi says he asks about you and wonders when you are coming home. The Donatus should be printed in Mainz, Uncle says. We all miss you so much, Henne, and hope your work continues to be successful. We are so proud of you. I am fine and Claus, too. We both send our love. Thea had kittens again. Your loving sister."

Gutenberg smiled. Uncle Otto was right. And so was Friele. He would say prayers for Little Else at St. Odile.

CHAPTER 26

The pilgrimage to St. Odile was the main topic of conversation in St. Pierre churchyard Sunday morning. Because it was the oldest church in Strasbourg, St. Pierre would have the honor of leading the delegation from the city that year, and the people stood in groups under the chestnut trees talking about their plans to go. The Beildecks were among them, but in obvious disagreement.

"We should go with the monks from St. Arbogast," Mme. Beildeck said.

"But I have promised to help carry the statue of Our Lady from St. Thomas church," Beildeck answered.

"You shouldn't have done that!" his wife scolded.

"The Master can walk with the monks, if he wants to," Beildeck said. "Master Hultz, too." They wanted to buy bread, he reminded her. Bread was for sale every Sunday morning in the cathedral square, and they must hurry or it would be gone.

"I will still cook for the Master," Mme. Beildeck said. "The monks don't eat enough"

"You are right about that," Beildeck laughed, as they started walking toward Notre-Dame. "The Master works too hard, you know. The mountain air and exercise will be good for him."

In better humor now, Mme. Beildeck took her husband's arm. "A pilgrimage is for prayer, not exercise," she corrected, but she agreed that Master Gutenberg did work too hard and looked very tired. She was glad he was going with them.

The convent of St. Odile drew thousands of pilgrims every year from Strasbourg and the many towns and villages in the district. Some people went every year. Most had been more than once. It was impossible to find an Alsacian who had never been to the Mount St. Odile in his lifetime.

Devotion to the saint went back 700 years. On February 14, young girls made a special visit to the shrine because it was believed that nine turns around the tower would assure them of being married within a year. Most pilgrims, however, came to drink from the miraculous spring called The Source, at the foot of the mountain, because these waters were believed to cure diseases of the eyes.

The Castle of Hohlenbourg, which became the convent of St. Odile, was built by Odile's father, Duke Adalric of Alsace, in 685. Situated on a steep, wooded slope in the Bloss mountains west of Strasbourg, it overlooked the whole vast plain of Alsace. On a clear day, one could see the cathedral spire and the meandering dark ribbon of the Rhein. To the south, the Schwarzwald and the great mountains of Switzerland were visible, and to the northwest, the Vosges.

As the story was told, and it became a legend, the Duke and his wife, Bereswinde, had a daughter who was born blind. Adalric ordered the child killed, but Bereswinde gave the baby to a nurse who took her to the convent of Baume-les-Dames, near Besancon. When the girl was 12 years old, she was christened, and during the ceremony immediately regained her sight. She was given the name Odile, which means "child of light". From Baume-les-Dames, the sisters took Odile to the Bishop of Regensburg, and news of the miracle spread quickly throughout Alsace.

At Hohlenbourg, meanwhile, Adalric had killed his son, Hugues, in a fit of anger. While Adalric was doing penance and suffering remorse for his violent deed, Bereswinde dared to approach him and told him that the child whose sight had been restored was their own daughter she had spared from death. The repentant Duke was overcome with joy. He sent for Odile and gave her the castle of Hohlenbourg that she might make it into a convent.

When Odile returned home, she brought several nuns with her. They nursed the poor and the sick, giving generously of food and alms to everyone who came to Hohlenbourg. Odile built another chapel, Niedermunster, at the foot of the mountain, and it was here one day that a spring suddenly appeared where Odile struck a rock. Later a blind man, washing his eyes at the spring, recovered his sight. From that day, and throughout the centuries, pilgrims had come to The Source, to pray for miraculous cures and to visit the tomb of St. Odile.

It is said that Odile had a vision of her father in Purgatory and that her tears and prayers delivered him. Her parents are buried at Hohlenbourg in the crypt of the Chapel of the Cross. St. Odile died on December 13, 730, and her body rests in the Chapel of St. John the Baptist.

Near St. Odile are two relics from Roman days, the Pagan Wall and the Beckenfels Rock. The great stone wall, standing three meters high in places, encircles over 200 acres and is on a plateau about one kilometer from the monastery. The oak pegs which originally fastened the stones together have long since rotted away, but the connecting holes are plainly seen. The Wall is believed to have been built by the Celts in the first century as a refuge against the Romans, who in turn enlarged it as a defense against the Germanic invasions. The immense Beckenfels Rock is a natural landmark near the Wall. It is 10 meters in height and has been used as an observation point for hundreds of years.

On the morning of the pilgrimage, everyone gathered at the west gate of the city to await the archbishop's blessing. The episcopal guard on horseback would act as escort and lead the procession, to be followed by groups from every church and religious order. Gutenberg, Hultz and his family walked with the monks from St. Arbogast, who carried a statue of St. Benedict. When the archbishop arrived, he blessed the pilgrims.

Then trumpets sounded and pipers and drummer played cheerful martial music as the crowd moved slowly on to the road.

The group from Strasbourg numbered about 300 and was a colorful parade of friars, cowled monks, monsignori, acolytes, tradesmen and craftsmen, and families with children. Some patricians rode in carriages. The sick and the old rode in carts drawn by donkeys or oxen. Penitants walked barefoot and were dressed in black, some carrying chains or crosses. Most townspeople wore the traditional Strasbourg dress and carried flowers or liturgical banners.

It was not a sad or somber group of pilgrims, Gutenberg noted. Many sang hymns or songs the children knew. When the monks chanted the prayers of their office, everyone kept silent but joined in the great Amens. At each village along the way, other pilgrims joined the procession, bringing their banners and statues carried on the shoulders of strong young men.

It was a full day's walk to Obernai where they would stay overnight, and after a brief stop at noon to eat and rest, the pilgrims arrived at the village about an hour after Vespers. Tiredness was soon forgotten as they were welcomed at this rendezvous point.

Now hot food could be cooked and eaten at leisure. Campfires were started, and soon the smell of soup and roast meat filled the evening air. People prepared to sleep in the fields or the churchyard, but some stayed in town to buy wine and candles to take with them the next day. Gutenberg and Hultz' family stayed at the inn but doubted if they would get much sleep. Most of the young people danced and sang in the square until long after nightfall.

Rising before dawn, the pilgrims continued their journey of a few kilometers to Niedermunster, the chapel at The Source where Mass was celebrated. For some, this was their destination because they could not make the steep climb up the mountain to the convent of St. Odile.

A pilgrimage wasn't an endurance contest, Hultz said. "Many believe that the healing miracles only happen here, at the holy spring, and will keep vigil at The Source. We must pray for them."

The pilgrimage had swelled to more than 1000 persons. Everyone walked barefoot now, winding their way slowly and silently up the forest-enclosed path. It was a difficult climb. Hultz and Gutenberg helped Beildeck and the monks carry their statues but stopped often to rest.

"Do you really believe in miracles?" Gutenberg asked.

"It is a miracle the shrine is still here," Hultz answered with a smile. "It is a miracle that people still come! Their faith is more important than any cure. Though there have been many cures. Yes, I believe in miracles! St. Odile was a holy woman. She received much grace from God. The Lord has blessed this place and will continue to bless it, even when the spring is gone."

Gutenberg would take some of the water from The Source, he said, to bathe his eyes. "I don't need a miracle. But I need the grace and the fresh air! I also want to see the Roman Wall."

"They call it the Pagan Wall, Johannes," Hultz laughed. "You are a Christian pilgrim and are thinking about a pagan wall. May St. Odile forgive you!"

Gutenberg and the group from Strasbourg reached St. Odile in the early afternoon. Many pilgrims had preceded them, and there was much activity as the nuns hurried about getting the visitors settled. Long tables of food had been set up in the yard, heaped with bread, cheese, fresh fruit and milk for the children. Blankets were distributed to the men who would sleep outdoors, and the hallways and refectory of the cloister were turned into dormitories for the women and children. Patrician families were given private quarters, and Gutenberg and Hultz had a large, comfortable room in the old castle which they shared with the Beildecks. The soldiers, bishop's guard and their horses encamped in a field beyond the cloister.

The convent area was large, and there was much to see - the saint's tomb, the three chapels, the cloister, the tower and courtyard. The view from the precipice was spectacular. Over a low wall at the very edge, the forest fell away, revealing tree tops and dark ravines, and far beyond, the plain of Alsace spread like a golden carpet in the sun.

Many of the pilgrims sat quietly under the trees to say their prayers and to rest from the exhausting trek. Vespers was sung by the nuns and monks in choir. Then after a light supper and the singing of Compline, everyone went to bed. In the cool night air, quiet and darkness, sleep would come easily. Gutenberg was glad he had come.

CHAPTER 27

The next morning Gutenberg was up early and set out by himself to explore the Roman Wall. He came on it a short distance from the convent and discovered other pilgrims there too. Children were playing soldiers' games - charging and defending the wall in mock battles - or playing hide and seek and peering through the peg holes and the Minnelstein "eye".

Gutenberg marveled at the giant stones set without mortar. The wall was indeed an incredible structure and reminded him of the Roman aqueduct in Mainz which he and Freile had explored when they were boys. The whole mountain of St. Odile, in fact, reminded him of the Taunus mountains, and he enjoyed the familiarity of landscape and peace of mind that comes with solitude in a place of quiet. natural beauty.

It was not difficult to imagine the real battles fought outside and within these walls centuries ago. But now, the pain and blood and death these fields had borne were buried forever beneath the grass and expansive blue sky. "God has changed a battleground into a monastery yard," Gutenberg thought. "That's a miracle, too."

Standing in this place, the past, present and future seemed to be one. Places and people change, still nothing changes. The Wall would be here another 1000 years, yet the hilltop would change. It was a paradox and a mystery. Gutenberg thought of his home, family, his life and work in Strasbourg, Ennelin. Where was she now? The unhappiness had disappeared with time just as the sorrows of war finally disappeared when the wars were over. God healed wounds on the face of the earth. He healed human hearts also. The Donatus had been printed and reprinted, which was satisfying. But he would like to print something else - a Missal perhaps, or the sermons of St. Bernard. A Cistercian monk was going to preach at the Mass on Sunday. Gutenberg hoped to speak with him.

At this moment, however, Gutenberg couldn't think about the future. His senses were filled with the beauty around him-the warmth of the sunshine, the breeze bending the grass in graceful waves down the slope, the hawk circling slowly in the sky. Gutenberg had walked the entire length of the Wall without realizing how far he had gone. Now he was very tired and sat down in the shade, took off his boots and quickly fell asleep.

Gutenberg woke to the ringing of the chapel bell. It was noon. Standing up and looking once more across the plain, he was startled to see the cathedral tower of Strasbourg in the distance. The morning haze had lifted and the spire was clearly visible.

"I wonder if Johann knows you can see the spire today," Gutenberg said aloud. "I must tell him!"

This discovery and the tolling bell made the past disappear in an instant and the present became exciting reality. To see the spire gave Gutenberg a happy, dizzy feeling of hope. Hultz had built a spire for Notre-Dame, maybe one day he would print the Missal monks read during choir at Notre-Dame. Gutenberg walked rapidly back to the cloister, carrying his boots in his hand.

The White Monks of the Cistercian Order came from the famous abbey of Citeaux in Burgundy. Founded in 1098 by monks from the abbey of Molesme, Citeaux was the mother house of more than a thousand abbeys and congregations throughout the Empire. This great expansion was largely due to the work of St. Bernard who, in the 12th century, founded the abbey at Clairvaux and more than a hundred others.

The Cistercian monks lived in silence and solitude and kept strict observance of the rule of St. Benedict. They were devoted to serving God through prayer, study of the Holy Scriptures and devotion to Christ's Passion. They were not engaged in teaching or helping the poor and the sick but offered their spiritual work of prayer for all men, while sustaining themselves by growing their own food and tending their own flocks.

The monks still lived austere lives of personal poverty, but their lands and productivity had increased so much in 300 years that commerce now was also a part of their monastic life. The two White Monks at St. Odile were returning from a journey to Strasbourg where they had sold the surplus wool, wheat, and wine from several abbeys at the annual provincial fair.

Honored to have the Cistercians among the pilgrims to St. Odile and because it was the feast of St. Bernard, the prioress had invited them to speak. The younger monk accepted and was eagerly awaited by the crowds who gathered in the courtyard to hear him.

The Cistercian was not an austere looking man, Gutenberg thought. He was tall and slender, forty years old perhaps, and youthful in appearance. He was tonsured and his face and hands were brown from the sun. He had an alert, friendly face and looked out over the people with quiet, intent blue eyes. He saw everyone. Speaking in a slow, clear voice, he began by asking a question.

"Do you think of God as a loving father." he asked, "or as a stern and powerful king, anxious to punish those who do wrong?"

The monk paused. "Think about it," he said.

Gutenberg thought immediately of the bishops he had seen who looked like kings in their gold embroidered robes and miters, but none of them had ever spoken as a loving father. The monk in his simple white robe and gentle manner was a sharp contrast.

"Who is God?" the monk asked. "He is the creator of heaven and earth, you answer. That is right. And we are God's creatures. His creations, His children. And because He created us, He loves each of us very much. A king wants allegiance. God wants love and faith. A king has subjects. God has a family.

"How do we show God we love Him?" the monk continued. "By going to Mass? Coming to St. Odile to honor one of His saints? Acts of penance? Sacrifice? Yes, but I say you do not need to wear a hair shirt or fast severely to show your love for God. You love God when you keep His commandments. You love God when you care for the sick. You love God when you are kind to a stranger, your neighbor, your servant, your master. You love God by carrying the cross He gives you. You love God when you offer your work, prayers and sufferings of every day as a gift to God. Whether it is preaching as I do, or plowing a field, cooking a meal or caring for a family as many of you do. Whatever your work is, do it with love and to please God most of all.

"Being here with you is a great joy to me because we can share our love for God together. When we return to our homes, we shall remember these days at St. Odile lovingly. They will remain sweet for us because we prayed together, sang God's praises together, and received Him in Holy Communion together. We met as strangers, we leave as friends because we came as a family to worship in love, the Father of us all. And to share in the holy banquet of the Eucharist which is the salvation of us all. The Eucharist is truly the feast of love to which God invites us, his dearest children, his dearest family.

"We know that the waters of St. Odile are known as healing waters," the monk went on. "But they are not the same as the water of Baptism. Water that restores the soul to God and washes it clean of original sin does not come from a spring but from the true source, which is God in the three persons of the Blessed Trinity, Father, Son and Holy Spirit, in whose names we were baptized. From these waters we receive the grace of God and His promise of everlasting life.

"You know that the purest water comes from the deepest well. Look deep into your hearts then, and let your love for God be as pure as the water drawn from the deepest well. Then, because He is God, He will change this water of our human love into the Wine of His own love which we shall taste forever in heaven. This is the living water that Christ promised to the Samaritan woman. It is the water of eternal life which is promised to all those who love God.

"Like the Samaritan woman, we may ask, 'How do I obtain this living water?' Through our gifts to God of faith and love. Ask God to increase your faith. Ask Jesus, His Mother and St. Odile to make your hearts more open to Him and to fill your hearts with more love for Him. Then the promise will come true, and heaven will be ours to share with God and his friends forever.

"God bless you all. Go in peace, to love and serve the Lord, with joy!"

The pilgrims had sat quietly, listening to every word of the monk's message. It was a refreshing message, Gutenberg thought. The White Monk had not talked about sin, damnation, death or hell, but about life and love and God's family of lovers. His words were not frightening, but reassuring!

To Fr. Sebastian, the Cistercian was a man who had found friendship with God. At Citeaux, the monks drank from the deep waters of contemplation, and it was good to see that this rare vintage of men still lived. Someday he would like to visit their abbey and taste those waters for himself.

The candlelight procession Sunday evening was the high point of the pilgrimage for Mme. Beildeck. She loved the pageantry and the singing. "It makes you feel like all the angels in heaven are with you," she said.

After the sun had set, a seemingly endless line of pilgrims encircled the monastery yard, each person holding a lighted taper which twinkled and glowed like hundreds of fireflies in the night. The pilgrims sang the Divine Praises in one full voice that resounded over the hills. Incense floated on the air with the intoxication of perfume, and lingered there. But it was the sight of the dazzling Monstrance, surrounded by candles, which held everyone's heart absolutely still for a moment.

You would have to be made of stone, Gutenberg thought, to remain unmoved by this procession, always beautiful in church, but overwhelming in beauty here in a forest cathedral with stars bright overhead. How good it was to say goodnight to God this way and know He blessed the night as He had blessed the day.

The pilgrimage ended, but Gutenberg and his friends did not walk back to Strasbourg. At The Source, Gutenberg and Hultz obtained horses for themselves, while Hultz' family and the Beildecks rode in a carriage. They traveled quickly, retracing the route through Obernai to Strasbourg in just a few hours. A feeling of exhilaration touched them all. It was like an emotional chord had been struck which made everyone happy and light-hearted and wishing somehow that they might have stayed on the mountain a little longer. Gutenberg rode at full gallop with Hultz, ahead of the carriage, laughing at their own exuberance.

CHAPTER 28

In the months following the pilgrimage to St. Odile, Gutenberg resumed printing of the Donatus. He was in need of paper to begin the third edition, so Hultz and Martin Brechter helped to arrange a loan of 80 pounds denari from the Franciscan brotherhood. On the feast of St. Francis, October 4, Gutenberg became a member of the St. Thomas chapter.

The third edition of the Donatas should be 28 pages, Gutenberg explained to Fr. Sebastian, and surprisingly, the monks did not object to removing some repetitious pages from the book. Nor, as it turned out, did Gutenberg have to add four lines to each page. The monks took out seven pages and Gutenberg made the pages 27 lines, adding only one line to each page.

The changes had taken so much time, however, that Heilmann lost patience. The Master was too particular about these shoolbooks, he told his brother. "We do them over and over," he said. "I know the lessons by heart and wish we would print something else! I think the Master does too. He talks about printing the Gospels or the sermons of St. Bernard."

Fr. Anthony objected to Gutenberg printing the Gospels and to printing for the Cistercians. "He could print the Doctrinale Advanced Grammar," Fr. Anthony said. "That book is needed in our schools also. I will talk to him."

The partnership agreement between Gutenberg, Riffe and Andreas Heilmann expired in 1443. The five years since Andreas Dritzehn's death had passed quickly. It seemed a long time ago that the two Andreas had polished stones and made mirrors for the pilgrimage to Aachen, Fr. Anthony thought. Sale of the Donatus had repaid Riffe and Andreas Heilmann their investments in the new work, but it was time to reassess their working relationship, and Fr. Anthony was concerned about Gutenberg's plans for the future. Liturgical books like the Gospels, or even a Missal, were much too ambitious.

"Andreas has completed his apprenticeship, and has been accepted as a member of the bookbinder's guild," Gutenberg told Fr. Anthony. "He presented a copy of the Donatus to the guild as an example of his work. I am proud of him." Now, as a master printer, Andreas would be entitled to master's wages, which Gutenberg would pay as long as they worked together, he said, whether Andreas was a partner again or not.

"I would like to print other books, yes, and will consider the Doctrinale. But if the Cistercians request a St. Bernard I shall not refuse them. It should not matter to Andreas what I decide to print!" Gutenberg said irritably. "I need more apprentices and Andreas can help me train them."

Gutenberg planned to discuss the new partnership with Count von Ramstein and Johann Riffe, he said. The partnership could be changed, the shop could be enlarged. There were several things he wanted to do. They would continue to print the Donatus, however, as long as there were customers for it.

"In my opinion, Johannes," Riffe said, "you should move the shop back into town and take on new apprentices, but not print any more books. There is more money to be made from printing single sheet announcements. They take less time, are less expensive to produce and they sell quickly. You don't need to enlarge the shop."

Von Ramstein would like to invest in a new partnership, he said, and he agreed that the shop should be in town. Gutenberg could print both books and single sheets, he thought. The Donatus did take time. New apprentices would pay for instruction. A new partnership might only be for two years, not five. Did Gutenberg really need to enlarge the shop?

"We could print an astronomical calendar, I suppose," Gutenberg said, "and should sell hundreds of those. But we would have to cast more letters. a larger size, stars and symbols and things. It would take time getting ready. An edition of St. Bernard could be done with the Donatus letters."

"You are never satisfied with the letters, Johannes!" Riffe answered. "You have cast enough letters to make a suit of armor, and still you want more! More punches and matrices are needed for larger size letters. More metal! Always more metal! I thought you used the letters over again. Yet you have almost twenty pages of Donatus in forms. I don't understand!"

"If there is a war," von Ramstein said quietly, "you won't print anything except a Call to Arms. Louis Dauphin is on the march again, and Strasbourg may be under seige if he and the Armagnacs reach Alsace."

"The Dauphin is always fighting somewhere," Gutenberg replied. "There are always rumors. I refuse to believe them. I shall go on printing Donatus, if I have to, and St. Bernard, if I am given the opportunity!"

Perhaps they were foolish to discuss partnership now, von Ramstein thought, and he advised Gutenberg to think about what had been said. It seemed prudent to wait six months and then decide what might be done.

"I will invest in a partnership with you," Hultz told Gutenberg. "But Riffe and the count are right in what they say too. Print a Doctrinale rather than St. Bernard. Reprint the Donatus. Train new apprentices, but don't enlarge the shop just yet. And print as many announcements or pamphlets as you can. You must have money, Johannes, and you get money more quickly from small prints than from books."

"Riffe has been such a good friend, and Fr. Anthony too," Gutenberg said sadly.

"They are still your friends, and friends do disagree at times," Hultz answered. He was also fearful of the Dauphin's armies threatening Strasbourg. If that happened, he knew work inside and outside the city, trade and farming would be disrupted for a long while. Gutenberg might be casting weaponry instead of letters of the alphabet.

A new partnership agreement was not drawn up, but Andreas Heilmann and the three apprentices continued to work at St. Arbogast. Gutenberg printed two more editions of the 28 page Donatus. Eventually they managed to cast enough letters to have complete page forms for the entire book. Now reprinting could be done as frequently as necessary without composing the same pages over and over again. Also, new punches and matrices were made and new letters cast for a calendar.

Then the long awaited letter from the abbot of Citeaux arrived, requesting 25 copies of St. Bernard's commentaries on the Gospels. Gutenberg and his men were elated. The letter confirmed, however, that the Dauphin was moving up the Rhein valley toward Colmar.

"If it should not be possible for you to print this book for us, we shall understand," the abbot wrote. "we are praying for the people of Strasbourg."

VIII. THE INVASION
CHAPTER 29

Alsace was invaded by the Armagnacs early in 1444, led by the 21-year old heir to the throne of France. Son of Charles VII, Louis Dauphin had already acquired a reputation as an intelligent but villainous and cruel prince. His army of 40,000 mercenary soldiers, known as the Escourchères, had marched from Burgundy to Basel and advanced steadily up the Rhein valley toward Strasbourg.

The countryside erupted in a chaos of burning and looting as defenseless villages were stripped of their grain and livestock. In Rosheim and Riquewihr peasants had hidden in caves and eaten raisins to stay alive. Vineyards were destroyed, wine cellars emptied, the Dauphin making little or no attempt to discipline his troops. Refugees arriving in Strasbourg told terrible stories of murder and atrocities, and the city was soon crowded with 8000 homeless and starving persons.

Heilmann and the other apprentices were conscripted for military service. Gutenberg was required to provide money equivalent in value to half a horse for the defense of the city. He was also listed among the goldsmiths to serve in the militia. His bulk supplies of lead, tin and brass were sold to make weapons. The valuable store of punches, matrices and metal letters Gutenberg buried in the crypt of St. Arbogast chapel. Hundreds of printed and unfinished sheets of the Donatus and reams of blank paper were taken to the monastery scriptorium. Not knowing how long the seige would last, Gutenberg made plans to move into Strasbourg. The Beildecks would go with him.

"Your house is not safe," Fr. Sebastian told Gutenberg. "Our abbey may not be safe for us, but we shall stay as long as we can. If the Armagnacs winter here, and if Strasbourg does not get help, I'm afraid the city will be taken."

The Dauphin did not enter Strasbourg, however. Lewis IV, count-elector of the Palatinate in Heidelberg, came to Strasbourg's assistance, and with the help of the citizenry forced Louis to abandon Alsace and retire to France. Many of the Armagnacs were left behind. It was winter now, and the deserted soldiers pillaged the countryside a second time. This time the abbey and Gutenberg's home at St. Arbogast were not spared.

In a single day, the monastery lost most of the books in the scriptorium, and the monks watched helplessly as volumes were carried off, torn apart or stripped of their bindings. Some of the books were burned like logs. Pages of others were stuffed into boots or under clothing for warmth. Gutenberg's house was ransacked, the barn leveled, the well polluted. The printing press was chopped up for firewood.

Then before the river ice melted, the Armagnacs crossed the Rhein. They did not surrender, but acted like a conquering army and offered their allegiance to Lewis Palatin and the Emperor Frederick III. Ironically, Louis Dauphin was credited for escorting them out of France.

When the months of upheaval ended, Strasbourg was safe, but the land around in every direction lay scorched and desolate.

"The castings, punches and matrices are safe," Fr. Sebastian told Gutenberg when he and the Beildecks returned to St. Arbogast. "But every Donatus has been stolen or destroyed. We will replant and rebuild and replace what we can, but it will take time. What will you do, Master? We cannot spare anyone to help you now."

Gutenberg would repair the house and plant a garden, he said. He would buy a pig and a goat. The Beildecks wanted to stay.

A city under seige suffers almost as much as one that is overrun by an enemy, Gutenberg thought. Fasting for Lent was forgiven during the seige, but sickness, hunger and death remained. Scars would remain. Rebuilding lives was much more difficult than rebuilding barns and fences, and Gutenberg thought of his own future. It would be another year before he could think of printing again.

Heilmann had been severely wounded and did not have the use of one arm. The three young apprentices were needed at home to help their families. Fr. Anthony and his priests were busy caring for the sick. Riffe's farms in Lichtenau had been ravaged, and he would have to borrow money for seed and new grape cuttings. Von Ramstein could provide a place in town for Gutenberg to work, but would have to delay any investment in a new printing agreement until the following year.

Gutenberg unburdened himself to Johann Hultz. "I could get another press," Gutenberg told him. "The schoolboys would help with the printing. But Nicholas Heilmann has only three men left at the mill. I cannot get paper. Besides, I really don't have any heart for the work. Books aren't important now."

Hultz knew it was impossible to print more Donatus or begin the St. Bernard commentaries, even if Gutenberg had the men and equipment to do it. "Will you go back to Mainz?" he asked.

Gutenberg shook his head. "I don't know. I don't know. Perhaps I will go to Basel."

Gutenberg had experimented with large initial letters cast from two pieces of metal which, when inked separately then fitted together, made it possible to print the letters in two colors. He was never able to complete the work, however, because printing the Donatus had taken so much of his time. Now Gutenberg had the time but could not get the metal he needed.

Gutenberg had also seen the fine work of Master Wilhelm from Basel who had engraved maps and pictures on copper plate. If relief plates could be cast from the engraved plates, Gutenberg reasoned, it would be possible to print maps and pictures, just like words were printed from relief letters.

"I would like to work with Master Wilhelm," Gutenberg told Hultz. "If pictures can be cast successfully on copper relief plates, think what this would mean! Words and pictures could be printed at the same time! Everything on a page could be printed at once - the text, initials, and illustrations - and in three colors!"

It was an extravagant idea, although Hultz was not surprised to hear Gutenberg speak of such things. Pictures were printed from wood, so they could be printed from metal also, he thought.

"You should go to Basel, Johannes," Hultz said. "I will go with you, in fact, as far as Freiburg. The Master there has invited me many times to see their openwork spire. Now I shall go. You can buy copper and other metal too, in Freiburg."

Fr. Sebastian also encouraged Gutenberg to visit Basel because the great Church Council was still in session there. Gutenberg was sure to meet important men who might be interested in printing.

"I will give you letters to some of the bishops," Fr. Sebastian said. "Show them the Judgment, a Donatus and the Pater Noster. Take some letters and a small press with you. You may be asked to print one of the communications of the Council!"

Gutenberg had spent 17 years in Strasbourg. He was 46 years old. The chance to go to Basel was tempting. Still he pondered his decision. Perhaps he should concentrate on printing in Mainz, Gutenberg reflected. The guilds would be more friendly now, and he could open a larger office with more men. Friele and Else would be happy to know he was coming home. The prospect of learning to cast copper relief plates, however, and printing illustrations and text together was too exciting, too important to be dismissed or put off. He might never have another opportunity to work with Master Wilhelm.

Now that Lewis Palatin had secured Strasbourg. it was possible for

Rhein barges to come and go again and for messages to be sent in and out of city. Gutenberg wrote to his brother in Mainz. He knew his family had heard about the turmoil in Alsace and anxiously awaited word that he was safe. Friele would be relieved but disappointed to learn that he was going even further away.

When letters arrived from Mainz, some were dated almost a year earlier, and were from Claus and Friele. None from Else. Gutenberg read eagerly, with shock and then grief - his sister, dear Else, had died. Her death was very sudden, Claus wrote. She had complained of a headache and went to bed. The following morning she collapsed in the kitchen. "My sweetheart, my bride is gone. Please pray for her," he wrote.

Else was not 50 years old, Gutenberg thought sadly. He remembered the last time he had seen her, and how unhappy she had been when he left Mainz. Else and Claus had been married 30 years. How lonesome it must be without her! Gutenberg could not have gone home for Else's funeral, he thought, and he couldn't go home now. Next year, next year I will, he promised himself.

Claus was in Frankfurt, Friele wrote, visiting Little Else and her husband. "Else's baby died, and she wants her father to live with them," Gutenberg read. "There is a caretaker at Hof zum Gutenberg. Should the house be sold?"

"The house must not be sold!" Gutenberg answered Friele. "It has been Claus' home for many years and he is like a brother to us. Nor will I accept rent from the man who took care of our mother and sister. I shall urge Claus to come home whenever he can."

Gutenberg wrote to Claus inviting him to live at Gutenberg Hof. He would have Masses sung for Else and the baby at Notre-Dame and St. Arbogast, he said.

I have responsibilities in three places now, Gutenberg thought. Mainz, Strasbourg and Basel. Friele would be glad Claus had been asked to stay at Gutenberg Hof, and Gutenberg hoped Claus would decide to stay. Perhaps when I return, he will come. It was too difficult now, and Little Else needed him.

CHAPTER 30

Coming out of Notre-Dame one morning, Gutenberg was surprised to see Ennelin's brother ride into the square with a group of young men from the grenadier guards. Recognizing the yellow and black insignia on Raoul's uniform, Gutenberg noticed that he also wore an officer's sash and ribbons for gallantry on his sword.

Gutenberg found himself staring as Raoul shouted orders sharply to his men. The exuberant officers dismounted and went into the Kammersell. Sitting tall and straight in the saddle, Raoul looked handsome, but when he dismounted, Gutenberg saw that he limped badly, dragging one leg. The boy had been injured in the seige of Strasbourg, Gutenberg realized. And he seemed arrogant. Raoul zur Iserin Tur was not the happy cheerful lad Gutenberg remembered.

Eight years had passed since Gutenberg's romance with Raoul's sister and the breach of promise suit. Gutenberg knew that Ennelin had not married and still lived on the Vieux Marché aux Vins with her widowed mother. He had only seen her a few times, briefly and at a distance. On Fr. Sebastian's advice, Gutenberg made no attempt to speak or correspond with her. He had not mentioned Ennelin's name, in fact, or discussed the lawsuit with anyone.

It saddened Gutenberg somehow that he had thought of Ennelin less and less as the years went by. "I was capitvated by a lovely girl," he thought, "but have been able to live without her. My work has taken all of my time and attention."

Now Gutenberg was curious to know more about Ennelin. He must speak with Raoul.

Entering the Inn, Gutenberg walked over to where Raoul was sitting. He had ordered cognac, Gutenberg noted, and it was still early in the day. Gutenberg took no notice of Raoul's leg and apologized for interrupting. "Master Raoul!" he said, saluting him. "I am so glad to see you!"

Raoul recognized Gutenberg immediately. Without help or hesitation, he stood up and extended his hand.

"It's a pleasure to see you, Master!" he said. Motioning his companions to leave, Raoul invited Gutenberg to sit down and ordered a cognac for each of them.

Raoul always liked the goldsmith who had courted his sister, who played games with him and took him fishing when he was younger. He never understood completely why Gutenberg had not married his sister. The Master's red hair and beard had faded a little, Raoul noticed, but he still walked with a firm stride and had the same friendly smile.

"I am proud to see you have served in the militia," Gutenberg began, "With honor."

"Ennelin nursed me or I would have died," Raoul said. "But my leg is useless."

"I wanted to ask you about Ennelin," Gutenberg said. "Is she well?"

"My sister left the convent when my father died. She takes care of my mother. She has not married. I shall not marry. This makes our mother unhappy. We have been a great disappointment to her."

Gutenberg was surprised by the frankness of Raoul's remarks. "Your mother should be proud and grateful to both of you," he replied.

Raoul shrugged and changed the subject.

"We know about your work, Master," he said. "I have a Donatus. Ennelin insisted I buy it. Remember when you took me to see the spire before it was finished? I was the only boy in school to see it." Raoul smiled for the first time.

"I wish Ennelin had married," Gutenberg said.

"She wanted to marry you," Raoul answered. "I never knew what happened, Master. I remember my sister cried a lot. Mama and Papa argued a lot. Something about your citizenship, I think."

"Yes," Gutenberg said. "I would not, could not, become a citizen of Strasbourg. I had to release Ennelin from her promise to marry. It was a very unhappy time, for her and for me."

Within the month he was leaving Strasbourg, Gutenberg continued. It was impossible for him to print books now, and he wanted to try some new work with metal engravings. "First I shall go to Basel," Gutenberg said. "Then I will return to Mainz to live."

Raoul was pensive. "I shall tell my sister I saw you, Master. She never hated you and would want you to know that. I'm glad we had this talk."

"Thank you, Raoul," Gutenberg said. "You are head of the family now. Take care of Ennelin."

"I will, Master," Raoul answered.

The conversation had been brief. Gutenberg had expressed no desire to see his sister or to say goodbye to her, Raoul noted. Yet he was interested in her welfare. Ennelin would be glad he had seen Master Gutenberg, but he would not mention the meeting to his mother.

I am free to live my own life, Raoul thought. Ennelin is the prisoner, yet she doesn't complain. She has never complained. Ennelin was the only person Raoul completely trusted and loved.

Gutenberg's heart ached for Raoul whose gentleness and mischieviousness had been replaced by cynicism and a foolish decision not to marry. Ennelin had saved his life. Perhaps in time she could also renew his spirit. I would like to see her again, he thought, but I shan't try to see her. It was enough to know that Ennelin was well and that Raoul would always look after her. Mme. Iserin Tur had become a martyr.

CHAPTER 31

Packing the metal letters and other equipment that had been stored at St. Arbogast was more difficult than Gutenberg anticipated. The brass punches were heavy and bulky. The lead matrices were heavy, but could be packed in neat rows like squares of chocolate. Many of the letters were still in the Donatus page forms, and Gutenberg decided to leave them that way at the monastery. The rest of the letters were sorted out, put into separate small bags and hidden in Gutenberg's boots with his personal belongings. The casting molds were taken apart and placed in Gutenberg's trunk.

When Gutenberg got ready to leave, the trunks were so heavy that Beildeck and the monks helping him could hardly lift them.

"This is as heavy as lead," one of the monks remarked. Beildeck frowned but laughed. "That's just what is in the Master's trunks," he said. "Lead, iron and brass tools! I hope the customs men won't think he is smuggling gold out of Strasbourg!"

Lorenz Beildeck was sad to see Gutenberg leave but envious also. He had always wanted to travel up the Rhein but had never been further from home than Haguenau and St. Odile. Mme. Beildeck, however, was certain that no city could be as fine as Strasbourg and no place as beautiful as the Vosges valley. She could not understand her husband's longing to see strange places.

Gutenberg planned to send some wine from Basel, he told them. He knew that Beildeck would savor it and only drink it on special occasions, while his wife would say it could never compare with Alsace wine. People are so different, he thought. Some have roots so deep they can't imagine ever going far from where they've lived all their lives. Others, like Beildeck and himself, found excitement in walking unfamiliar paths and experiencing new sights and surroundings.

"When I come back, perhaps you both will come to Mainz with me," Gutenberg said.

"We may be too old to serve you, Master," Beildeck answered, but he was pleased with the invitation. "I would go," he added, "but I could not leave Mama. We must live and die together."

Mme. Beildeck was touched but pretended to be offended to think her husband would want to visit Mainz, or Basel, if he could, without her. They must look after the house and help the monks harvest their grapes, she said. Work at home was more important than riding up and down the river.

Beildeck was to keep the horse and harness and the dog. "I will take one of Madchen's puppies with me," Gutenberg told him. "A Bernese dog should see where he came from, I think." These beautiful mountain dogs with the long, wavy black coats and white blaze on their chest, face, feet and tip of the tail, were common in the Swiss cantons and trained as harness dogs.

"I will train Fritz to pull a cart for us," Gutenberg said. "When he has grown a bit."

Driving a small carriage with Raoul on horseback beside her, Ennelin and her brother rode in silence to St. Arbogast. Ennelin had asked to go when Raoul told her that Gutenberg was going to Basel. "I want to say goodbye" she said. "We never said goodbye."

Raoul knew his sister hadn't seen Gutenberg in ten years. She was 26 years old, but a pretty woman, he thought. He was glad she wanted to visit St. Arbogast again.

Ennelin was dressed stylishly in brown with a brown cape lined in white silk over her shoulders. Her dark hair was covered with a lace shawl. The only jewelry she wore was an amber cross on a gold chain around her neck.

As they approached the monastery yard, Ennelin saw Fr. Sebastian coming out of the cloister. She reined the horse and waited for Raoul to dismount and help her from the carriage.

"Come," she said. "I shall tell Father why we are here. I'm sure he remembers me."

The monk walked toward them and recognized Ennelin at once. "My dear Miss Ennelin," he said, and raised his hand in blessing. "What a joy it is to see you and your brother."

Ennelin explained why they had come, and the monk nodded approvingly. "Wait here," he said, "I'll send word to Master Gutenberg that he has visitors."

"Ennelin is in the cloister?" Gutenberg exclaimed. He had been helping Beildeck in the barn and his hands were dirty, his clothes mussed. He stared at the young novice waiting patiently for an answer.

Well, I must go, Gutenberg thought. I must go. I can't refuse. "Tell Father I'll be along. In a few minutes."

When Gutenberg arrived at the monastery, he had washed and changed his coat and boots. Mme. Beildeck was away, and he was glad no explanation had been necessary. Walking into the monastery yard with a casualness he did not feel, Gutenberg stopped to adjust his hat. Why was he hurrying? Then he saw Raoul leaning against the wall.

"My sister wanted to come," Raoul said.

Fr. Sebastian came out of the chapel then with Ennelin beside him. "Isn't this a wonderful surprise," the monk said smiling.

Ennelin offered her hand. "I want to wish you well in Basel, Johannes," she said. "Master Gensfleisch zum Gutenberg!"

"My dear Ennelin," Gutenberg answered, bowing a little stiffly. "How kind of you to come!" He found himself staring. The lovely young girl he had known was now a lovely young woman, and she was wearing the amber cross he had given her. "You look beautiful!" he said finally. "Beautiful! I am so happy to see you!"

Ennelin wore her hair differently, but her voice was the same and her eyes smiled in the same teasing way Gutenberg remembered so well. Ennelin had never been shy. He saw no trace of bitterness, longing or self pity in her face.

They walked into the garden then, chatting easily, like they had only seen each other the day before. When they returned, Fr. Sebastian gave Ennelin a large bouquet of lilacs.

"The Armagnacs couldn't eat our flowers," he said. "Please come to St. Arbogast again, my dear. Your brother too. We will always be happy to see you."

Gutenberg helped Ennelin into the carriage. "God bless you," he said, and kissed her forehead. This spontaneous gesture was met by a quiet, warm, lingering gaze. "And you," Ennelin answered. "Goodbye, Johannes."

Gutenberg stepped back as Ennelin took the reins and followed Raoul's horse down to the road. He and Fr. Sebastian watched and waved until they passed from sight.

Ennelin had been at the monastery scarcely an hour, but seeing her made it easier somehow for Gutenberg to leave Strasbourg. By coming, he thought, she had given them both a lasting moment of sweetness, a memory to erase all their past hurt and unhappiness. Remembering would no longer be painful.

"Ennelin left something for you, Johannes," Fr. Sebastian said. "She asked that I give it to you after they had gone."

Fr. Sebastian handed Gutenberg a small package. Gutenberg opened it and inside, wrapped in fine linen, was an alabaster statue of the Virgin and Child. It was a rememberance he would always treasure.

CHAPTER 32

The day was going to be hot, Gutenberg knew, as he waited for Beildeck to bring the horse and wagon around to the yard. Madchen stood expectantly at the gate, watching her puppy that barked and danced around Gutenberg's feet.

"We'll be back," Gutenberg said, fondling the big dog's ears. "You take care of the house. I'll take care of Fritz."

Madchen whined and wagged her tail. Her eyes told him she knew they were going without her but that it was all right.

Gutenberg and the Beildecks didn't speak as they headed down the road toward Strasbourg. The sun was barely up, but already people were on their way to market. Soon other carts and wagons, loaded with produce, joined them, the drivers waving and calling friendly greetings. Flocks of geese and ducks were guided down the road by impatient children. At the bridge where the Rue de la Plaine des Bouchers crossed the canal, they encountered farmers driving their calves and sheep to the abattoir for slaughter. The activity helped raise the Beildeck's spirits.

Crossing the bridge, Beildeck headed for Quai Thomas, where the barge was waiting. After Gutenberg's baggage had been put on board, Mme. Beildeck hurried off to the market while her husband stayed behind to watch the trunks and the dog. Gutenberg was going to visit Notre-Dame, he said.

"We leave at 8 o'clock," the captain told them. "All passengers must be here a half hour before. Don't be late!"

Today Gutenberg could see storks circling down to their nest on the roof of the nave. Monks and friars were arriving for Mass and Gutenberg followed them into the church.

They entered the St. John chapel while he purchased a candle and walked slowly down the dark vault to the steps in front of the choir. He placed the candle in a holder and knelt on the stone floor, facing the apse and beautiful stained glass window of the Virgin with outstretched arms. Truly this is the house of God and the gate of heaven, he thought.

Gutenberg was not going home. He would be coming back to Strasbourg but didn't know when. He hoped the trip to Basel would be worthwhile. I wonder if I shall ever be allowed to print something besides the Donatus, he thought. My work in Strasbourg has taken so many years. I would like it to be a blessing to God, like Johann's spire, and a blessing to you, most Holy Mother. Gutenberg looked at the crucifix. May the work I have started be a blessing to You, he murmured and crossed himself.

Gutenberg stood up and saw Hultz and his son coming out of the chapel. The lancet windows were ablaze now with morning light and the walls of the vault were brushed with a soft pink glow. The acolytes' bell sounded and the monks filed into the choir to sing the office of Prime.

On the quai, Gutenberg and Hultz were surrounded by friends and family who had come to see their departure. Workmen from the cathedral and monks from St. Thomas, St. Pierre and St. Arbogast had come too. Von Ramstein, Riffe, Fr. Sebastian, Bro. Gerard, Fr. Anthony, Andreas and Nicholas Heilmann, Konrad Sahspach, even Master Lebert from the guild were there.

"Most people leave Strasbourg for the hereafter," Fr. Anthony said with a smile. "We expect to see both of you again soon!"

Beildeck had his arms full of packages. Mme. Beildeck was weeping.

"I know you'll take care of things, Renz," Gutenberg told Beildeck. He kissed Mme. Beildeck and the tears came harder.

"Be careful what you eat, Master," she warned. "You may be poison-ed before you get to Basel!"

"Don't worry, Mama," her husband reassured her.

The captain of the barge was impressed by the large gathering who had come to say farewell to two of his passengers. Finally he sounded the bell, and Gutenberg and Hultz stepped on board.

"Give us your blessing, Father?" the captain asked from the deck.

All the monks and friars obliged and everyone cheered.

"I doubt whether a bishop ever received so many blessings," Hultz laughed.

Gutenberg stayed close to the rail to watch as the mooring ropes were loosened. The four tow horses on shore were aided by oarsmen on the boat who leaned and pushed on poles held over the side. Children and dogs followed their progress, running along the embankment to where the channel turned into the canal Zurich and southward to the L'Ill and the Rhein. Small fishing boats following alongside, added to the excitement of departure.

When they left the canal and entered the river where the current swelled. Gutenberg and Hultz were still on deck, looking at the cathedral spire and the sun shining on the golden statue of Our Lady. A light breeze brought the scent of apple blossoms over the water.

Just as they passed the last point of land, Gutenberg saw a man on horseback, alone and waiting quietly till the barge went by. He was in silhouette, then turned and his yellow sash was caught by the wind and flew behind him. Raoul saluted and Gutenberg returned the salute.

The plain between the Vosges mountains to the west and the Schwarzwald to the east was about 80 kilometers wide, a broad expanse of fertile farmland, vineyards and orchards. It is like a garden, Gutenberg thought, as he watched the panorama of natural beauty unfolding before them.

They should reach Freiburg in a week, Hultz said, if there were no delays. It was 75 kilometers to Beisheim where they would cross the river by ferry to Breisach. From there, Freiburg was a two hour ride or half day's walk, and he hoped they could get horses in Breisach.

"The peaks around Freiburg all have names," Hultz went on. "And, I'm told, even the devil prays at the door of Freiburg munster!"

Gutenberg smiled at his friend's knowledge and enthusiasm. "We should have traveled up the Rhein long ago, I think," he said. "Why don't you come on to Basel with me?"

"No," Hultz replied. "I shall go to Ottmarsheim on my way home. I want to see the octagon church there. It has no great spire, but is 11th century Roman style and copied after the chapel at Aachen."

Hultz sounded like a schoolboy planning a holiday, Gutenberg thought.

And it would be a holiday of sorts for both of them: Hultz visiting monks and munsters while he saw goldsmiths and guild workshops. They would have much to tell each other when they got back to Strasbourg.

IX. THE RELIEF PLATES
CHAPTER 33

Basel, like Mainz, was built on the west shore of the Rhein where the river made a broad sweep eastward. Once the site of a Roman camp, the city was founded in 374 and became important when the bishop moved his see to Basel in the 5th century. After the breakup of Charlemagne's empire, it became part of the kingdom of Louis the German. The foothills of the Jura mountains were to the south, and rivers and passes from Basel led through the Alps to Milan and Rome.

Basel was the capital of the most northerly Swiss canton and had become a free imperial city in the 14th century. The country had had a long history of struggles against Austrian domination, and Basel, though not a member of the Swiss Confederation, helped to win these wars.

It was a cosmopolitan city, known for its textiles, muslin, embroidery and fine woodcraft. But when Gutenberg crossed the Rhein, he felt he was entering a different world. The language was different, the food and the people were different. These tall, brawny men of few words seemed suspicious of strangers. Only the timbered houses and fountain squares were familiar. The Romanesque munster had new twin towers, Gutenberg noted, though they were half the height of Notre-Dame.

Gutenberg rented a room at an inn, and after making inquiries at the guild, succeeded in meeting Master Wilhelm. The engraver was flattered that Gutenberg had come all the way from Strasbourg to see him, yet was modest and reticent to talk about his own work. Wilhelm did not know how books were produced, he said, but he had heard about Gutenberg's new printing with metal letters. The idea of casting copper relief plates from engraved plates to print pictures, he found original and intriguing.

He would engrave some scrollwork designs, Wilhelm said, which Gutenberg could use as the matrices for relief castings. He would also allow Gutenberg to share his workshop and would introduce him to other guild members.

Master Wilhelm had a fine reputation, and Gutenberg was honored to have been welcomed so cordially. The guild masters in Basel were familiar with every aspect of working with metal, it seemed, and Gutenberg listened with interest to what they had to say. Wilhelm and Gutenberg said nothing, however, about the relief plates.

Six months later when Gutenberg wrote to his brother, he could report progress but the work had been difficult. "The lines on an engraving are not cut as deeply as the matrix for a letter so the relief plates are not as sharp as a letter casting. There are so many fine lines that small details, like bird feathers and some flower petals, are missing. Vines and scrolls are simpler and the plates and prints come out well. As long as the outlines and most important features print clearly, however, they will serve as a guide to the artist who can fill in the details and colors by hand.

"We've made individual plates which can be printed together, and sometimes we have put several pictures on one plate, then cut the prints apart. Laying these prints under lines of text shows how an illustrated and printed page might look. Of course, to print the pictures and text at the same time, the relief plate has to be nailed to a block of wood so it's the same height as the metal letters! There's much work to be done, as you see. The copper plates are expensive, but the results will be worthwhile."

Gutenberg had presented his letters of introduction to four bishops, he wrote Fr. Sebastian, and hoped to meet one of them soon. "At one time, Master Wilhelm says, there were a thousand prelates here, now only half that many, but the city still seems crowded with red and purple hats. There is much intrigue among the churchmen. As I understand it, the group still here is angry because Pope Eugene IV returned to Rome and because Duke Amadeus of Savoy, who they had crowned pope, was not recognized. So they continue their efforts at schism and against papal authority. Even Emperor Frederick III made his peace with Eugene and has left these stubborn men to fight among themselves. They will have to disband soon, everyone thinks."

"I have met the bishop of Konstanz!" Gutenberg wrote in another letter to St. Arbogast. "He has shown the most interest in my work and I have printed two communiques for him. He is greatly interested in the arts, more than in politics, I think. He asked if it might be possible to print a Missal! I told him 'yes'! But he is reluctant to authorize the printing of any liturgical book. Perhaps he will change his mind."

"The bishop is also acquainted with the papal nuncio who is from Kues, near Trier," Gutenberg went on. "Nikolaus Cusanus has a splendid reputation as a scholar and scientist and is highly respected by everyone. The bishop has been trying to meet with him for some time. You see, Master Wilhelm engraved an heraldic coat of arms for Cusanus, and I made the relief plate and prints from it. It is the sign of the crawfish or crab, Krebs, which is his family name. I should be very happy for the papal nuncio to see it as well as the Donatus and Paters I gave to the bishop. But they must be presented by the bishop."

Months went by without any news from Konstanz. Gutenberg had been in Basel more than a year and was increasingly frustrated waiting for a commission from the bishop and wondering if the bishop had ever met with Cusanus. Repeated inquiries finally brought word that Cusanus had returned to Rome and the bishop to Konstanz. Bitterly disappointed, Gutenberg told Wilhelm he was returning to Strasbourg.

"I had too high hopes of getting the support of influential people," Gutenberg wrote to Count von Ramstein. "And without their help, there is nothing we can do. Master Wilhelm and I have accomplished a lot, but the opportunity to meet Cusanus or print a Missal may never come again... Wilhelm insists I see the great Alps before I leave, so next week we shall go. We'll be gone about a month and then I depart Basel forever."

CHAPTER 34

In June, when the snows had melted and the mountain roads were open, Gutenberg and Master Wilhelm made the journey on foot to Luzern. Walking the valleys and gentle slopes from Basel would be pleasant, Wilhelm assured his companion, and prepare them for climbing the higher land later on. Wearing a new collar and waving his tail, Fritz led the way.

Luzern was on a large lake and presented a breathtaking view of the surrounding mountains. Reflected in the water, the snow-capped peaks of Pilatus and Rigi were an unforgettable sight, the highest mountains Gutenberg had ever seen. Walking along the ramparts and covered wooden bridges, even getting lost in the narrow, winding streets was an adventure in this beautiful town.

At Interlaken, Gutenberg wrote glowingly in his journal. "We did not climb the Jungfrau, but we saw it! There were clouds for two days, then all at once, there it was! A magnificent white pyramid, twice the height of Pilatus! There are many rivers, lakes and waterfalls. The air is wonderful! Cows and goats are in the high pastures now, and you can hear their bells everywhere. And people living on the mountains send greeting across the valleys by blowing horns that are as tall as a man and reach to the ground. I've never seen anything like them."

Gutenberg got a little cart for Fritz to pull and to carry their knapsacks that became heavier and bulkier as they collected cheese, wood carvings and silk banners from each of the cantons they visited. When they reached the Bernese Alps, Fritz seemed to know he was home.

"We shall see another Fribourg before we get to Bern," Gutenberg wrote, "and then cross the Jura mountains into Basel. Wilhelm has been good company and is an excellent guide. He has made many sketches of the places and people we've seen along the way. I wish we could make engravings and relief prints from his pictures. The man is truly an artist."

When they reached Basel after nearly eight weeks, Gutenberg's boots were worn out and Wilhelm had used his last piece of precious paper to make a drawing of Fritz and his cart.

Several messages were waiting for them in Basel. Gutenberg had a letter from Claus saying that Friele was not well and that Odilgen had become a novice. She had left Mainz and was living with the sisters at St. Odile in Alsace!

Wilhelm had a letter from the bishop of Konstanz. "He wants us to meet him at his residence in Schaffhausen," Wilhelm read aloud. "Before August 15. Surely we must go, Johannes. He must have news for you."

"Why didn't the bishop say what he wanted to discuss in his letter," Gutenberg answered irritably. It would take at least a week to reach the city by boat, up the Rhein to the Rhein Falls, and Gutenberg did not want to postpone his return to Strasbourg and Mainz any longer. "I don't want to go to Schaffhausen!" he said. "If the bishop wants me to print a Missal, he should say so! Does he mention Nikolaus Cusanus?"

"The bishop must talk with his abbots," Wilhelm said, "A decision about printing the Missal must have their consent also. And he did see Cusanus. Listen. 'The papal nuncio is pleased with your work and thanks you for the engraving and prints of his family coat of arms. He sees great benefits from using Master Gutenberg's printing press because it would establish uniformity of texts and hasten distribution of important church papers.' "

"That is true," Gutenberg acknowledged.

Wilhelm continued reading. " 'I will show my abbots the copy of the Donatus and other prints you gave me, and think I can promise Master Gutenberg a favorable answer - to print a Missal for our Diocese.' Now, what did I tell you!"

"The bishop is a good man, Wilhelm," Gutenberg replied, "and I'm sure he means what he says. But promises made cannot always be kept."

"Will you change your mind about visiting Schaffhausen?" Wilhelm asked.

"No. You must go, because you are a citizen of Basel and cannot refuse his invitation. I shall give you a letter," Gutenberg said. "I am worried about my brother's health, and the bishop will understand my duty to him. Should I be given the commission to print the Missal, I will print it in Mainz."

Wilhelm would go to Schaffhausen, he said. And he would also come to Mainz whenever Gutenberg needed him. The two men had become good friends, and working together to print books and pictures was a tantalizing thought for the future.

X. THE RETURN
CHAPTER 35

When Gutenberg returned to Strasbourg, he went to see Odilgen first of all. It was a bittersweet meeting. They talked about the family and why she had chosen the community of nuns at St. Odile. Odile was her name saint, the girl said simply, and she was happy caring for the sick and the poor who came to the monastery for help. Gutenberg was to tell her parents she prayed for for them every day.

Odilgen was a little thin, Gutenberg thought, and he gave her money, chocolate and a warm sweater for winter. If she got sick or needed anything, she was to write to Fr. Sebastian. And she would have visitors, he assured her. The Beildecks, Hultz and Fr. Anthony would come as often as they could. Gutenberg and his niece both cried when he had to leave, knowing in their hearts they might never see each other again.

Gutenberg's friends in Strasbourg were pleased that he had accomplished so much in Basel, but his reunion with them was brief also. Fr. Sebastian, Fr. Anthony and Count von Ramstein were away from the city, and when he boarded the barge this time, only the Beildecks, Hultz, Andreas and Nicholas Heilmann were there to say goodbye. It was another painful farewell.

As the barge made its way to the Rhein, Gutenberg thought of the trip thirteen years before, when his mother was dying. He had been sad and uncertain then about the future. Now he was still uncertain, but more hopeful somehow. He was glad to be going home at last, and he would always cherish the many friends and good memories he left behind in Strasbourg.

The high single tower of Notre-Dame was still in view. It had welcomed them to Strasbourg and was the last thing he would see of Strasbourg. Gutenberg stayed on deck a long time. By night fall the spire too would be a memory.

"My name is Beck," the captain said. "You are going to Mainz, Master?" Gutenberg nodded. "A fair city, Mainz," Beck answered.

The sun was directly overhead now and cast bright sparkles on the water. There was a slight breeze and the captain hoisted a sail so the horses on shore could pull more easily.

Der Vogel was a good boat, the captain said. Had the Master seen the picture of a bird painted on the side? Yes, Gutenberg said, and Der Vogel was a good name. Some birds were like boats, he thought, floating, riding the current, resting, then moving on.

Finding Gutenberg a good listener, Captain Beck continued the conversation as he maneuvered the barge expertly past sand bars and small islands. He was from Speyer, Beck said. In their cathedral, eight kings and emperors were buried. Strasbourg had the high tower, but no kings in the crypt! he laughed. No, he had never climbed the Strasbourg tower. Heights made him dizzy, and he felt much safer on water. How long had he worked on the river? More than twenty years. "I know every island, rock and reef on both sides of the meandering Rhein," Beck said. "I know which toll masters are honest and which are not. Beyond Mainz all the castle barons demand tribute and some of them are pirates!" Beck spit over the side in disgust.

At Speyer, Gutenberg decided to go ashore to visit the Dom and see the royal crypts. There were few people to meet the barge, however, and the street leading into town was strangely deserted. Why? Gutenberg wondered. Soon he knew why. At the Altportal, he met a loud, jeering crowd following two criminals to their public execution. Gutenberg got a glimpse of the men in chains and the scaffold where they would be hung. He shuddered and turned away.

Watching people put to death held an attraction for some people, which Gutenberg could never understand. In Strasbourg, women found guilty of adultery were drowned and their screams deadened by the roll of drums and cheers from the crowd. Only a few wept. Gutenberg had seen the remains of bodies that had been butchered and dismembered. He remembered the cruelties inflicted by Louis Dauphin and the Armagnacs on the peasants of Alsace. Torture and brutality sickened him.

So many people endured sickness, disease, hunger and pain as part of everyday life. Additional agony and suffering, deliberately inflicted, was the work of the Devil! he thought angrily. The condemned men could be murderers. They might have tried to escape from prison. They could be innocent! Whatever their crimes, forgive them, Lord, Gutenberg prayed, and take their poor souls to heaven!

Gutenberg returned to the barge without seeing the Dom. There he found Beck's daughter, a pretty girl in her teens, hanging out the wash and singing to her canary. The bird, in a cage, responded with sweet trills and whistles and fluffed its feathers. The girl smiled shyly to Gutenberg and he waved his hand. Having a canary instead of a gander or a rooster for a mascot, revealed an unexpected side of Captain Beck.

The barge stopped briefly at the large island of Opaw across the river from Mannheim and then at Worms. There was an old Jewish cemetery at Worms near the Dom, Gutenberg remembered. The Andreasring, it was called. Jews had been blamed for the Black Death 100 years before, and thousands had been killed. Jews were no longer permitted to live in Strasbourg. Those were terrible days, he thought, yet good and beautiful things had survived also. Like the windows of St. Katherine's church in Oppenheim.

At this last stopping place, Gutenberg went ashore again to visit the church and light a candle for his sister. The sanctuary was half the size of Notre-Dame, and the windows were eye level instead of high overhead. As the sun shifted, patterns of red, blue and gold warmed the stone floor and anyone standing on it. St. Katherine's was a jewel, Else had often said, and she was right.

What was new in Mainz, Gutenberg asked the captain the next morning as they began the last day of their journey. Standing on deck where he could see every bend of the river, Gutenberg was anxious for information which he knew Captain Beck would gladly supply.

"The Holzturm is new," Beck said. "But it is wood, not stone, and doesn't match the other tower. Business is very good, and there are many new shops. Everyone trades in Mainz!"

They passed a barge leaving the city and saw one approaching from the opposite shore. Many small boats were headed for the fischtor where fish would be sold and other produce unloaded for market.

The captain liked Mainz because it was a busy place. "Here people don't sleep their days away," he said. "They are friendly and cheerful. Like you, Master. Would you like to help me raise the flag?"

"Oh, yes!" Gutenberg smiled broadly. "Thank you, Captain!"

Beck lowered the Worms banner and unfolded the large double wheel, red and white emblem of Mainz. Gutenberg affixed the rings of the banner onto the rope, hoisted it, and watched it unfurl quickly into the wind. Now the Vogel flew the flags of all Rhein imperial cities from Basel to Mainz.

As they passed the castles of Nerstein, Schwabsburg, Nakenheim,

Haxheim, Laubenheim, Weisenau, Gutenberg remembered all their names. And on the right bank where the Main river joined the Rhein, stood the fortress Gustavsburg.

Gutenberg was home!

What if things had changed during his absence! People were always building something new or repairing something old. The bells still rang at the same time every day. St. Christoph's churchyard still smelled of lilacs in the spring. No wars had destroyed the city gates. No plague had filled the cemeteries. Boys still played on the Roman aqueduct and tried to scale the Jupiter column. Gutenberg strained his eyes for a first glimpse of the Dom and St. Stephan's on the hill.

"Oh, it is good to be home again!" Gutenberg exclaimed. "To see everything as I remember it or not! In its same place or not! Painted new or not! We must hurry, Captain Beck! Tonight I shall sleep in my beloved Mainz. Golden Mainz am Rhein!"

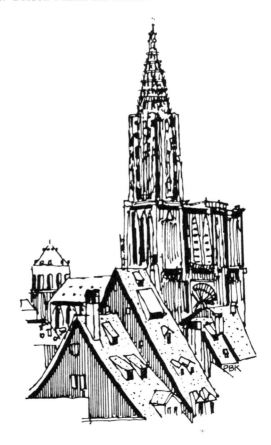

MAINZ
1446-1468
The Printed Bibles

XI. THE HOMECOMING
CHAPTER 36

When Gutenberg disembarked at the fischtor in Mainz, his brother, Friele, Friele-Else, young Orte, and his brother-in-law, Claus Vitzthum were there to meet him. It was a joyous reunion. Friele was thinner, Gutenberg thought. His hair was gray, and he used a walking stick. Friele-Else seemed more solicitous than usual, and Gutenberg sensed a feeling of relief in their warm welcome. He had seen Odilgen, he said, and assured them she was well and happy. Orte was a handsome officer, taller than his father and reminded Gutenberg of Raoul.

At Hof zum Gutenberg, dinner was waiting, and they sat for a long time, talking and drinking wine as Gutenberg told them about his trips to Basel and St. Odile, and his reasons for leaving Strasbourg. He was home at last and home to stay, he said.

Since Else's death, Claus continued to live at Hof zum Gutenberg but went to Frankfurt frequently to visit his daughter. Little Else thought he should move to Frankfurt, Claus said, now that Gutenberg was home. Did he wish to sell the house or would he live in it, Friele wanted to know.

"Of course, I shall live here," Gutenberg told them. "And I would like you, Claus, to live with me. This has been your home for many years. Lonely, now I know, and it would be lonely for me. I intend to open a printing office in the house. We have always got along well, Claus, and I will need your help and advice. Will you stay?"

"Little Else is very good to me and Henne too," Claus said, "but Mainz is my home. Old friends are here. Else is still here. I would like to stay and help you, Johannes, if you think I can."

The arrangement was pleasing to Friele. "I would not have sold the house," he told his brother, "as long as you were away. I'm glad you don't wish to sell it. I knew you would be home one day, and now you and Claus can look after each other."

Gutenberg's intent to live permanently in Mainz seemed providential, Friele thought. It meant that a Gensfleisch would still inhabit the family home. They were a small family, and could easily visit one another now that Johannes was back. Eltville was only an hour's journey down the Rhein and Frankfurt was two hours up the Main river from Mainz.

"We will visit you and Little Else too," Gutenberg said, "and our friends can visit us here at Hof zum Gutenberg. Claus and I will be glad to have company, though I expect to be very busy."

It was late before the last bottle of wine was consumed and everyone went to bed. As they took candles and went upstairs, Gutenberg had a warm, deep feeling in his heart that his return to Mainz at this time was indeed providential and that the future would be good for all of them.

In the next two months, Gutenberg and Claus turned one room of Gutenberg Hof into a small printing shop like he had done at St. Arbogast. The letters and equipment were unpacked, the foundry set up, and Gutenberg ordered another printing press and letter cases to be built. With his cousin Rudi Sorgenloch's help, he hoped to interest other goldsmiths in working with him. He would instruct them in the new work as he had Dritzehn and Heilmann in Strasbourg.

Inside of a year, Gutenberg had four apprentices and had printed three editions of the Donatus, using the page forms and letters he had brought with him. He also began work on an astronomical calendar in German for the year 1448 and had cast new letters for this. Gutenberg was pleased by the aptitude and enthusiasm shown by his pupils in learning their new skills. Even Claus became a careful reader of the pages before they were printed and enjoyed the activity.

Before the calendar was complete, however, on Assumption Day, August 15, 1447, Friele Gensfleisch died. The family was grief stricken. Gutenberg knew that without his brother's help, he would not have been able to pursue the work with metal letters. Generous, loyal, and with unfailing confidence in whatever Gutenberg did, Friele had also provided the money for paper and equipment so Gutenberg could begin printing again in Mainz. In his will, he bequeathed an additional annuity so the work could continue.

Friele Gensfleisch was buried in Eltville, a respected member of the Mainz council and servant of the diocese of Mainz. His widow was unconsolable.

Gutenberg resumed printing, but it was discouraging because the scriptorium monks were critical and depreciating of what they considered "artificial writing." The Donatus were acceptable and useful as school books, they said, but only manuscript was considered fine enough for anything else. Even the Doctrinale advanced grammars continued to be written by hand. Gutenberg longed to print a liturgical book, but the abbots of Mainz refused to listen or even consider such a proposal.

The need for copies of the Missal in quantity was as great as the need for Donatus in schools, Gutenberg believed. The Missal was used daily in monasteries and by the local clergy. It was constantly being copied and recopied by hand. That no one in Mainz seemed interested in printed books, aside from the Donatus, was infuriating.

By now Gutenberg had printed no less than 24 editions of the Donatus, the latest being 24 pages instead of 28 pages quarto. He had learned how to adjust the number of lines on a page to conserve paper. He had demonstrated that it was possible to publish many copies of one book in a short length of time. He was also constantly improving and enlarging his supply of metal letters. His printing was far superior to wood block printing, yet Gutenberg was not given any new work of importance. He published fifty single pages in German listing the fast and abstinence rules for Lent for Fr. Hermann Gunther of St. Christoph church, but that was all.

Then in 1448, Gutenberg received a letter from Konstanz. The bishop requested that fifty copies of the Latin Missal be printed for his diocese.

Gutenberg was elated. This book would be ten times larger than a

Donatus. He would make new punches and matrices and cast new letters for the Missal, Gutenberg said, including the two-and three-line initials, if possible, like those in the manuscript book he would copy. He would work with the monks at St. James, he told Claus, and have them read the text before it was printed to be sure it was perfect. And he would print 60 copies, Gutenberg decided. There must be copies for Mainz as well as Konstanz. His funds were inadequate, however, to purchase all the metal and paper he would need, and Gutenberg turned to his cousin, Arnold Gelthuss, who borrowed 150 gulden on his own security, enabling the work to begin.

When the Missal appeared the following year, it contained 192 leaves or 384 pages quarto size, and the 60 copies had required 6000 folio sheets of paper. Some lines and words were printed in red. Several combination letters and abbreviations had been used so the columns were as even on the right as on the left. The improvement in appearance over the Donatus pages was striking. Even the monks were forced to admit that the letters and pages of the printed Missal rivaled the finest manuscript.

Recognition of the Missal's excellence came from clergy and guild members alike. The book was widely praised in Mainz, even by former critics, and friends felt certain that now Gutenberg had established himself as a printer of repute.

Hopeful that he would be asked to print a second edition, Gutenberg kept the Canon and as many of the page forms intact as he could so that reprinting of the Missal might be accomplished more quickly in the future.

CHAPTER 37

"We have received the Missal with great joy," Count von Ramstein wrote from Strasbourg. "Fr. Sebastian, Fr. Anthony, Master Hultz and I congratulate you on this truly magnificent volume! Master Hultz especially wanted you to know how happy and proud he was of your success. The Missal arrived shortly before his death. He is buried in Notre-Dame. I regret this sad news, Johannes. Pray for him."

Gutenberg was stunned. The dear friend with whom he had shared his first ideas about printing and the metal letters was gone. Ten years had passed since the cathedral spire was completed, only three years since they had gone to Freiburg together. And in Mainz, Claus Vitzthum was dying.

In five years, Gutenberg reflected sadly, he had lost four people close to him - his sister, brother, Hultz and now Claus. Each of his printing achievements had been marked or marred by death.

Little Else had come from Frankfurt to care for her father, and now after the funeral she and her husband, Henne Humbrecht, would be returning to Frankfurt. Gutenberg hated to see them go. It was nice having young people in the house. Gutenberg Hof would be lonely indeed without them. Else too was concerned about leaving her uncle.

"His work is so important to him, Henne," she said. "I wish we could stay with him."

"It would mean renting our house in Frankfurt," Henne answered. "Would you want to do that?"

"Yes, and you have as much business in Mainz as you have in Frankfurt," Else said. "It's just if we leave, Uncle will be alone. I don't think he should be, not anymore. Besides, we understand Uncle. Mama and Papa did too. Aunt Friele-Else never did, and she won't leave Eltville, I know."

Henne kissed his wife and hugged her. "I might have more business in Mainz," he said. "I'll speak to your uncle."

"Else and I have talked it over, Master," Henne told Gutenberg, "and we don't think you should live here by yourself."

"I won't be by myself," Gutenberg protested. "The servants are here, and the printers. I'll be busy." He was pleased by their concern, however, and hoped they would visit him often.

"We thought, Uncle, you might want us to stay," Else said.

"With an old bachelor and in a house that is a workshop? I can't ask Henne to do that. With your father, it was different."

"We'll come if you want us," Henne said.

Gutenberg could see Henne was sincere, and Else, too. "You will inherit Hof zum Gutenberg one day," Gutenberg told his niece.

"Then we shall live in it" Else said happily. "I love Mainz and this old house, and Henne does, too. We'll rent the house in Frankfurt."

"You really would like to come?" Gutenberg asked Henne.

"I have family here too, you know," Henne answered. "It won't be difficult for me to work in Mainz."

"I'll move the printing shop!" Gutenberg told them. "Then there will be plenty of room for all of us." He embraced Else and put his arm around

Henne's shoulders. "I love you both, you know," he said smiling. "You've made me very happy."

XII. THE PROPOSAL
CHAPTER 38

Soon after being named cardinal and papal legate to Germany in 1450, Nikolaus Cusanus visited Mainz. His mission was to win support of the Rheinland bishops to the policies of Pope Nicholas V.

Considered one of the greatest intellectuals of his day, Cusanus had performed some of the first scientific experiments, outlined the mathematics of calculus, and, on his return to Rome from Constantinople, brought many Greek scholars with him. He played a prominent role at the Council of Basel and was widely respected as the most capable and influential man serving the Papacy. Born in the town of Kues not far from Trier, Cusanus came from a family of immense wealth, although his father was a commoner and called himself a simple fisherman.

The four archbishop-electors of Mainz, Cologne, Trier and the Rhein Palatinate were headquartered in Mainz, under Count Dietrich von Erbach, archbishop and grand elector of the Holy Roman Empire. These men had favored conciliar church government as decreed at the Councils of Basel and earlier at Constance. Opposing this view were the Pope, Emperor Frederick III and the lay electors of Saxony and Brandenburg, who wanted strong central government from Rome.

The Rhein electors sought to keep civil and church authorities within the Empire and free of Roman domination. The questions of revenues, courts, and liberties of the German church and national government had been debated at length by the clergy, but neither the Pope nor the Emperor would listen to their grievances. Frederick, in fact, had sided with Rome against his own bishops and deliberately avoided meetings with them by residing outside the Empire most of his long reign.

After the many years of the Avignon Schism, popes and anti-popes, the election of Nicholas V in 1447 had really marked the end of the Conciliar movement. Cusanus himself now favored the papal position. The Pope planned to celebrate the unity of the Church at a Jubilee to be held in Rome in 1450.

Son of a country physician, Pope Nicholas was a scholarly, pious man. He was a patron of the arts and wanted Rome to be the cultural, as well as the religious center of the world. He took a great personal interest in books and reading. His large collection of over 1200 manuscripts would become the nucleus of a Vatican library.

Cusanus was acquainted with Archbishop Erbach, now nearly sixty years of age, and with Diether von Isenburg, provost of the collegiate churches of St. Victor and St. John in Mainz. Not yet forty, Isenburg was a brilliant, ambitious man, also opposed to papal encroachments against the church and civil government in Germany, and known to be an ally of Duke Sigismund, unfriendly to Cusanus.

The cardinal met with the Mainz hierarchy and the banker, Johann Fust, who was the collector of papal revenues in Mainz, and let it be known that he was not unsympathetic to the Rhein electors' strong resentment concerning the large share of revenues paid by Mainz, Trier, Cologne, and other German archbishoprics.

To Mainz, came all transportable produce and goods which Fust exchanged into monies that were then passed on as revenues to Rome. Revenues from the Holy Roman Empire, in fact, were much larger than those collected by the Medici in Burgundy and from England, France and Italy, and represented the single, most important source of papal income. The manner of their collection and transmission was an extremely well-guarded secret.

The cardinal was prepared, he said, to offer a sizeable reduction in the amount of revenues contributed by Germany.

The cardinal then went on to make another proposal which he believed would bring great prestige to Mainz and also demonstrate cooperation between Mainz and Rome. Copies of the printed Missal had been received in Rome and were greatly admired by the Holy Father, Cusanus said. It was a remarkable volume and convinced the Pope that the new art of printing could serve the Church in tremendous ways. How better to demonstrate this than for Master Gutenberg to print the Bible.

It was an audacious idea, the cardinal admitted. There were many questions to be answered, many objections to overcome. Would Gutenberg be able to print a book of so many pages? He would surely need more men and equipment, and was financial help available to him? Of course, scriptorium monks must read and approve the printed text, and the work done under the archbishop's authority. It was impossible to know how many Bibles could be printed or what the costs might be. For his part, to show his own support of the Pope and faith in the project, Cusanus would contribute 1000 gulden from his own funds to buy paper and vellum.

The cardinal's listeners could hardly believe what they were hearing. They waited for the archbishop to speak, and when he said nothing, Cusanus continued. There was a great need for more Bibles in the Church, he said, and manuscript Bibles took too long to produce. No two hand-written books were exactly alike, but printed texts were identical. The cardinal believed that all liturgical books should be identical, that this was as important as the uniform celebration of the Mass.

Cusanus was going on to Trier, he said, and would return to Mainz on his way back to Rome. At that time, he hoped to have a definite, affirmative answer for the Holy Father.

The thought of printing the Bible was so overwhelming, that discussion of the concession in revenues was momentarily forgotten. Isenburg thought printing the Bible was an inspiration. The Collegiate abbot was incensed. Tradition dictated that only monks copy the sacred scriptures! Such work was never entrusted to laymen! The Missal contained many passages from Scripture, the Benedictine abbot reminded him. The monks of St. James had assisted Master Gutenberg with this book and would be willing to do so again, he said. Fust remarked that 1000 gulden would buy 100 country houses. Archbishop Erbach said he would appoint Isenburg to be in charge of the project. He had disagreed with Rome about many things, but after the assurance of lower revenues, he would not oppose the Pope's wishes here. He thought the decision really rested with Gutenberg, however, and directed the Benedictine abbot to speak with him.

When Gutenberg arrived at St. James monastery, he was hopeful that the abbot wished to proceed with printing of a Psalter. They had talked about it, but no decision had been made because of the costs involved. Perhaps now he could begin.

"Cardinal Cusanus, the papal legate, has been in Mainz." the abbot began. "He had received a copy of the Missal from the bishop of Konstanz and was most impressed with it. The Holy Father was impressed with it. The cardinal has requested that you print another book, Master. Much larger than a Psalter. He has asked that you print the Bible."

Gutenberg stared at the abbot in disbelief.

"This is not the time for modest aspirations, the cardinal said. A printed Psalter can follow, but must not precede publication of the Holy Scriptures," the abbot continued. "Is it possible for you to print the Bible, Master?"

"The Psalter is only one book of the Bible," Gutenberg answered. "The complete Bible is the largest book in the world! And the most precious. I would never consider printing it on my own initiative."

"A Cardinal of the Pope has taken the initiative," the abbot replied. "He is a man of great vision and courage and hopes it can be done. Will you do it?"

"The Bible would be the most difficult book to copy and print without errors." Gutenberg said. "Yes, it can be printed, but I will not take responsibility for the accuracy of the Latin text. The monks must read the pages and make all the corrections."

"That was the cardinal's thinking also," the abbot answered. "I have assured him that we will cooperate with you in this regard. We will share the responsibility."

"Where will the money come from?" Gutenberg asked. "Yes, I can print any book, any size, in any quantity, providing I have the men, money and materials to do it. I will need metal, equipment, a large printing office.."

"You will have everything you need," the abbot replied. "The cardinal wishes it so. Herr Fust, I am sure, will provide for the metal and equipment. The cardinal himself has pledged a large sum of money for paper and vellum."

"Then I cannot refuse," Gutenberg said. "To print the Bible is a great honor."

"It is work for the greater honor and glory of God, Master," the abbot told him. "We shall all pray for success."

"Thank you, Father Abbot," Gutenberg answered soberly. "I will need God's help in a tremendous way!"

At the abbey of St. Victor, the Collegiate abbot was still outraged by the cardinal's request. The idea of printing the Bible, of all books, was preposterous, he told Isenburg, and he could not believe that the Pope had approved it.

"I respect tradition too," Isenburg answered, "but think what printing will mean to the Church. The manuscript books are beautiful, but it takes so long to produce them, one at a time."

"How many Bibles will be printed?" the abbot asked. "Which manuscript Bible will Gutenberg copy? His men don't read Latin. There will be thousands of mistakes!"

"Monks will read the Bible pages before they are printed," Isenburg answered, "You heard the cardinal say this must be done." Isenburg did not wish to argue. The abbot was a good man, a good priest, and devoted to preserving Sacred Scripture. The Collegiate monks published some of the finest manuscript books in Mainz.

"I came to ask that you lend Master Gutenberg the St. Victor Exemplar Bible to copy from," Isenburg said. "The text is the most perfect we have."

"Lend the Exemplar?" the abbot's voice rose with indignation. "Never! Gutenberg can copy the archbishop's Bible! The Exemplar will not leave our monastery!"

Archbishop Erbach was pleased about the reduction in papal revenues promised by Cardinal Cusanus. The other electors would be pleased also, he told Fust. They had waited a long time for the Pope to remedy the situation.

"Cardinal Cusanus is a shrewd strategist," Fust answered "Very shrewd. And if the revenues are less, my fees will be more."

"I hope you will continue to favor Mainz as you have done in the past," Erbach said. "Now we must do the cardinal a service and support his desire for a printed Bible. Assistance to Gutenberg will be remembered."

"It is an ambitious project," Fust replied, "and there are many risks. The work may never be finished. What if Master Gutenberg should die? Half a Bible is worthless!"

"The equipment can be used for other things," Erbach answered. "Someone else can carry on the work, if necessary. That doesn't concern me. But the work must be kept secret. Gutenberg is printing books for the Church. It is not necessary to say what these books are. Even if the Benedictines take responsibility for the text, I will not alienate the powerful abbots by giving official support to the Bible printing. It is in direct competition to manuscript! Therefore, I shall withhold any acknowledgement or blessing of the books until they are printed. If and when they are printed."

If he put money into the project, the Bibles would be printed, Fust declared. And surely the metal and printing equipment would not cost 1000 gulden. Erbach did not wish to be embarrassed if the project should fail, Fust thought. And if it was successful, Cardinal Cusanus will be indebted to me. The benefits possible far outweighed the risks involved. Fust would meet with Gutenberg and arrange a loan agreement, he said.

When Cardinal Cusanus returned to Mainz, he met Gutenberg at the abbey of St. James. The abbot kept the meeting informal, and Cusanus wore his white monk's habit and was not dressed like a prince of the church. He was an Order priest, after all, and had achieved his cardinal's appointment by many years of hard work. Despite his personal fortune, Cusanus had not bought his red hat.

Gutenberg was immediately at ease. The cardinal's interest in printing was genuine, and he listened intently as Gutenberg showed him some of the letters, punches and matrices and explained how they were used. Cusanus looked forward, he said, to visiting the printing office and seeing the Bible pages being printed next time he came to Mainz. This first printed Bible would be treasured by His Holiness, Cusanus said, and gave Gutenberg his blessing.

It was reassuring for the Cardinal to see that Gutenberg did not approach printing of the Bible as a work for his own self-esteem. He had not been flattered by the proposal and was fully aware of the enormous problems facing him. It would take several months before he could begin, Gutenberg said, and perhaps a year before the Bibles would be completed. The Master hoped that Cusanus would be patient.

The cardinal knew that smaller books, like the Missal and Psalter, could be printed in much less time, yet Gutenberg had not argued this point as he might have. Cusanus knew also that Archbishop Erbach and Fust were willing to cooperate for political reasons that were profitable to them. Isenburg was enthusiastic and highly capable, but was his enthusiasm grounded in sincerity, the cardinal wondered, and did he have the fortitude to see the project through? Gutenberg knew the Custos by reputation only, but said he looked forward to his counsel and help. It remained to be seen what would happen. Cusanus had faith in Master Gutenberg, the abbot, and yes, even in Isenburg. He would pray for success.

CHAPTER 39

The agreement between Fust and Gutenberg was reached without complication. Gutenberg estimated he would need 800 gulden - 500 for metal and equipment, 300 for wages and expenses for one year. It would take that long to make the new letters, and equip the printing office, he said. His only request was that the metal and equipment he would make be accepted as collateral for the loan and returned to him when the loan was repaid. Fust agreed, and in 1450 a loan for 800 gulden, at six percent annual interest, was signed by both men.

"We both work in gold, Master Gutenberg," was Fust's way of stating the bond between them. "You are the goldsmith who makes things *from* gold. I am the banker who exchanges goods *into* gold! Together we shall produce Bibles for the Church!"

"I print the Bibles for God and His Church," Gutenberg answered solemnly. With letters of lead more precious than gold, he thought to himself.

"It is a tremendous opportunity and a tremendous burden," he told Fust. "The project will be long and difficult."

"We all have confidence in you, Master," Fust assured him.

Gutenberg was satisfied with their agreement. The loan was large but could be repaid when the books were sold. Then he could use the equipment for work of his own choice. He was particularly grateful for the Cardinal's generous gift. No one was to mention it, however, and the paper and vellum would be assumed to have been provided by the monasteries in Mainz.

With his friends, Gutenberg was enthusiastic. "Now I will have a real printing office and be master in my own shop! Rudi will come and work with me. The guild will supply all the metal I'll need. I'll order paper from Strasbourg. And I know the Benedictine abbot and the monks at St. James will help as they did with the Missal."

Gutenberg's cousin, Arnold Gelthuss, was impressed by Fust's participation in the project. "Eight hundred gulden is a fortune!" he said.

Dr. Humery was reassured to learn that Custos Isenburg would oversee the project. It was without doubt a great and unusual undertaking, he said, and the custos was trustworthy.

The amount of money involved and the work itself must not be talked about, Gutenberg cautioned. There were members of the clergy who did not approve of the Missal and who would be pleased if the Bible project should fail. "Others, like the abbot, think our work is the will of God and cannot fail. I prefer to believe him!" Gutenberg said. "You made the Missal possible, Arnold. Isenburg arranged the meeting with Fust. May this association be as successful as ours!"

Gelthuss laughed and answered, "You are privileged, Johannes! Usually Fust only has business with abbots and bishops. He must have higher regard for the Bible than we give him credit for."

"You serve God. Herr Fust serves himself," Dr. Humery replied. "Remember that, Johannes!"

There was much preparatory work to be done before the Exemplar manuscript Bible pages arrived and printing could begin.

Gutenberg rented a building across the street from the Bishop's palace and spent the next three months equipping the new space and hiring workmen. When the letter designs were finished and the punches and matrices cut, the foundry could begin operation. He ordered the large amounts of lead and brass needed, plus the lead, tin and antimony used for the letter castings themselves. Additional hand-casting instruments were made, and the letter cases and presses constructed.

The printing office would consist of a foundry for mixing metal, making the castings, and finishing the punches and matrices. A storage room that was dry and clean would be used for the bulk paper and finished quires. Printing and composition would be done in one large room where the compositors and printers had easy access to one another. Here, would be three double letter cases for six compositors. There were six presses, each with a long sliding top table attached to hold the page forms. The tympan would hold the paper in proper position. The unprinted and printed sheets would be placed on shelves on either side of each press.

Gutenberg acquired a staff of about 30 people. They included two punch carvers, two foundrymen who mixed metal and made the matrices, two letter casters, six compositors and twelve pressmen, two men on each press. One pressman would handle the screw and make the prints, while the other would ink the letters and position the paper properly. There were two page handlers to keep track of the sheets used by each printer. Finally, there were three or four young apprentices who helped the compositors put new letters into the cases then replace the letters after the page forms had been printed. They also cleaned ink from the printed forms and refilled the ink balls for the printers.

The punch carvers and letter casters were master goldsmiths. The compositors and pressmen who had to be specially trained for their work would become journeymen. All of Gutenberg's men belonged to the guild of St. John and St. Luke, which included copyists, papermakers and book binders.

Everyone in the shop would have specific responsibilities, Gutenberg explained to Fr. Gunther. Three of his experienced men would supervise the casting, composition and printing. The work would be divided so there were fewer chances for mistakes. It was also essential for the work to be coordinated.

"Some men will be proficient in everything," Gutenberg said, "but

I want the office to function as a group working together. Only then will the entire operation go smoothly and efficiently."

"As in a monastery?" Fr. Gunther remarked.

"As in a monastery!" Gutenberg smiled.

The most important things, he said, were for the compositors to copy text correctly, and for the printers to keep the four pages on each sheet and the four sheets in each quire in order. Then all would be well.

"I do want someone here in the shop to read all the pages before you do," Gutenberg said, "and I need someone to make the new letter designs for me. Would two of the monks be able to do this?"

"Fr. Cremer could design the letters, but he has been ill," Fr. Gunther replied. "I know someone else, who is not a monk, but he could do both jobs for you, I think. His name is Peter Schoeffer. He is from Gernsheim and is a talented young copyist. He studied in Paris, his manuscript is beautiful, and he reads Latin well. Would you like Peter to come and see you?"

Gutenberg and Schoeffer liked each other immediately. Gutenberg found the young man to be intelligent, friendly, and intent on learning everything he could about printing. Schoeffer had seen the Missal, he said, and was fascinated by the whole idea of printing from metal letters. He already knew how books were produced in quires of 16 pages each and how they were bound, but transforming handwritten letters on paper into metal and then back into printed words on the pages of books was the most exciting thing he had ever heard of.

Schoeffer was eager to begin working with Gutenberg and wanted to master every process. He would learn how to carve the letters on the brass punches, to pound them into the matrices, cast them, compose them into words, and then print the words on paper. But first, he would design the letters to be used in the printed Bible, Gutenberg told him. That was the first important step.

Assisting Master Gutenberg was the opportunity of a lifetime, Schoeffer boasted to his friends. Printing the Bible would be the accomplishment of a lifetime! He was proud to have been chosen to design the letters. Some of his friends, however, thought Schoeffer was foolish to give up a good living as a copyist. How many letters were in the alphabet, they asked? Designing them would take only a day! Why give up steady work with the monastery to learn something new?

Wasn't it more foolish to copy and recopy the same pages by hand, Schoeffer argued, when by using metal letters, many copies, many pages, could be printed at one time? Fine manuscript letters could become fine printed letters, he told them, and printing the Bible would take months. No, he would not miss this chance to master a new art.

CHAPTER 40

"How many letter designs will you need, Master?" Schoeffer asked, "and how big should they be?

"I'd like two sets of capitals," Gutenberg answered, "and all of the small letters, of course. I also want combination letters, abbreviations, the numbers, and punctuation marks, and letters with accent marks. Everything written by hand must be duplicated in metal. The Bible letters should be smaller in size than the Donatus and Missal letters. About 30 letters in a line is what we'll want."

"How many castings will be needed?" Schoeffer wanted to know.

"To start, about 200 of each letter. We'll need more of some letters than others. The e's, a's, i's, t's, and s's, for example, are used most frequently."

"But you use the letters over again," Schoeffer replied.

"That's right, and I plan eventually to have 24 pages in forms at one time. If we use between 2000 and 2500 letters on each page, we'll need 50,000 to 60,000 castings."

"Thousands of letters, Master?" Schoeffer couldn't believe Gutenberg was serious.

"Yes, when the six presses are in operation," Gutenberg told him. "There will be six pages being composed, six pages being read for mistakes, six being corrected before final printing, and six pages being printed; that's 24 pages."

Gutenberg said that the punches and matrices would be made and the letters cast while the presses were being built. Composition of the first pages would begin as soon as possible so they could see how the pages cast in metal and the manuscript pages compared in length.

"Printing won't begin," Gutenberg explained, "until we know the number of lines on each page, the number of pages in each Bible, and how many copies of each page will be made. The number of Bibles we can print depends on how much paper and vellum we can afford to buy."

"When do you think we can start printing?" Schoeffer asked.

"Six months, maybe a year. The preparations take time. You must be patient," Gutenberg smiled.

Peter Schoeffer reminded Gutenberg of Brother Paulo in Strasbourg who had been so eager to print the Pater Noster. What would Paulo think now, if he knew they were planning to print the Bible!

When Gutenberg went to the Collegiate abbey to see the Exemplar manuscript Bible, the abbot made no attempt to hide his opposition to what Gutenberg proposed to do. These were the sacred words translated into Latin Vulgate by St. Jerome, in Bethlehem, 1000 years ago, the abbot said. The Exemplar text was the most perfect in existence. How did Gutenberg dare to print the Bible! How did he ever hope to print it correctly! Because of his vow of obedience, the abbot must abide by the wishes of Cardinal Cusanus and the archbishop, he said, but he was personally convinced that printing the Bible was morally wrong and an impossible task that could only end in disaster.

Gutenberg had been unaware of the abbot's feelings, and he knew it would be useless to try and defend his work. Instead he expressed reverence for the holy text and admiration for the men who for centuries had faithfully copied the Sacred Scriptures. Their love and devotion, and the Holy Spirit, he said, had preserved God's Word for all men. Printing could do the same.

The abbot nodded. The Master was sincere but impertinent. Gutenberg could not touch the Exemplar Bible, the abbot responded coldly, but he would be allowed to see the volume the monks were presently copying in the scriptorium. The loose sheets and quires of these new pages, before they were bound and the Bible blessed, would be made available for Gutenberg's men to copy.

Gutenberg wanted to count the number of folios or leaves in the Exemplar Bible and also the number of lines in each column on one page. He had to determine the number of sheets used for the book in order to make his own size and quantity estimates for the printed Bibles. How could he do this, if he was forbidden to touch the Exemplar!

One of the monks supplied the information he needed. The Exemplar Bible consisted of 70 quires, he said. This meant that the book had a total of 560 folios or 1120 pages, and that 280 sheets had been required for the two volumes. The pages, the monk told Gutenberg, had 48 lines in each column.

The monk leafed slowly through Volume I of the Exemplar which ended with the book of Psalms, Gutenberg noted. The art and workmanship were exquisite, especially the opening page of Psalms with the magnificent initial letter B for Blessed, the first letter of the first word which had been colored in gold. Gutenberg found it difficult to concentrate on sheets and lines and numbers, realizing that David's words were first written 2000 years ago! We too shall copy these words, he thought. But we won't make just one copy. We shall print many copies! Many pages, many Bibles, for the honor and glory of God!

On his way out of the abbey, Gutenberg went into the chapel and prayed. It was the feast of St. Michael, the archangel who defended heaven and defeated the Devil, and who continued to help mortals in the everlasting battle between good and evil on earth. St. Michael, protect my work, Gutenberg prayed. This saint and the Holy Spirit, he thought, will help us ordinary men do what has never been done before. It is not impossible. It is not a sin. It might be a sin if we didn't print the Bible when it is possible to do so.

At age 52, I begin the greatest work of my life, Gutenberg reflected. Others will have a part, but I will be responsible for the final success or failure of this printing. Johann Hultz said a prayer every morning before mounting the spire in Strasbourg. I must do the same. I must do the same. God help me!

CHAPTER 41

Bible pages, Gutenberg explained to Schoeffer, were folio size. Two folios could be cut from one sheet, and two sheets could be cut from one calfskin. One folio or leaf was two pages, called folios a and b.

"This means we get two sheets, four folios or eight pages from one calfskin," Gutenberg said. "You always double the folios for the number of pages and halve the folios for the number of sheets. Half of the number of sheets shows the number of calfskins you will need. Do you see?

"If the Bible has 560 folios, that's 280 sheets, or 140 calfskins," Peter said, "and 1120 pages."

"Yes," Gutenberg answered, "that's right."

"Then 10 Bibles this size would require 2800 sheets," Peter said, "and

100 Bibles, 28,000 sheets!"

"That's right," Gutenberg told him. "And if we printed 25 copies on vellum, they would require 7000 sheets or 3500 calfskins."

"Would you really print 125 Bibles, Master?" Peter asked.

"I'd like to print 200 Bibles," Gutenberg replied with a smile.

The fewer lines on a page, the more pages and the greater number of sheets were needed, he explained. Likewise, the more lines on a page, the fewer pages and the lesser number of sheets were needed. It was just like writing a letter. In a book the size of the Bible, with over 1000 pages. more lines on each page were desirable, and this was the reason why some Bibles were written in very small handwriting.

At the same time, Gutenberg went on, the more pages in a book, the more copies should be printed.

"Why?" Peter asked.

"Because if you print only 50 copies of a book that has 1000 pages, it takes longer to compose the pages than it does to print them," Gutenberg said. "On the other hand," he added. "200 copies of a Bible 560-folio size, like this one, would require 56,000 sheets of paper and vellum. Too few or too many copies would be inefficient."

Gutenberg had had experience adjusting the number of lines on the Donatus pages, from 26 to 27, 28 to 30 lines on each page, with a resulting fewer number of leaves, pages, and sheets needed in each edition. The Bible pages, however, were folio size, twice as large as the Donatus quarto leaves, and the number of pages in the Bible was many times greater than in a Donatus.

"We must print as many Bibles as we can, Peter," Gutenberg said, "but first we must consider the number of lines on each page and the number of folios and sheets needed for one Bible."

"The new letters we have cast are about the same size as these hand-written letters," Peter observed.

"Yes, they are," Gutenberg answered, "but we shall make our columns slightly wider, so the number of metal letters in a line will be the same as the number of handwritten letters. Also, the lines of metal letters will be further apart than the lines of manuscript. We can't duplicate the same amount of text in the same number of lines, using metal letters, Peter. And the fewer lines on a page, the larger the book will be. The first thing we shall do is compose a page of Genesis and see how it compares in size and space to the manuscript text."

Gutenberg thought that perhaps 48 manuscript lines would be equal to 45 printed lines. Using algebra, he figured that a Bible with 45-line pages would have 597 folios, or 1194 pages. It would be 37 folios larger than the Exemplar Bible. Three lines less on a page made quite a difference.

After the test page of Genesis was completed, however, it turned out that 45 printed lines were three lines longer than 48 handwritten lines, and 48 printed lines were six lines longer. Only 42 lines in metal letters were the same depth as 48 lines in manuscript.

"Well, how many folios would be needed?" Gutenberg asked Peter.

Using algebra again, Peter found the answer. "A Bible with 42-line columns would require 640 folios, 320 sheets, and have 1280 pages," he answered. "It would be 80 folios larger than the manuscript Bible."

Gutenberg felt that both the 42- and 48- line columns were too long, however. The width of the columns was satisfactory, he said, but he didn't want the text to fill the page so much. He would make the top and bottom margins larger, leaving room for titles at the top and more room for illustration at the bottom.

The monks' manuscript Bibles had small margins, Gutenberg explained, because vellum was so expensive and couldn't be wasted. Most handwritten books, in fact, had small margins because the monks were just as saving with paper.

"I want the printed Bibles to have generous margins," Gutenberg told Peter. "I'd end the columns here - at 40 printed lines or 46 manuscript lines. The balance of text and margin is much better."

"That's only two lines less," Peter said, "and 40-line columns make the Bible even larger. It would have 672 folios, 1344 pages, and require 336 sheets. That's 33,600 sheets for 100 Bibles..and 25 on vellum would require 8400 sheets. That is 42,000 sheets, Master!"

"From 50,000 sheets then, we would get about 150 Bibles." Gutenberg replied. "A ream is 500 sheets. If I bought 100 reams, I might print 150 Bibles on paper, and still print 25 on vellum. It's possible that we could print 175 Bibles, Peter."

The difference of 32 folios between books with 42-line pages, 640 folios, and 40-line pages, 672 folios, interested Gutenberg. This difference of 32 folios or 16 sheets meant that from 1600 sheets five Bibles 42-line size could be printed. In other words, from 33,600 sheets, he could get 100 Bibles 40-line size, but 105 Bibles, 42-line size.

Gutenberg preferred the 40-line pages with the larger margins, and 1600 sheets were only three reams of paper, after all. Still, five additional Bibles from the same amount of materials could not be ignored. He would have to study these figures more closely and see what the difference in cost would be.

Gutenberg decided to figure the number of sheets of paper and vellum needed and the cost for 100, 125, and 150 Bibles on paper and 25 Bibles on vellum - for both 640 and 672 folio-size volumes. The size of each volume, whether 40-or 42-line pages were used, would be Gutenberg's decision. The number of copies printed, the size of the edition, would be Isenburg's decision. Both decisions would be determined by the costs involved and the amount of money available. Perhaps 175 Bibles would be too expensive, Gutenberg thought. Certainly the quantities of paper and vellum needed would be staggering.

Paper cost 12 gulden a ream..100 reams or 50,000 sheets (10 bales of 5000 sheets each) cost 1200 gulden. An allowance of about five percent, 2000-2500 sheets, must be added for waste paper, test pages, corrections and reprinting.

For 150 Bibles 40-line size, (336 sheets each) Gutenberg would need 50,400 sheets, or 105 reams, costing 1260 gulden. For 150 Bibles 42-line size, (320 sheets each) he would need 48,000 sheets or 100 reams, including waste, costing 1200 gulden. From 50,000 sheets, he discovered he could get 156 Bibles 42-line size.

Vellum cost about a third more than paper, or 33.5 gulden for 1000 sheets. No allowance for waste was figured. Gutenberg needed 8400 sheets of vellum for 25 Bibles 40-line size, but 8000 sheets for 25 Bibles 42-line size. The cost was 282 gulden and 268 gulden respectively.

Total cost then for 175 Bibles, 40-line, was 1542 gulden, and for 175 Bibles 42-line, 1468 gulden, or 74 gulden less.

If he elected to print 156 Bibles 42-line on paper, using 50,000 sheets plus 2000 for waste, costing 1248 gulden, and 25 Bibles on vellum, his total cost would be 1516 gulden for 181 books. He would get six more Bibles for 48 gulden. And the cost of 181 Bibles 42-line size was 26 gulden less than the cost of 175 Bibles 40-line size! The 42-line pages must be considered.

Doing so much arithmetic again reminded Gutenberg of the long, difficult hours he had spent in Strasbourg working at similar size and quantity figures for the Donatus. At least this time, it is easier, Gutenberg thought to himself. Still there was no easy way of estimating the size and cost of a book. The number of lines on a page determined the number of pages, and the number of pages, folios and sheets per Bible, times the number of Bibles considered, gave the total amount of paper and vellum needed.

Or put another way, he could determine how many books could be printed from a given amount of paper and vellum. The number of sheets needed for 175 or 181 Bibles would cost in the neighborhood of 1500 gulden!

Peter was quick with figures, but the Bible estimates Gutenberg had to do himself. And getting the figures was not enough. The numbers had to be read, like words, to get the true picture of what could and could not be done.

There was too much activity at the shop for Gutenberg to concentrate, so he worked on the cost estimates at home. Little Else and Henne did not bother him. Fritz and Thea were company. The dog followed him everywhere, and the cat was usually close by also, sometimes stretched out on a sunny spot on the floor or the window sill.

It was interesting to see the difference two lines in each column, four lines on each page, made in the overall number of sheets needed. More vellum Bibles would be highly desirable, Gutenberg thought.

How many Bibles could he get from 10,000 vellum sheets, he wondered. The cost, 335 gulden, was expensive, to be sure, but would be offset by the higher selling price of each vellum book. Gutenberg learned that 30 Bibles, 40-line, and 31 Bibles, 42-line, could be printed from 10,000 sheets. Again the increase, using the 42-line pages, was six books - from 25 to 31, over his original figures.

How many sheets would be needed for 35 Bibles on vellum? Ten Bibles, 40-line, required 3360 sheets, costing 113 gulden, and 25 cost 282 gulden. Ten Bibles, 42-line, required 3200 sheets, costing 107 gulden, and 25 Bibles cost 268 gulden. Vellum cost for 35 books, 40-line, was 395 gulden, and for 42-line, 375 gulden.

Total cost for 185 Bibles, 40-line, was 1655 gulden, and for 185 Bibles, 42-line, 1575 gulden - or 80 gulden less! The 185 Bibles, 42-line, cost only 33 gulden more than 175 Bibles, 40-line, and 35 not 25 were on vellum.

Gutenberg rechecked his figures. The 40-line pages required sufficient additional sheets, he noted, to make the number of sheets and the cost of paper and vellum across the board increasingly more expensive.

Ordinarily, he thought, 10,000 vellum sheets would be a good quantity to buy, like 50 or 100 reams of paper. But 30 Bibles, 40-line, required 10,080 sheets, and 31 Bibles, 10,416 sheets. The 30 Bibles, 42-line, required 9600 sheets, and 31 Bibles 9920 sheets. The additional 500 sheets of vellum in each case, in 40-line Bibles, cost 17 gulden more.

Further comparisons between 42-and 40-line books revealed other startling differences in cost. If 10,000 vellum sheets were used, 30 Bibles

(335 gulden) plus 150 on paper (1260 gulden) 40-line, would cost 1595 gulden. But 31 vellum Bibles (335 gulden) plus 150 paper (1200 gulden) 42-line, cost 1535 gulden! One Bible more cost 60 gulden less! Because, Gutenberg saw, the 40-line books required five additional reams of paper.

He compared the costs between 185 Bibles (35 vellum) 42-line, 1575 gulden, and 180 Bibles (30 vellum) 40-line, 1595 gulden. Five more Bibles cost 20 gulden less!

The break-even point, where 40 and 42-line Bibles cost the same, Gutenberg found, was with 175 Bibles - 150 paper and 25 vellum, 40-line, costing 1542 gulden, and 182 Bibles - 150 paper and 32 vellum, 42-line, costing 1543 gulden. And vellum copies increased by seven.

There was more arithmetic, and algebra, involved in estimating the size of books, amount of material needed and their cost, than Gutenberg ever imagined. Never before had he done so much work with numbers. The Donatus and Missal estimates had been simple by comparison. His notations concerning the lines on each page, the number of folios and sheets in each Bible, and for different numbers of Bibles, on paper and on vellum, filled many pages. The cost comparisons were especially important.

It was possible to print 50 more paper Bibles, using 33 reams, for 396 gulden, plus 10 more vellum Bibles for 107 gulden. A total of 60 more Bibles, 42-line size, could be printed for 503 gulden. The 100 paper Bibles this size, 67 reams, cost 804 gulden, and the 25 on vellum cost 268 gulden, for a total of 1072 gulden. The total of 1575 gulden for 185 Bibles checked with the other figures he had made.

Somehow, Gutenberg thought, he must persuade Custos Isenburg that despite this large expenditure, 150 Bibles on paper and 35 on vellum, each book with 42-line pages and in 640 folio volumes, should definitely be considered. But first he would tabulate some percentages and go over his figures with Dr. Humery. Had he overlooked anything?

CHAPTER 42

"You suggest printing 185 Bibles, Johannes?" Dr. Humery said, "For 1575 gulden? You must be mad! Where will Isenburg get the money? He might consent to 1000 gulden. How many Bibles can you print for 1000 gulden?"

"I told you, 125," Gutenberg answered. "The cost is 1072 gulden."

"Then start with that figure. Don't start with 185 Bibles. That's an odd number. Why not a total of 150 or 175 books?"

Gutenberg explained his comparisons between 175 and 185 Bibles, with 40 and 42-line pages. Many things must be evaluated before the whole picture became clear, he said. The 125 Bibles, for example, included 20 percent vellum, or 25 books. If the number of paper copies increased and the number of vellum stayed the same, the percentage of vellum to total books would become smaller. The increase should be in both paper and vellum, Gutenberg thought.

"And it would be wrong to simply increase the total by, say, 20 percent," Gutenberg said. "Increasing 125 books, for example, by 20 percent, is 25 books. But what are they? 50 vellum with 100 paper? That combination would cost 1340 gulden. The cost for 125 paper and 25 vellum is 1276 gulden, because paper costs less to buy. In the first case, you have a third in vellum, and in the second case, 17 percent vellum. I think 80 percent paper and 20 percent vellum is the best proportion."

In the total of 185 books -150 vellum and 35 vellum- he had 19 percent vellum and 81 percent paper. He had increased the paper copies 50 percent, from 100 to 150. and increased the vellum copies 40 percent, from 25 to 35. The increase of 60 Bibles, from 125 to 185, was 48 percent. The increase in cost, from 1072 gulden to 1575 gulden - 503 gulden- was 47 percent.

"All right," Dr Humery replied, "that's fine. You have most of the answers in your mass of figures, I see. And the more books you print, the larger the profits. Do you know what Bibles sell for?"

"Paper Bibles sell for 35-40 gulden each and vellum Bibles 50-60 gulden each," Gutenberg told him. "the cost of the paper and vellum is included in the selling price. The 10 additional on vellum cost 107 gulden and will sell for 500 gulden. The 50 additional on paper cost 396 gulden and will sell for 1750 gulden. That's a cost increase of 503 gulden for 60 books, and the sales increase 2250 gulden."

"And what will sales from 125 and 185 Bibles be?"

"Just a minute," Gutenberg answered. Doing arithmetic again, Gutenberg found that 125 Bibles, 100 paper and 25 vellum, costing 1072 gulden, would sell for 4750 gulden. And 185 Bibles, 150 paper and 35 vellum, costing 1575 gulden, would sell for 7000 gulden.

"Your gross profit then from 125 Bibles is 3678 gulden, and from 185 Bibles, 5425 gulden," Dr. Humery said. "Now I'll do some percentages for you." With pen and paper, Dr. Humery wrote the numbers he wanted, looking at Gutenberg's figures as he did so.

"Your cost goes up about 50 percent, yes. Sales go up 47 percent and profit 47-1/2 percent - all about the same." Dr. Humery made more notations. "Your cost in each case, 125 and 185 Bibles, is 23 percent of sales, and the gross profit is 77 percent of sales."

The cost, Gutenberg reminded his friend, was based on materials only. It did not include the time and wages of the men. Printed Bibles would sell for the same price each as manuscript Bibles, although he thought they could be sold for less and still show a nice profit.

"What does each Bible cost for materials?" Dr. Humery asked.

"The 150 on paper cost 1200 gulden or 8 gulden each," Gutenberg said.

"The 35 on vellum cost 375 gulden or 10.7 gulden each. Paper Bibles sell for four times cost -35 gulden each, and vellum Bibles sell for five times cost -50 gulden each."

"And both 125 and 185 Bibles sell for more than four times their cost," Dr. Humery added. "Johannes, I hope you can print 185 books and will get the money you need to do it. It is a matter of choice. The 60 more Bibles are important. Are they worth 500 gulden additional cost? Are 185 Bibles worth spending 1575 gulden to print them? That's the choice Isenburg must make."

The two men looked at each other and smiled. Gutenberg reached for the bottle of brandy and filled Dr. Humery's glass. "Thanks to you," he said, "I will know what to say to Custos Isenburg."

It had been most important, Gutenberg told him, to determine at the outset how many Bibles it was practical to print, not only in terms of sales and profits, but in terms of the number of sheets needed, time involved, and obtaining a sufficient number of copies, paper and vellum, that justified the time and expense.

"I'd like to print 200 Bibles," Gutenberg said, "and 150 paper and 50 vellum would cost 1736 gulden. That's 25 percent vellum. Increase the number of paper copies, decrease the number of vellum, and the total cost is less. With 175 paper and 25 vellum, the cost would be 1672 gulden. Only 64 gulden less. And only 12- 1/2 percent vellum. If we printed 165 paper and 35 vellum, the cost would be 1695 gulden, and 17-1/2 percent vellum.

"Where would we get 16,000 sheets of vellum for 50 Bibles?" Gutenberg went on. "An initial cost of 1736 gulden is far too much. It would also take twice as long to print 50 books as 25, but 35 we could manage. I'm very satisfied to have determined that the Bible pages will be 42 lines. The number of books and cost comparisons were necessary. Now it's a matter of how many 42-line Bibles to print."

"You have sound arguments for printing 185 Bibles," Dr. Humery said, "and I agree that 150 paper with 35 vellum is the best combination. But Isenburg may think that 125 Bibles are enough. He supports the project. He will listen to you. It will be to his credit as well as yours to print as many Bibles as possible. I wish you well!"

Isenburg was going to Rome, he told Gutenberg, as the archbishop's representative at the coronation of Emperor Frederick III. Archbishop Erbach could not attend, he said, because of ill health, and Isenburg would lead the delegation from Mainz.

The truth, Isenburg knew, was that Erbach still refused to attend the Pope, and pleaded poor health and the long journey as the reasons for his absence. Isenburg, however, was glad for the opportunity to take Gutenberg's report with him and to speak with Cardinal Cusanus himself about the Bible proposals.

"I must explain first," Gutenberg said, "that my estimates for the amount of paper and vellum needed, the number of Bibles to be printed, and the cost are figured in essentially the same way as the monks in the scriptoriums estimate their costs for materials and the number of books that can be produced. But with one important difference. We must know before we start printing exactly how many Bibles will be printed. With no increases or decreases in quantity after printing begins."

RECAP OF THE FIGURES DISCUSSED BY GUTENBERG AND DR.
HUMERY

Comparison of total costs for 40-line and 42-line Bibles in various
quantities of paper and vellum

40-line

Bibles	Paper	Vellum	Gulden
185	150	35	1655
180	150	30	1595
175	150	25	1542
150	125	25	1338
125	100	25	1122

42-line

Bibbles	Paper	Vellum	Gulden
185	150	35	1575
181	150	31	1535
175	150	25	1468
150	125	25	1276
125	100	25	1072
200	150	50	1736
200	175	25	1672
200	165	35	1695

Comparison of cost and projected sales for 125 and 185 Bibles 42-line
size on paper and vellum

Bibles 42-line	Cost	Projected Sales
100 paper	804 gulden	3500 gulden
25 vellum	268 gulden	1250 gulden
125 Bibles	1072 gulden	4750 gulden
	3678 gross profit	
150 paper	1200 gulden	5250 gulden
35 vellum	375 gulden	1750 gulden
185 Bibles	1575 gulden	7000 gulden
	5425 gross profit	
50 paper	396 gulden	1750 gulden
10 velum	107 gulden	500 gulden
60 Bibles	503 gulden	2250 gulden
	1747 gross profit	

The monks usually knew, he explained, the size of each book they would copy, how many titles they planned for one year, for example, and how much paper and vellum they would need. If they were short of paper, they could order more, or fewer titles would be produced. If they had paper left over, they could use it the following year or for another smaller book, perhaps. Any increase or decrease in the number of titles created no major problem.

"Think of it this way, Your Grace," Gutenberg went on, "printing is like having 100 monks copying the same book at the same time. Printing, however, involves two steps, not one. Copying or composing each page in metal letters is the first step, then printing that page is the second step. The number of copies printed is the number of books in that edition. If the edition is increased, more copies can be printed of the page still on the press and all subsequent pages. But those pages already printed have to be composed over again and printed over again. Much time is lost, and our estimates for paper and vellum are lost also. To decide to print fewer books later on means wasting many of the pages already printed. Do you understand? Hundreds of sheets could be wasted, or thousands of more sheets could be required."

"I think I understand," Isenburg replied. "Now tell me what you recommend, Master."

"I hope we can print 185 Bibles," Gutenberg began. "200 Bibles are too expensive."

Isenburg was dumbfounded. "200 Bibles!" he exclaimed.

"I will show you my figures," Gutenberg said. "You may take them with you. We can print 125 Bibles for 1072 gulden, but I strongly recommend that we increase the edition by 60 books, to 150 on paper and 35 on vellum. The additional cost is 503 gulden, or a total cost for 185 Bibles of 1575 gulden. Is this money available, from the abbots, the archbishop or the cardinal?"

Each Bible would have 42-line columns, Gutenberg added, and 640 folios. The original estimate was for 100 Bibles on paper and 25 on vellum. The books would be larger than the Exemplar Bible but smaller than a Bible with 40-line columns.

There could hardly be much difference between 42-line and 40-line pages, Isenburg remarked. But the savings in the total number of sheets used, made an important difference, Gutenberg said. So important that he would file some of the letters to get 42 lines in the same space. From the same number of sheets, he could print more Bibles if they were 42-line size, and he could keep the larger margins.

"But why the increase of 60 Bibles?" Isenburg wanted to know. "Why not 50 or even 100? How did you arrive at 185? Such an odd number."

"That's what Dr. Humery said," Gutenberg smiled. "Because 150 Bibles on paper can be printed from 50,000 sheets. And 10 more Bibles on vellum gives us a percentage of 81 percent paper and 19 percent vellum, which is the best proportion, and keeps the overall cost under 1600 gulden. Also, we wouldn't be able to get 8,000 calfskins for 50 vellum Bibles, but we can get, I believe, I hope, 5,600 for 35 on vellum. To increase the number of Bibles on vellum is important because they sell for more money."

Gutenberg gave Isenburg a copy of his figures to study. "This will show you how the costs compare," he said.

"You have become a mathematician, Master," Isenburg said. The cardinal will appreciate your work here, which he understands better than I. I never knew printing involved so much analysis and planning to find the best use of sheets and calfskins!"

"And it's because we must have these answers before we begin work that they are so important," Gutenberg answered. "The lines, pages, sheets all determine how many books are most economical and practical to print. I have learned some amazing things, Your Grace."

"It will take longer to print 185 Bibles," Isenburg said.

"Yes, and I have not figured the cost in time," Gutenberg answered. "The figures are for materials only. I would like to order the paper from the Strasbourg mill owned by my friend Nicholas Heilmann. His prices will be less than if the sheets came from Augsburg. But the monks, the abbot, could help place the orders for vellum. Production is seasonal and several sources of supply are needed."

Gutenberg went on to explain that all orders for paper and vellum must be placed in advance and arrive on a regular monthly schedule so printing would not be held up and the men idle and unable to continue work. He would pay on delivery. Isenburg suggested that all orders and bills be sent in his name, and assured Gutenberg that they would be paid promptly. The materials would be delivered to Gutenberg who would authorize payment. Isenburg would affirm the recommendation to print 185 Bibles, he said, and make every effort to provide the additional funds needed.

"But as you have demonstrated, Master," he cautioned. "the Bibles must be cut to fit the cloth, and the cloth is expensive. At this time, I can only approve 125 Bibles and 1000 gulden. When I return from Rome, then we shall talk again."

"We shall file the letters and build other presses while you are away," Gutenberg answered. "If all goes well, we shall be ready to print when you return. I shall not begin until I have your final decision."

"May I take the page of Genesis with me?" Isenburg asked. "The first page of the Bible tells the beginning of God's work and of yours. Do not be disappointed, Master, if we cannot print as many Bibles as we both would like, however. Nearly 200 Bibles would be a miracle, like the loaves and fishes, Pope Nicholas will say. Let us hope you will be allowed to perform that miracle for us."

At St. James, the abbot was shocked by Gutenberg's proposal. The numbers, the quantities, the costs Gutenberg spoke of were fantastic. Thousands of sheets. Hundreds of gulden. Each book would have 640 folios, 1280 pages! And Gutenberg thought 125 Bibles were too few!

"Do you realize, Master," the abbot said, "it would take ten monks more than eighteen years to copy 185 Bibles? Ten monks can copy ten Bibles in one year. We would need 185 monks working all year 'round to produce so many books!"

In the scriptorium, he said, each title was a complete book and copied one at a time. Several monks might copy the same book, at the same time, and if the edition was increased, more monks would join them. And when monks died, others continued their work. Sometimes ten monks worked on one Bible or one large book.

Printing 185 copies of each page as they went along, Gutenberg said, meant that no one printed book was complete until the first print of the last page was made. Printing had certain restrictions too, although the benefits far outweighed these restrictions.

Only the Lord Himself could help Gutenberg get so much money and print so many Bibles, the abbot told him. And it would take Gutenberg years, too, to make 185 copies of so many pages. The monk admired the scope and detail of the Master's plan, yet it seemed impossible that such hopes and dreams could actually be realized.

Schoeffer was very surprised when Gutenberg told him that he wanted to file down some of the letters. "You want to get 42 lines in the same space as 40 lines?" he asked. "That's impossible! Why? Which letters?"

It was possible, Gutenberg explained, by filing down the body of the capitals, of the tall letters - b, d, f, h, k, l, and t, and those that hung below the line - g, j, p, q, y. With the lines closer together, the margins would stay the same.

"The 42-line columns mean a great savings in the number of sheets used in each Bible and in the total number of Bibles we print," Gutenberg said. "And I don't want to make margins smaller by just adding two lines to each column.

"The printed Bible must be outstanding for its margins as well as the text," he said. "Margins and text should balance geometrically, Fr. Cremer told me, according to rule. So we will keep the 40-line depth we have now, but will get 42 lines in that depth. The margins won't change."

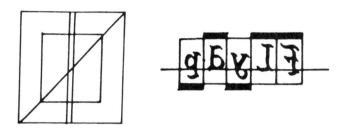

XIII. THE BIBLES
CHAPTER 43

The men in Gutenberg's shop were a talented, cohesive group. Two sets of brothers - Johann and Wenderlin von Speyer, and Heinrich and Nicolaus Bechtermuntz from Eltville, had worked with Gutenberg on the Missal. They were joined by Heinrich Eggestein from Strasbourg, Ulrich Zell from Cologne, Heinrich Kefer and Bechtolf von Hanau. Conrad Sweynhelm and his friend Arnold Pannartz, Albrecht Pfister from Bamberg, Berthold Ruppel from Basel. Johann Mentelin and Adolf Rusch were among the recent arrivals.

Some of the men were master goldsmiths and bookbinders, some were journeymen woodcarvers. The most experienced were put in charge of the letter casting, composition and printing. Every man was required to learn each procedure before being assigned to a job based on his particular ability or background.

To have been selected by Gutenberg to work on the Mainz Bibles was considered a great honor, and all of the men pledged themselves to faithful service until the books were published.

Gutenberg's decision to file some of the letters was not received with enthusiasm, however, and for the first time, Gutenberg's judgment was questioned by the senior goldsmiths. How was it possible, they wondered, to get 42 lines in the same space as 40 lines? To attempt to do so seemed fruitless. The 40-line page of Genesis looked fine. Why should the Master insist on printing 42-line pages?

"We could recast the letters much faster," Pannartz argued. "Or simply add two lines in each column."

"No," Gutenberg told him. "I want to have the larger margins. And I think the filing of the letters will be sufficient."

Most important, he said, were the considerable savings in sheets and money if 42-line pages were used. And the margins were important also. If they must recast some letters later on, they would.

For his part, Gutenberg would make up a schedule for the flow of work from compositor to scriptorium, back to the shop for corrections, final reading and final printing. He also had to determine the number of pages in each book of the Bible and where the books began and ended within each quire.

Peter Schoeffer would be responsible for the ordering, storage and distribution of paper, vellum, and the various metals. He would act as liaison between the monks and men in the shop and double check the corrections.

Before the printing began, however, Peter helped to file those letters which were too tall or too long. Only 12 small letters and the 26 capital letters were involved, but more than 200 castings have been made of each one. The filing would take time. It would take less time, Peter thought, to make new punches and matrices and cast new letters. Moreover, he was often dissatisfied with the castings because not all of them were as sharp as his letter designs.

"Why does this happen?" Peter asked the goldsmith Ruppel. "I don't understand it."

So many letters had been cast for the Bible, Ruppel explained, that several matrices had to be replaced. The punches stayed sharp, but the matrices wore out from continuous use.

"When they do," Ruppel said, "the castings are flawed, and we make new matrices. It is costly, however."

"Would using a different metal for the matrices be the answer?" Peter asked. "Instead of lead, use copper."

"Copper would be more expensive!" Ruppel answered. "And the punches would have to be made of a harder metal. Steel, possibly. The cost for this, Master Peter, would be very expensive."

But the tools would last longer and produce finer letters, Peter argued.

The castings were as sharp as the tools used for making them, Ruppel admitted. But brass and lead had always been used for most punches and molds, he said. Steel and copper were only for fine, intricate work.

"Letter castings are fine, intricate work," Peter said. "I'd like to try carving some steel punches and to make some copper matrices. If the matrix lasts longer and sharper castings can be made, the money will have been well spent. Will you help me, Master Ruppel?"

The goldsmith was hesitant. It was a waste of time, he thought. There might be no improvement in the letters. Still, the idea had merit.

Peter would pay for the metal himself, he said. "I want to try," he repeated. "There's no harm in that, surely. Will you buy the metal for me?"

Ruppel liked Peter and was persuaded to encourage him. "We must work secretly," he cautioned. "The other goldsmiths must not know what you are doing."

If the experiment was successful, they would demonstrate the results to Gutenberg, Peter said. Until then, it would be their secret.

Peter would design the letters P, T, L and Q, he said, both small letters and capitals. These were four of the letters that had to be filed top or bottom, and if the matrix was changed somehow, maybe the body of the letters need not be filed.

"I can accomplish two things perhaps," Peter told Ruppel. "But first I shall hope to show that letters need not be cast with faults and look worn before we have even printed with them!" He did not need and could not afford a lot of metal, he said, and would make the punches and matrices at home.

Ruppel agreed to substitute the copper matrices in the mold he was using and to make 20 castings from each one. They should be able to compare the results rather quickly, he thought.

CHAPTER 44

Herr Fust was an infrequent visitor at the printing shop. When he did come, Gutenberg was usually absent or absorbed in an immediate problem so that Fust had to wait, or found himself conversing with Peter Schoeffer. Fust did not like to be kept waiting, even though the young man was courteous and informative about the work being done.

Fust arrived one day just as Gutenberg was leaving. "I'll be right back," Gutenberg said, hurrying out of the shop.

Affronted but determined to stay, Fust allowed Schoeffer to show him through the shop.

They had had trouble with the letters, and margins, Peter said, and printing of the Bibles had been delayed until the letters were filed.

"We're using 42-line columns, you see," Peter explained, "because of the savings in materials. We can get more Bibles from the same amounts of paper and vellum. And with the lines closer together, we will also keep the larger margins the Master wants."

Fust was not sympathetic to the difficulties encountered. He was particularly irritated by delay for any reason and by Gutenberg's insistence that the letters be filed. "Why is it necessary to file the letters?" Fust demanded. "If the columns must be 42 lines, the margins can be smaller!"

A year had gone by, he said, and nothing had been printed. When did Master Gutenberg intend to start printing? Fust had come for some answers. "I've been patient long enough!" he said angrily.

"Custos Isenburg has approved 125 Bibles as the quantity to be printed." Peter replied. "But we may print more than that. When he returns from Rome...."

"You could start printing now then," Fust interrupted. "What does it matter whether the columns are 40 or 42 lines? Who is going to count them! I say start printing something!"

Most of the letters had been filed, Peter responded. But the Master would wait on the printing until Custos Isenburg came back to Mainz. "Talk with Master Gutenberg, Herr Fust, and he will tell you why it is best that we wait," Peter said.

"I'm tired of waiting! For the books and for the privilege of speaking with Master Gutenberg!" Fust answered sarcastically. "I say don't wait on the printing! 125 Bibles? How many more do you expect to print! You may tell Gutenberg that further delay is against my wishes, and I shall advise Archbishop Erbach of that fact. I should have something to say about how the work progresses, and I'm sure the archbishop will agree with me!" Fust turned and strode out the door, banging it behind him.

Gutenberg said he would talk to Fust immediately when Peter told him what had happened. He could appreciate Fust's impatience but resented his interference. "The number of lines is important, and the number of books just as important," Gutenberg said. "Fust will surely understand that 185 Bibles will be more profitable than 125! But that is not our decision to make!"

Fust, however, was unavailable when Gutenberg tried to see him. Two days passed, and Gutenberg received a letter from Fust stating the archbishop's request that printing of the Bibles begin at once.

"I am not ready!" Gutenberg told Fr. Cremer. "If I begin printing with 40-line pages, all the estimates will be wrong! I begin with letters the wrong size, lines the wrong depth, and possibly the wrong number of copies! I will not start 42-line pages with the letters I have now! I will not print books with different margins! And the margins will be as I want them to be!"

For some pages in the Bible to be 40 lines and others 42 lines was contrary to everything a copyist would do, Fr. Cremer said. Even if the difference wasn't apparent to the naked eye, or no one would count the lines, it was sloppy work, he agreed, reflecting trial and error.

"The monks don't change the number of lines on each manuscript page as they go along!" Gutenberg said. "It's not the proper way to begin, particularly if we print more than 125 books. I won't know how many copies to print until Isenburg returns. And if filing doesn't work, we must recast the letters."

Being pressured by those who did not understand what was involved was as frustrating to Gutenberg as waiting for a definite answer from Isenburg about the number of books to be printed.

"Custos Isenburg perhaps fails to appreciate the urgency for an answer about increasing the edition," Fr. Cremer said. "Even if you began with 42-line pages, it means doing them over a second time, doesn't it, if you print more than 125 copies?"

"Yes! It's double work," Gutenberg answered. "I explained this to him, and he said to wait."

"But now you can't wait, Master," Father said.

Fr. Cremer had accommodated himself to the abbot, and the abbot to the archbishop, many times, he said, under difficult circumstances. Sometimes decisions were made arbitrarily, or influenced by another, sometimes they proved to be wrong, but rarely were they questioned.

"We live under obedience," Fr. Cremer told Gutenberg. "You have worked independently most of your life. You are not a politician! Now you must accept another's decision, even though it is ill advised."

Fust undoubtedly resented Isenburg's authority in the Bible project, the priest said. "He wants to show the custos, the cardinal and you that he and the archbishop have authority too, and can make judgments when they think you are delaying the work unnecessarily."

"Isenburg favored my proposal," Gutenberg said, "and I trust him to present it fairly. I am more anxious than anyone to start printing, but at the right time!"

"Begin with 40-lines, if you have to, Master," Fr. Cremer advised. "Let the archbishop know you've made a start. When the letters are filed, you can switch to 42-lines. And if 125 Bibles are approved, so be it."

"I am hoping we can publish 185 Bibles," Gutenberg answered.

"If you must reprint some pages, then reprint them," Fr. Cremer said. "But first, I suggest you write Isenburg and tell him you are being forced to begin, and by whose authority. Remind him that reprinting, if the edition is increased, is expensive. Ask him again what final quantity has been approved. Explain why you must have an immediate answer. The custos will appreciate your position and your frankness."

The conversation reminded Gutenberg of his talks long ago in

Strasbourg with Fr. Sebastian and of the troubles Hultz had had with Archbishop von Diest building the spire. Hultz had been unable to work on his own but had managed, despite rivalries, pressures, alliances which made the work more difficult. I have been independent, until now, Gutenberg thought, and Father is right, I am not a politician. I am a goldsmith who must serve the church as well as God and myself. But obedience is one thing, coercion is another!

Gutenberg would send a letter to Isenburg, he told Fr. Cremer, and explain the situation. Erbach may have exceeded his authority.

Within a week, reluctantly, and with much misgiving, Gutenberg began composing Quire I, Genesis, and the first pages of Kings, Quire XVII, which would be printed on a second press. There was much excitement and confusion as the work began. The compositors could only hold 20 lines of text in the tray of letters because 40 lines of metal letters were too heavy, and it seemed to take a lot of time for even the experienced men to complete one column. Everyone was concerned about Genesis because it was the first book of the Bible, and four test prints were made before Gutenberg and Fr. Gunther were satisfied with the text and appearance of the opening page.

Fr. Gunther knew the story of creation from memory, but he read it several times to be sure nothing had been left out. When the page ended with the word "bona," and the sentence "God saw all that he had made and it was very good," he thought this was a good omen. The line that followed, "And there was evening and morning, the sixth day" would start the second page.

It took three days to compose and correct the two first pages of Genesis and Kings. In another three days, 100 copies on paper and 25 on vellum, had been printed of each page. Everyone, except Gutenberg, was happy and thought the pages were beautiful.

"God was pleased to have made the world in six days." Gutenberg said. "But I can't be pleased to have printed two pages of the Bible in six days when I know it is not good, that we begin too soon! Too soon!"

Not all the letters had been filed, and Gutenberg took no satisfaction in knowing he would have to continue printing 40-line columns until they were. He would be satisfied when they began 42-line pages, he said, which he hoped would be when the men returned to the shop after Pentecost, and when Isenberg confirmed the number of Bibles to be printed.

CHAPTER 45

In the weeks before Whitsun, Gutenberg's men composed and printed seven pages of Kings and nine pages of Genesis, 40 lines. The tenth page of Genesis was composed, using the newly-filed letters. Despite all their efforts, it was only possible to get 41 lines in the same space as 40 lines. It was a terrible disappointment.

Gutenberg printed the 41 line page, but he refused to print any more. Until he could print 42 lines, as intended, they would not continue with Genesis or Kings, he said; nor would they start Proverbs which was the first book in Volume II, and ready to be printed on Press 3.

Of the 17 pages that had been printed thus far, 16 were 40 lines, one was 41 lines. To Gutenberg, that more than fulfilled his obligation to begin. He felt obliged now to stop the work before all the savings and advantages gained from 42 line pages had been lost.

"I will not begin printing again with less than 42-line columns!" Gutenberg told Pannartz. "You were right. Filing is not the answer. We will recast the letters we need."

Pannartz was annoyed because two pages of Proverbs had already been composed, but he agreed that it was best to stop work completely. They were so close with 41 lines, recasting the letters might give them the 42-line columns Gutenberg wanted.

Gutenberg ordered Kefer to stop printing. "We must stop somewhere, whether Fust likes it or not. We will finish the two quires we started later."

"We are waiting for paper," Kefer said. "We have to stop now, anyway, until a new shipment arrives."

"Good!" Gutenberg answered. "Good! That gives us time to recast the letters."

Custos Isenburg had been delayed, Gutenberg learned, but was expected back for the feast of Corpus Christi. They would resume printing after Isenburg returned, Gutenberg told his men. And then every page would be 42 lines, whether they printed 125 Bibles or 200 Bibles.

Fust was in a rage when he learned that Gutenberg had stopped printing. This time he went to Gutenberg's home and demanded an explanation. On whose authority had Gutenberg acted!

"The decision is mine," Gutenberg told him. "I take the responsibility. Erbach is master in the Dom, Herr Fust, but I am master here! We began printing against my better judgment. Now it is my judgment that we wait for Custos Isenburg, who may approve 185 Bibles. If he does, we shall have to recompose and reprint the 17 pages already printed, but no more than that. If he doesn't, we'll continue printing 125 copies, but all pages will be 42 lines, my original plan. We may have 60 more Bibles to sell and I think Isenburg's decision is worth waiting for. In the meantime, some of the letters will be recast."

"And when is the Custos expected in Mainz?" Fust asked.

"In two weeks. Printing is halted only temporarily, Herr Fust."

"You are a stubborn man, Master, and you are losing time and money," Fust answered. "But you are right about one thing -60 Bibles are worth waiting for. Tell me what Isenburg has to say."

Several weeks after their decision to experiment with the steel punches and copper matrices, Schoeffer and Ruppel succeeded in making and testing the new tools. Even after repeated casting, neither the new matrices nor the letters showed any sign of deterioration. It was clear that tools made from the higher quality metals would last longer and produce superior castings. Changing the metals of the tools had definitely solved the problem of less than perfect castings from less than perfect matrices. Both men were pleased with the results.

Schoeffer placed a row of the small letters directly above and below a row of the capital letters. There was virtually no space between each row. The tails of the small p and q filled the face of the castings to the bottom edge. The capital letters and small t's and l's filled the face of the castings to the top edge. Small l's could be placed directly below small p's without the letters touching.

"All I did," Schoeffer told Ruppel, "was to make the height and depth of the letters fill the face of the casting completely. No letters are taller than the capitals, and none longer than the small p's and q's. Casting the letters with no excess metal top or bottom will bring the lines closer together."

Would Gutenberg be pleased, they wondered.

The copper matrices would surely last longer, Gutenberg told them, and the castings would be better also. But what excited him most of all was that it appeared the lines of letters would be closer together. He was concerned, however, that the base of the letters would not be even across the bottom.

"We shall make a print of the letters you have in the form," Gutenberg said. "If this means we can get 42 lines of letters in a column, it will be worth the cost of changing to steel and copper. You may have solved two problems instead of one, Peter."

Other Masters would have been very displeased by such independent activity, but Gutenberg respected the bold initiative Schoeffer and Ruppel had taken. Following through and testing the new idea appealed to his own creativity and sense of independence. The test print was like the very first one he had made, Gutenberg thought - rows of the same letters in a print that looked like a copy book. The print of Peter's new letters was encouraging indeed.

They would recast all the tall and long letters, Gutenberg decided, using the new punches and matrices, then insert these letters in the first page of Proverbs waiting to be printed. Eggestein, the compositor most skilled in removing and inserting individual letters, made the replacements of l's, t's, p's, j's, k's, b's, d's, y's, etc., on the Proverbs page. Then he made each column 42 lines. Would the slight difference in space between lines be enough to get 42 lines in the same space as 40 lines? Everyone in the shop anxiously awaited the result.

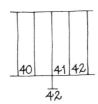

When the form was measured against a 40-line form, it was the same depth. A test print quickly confirmed the measurements. The first 42-line page of Proverbs was the same depth as the 40-and 41-line pages of Genesis.

Gutenberg was jubilant. Those printers who thought it couldn't be done, and those who had spent days filing the letters, were equally thrilled and amazed by what had been accomplished. Schoeffer had made a major contribution, and the Master had done the impossible.

The filed letters would be melted down, Gutenberg said, to be sure none of them got mixed in with the new ones, and the metal used for the new letters. The goldsmiths would begin recasting a supply of the tall and long letters immediately so the compositors could continue with 42-line pages in Genesis, Kings and Proverbs.

Finally, the work could proceed with letters the proper size, and columns, pages and margins the proper depth. Every page of the Bible from then on would have 42-line columns of text. Eventually, all of the punches and matrices would be remade in steel and copper, and Gutenberg was confident that every casting would be better and last twice as long as before.

The attitude of every man in the shop was uplifted in the knowledge that Gutenberg was satisfied at last with the letters and pages of the Bible. The many problems they had - composing words correctly, the filing, the forced delays until paper and vellum arrived, making corrections and reprinting that had taken so much time - none of this seemed to matter anymore.

Gutenberg rewarded Schoeffer by making him his chief assistant, and he accepted Ruppel's son as an apprentice goldsmith. And because the Bechtermuntz brothers were the first young men to finish their apprenticeship and join the guild, Gutenberg declared a two-day holiday.

The guild ceremony took place on St. John's Day, June 24, in the guild hall, with Master Gutenberg as sponsor. The other printers, however, planned a ceremony of their own which they thought more appropriate to the feast of St. John the Baptist. When the new guild members emerged from the hall, they were escorted to the printing shop where a large wine tub, filled with water, stood in front of the door. The Bechtermuntz brothers were told they could not enter until they had been baptized. Their protests were overcome by spirited determination as the two were blindfolded and their fine coats removed. As they were dunked in the tub, the onlookers cheered. But the newly baptized retaliated, and soon everyone was wet, choking and laughing.

Gutenberg and Ruppel watched the fun from across the street, with no intention of interfering. The melee was not malicious, everyone liked the Bechtermuntzes, and this good natured comraderie helped relieve tensions after the many weeks and months of hard work.

Next year Schoeffer and Eggestein would also join the guild, Gutenberg said. The official recognition of his men made Gutenberg very proud, especially of Peter Schoeffer. Not since Andreas Dritzehen in Strasbourg had he known anyone with the same intensity and capacity for becoming a master craftsman and master printer. Like father, like son, Ruppel remarked; nor did he think Gutenberg's confidence was misplaced. A promising future lay ahead for the young man from Gernsheim.

The success, pride and happiness Gutenberg enjoyed was dampened, however, soon after, by sad family news which arrived by letter from Strasbourg. Orte and Odilgen Gensfleisch had both died. There had been an epidemic of dysentery, and while visiting his sister at St. Odile, Orte too became fatally ill. Friele-Else insisted on making the journey to Strasbourg to visit their graves, and Little Else accompanied her. Gutenberg was unable to go with them, but deeply mourned the tragic loss of his niece and nephew.

CHAPTER 46

Delivering pages to the monks at St. James scriptorium, Peter often saw a girl leaving or going into the monastery. He saw her only briefly and didn't know her name. Sometimes she was alone, sometimes with a companion. She was tall, about 17, Peter thought, and had beautiful blonde hair. A wealthy girl, judging from her clothes. Why did she come to the monastery, he wondered. Peter found himself longing for an opportunity to speak to her, and one day asked Brother Jean-Marie who she was.

"Christine had asked about you also," Brother Jean-Marie smiled. "She is Christine Fust, Herr Fust's daughter. She and her friend have been helping the Sisters sew vestments for us, and Christine reads to old Fr. Simeon, who is blind. You have never met?"

"No," Peter answered. "I would like to meet her."

"She comes again on Tuesday," the young novice said. "I will introduce you."

When Peter and Christine did meet, they were half in love. Christine was a happy person. She had a wonderful smile, yet was modest and soft-spoken, unlike her father, Peter thought, and she had spirit. Christine had been coming to St. James over her father's objections, she said, though her mother approved and did not try to keep her at home all the time.

"I'm not rich," Peter told her. "I have no title, no large inheritance. Your father is one of the most important men in Mainz. He would never consent to our seeing each other."

Marriage would be impossible, Peter told himself. He could not marry anyone until the Bibles were published, and that wouldn't be for at least two years. It was a hopeless situation, he thought sadly.

"Papa must get to know you better," Christine said. "The monks have told me you made some punches and letters the Master praised you for. Papa will be pleased, too, when I tell him. You will be an important man when the Bibles are finished, Peter, and Papa likes important men."

"By then you will be promised to someone," Peter answered.

"My father spoils me and protects me," Christine replied. "He will not force me to marry anyone I don't love. He knows I will enter a convent if I do not marry."

Perhaps one day Master Gutenberg would make him a partner, Peter thought. Or he could open a printing office of his own in Gernsheim. Two years was a very long time! But in that time, if he worked hard, Christine's father might consider him worthy of his daughter.

Peter and Christine continued to meet secretly at St. James and to pray for each other. Their private betrothal was sealed in an exchange of letters hidden in a prayerbook.

Peter said nothing to Gutenberg about the romance. Only the sacristan and Brother Jean-Marie observed the trysts in the monastery chapel and kept their silence.

When Custos Isenburg returned to Mainz, he went directly to Archbishop Erbach and reported the events of the Emperor's coronation. The festivities were magnificent and the Grand Elector was missed, Isenburg said. Cardinal Cusanus and the Holy Father both hoped his health had improved. Erbach made no comment.

Isenburg had also discussed the Bibles with the cardinal, he said, and had received his recommendations concerning the number of books to be printed. After studying Gutenberg's figures, Cusanus thought 185 copies would be highly desirable and practical, given the circumstances. He would contribute another 500 gulden so the edition could be increased by 60 books.

"What will 185 Bibles cost?" Erbach asked. "And what will they sell for?"

"The 185 Bibles will cost 1575 gulden, for paper and vellum, Your Grace," Isenburg replied. "And 185 Bibles will sell for 7000 gulden."

"That much?" the archbishop exclaimed. "Are you sure?"

"Yes. The 150 paper Bibles will sell for 5250 gulden, and 35 on vellum, 1750 gulden. The 100 paper Bibles with 25 on vellum would cost 1072 gulden and sell for 4750 gulden," Isenburg said, sure of his facts and taking pleasure in reciting them.

"In other words," Erbach said, "For half again the number of books, sales will increase about 50 percent."

"From a cost increase of 500 gulden, the sales increase 2250 gulden," Isenburg answered. "Gross profit is 5425 gulden."

	COST		SALES	
185 Bibles	1575 gulden		7000 gulden	- 5425 profit
125 Bibles	1072 gulden		4750 gulden	
60 Bibles	503 gulden		2250 gulden	
	50 percent increase		50 percent increase	

"Incredible!" Erbach said. "Monks might complete 185 books a year, but not Bibles, and not for so much money."

"The Benedictine abbot will give 100 gulden," Isenburg said, "to purchase the vellum sheets needed for 10 Bibles."

"I am sure the Benedictines are richer than the diocese," Erbach remarked. "We know that Cardinal Cusanus has great private wealth. Master Gutenberg is fortunate to have his support, and support from Herr Fust as well. Whether 125 or 185 Bibles are printed is of no difference to me. I hope they are completed, that's all. Does Herr Fust know the edition will be increased?"

"I shall tell him, Your Grace," Isenburg replied.

At that moment Fust joined them. He apologized for the interruption, but the archbishop did not seem disturbed.

"Your Grace," Fust acknowledged. "Custos Isenburg! You are back, finally!"

"The Custos brings news, Herr Fust," Erbach said. "Cardinal Cusanus will give 500 gulden more so that 185 Bibles can be printed."

"Well, perhaps now the work will get under way at last," Fust said. "Master Gutenberg began printing because the archbishop and I insisted. Now he has stopped printing completely -waiting for your report."

"None of us fully understood his reasons for not beginning to print until the exact number of books was determined," Isenburg answered. "I hope there won't be serious difficulties."

"The books will sell for 7000 gulden, Herr Fust," Erbach told him.

Isenburg noted Fust's privileged access to the archbishop and their obvious rapport. He would leave them, he said, to speak with Gutenberg. The Custos was dumbfounded that Gutenberg had stopped printing and had dared to go against Erbach's wishes, and Fust's! Isenburg smiled to himself. No other Master in Mainz would have done that.

"Of course, I'm pleased," Gutenberg told Isenburg, "and I am most grateful for the cardinal's added financial support. And the abbot's. I'm glad the cardinal agreed that 185 Bibles are desirable and worth the cost. I only wish I had known sooner!"

"I understand, Master," Esenburg replied. "At least I did when you explained the situation in your letter. I regret you had to start printing when you did. I'm also glad you stopped when you did!"

"It was foolish to continue," Gutenberg said. "A waste of time and materials. But, what is done, is done."

"We are committed to 185 Bibles, Master," Isenburg assured him.

"Everything should go well from now on. Were you able to file the letters and get the 42 lines you wanted?"

"We have recast some letters and made new punches and matrices," Gutenberg said. "We have 42 lines in the same space as 40 lines."

"How did you manage to do that?" Isenburg asked.

"I'll show you. Peter Schoeffer made it possible," Gutenberg answered. "Would you like to see the other pages of Genesis?"

Gutenberg would move ahead, using five presses for the 42-line pages and one for reprinting 60 copies of the 40-41 line pages. It rankled him that these 17 early pages had to be done over exactly as they were, but he could not go back and change them to 42 lines, because throwing away the 1000 sheets already printed in Quires 1 and 17 would be an unforgivable extravagance.

Getting the additional amounts of paper he needed every month would be a problem. Gutenberg hoped the Strasbourg mill could deliver 100 reams of paper, 50,000 sheets, 10 bales, for 150 Bibles. It was a huge order, an increase of 16,500 sheets from the original 67 reams.

Getting the additional 3200 vellum sheets was his biggest concern, however. A total of 11,200 sheets, 5600 finished calfskins, would be needed for 35 Bibles.

In the printing shop, Gutenberg had to revise his production schedule because it took longer to print 185 copies of each page. The rate of production by each printer had improved, however, so the work would go faster, he believed. Mercifully, the original book-size estimates would not change too much, if at all. Each Bible should still have 640 folios, despite the 17, 40-line pages.

In his report to Cardinal Cusanus, Isenburg confirmed that 185 Bibles would be published and that the Abbot of St. James was contributing to the cost of the vellum. Archbishop Erbach still had not offered any money whatever. A review of the expenses showed a total of 2400 gulden received and spent as follows: 800 gulden from Fust to Gutenberg for metal and equipment; 1000 gulden plus 500 gulden from Cusanus and 100 gulden from the Benedictines for paper and vellum. The cardinal and abbot would each receive gratis a number of the printed Bibles, Isenburg wrote.

"We are grateful to Master Gutenberg," he added, "for insisting on 42-line pages and showing us why so many Bibles could be considered.

We are beholden to you, Your Grace, for providing the inspiration and most generous financial help."

The opening pages of Genesis, Kings, and Proverbs were magnificent, Isenburg wrote. He hoped the cardinal would be able to return to Mainz and see the Bibles for himself. He did not mention Gutenberg's premature start with 40-line pages.

CHAPTER 47

In 1452, printing of the Bible was finally going smoothly. It had taken almost two years of preliminary work, but now that Gutenberg had sufficient letters the right size, every page of the Bible was being printed with 42-line columns. Good quantities of paper and vellum were on hand, and six presses were in operation.

The compositors and printers worked in teams. In Volume I, Team 1 worked from Genesis to Kings; Team 2 from Kings to Esdras 1. In Volume II, Team 3 started at Proverbs, and Team 4 would start Quire 17 at Daniel. Team 5 would complete Volume I, from Esdras through Psalms. Team 6 would complete Volume II, starting at Romans.

Each pressman printed one quire, or 16 pages, at a time, making 185 prints of each page, one by one, in sequence. The quire consisted of four sheets, four pages on each sheet, which when nested and folded once through the center made eight folios or 16 pages. The printers worked with flat sheets and needed 185 each of four sheets to print each quire.

One printer, averaging 10 prints an hour in a 12-hour workday, could make 185 prints in a day and a half, or print two pages in three days, four pages a week. At this rate, he could complete 16 pages or one quire a month.

A compositor could compose one page in a day or five pages a week, allowing the sixth day to make corrections. Working ahead of the printer always, a compositor would be starting page 8, for example, when the printer was beginning page 4.

If six compositors maintained a completion rate of 30 pages a week, the 1280-page Bible would be composed in less than a year. If six presses were in continual operation, Gutenberg could estimate six quires completed each month or the 80 quires printed in 13-14 months. Another estimate based on an average of 700 prints a day indicated that 185 prints of 1280 pages meant 236,800 page prints, and would require 338 days to complete.

Production was less in the winter and more in the summer because of the shorter and longer daylight hours. And a normal six-day work week was not consistent throughout the year. Excluding Sundays, the octaves of Christmas and Easter, the major feasts of Pentecost, Corpus Christi, and All Saints, the Marian feasts and local saint's days, the actual number of workdays annually was about 280. Allowing for illness, repairs, composing a second time and reprinting the 40-41 line pages, Gutenberg figured it would take about two years to complete the Bibles.

Accuracy in composition was always important, and the compositors were rewarded for their perfect pages or for the fewest number of errors made in a week. They were penalized also if errors or corrections were overlooked and a page form had to be corrected a second time.

Accuracy in printing was even more important. "The proper page on the proper sheet" became a byword with each printer. A page printed out of sequence could mean that one, two, or three pages on that sheet had to be composed again and reprinted. It meant throwing out, however, many sheets that had been printed, possibly 185, replacing them and starting over. If this should happen, the printer was penalized the cost of the paper or vellum lost and forfeited his wages for the time spent to print the pages again. Sometimes the pages looked very much alike, and if they were not identified properly, misprints could occur.

The text, of course, was continuous. Books of the Bible began and ended anywhere on a page, at the top of a column or within a column. Some books began a new page. Rarely did books begin a new quire. Gutenberg spent many hours carefully estimating the number of pages in each book and noting which books comprised each quire. The more 42-line columns and pages that were composed, the more accurate his figures became. The short lines around the two-line capitals and the larger initial letters followed the style of manuscript Bibles.

The flow of the pages from compositor to printer for a test print, to monk reader, back to compositor for corrections, a second test print read and approved, and final printing of 185 copies developed into an efficient, routine operation. Only if a printer lacked the 740 sheets he needed for each quire would work be held up.

To print 150 paper Bible pages, a printer needed 600 sheets of paper, and for the 35 vellum Bibles, he needed 140 sheets of vellum. For his six pressmen, Gutenberg had to have 4000 sheets of paper and 1000 sheets of vellum on hand every month. If deliveries were late or there was not enough paper and vellum in reserve, printing would stop. And if two or more presses ceased operating, even temporarily, the work schedule fell far behind.

Such delays affected the compositors also, because should a printer run out of paper or vellum before 185 prints had been made, the page forms could not be taken apart and the letters reused immediately. More than once Gutenberg and Schoeffer ran down to the Fischtor to meet the Strasbourg barge and rushed reams or bales of paper back to the shop so work could resume.

The monks' cooperation had been excellent. They were seldom responsible for not delivering corrected pages on schedule. Fr. Cremer was impressed by Gutenberg's careful attention to detail as he noted the left and right edges of each column, which were straight as an arrow, and the 42 lines which were amazingly the same depth as 40 lines.

Monks who still refused to admit that printing had merit or that printed pages were equal to manuscript began to change their minds as 740 finished sheets arrived week after week at the scriptorium. Here the sheets were collated into 185 quires. Only as the collection of finished quires grew and filled the shelves of the storage room did the bulk of these pages begin to present the visual evidence that not one but 185 Bibles exactly alike were being completed at one time.

The monks were responsible for putting the individual quires together. There had been 100 copies of the 12 quires in each Missal. There would be 185 copies of the 80 quires in each Bible.

The monks had learned from collating the Missal that it was more difficult to gather four printed sheets in proper order than it was to gather four blank sheets together, as was done for their own manuscript quires. The printed sheets must be placed face up or face down, folded in or folded out, or the pages would be mixed up. The system they developed worked out well, providing everyone paid attention to what he was doing.

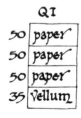

The 185 prints each of sheets 1-2-3-4 were placed in four piles. One sheet from each pile was picked up, nested together with sheet 1 on top, then folded once through the center. Each quire was then numbered and stacked according to number. The 150 paper quires were stored on three shelves, and the 35 vellum quires on one shelf. Eventually the entire room would be walled by Quires I through LXXX, a prospect which even the abbot of St. James found awesome.

At a conference attended by the bishops and abbots of Mainz, the abbot of St. James was questioned about Gutenberg's work. The abbot of the Carmelite monastery was unimpressed by what he had heard. His monks, he said, had begun work in April on a new manuscript Bible which would be known as the Great Bible of Mainz. On vellum, with 60 lines to a page, it was a work of art, he boasted, and would be completed the following year.

"I am sure the Great Bible will be a work of art," the abbot of St. James replied politely, "and I predict it may also be the last manuscript Bible produced in Mainz."

The Carmelite was shocked. "The last! Impossible!" he said scornfully. "The printed Bibles of Master Gutenberg are far from finished. Will they ever be finished? He has already been at work two years."

"Gutenberg's Bibles may not be finished until 1453," St. James' prelate answered. "But when they are, there will be not one, but 185! All of us can rejoice in that. There must not be rivalry between us, Father Abbot. Each Bible is precious in the eyes of God."

"Each complete Bible is precious," the Carmelite replied. "I seriously doubt that Master Gutenberg will be able to print the entire Bible or that he will produce 185 copies. The money, time, and paper wasted if he should not, will be enormous. I have reservations about his success, that is all."

Drawn into the conversation was the abbot of St. Victor who had given Gutenberg the Exemplar Bible quires to copy from. "I too, have reservations," he said, "about the accuracy of the printed text. There are many mistakes, I'm sure. Laymen should never be allowed to copy Holy Scripture!"

"We found and corrected some mistakes in the Exemplar Bible," St. James' abbot replied cooly. "The monks who read the text have been extremely careful, which is one reason the work has gone slowly. I tell you both, the entire Bible will be printed. The 185 books will be printed. We must wait and pray for that day. In a thousand years, in all the Empire, I wonder if 185 Bibles have been written by hand in a single year!"

The lack of confidence in Gutenberg's work by his fellow prelates was disturbing to the abbot of St. James. Only the abbot of St. Stephan's offered a word of support.

"The master's work is of great importance," he said., "and you are right to defend it. We are all disciples of St. Jerome, you know, and I believe God will protect His Book and all who reproduce it, whoever they are." When the Bibles were completed, then they would have the physical evidence which would erase all doubt, apprehension and criticism, the abbot said.

The abbot of St. James was grateful for this expression of good will, coming as it did from the senior abbot of St. Stephan's. The work had been difficult from the beginning and he had had doubts himself about laymen copying and printing the Holy Text. Seeing how Gutenberg and his men worked, however, had given him great respect for their ability and dedication. He dared to envision the time when there would be universal monastic acceptance of the printing process.

CHAPTER 48

Gutenberg knew that his Bibles would not be published the following year. In fact, he needed more money to meet expenses so the work could go on. Of the original 800 gulden loan from Fust, he had spent 500 gulden for metal and shop equipment and 300 gulden for wages and rent. He had paid the men from his own funds the past few months, but was no longer able to do so. With two years' work remaining, another 600 gulden was needed for operating expenses.

"I am reluctant to increase my indebtedness to Herr Fust," Gutenberg told Isenburg, "because I have not repaid any part of the loan thus far. But I can raise the money myself. I can reprint the Missal, and I can get a new loan from my friends in Strasbourg. I know they will help me."

Custos Isenburg showed little enthusiasm for either proposal, however. "The money should come from Mainz," he said, "and rather than print another Missal, I think Herr Fust would consent to an additional loan, if he knew you had been asked to publish a Psalter."

"A Psalter?" Gutenberg replied with surprise. "Cardinal Cusanus said that the Bibles must come first."

"But you could begin casting the letters for a Psalter now, couldn't you? And print the Bibles at the same time," Isenburg suggested.

He would have to design larger letters for a Psalter, Gutenberg said. He would need more metal for the punches and matrices, and for the castings themselves. But yes, the men in the foundry could be casting the Psalter letters while the Bible pages were being printed.

"How much will the metal cost?" Isenburg asked

"At least 200 gulden, I'd say," Gutenberg answered.

"Then I shall tell Herr Fust that you need 800 gulden - for expenses to finish the Bibles and to cast new letters for a Psalter," Isenburg said. "I am sure he can arrange a second loan. The Missal and the Bible are not the only books you shall print for the Church, Master."

Gutenberg was astounded at Isenburg's suggestion, yet the idea was a good one. And Isenburg sounded confident of Fust's cooperation. The work on the Bibles would not be delayed, and they would be ready to print the Psalter as soon as the Bibles were finished. Gutenberg did not like the thought of owing Fust so much money, however, and rather wished he had insisted on getting help from Strasbourg. Still, it would be easier if the money came from Mainz.

Gutenberg thought he would consider 200 gulden only as an additional loan for equipment, and the other 600 gulden for expenses might be considered an investment in the Bibles. I don't wish to have any partners, Gutenberg thought. The equipment will belong to me, but Herr Fust and I could share in the Bible profits. I shall suggest this to him if he agrees to Isenburg's proposal.

Isenburg knew that printing the Psalter would be an inducement to Fust to further support Gutenberg's work, and there was also the possibility of future printing from Rome. Fust had offered additional money to the Bible project, if needed. Now he had the chance to fulfill that offer. Isenburg asked Fust to come and see him.

"You mean to say Gutenberg must have another 800 gulden?" Fust exclaimed. "And you want me to loan it to him!" Prelates were never shy about asking for money, he thought, but Isenburg's proposal took Fust completely by surprise. "For operating expenses and a Psalter. A Psalter, yes, that would be profitable. But expenses for two years? The Bibles should have been printed by now!"

"It would be a good investment for you, Herr Fust," Isenburg continued. "If you and Master Gutenberg can negotiate a second agreement, it would benefit both of you. Cardinal Cusanus gave additional money for the Bibles, and he has hinted that Mainz could receive considerable liturgical printing from Rome. He wants the printing of the Bibles and the printing shop to be successful."

It was true, Fust reflected, that the cardinal and the abbots in Mainz had shown supreme confidence in Gutenberg's work, in spite of the problems with the Bibles so far. Yet printing from Rome was something Fust had not anticipated. Printing books and church papers of all kinds could become a very lucrative business. Suddenly the delays and Gutenberg's unpaid loan were unimportant. He might invest in the printing office, Fust thought, or even become a partner.

"You may tell Cardinal Cusanus I will raise the money," Fust told Isenburg.

"We all have an interest in the Bibles and Psalters," Isenburg answered. "The cardinal will be grateful for your continued support. Printing is expensive, but the rewards are great, wouldn't you agree?"

The new agreement between Gutenberg and Fust was on the same general terms as the 1450 agreement. The metal letters and equipment Gutenberg would make for the Psalters would be his security for a loan of 200 gulden. When the loan was repaid, the equipment would belong to Gutenberg. The 600 gulden for expenses would be Fust's investment in the Bibles, and they would share equally in the profits when the books were sold.

Gutenberg's debt to Fust was limited to 1000 gulden, an increase of 25 percent and agreeable to Gutenberg. The investment was agreeable to Fust. Sharing profits from the Bibles was acceptable to both men.

Fust did not mention a possible partnership to Gutenberg. Time for that when the Psalters were ready to be printed. He still had a lien on the printing equipment, he thought, which didn't even exist two years ago, and which had greatly appreciated in value. The printing office was fully equipped and provided ample security against 800 gulden which Fust knew he could raise without difficulty in Mainz.

The written agreement could be drawn up later, Fust told Gutenberg. A verbal agreement now was sufficient. The work must go on!

Gutenberg was pleased that the negotiations had gone well. Isenburg's request had been an excellent idea, and it had also solved the immediate financial problem.

Schoeffer could start designing the Psalter letters, Gutenberg thought. They had to be larger than the Bible letters because the words of the Psalter were sung in choir and must be big enough so several monks could read them at one time. Gutenberg himself would cast a set of the two-color initial letters he had made and perhaps even try to make some copper relief plates of border illustrations like those he and Master Wilhelm had done in Basel.

There were 150 Psalms and how many pages, Gutenberg wondered. But all the estimating of pages and sheets could wait, he thought thankfully. The new Psalter letters were the important things, and the men had time to cast letters that would be even finer than the Bible letters. They could even start composing the book of Psalms in the Bible, Gutenberg decided, which would familiarize the men with the text so that when they began the Psalter, the work would be easier. As usual, he was thinking far ahead and happy to be planning something new. The Psalter would be a beautiful book.

Dr. Humery was not enthusiastic about the Psalter, nor was he satisfied with Gutenberg's newest agreement with Fust. He was, in fact, very upset and angry that Gutenberg had not consulted him before going ahead on Isenburg's advice.

Gutenberg should have borrowed money from his friends in Strasbourg to repay Fust what he already owed, he told Gutenberg. Work on the Psalters could be put off.

"If you needed more money for expenses, why didn't you tell me?" Dr Humery asked. "Gelthuss, Rudi Sorgenloch and I could raise 800 gulden on our own security! The way it is now, Fust still owns the printing equipment. He can give the shop as security for his loan. And you intend to share Bible profits with him? Don't be a fool, Johannes!"

Dr. Humery was particularly concerned because he didn't think a verbal agreement was Fust's style. Nor could he understand Fust's willingness to overlook the interest on the first 800 gulden as Gutenberg reported.

"A written agreement must be made," he said. "The amounts and purpose of the loan and the investment must be clearly stated. A date for repayment of the 1000 gulden should be named after the Bibles are ready to be sold." These important points must be in writing, Dr. Humery insisted.

Did Gutenberg know if Fust was investing by himself or would others be involved, he asked, because if Fust or his associates demanded the money back before the Bibles were published, it would mean disastrous consequences for Gutenberg.

"Isenburg is protecting the Bibles, Johannes. But you must protect yourself!" Dr. Humery said. "You have no protection without a written agreement."

Gutenberg promised to let Dr. Humery approve the agreement before it was signed, but he was not apprehensive.

"We can trust Custos Isenburg," he said. "And when the Bibles are sold, I can repay everything I owe, and Fust will make a good profit on his investment besides. The most important thing now is to finish the Bibles without further interruption."

CHAPTER 49

By the end of 1453, work on the Bibles was showing considerable progress. Over half of Volume I and of Volume II had been completed.

Each volume was divided into three sections, and compositor-printer Team 1 had finished the section, Genesis to Kings. They were now reprinting the 17 early pages of Genesis and Kings that were 40 and 41 lines, making 50 additional paper copies and 10 additional vellum copies of each. Team 2 had finished the long section of Kings and was well into Paralipomenon (Chronicles). Team 5 was printing the four quires of Psalms as a unit before going back and printing Esdras where Team 2 would leave off.

In Volume II, Team 3 had completed Proverbs through Ezekiel. Team 4 had started at Daniel and finished the Old Testament. They were preparing to start the Gospels. Team 6 would print the Apocalypse, which was a single, complete quire of 16 pages, then go back and start Romans where Team 4 left off.

As each book of the Bible was finished, Fr. Gunther blessed it and read passages aloud to the men. He read about the Flood, Abraham, Jacob, Joseph and his brothers, the story of Moses, from Ecclesiastes and Proverbs. The Psalms of David and the Gospels would be more familiar, he said, but the printers liked hearing the Old Testament stories. The chance to reflect on the words they had copied and printed also served to remind them of the sacred content of the Bible.

It was often difficult to sustain this sense of sublime purpose, however, when letters fell on the floor, a page was misplaced, or one of the chapters was omitted. It seemed very strange to be composing and printing the story of Christ's Birth in the summertime and of His Passion and Resurrection in wintertime!

Fr. Heinrich Cremer of St. Stephan's had been selected to illustrate the Bible for the Archbishop of Mainz. He began by gathering the first 17 quires of Volume I together to plan where he would place the page titles, chapter numbers, initial letters, small capitals and decorative opening pages of each book. This was the first time a collection of consecutive quires had been made.

"The pages Genesis to Kings are so beautiful," the abbot told Gutenberg, "I think the monks and printers should see the results of their work. When Father has added the red and blue and other colors to these pages, I want you and your men to come to the monastery, and we shall look at the printed Bible together."

"You are very generous to give us this privilege," Gutenberg answered. "Most of the men will never see a bound Bible and can only imagine the final result." He doubted that they had ever seen Bible pages at all before beginning work on the printed Bible.

Gutenberg had seen the pages in metal forms, the prints before and after correction, and the printed sheets of each quire as they were finished. Again he used a guide quire of blank pages, as he had done in Strasbourg with the Donatus, and placed the corrected prints of each page in the guide so he could keep track of the sequence of pages produced on each press.

The printers saw 185 prints of one page, a page at a time, and the piles of four sheets printed on both sides as they were finished. After awhile, all the pages looked alike. The printers never saw the individual quires because collating was done at the scriptorium. The compositors, working their pages in sequence, book by book, only saw prints of their page forms when corrections had been made.

The monks read a few pages in sequence each time they were corrected, but from six different places in the Bible. Those who gathered the 185 copies of a quire together for storages saw only the four sheets of each quire in sequence.

No one until now, except Fr. Cremer and the abbot, had viewed a large portion of the Bible's printed and finished sheets in readable order.

The monks and printers waited patiently while Fr. Cremer placed the first illustrated pages on an easel in the refectory for the men to see. They eyed each other shyly, suspiciously, nervously, as the abbot rose to address them.

"This Holy Bible is your book to share," the abbot said. "All of you can be immensely proud to have created it."

Then, as Fr. Cremer slowly turned the pages, the silence was broken. A few comments, later spontaneous applause followed the display of each two facing pages. The monks were impressed by the clear, even black lines of text, the perfect matching of the margins and the number of short lines so carefully placed to allow room for the larger initial letters and the smaller two-line capitals. The printers, compositors, letter casters and punch cutters responded to the colors that had been added - the lines in red, the gold fringe and marginal flourishes that enhanced the black text. They were fascinated by the little fish with blue eyes that peeked out from many of the initials.

Sincere respect for each other's work was a result of the meeting. The monks and printers learned more fully what each had contributed, and Gutenberg was hopeful that former rivalry and distrust would now be replaced by a closer feeling of cooperation. Never again would his men or his work be held in contempt. Monks who had argued the merits of manuscript over printed liturgical pages could no longer depreciate printing with metal letters.

The archbishop's Bible was unique, the abbot pointed out, because no other Bible would be illustrated in precisely the same way. Yet the text in each of the 185 copies was identical! These books, the abbot said, were a blessing from God, and they all must pray for the successful completion of the pages still to come.

Special visitors to Fr. Cremer's exhibit of the Bible pages were the Carmelite abbot of the monastery that had completed the great manuscript Bible earlier in July and the talented scribe monk whose work it was. Both men were forced to concede that Gutenberg's letters and printed pages were remarkably well made.

Gutenberg had not seen the Great Bible, but Fr. Cremer had and was very complimentary. The volume was magnificent, Fr. Cremer said, on folios larger than those of the printed Bible, and written with round, Gothic capitals and small letters having firm vertical strokes. The scribe had used special quills, whittled into nibs with oblique points, he said.

Gutenberg and Schoeffer expressed a desire to see this Bible also and hoped that the printed Bible would match its beauty and accuracy.

"The engravers from Basel," the abbot said to Gutenberg, "Master Wilhelm and his son, started to illustrate our Bible, as you know, but did not finish. They had other work, they said, which was more important. I wonder what work could be more important than illustrating a Holy Bible, Master."

"They also worked on the illustration of one of the printed Bibles, Your Grace," Gutenberg answered, "but they did not complete that work either. We regret it as much as you."

The Carmelite abbot stubbornly refused to show enthusiasm for Gutenberg's work. "The Great Bible is on vellum, the Archbishop's Bible is on paper," he sniffed. "It is premature for any final judgement. Your Bibles are incomplete. I hope you can finish what you have begun, Master."

The scribe was more generous. "I wish my letters might have been cast in metal." he confided to Schoeffer.

Master Wilhelm had come to Mainz and made a set of engraved plates and the copper relief plates of figures which they hoped would be used to illustrate the Bibles. The small relief plates of flowers, birds, scrolls and decorative designs were nailed to blocks of wood to make them the same height as the letter castings, then arranged in the margins of a page. Text and pictures could be printed at the same time, and the pictures colored in later by hand.

Gutenberg had shown this work to the abbots, but they felt strongly that illustrations in the Bibles should be different in each individual volume. Also, there had been no time to do all the work involved without delaying the Bible printing, Gutenberg discovered.

To everyone's surprise, the Carmelite abbot consented to the decorative figures being used in the great manuscript Bible. Fr. Gunther also agreed to one printed Bible being illustrated in this fashion. Wilhelm's time and work in Mainz would not be wasted.

Wilhelm embellished 60 pages of the manuscript Bible, and his son half the pages in Volume I of a printed Bible, when disagreements developed. Wilhelm left the work abruptly, angry and disappointed. The engravers had stayed on a short time in Mainz to help Gutenberg with the two-color initial letters for the Psalter, and then returned to Basel.

CHAPTER 50

In 1453, the city of Constantinople, long a Christian bulwark against Islam, was conquered and occupied by the Turks, led by Sultan Mohammed II. Fearing that this catastrophe could lead to an invasion of Europe, Pope Nicholas issued immediate appeals to the Christian sovereigns and rulers for aid, urging them to send armies into the field to defeat the Sultan and protect Europe from the Infidels. Response to the appeal was apathetic. To induce cooperation, a special Indulgence would be given to those who contributed funds or personally took part in the Crusade.

Copies of the Indulgence must be distributed quickly throughout the Empire, and from Rome, Isenburg received instructions to have Gutenberg publish them as soon as possible.

"The printing press can serve the Church in another way," Cardinal Cusanus wrote, "though I do not wish Master Gutenberg's work on the Bibles to be disrupted. These are trying days and make it impossible for me to visit Mainz soon. Could some of the finished Bible pages be sent to Rome? It would hearten the Holy Father immensely to see what has been accomplished."

Gutenberg would send the Cardinal as many Bible pages as possible, Isenburg responded, and work on the Indulgences would begin immediately.

New, smaller and rounded letters would be cast for the Indulgences, but it should not take a lot of time to compose and print this single page, Gutenberg thought. Once printing began, they could produce a thousand copies in 10 days. He would continue to print the Bible on five presses and would print the Indulgence on the sixth press.

Composition and printing of the text turned out to be much more difficult than Gutenberg anticipated, however. The Indulgence was only 30 lines, but because the lines extended the full width of a page instead of being in two columns, it was hard to compose them and equally difficult to make corrections. The width of the lines also made the page forms hard for the printer to handle. Lines became uneven and individual letters shifted easily out of position. Fr. Gunther read and reread the text so many times, he thought he had earned an Indulgence himself. Six test prints were necessary before 1000 perfect copies could be printed.

All in all, it took two months to publish the one-page Latin Indulgence. When at last they were published, in October, 1454, everyone in the shop and in the scriptorium breathed a great "Amen!"

For Gutenberg, payment for the Indulgences was welcome because money for wages was no longer met by Fust's investment. And in order to have other income until the Bibles were published, he began work on a Turkish calendar, in German, for the year 1455.

Printing the Bible on five presses instead of six had not delayed that work appreciably, and at the beginning of 1455, only 100 pages in each volume remained to be printed. Now Gutenberg could predict with certainty that the Bibles would be finished before the end of the year.

As he watched his men work on the Bibles, Gutenberg was impressed by the speed and efficiency they had developed. In every phase of the work, fewer errors were made and printing progressed smoothly. The shop was a scene of constant activity, but there was no confusion. The men worked in silence. Only the presses were noisy, and there was a rhythm to the sound as the page forms were inked and slid into place and the heavy press screws lowered to meet the paper. As each page was printed and placed with the other sheets of the quire, it was fanned slightly to prevent the sheets from sticking together.

The reams of sheets had to be riffled also before they were printed or it was possible to pick up two sheets instead of one. Gutenberg noticed that the monks riffled the sheets again before making up the quires. No on knew why paper had this tendency to cling to itself, and paper cuts were common.

When 185 prints of each page had been made, the page forms were changed. Cleaned first with turpentine to remove the ink, they were un-tied, and the letters were carefully taken apart line by line and returned to the letter box. This was still painstaking work, but look-alike letters were seldom misplaced any more, Gutenberg noted with satisfaction.

Gutenberg had estimated the size of each volume at 640 pages, 320 folios or 40 quires. Actually, he believed now that Volume I would be half a quire or eight pages larger, 648 pages, and that Volume II would be a half quire less, 632 pages. By putting four teams of compositor-printers to work on the remaining pages instead of two, the Bible could be finished in half the time, Gutenberg reasoned.

Paralipomenon (Chronicles) through Job was 100 pages, Romans through St. Jude was 122-123 pages. Only 13-14 quires in all. Teams 1 and 3 were available, plus teams 5 and 6, now that the Indulgences were finished.

If the paper and vellum continued to arrive on schedule, if there were no further delays, Gutenberg told Schoeffer, they might have a Bible for Corpus Christi. The great June feast would be a splendid occasion, he thought, for announcing completion of the first printed Bible. Peter was happy at this prospect also because it meant that he and Christine could be married.

In the spring, Herr Fust announced the engagement of his daughter to Peter Schoeffer. Gutenberg pretended to be surprised, but Else and Henne knew of the romance and the men in the shop as well. The men liked Peter, but some thought he was seeking to further his own ambitions by courting Fust's daughter. Peter's family was not wealthy, but he was a guild member and Gutenberg's chief assistant. The bigger surprise was that Herr Fust had made no objection.

"A clever and enterprising fellow," was the way Henne Humbrecht described Peter. He and Else liked him and were sure they would like Christine also. Peter would become a master printer one day, Else said, which assured them that her uncle's work in Mainz would continue.

Sitting by the Fischtor one evening, Else, Henne and Gutenberg watched the barges tie up for the night. It was unusually warm for April and pleasant to feel the cool breezes and listen to the soft lapping of the water on shore. Everything on the east shore of the Rhein looked pink and gold as the sun set. Birds hidden in the trees above them were chattering goodnight. It was a peaceful time before shadows absorbed the river in blackness.

Cardinal Cusanus had requested another issue of the Indulgences, Gutenberg said. He was placing Peter in charge of the printing and felt that the experience gained from the first printing would make the work easier the second time. Gutenberg also confided that he intended to make Peter a partner when the Bibles were finished.

"The steel punches and copper matrices were his idea," Gutenberg said. "And as a full partner with me in the printing office, Peter will be respected even more by his father-in-law."

"It takes courage to accept Herr Fust as a father-in-law!" Else laughed. "A partnership would be a fine wedding present, Uncle."

"And I think a member of our family should be part of the business, too," Gutenberg went on. "I want two partners. I'd like you, Henne, to be a partner also. Peter will work in the shop and you would visit the abbots around Mainz to show them the Bibles and Psalters we have to sell. Would you like to do that, Henne?"

"You honor me, Uncle," Henne answered. "You honor us," he said, smiling at Else.

"Oh, you are a dear," Else cried and kissed Gutenberg on both cheeks. "Papa would be so proud!"

It pleased Gutenberg to think of having two young partners to share responsibilities in the printing office. At age 56, he must think of the future and provide for his heirs, he said. He wished that his nephew, Orte Gensfleisch, were alive and that Friele's son might benefit from the printing. But some things were not to be. One day Adam Gelthuss could join them.

When the Bibles were sold, Gutenberg would be free of debt. And he would have money from his share of the profits to enlarge the shop, to add a bindery, perhaps. A sense of well-being allowed Gutenberg to think ahead for the first time in four years. He would tell Fust at once about his plans for Peter.

CHAPTER 51

Fust came to the printing shop at Gutenberg's request, a bit surprised to be invited and wondering what the problem might be. Peter had told Fust about the second printing of the Indulgences. Publication of the Bibles would be delayed again, Fust supposed, and was not pleased at this prospect. Gutenberg should have paid him something on the outstanding loan from what he received from the first printing of the Indulgences, Fust thought. Could that be why the Master wanted to see him? To meet part of his obligations? At least Isenburg had not asked for additional funds. The work had gone on, Peter reported. Still, it must be something important for Gutenberg to want to see him.

Gutenberg offered Fust a glass of wine and began the conversation by saying that the Bibles would definitely be published in 1455. It had taken a long time, he admitted. He was pleased about the engagement between Christine and Peter.

"I have plans for Peter," Gutenberg said. "I have said nothing to him as yet, but I thought it would please you to know that when the Bibles are published, I shall ask Peter to become a partner. Your future son-in-law shall be more than my assistant, Herr Fust. This is my wedding present to him."

Fust put down his glass, plainly unprepared for such an announcement.

"Peter will be pleased, I'm sure," Gutenberg said, when Fust made no immediate comment.

"It is generous of you, Master," Fust answered, "but premature. You have mentioned partnership. I think it would be more fitting that you and I become partners. Before the Bibles are published. Peter has no money to put into the business!"

Gutenberg was astonished by Fust's proposal that they become partners. "I owe you a lot of money, Herr Fust," he said. "I would not presume to suggest partnership until you are repaid."

"Cancel what you owe me," Fust replied. "Consider the 1000 gulden as my investment in the Psalters, if you like. We will share the Bible profits. We could also share profits from the Psalters and all the books you will publish in the future. I know the printing office will be successful."

"I expect the Bible and Psalters to be profitable, yes," Gutenberg said. "But the equipment is worth much more than 1000 gulden, Herr Fust. If you wish to share in the Psalter profits, I suggest you reinvest."

"Reinvest!" Fust exploded. "You forget, Master, there wouldn't be any shop or any equipment if I had not lent you the money."

"There wouldn't be any shop if I had not made the equipment!" Gutenberg corrected. "I have also paid the shop expenses, wages and rent, myself this past year from the money I received for the Indulgences."

The Psalters would not be printed for some time, he added. He didn't know how many copies would be printed. "We can discuss partnership later, Herr Fust. But not now. Not now!" Gutenberg said. "And I never intended that Peter make an investment!"

Fust left the shop abruptly, and Gutenberg stood at the door, frowning and angry as he watched Fust walk down the street. Fust did not want Peter to become a partner, he thought, but to become a partner himself! Fust should cancel the loan and also increase his present investment to 1000 gulden, if he prized partnership and profits so highly! And why would a man of Fust's wealth and position even consider being a partner with a goldsmith? Fust was a guild member, but he was not a craftsman.

Gutenberg was still upset when he told Dr. Humery later that night what had happened. "I can hardly believe it," he said. "Cancel what you owe me! I'd never think of offering Fust partnership in exchange for cancelling my debt. The man would be insulted! And I choose my own partners! I always have and I always will!"

"Of course, 1000 gulden is less than the shop and the equipment are worth," Dr. Humery agreed. "If Fust wanted to share in the Psalter profits, he should reinvest. You are right about that, Johannes."

"Fust knows nothing about printing," Gutenberg went on. "He came forward with money for the Bibles and the Psalter letters because Cardinal Cusanus and Isenburg wanted the books printed!"

"But, Johannes," Dr. Humery answered, "don't you see? Fust knows you can pay him back when the Bibles are sold. And when this happens, you - not he -will own the equipment. Fust doesn't want to be repaid. He doesn't want you to bring in other partners. You made the equipment, yes, but he paid for it, and still has a lien on it. You used the money from the Indulgences for expenses. You should have reduced your debt to Fust! Fust wants to become a partner because he knows the Psalters will be profitable. Anything you publish in the future will be profitable to you alone, unless he is a partner."

"I don't want Herr Fust as a partner!" Gutenberg replied. "I thought he would be pleased about Peter."

"What if Fust demands payment now?" Dr. Humery asked. "If you can't repay the loan, Fust keeps the equipment and the books and shares nothing!"

"He shares nothing unless the Bibles are printed," Gutenberg said wearily. "We have a problem with the pages in Esdras and another in Romans. Any delay at this point means we won't be able to publish the Bibles by summer. I can't worry about Herr Fust, Conrad."

CHAPTER 52

So far Gutenberg's counts of the number of pages within the individual books of the Bible had been unfailingly correct. Some books had ended one or two lines short of a full column on a page, and this was acceptable. The Gospel of St. John had ended 12 lines short and compositor 4, ending this section, had begun Romans prologue properly in that space. The compositor of team 6, however, started at the top of a new column, and duplicated the 12 opening lines. When he had finished the 2-1/2 pages of the prologue, the text was 12 lines into Romans proper. The monk reading the test prints discovered the duplication. The compositors were angry with one another and blamed Schoeffer for the mixup.

Nothing had been printed, fortunately, and the page forms were adjusted so that Romans prologue ended a full column and Romans proper began a full column. This was done by removing the 12 lines that had been duplicated by compositor 6, and carefully moving lines back on three pages. It was a time-consuming job.

A more serious problem faced Gutenberg in Volume I. Here the two long books of Paralipomenon (Chronicles) and Esdras and the two pages of Oromanasses separating them, comprised one of the longest sections of the Bible, 136 pages, or 8-1/2 quires. Tobias to Psalms was 64 pages, four quires even, and Psalms by itself was also 64 pages, four quires. To expedite printing, Team 1, who had finished reprinting the 17 pages of Genesis and Kings, began printing a quire at Tobias while Team 5 completed the Psalms.

It had been difficult to know exactly how long Paralipomenon and Esdras would be. They seemed to be the same length, both 66 pages, though Gutenberg could not be sure. When Paralipomenon was finished, it was 66 pages and Oromanasses two pages. But would Esdras be 68 pages,

Gutenberg wondered.

"If Esdras is 66 pages, we'll have text on 134 pages and two blank pages," Gutenberg told Schoeffer. "If it is 67 pages, we'll have one blank page.

"That can't be possible, Master!" Schoeffer protested.

"I must have counted Oromanasses twice, that's all I can think of," Gutenberg said.

Schoeffer could see that Gutenberg was furious with himself, and he could not believe Gutenberg would make such a dreadful mistake. "Perhaps Esdras will be 68 pages, Master," he said. "Books 1-2-3 of Esdras, 40 pages, and Book 4, 28 pages."

"I don't think so. I hope I'm wrong, but we won't know for sure until the first three books are completed," Gutenberg answered. One or two blank pages were a certainty in Gutenberg's mind and where would they put them?

Agonizing over the situation wouldn't solve the problem, Schoeffer realized. A solution must be found. "Well, blank pages can't be together," he said, "facing each other or right and left. They must be separated. They must be on the left. And they can't be placed in the middle of a chapter."

"That's right, Peter," Gutenberg said, smiling at Schoeffer's quickness to assess the options open to them.

Any blank pages must follow a full right page, ideally at the end of a chapter, he thought. Nothing could be done, however, until they knew where chapters 1, 2 of 3 of Esdras ended, and if the number of pages matched the estimate. They must watch the work closely and be prepared to do what must be done.

"I'm sorry, Master," Schoeffer said sympathetically.

Gutenberg nodded. His assistant could handle a crisis, he thought.

At least the blank pages would be confined to Esdras. Perhaps they should not have started Tobias. If they had not gone ahead with Psalms, the blank pages would be at the end of the Bible. Gutenberg blamed no one but himself, but he knew Fr. Gunther would consider the fault his also. The work had been going too well, he thought. It could be ruined by errors like this.

Worn out from anxiety and tension, Gutenberg sat at his desk looking at some corrected pages Fr. Gunther had returned. The word Sanctus was misspelled in four places. Throwing the page aside, he turned his attention to other papers, bills, and statements which Schoeffer had passed on to him. Among them was a letter bearing Fust's seal on the back. Surprised and puzzled, Gutenberg opened it and read, then got up and walked suddenly out of the shop. A printer waiting to speak with him was dismissed without a word.

"What is it, Johannes?" Dr. Humery asked as Gutenberg appeared, his face flushed, and out of breath.

"You warned me. Now it has happened," Gutenberg said, handing him the letter. "Read this!"

Dr. Humery read the letter. Herr Fust was demanding that Gutenberg pay him 2000 gulden principal and interest within 90 days. Fust's statement listed two loans of 800 gulden each, 250 gulden interest on the first and 176 gulden interest on the second, for a total of 2026 gulden. Gutenberg was to be present at a hearing when the Mainz Council convened on the first Tuesday in May.

Dr. Humery was stunned. He sat down and read the letter again. He really did not think Fust would go so far, though the timing made his motives clear. It was less than a month since the conversation about partnership.

"Fust has included the whole amount, 1600 gulden," Dr. Humery said. "He makes no distinction between the capital investment for equipment, the loan for 1000 gulden, and his 600 gulden investment in the Bibles, the work for your joint profit. Plus 426 gulden interest! His figures must be proved."

"What can we do?" Gutenberg asked.

Dr. Humery suggested that Gutenberg be prepared to prove how the 1600 gulden was spent. No date was named for completion of the Bibles, he reminded him. No date was named for repayment of the loan.

"You aren't guilty of default or defraud, Johannes," Dr. Humery said. "The second agreement was never in writing, but in any event, I'm sure Fust can't insist on payment in 90 days."

Dr. Humery thought Gutenberg could refinance a loan for 1000 gulden, 2000 if necessary, through a bank in Frankfurt or in Strasbourg, with the Bibles as security.

"I'd need more than 90 days, I think, to do that," Gutenberg said, "and I would have to pay interest. Fust said I need not pay him any interest. Now he implies that the investment never existed! I'll talk with Custos Isenburg. The 600 gulden for expenses was not a loan!"

Else and Henne were horrified when Gutenberg told them of Fust's demands. Henne would go to Frankfurt at once, he said, and arrange for a loan.

"You must talk to Custos Isenburg and the archbishop, Uncle," Else said. "They must be told what Herr Fust is doing. It's stealing!"

"You have friends on the Council, too." Henne added, "and other friends who will help. Try not to worry, it's only a hearing."

They were encouraging, but Gutenberg was worried. And the work in the shop must go on. Schoeffer knows nothing about it, I'm sure, Gutenberg thought, and I won't tell him. I'll say nothing to the men either until after the hearing. Time enough then for them to know the Council's decision and whether it will affect the work on the Bibles and future printing.

Gutenberg did confide in the abbot of St. James, however, when he learned that Custos Isenburg was not in Mainz. The abbot was shocked. In his opinion, the Bibles were not in jeopardy, but Gutenberg and his shop might be. Clearly Fust's intentions threatened to ruin Gutenberg. The abbot would inform Isenburg immediately, he said, and keep him advised of what happened. He was confident that the Custos would do everything he could to help Gutenberg. Fr. Gunther and the abbot would attend the Council hearing.

Gutenberg was grateful for the abbot's assistance. Isenburg, he felt too, rather than the archbishop, would be most influential in his behalf.

Alone, Gutenberg could only think of Fust's offer of partnership. 'Cancel what you owe me,' Fust had said. Gutenberg did not regret declining Fust's offer. He did regret allowing the verbal agreement to stand. And what of his own time and work these five years? He had paid himself no regular salary. He had not borrowed 1600 gulden! The loan was for 1000 gulden and for equipment only. The Council must be fair, Gutenberg thought. They must determine what I properly owe and give me time to repay!

XIV. THE LAWSUIT
CHAPTER 53

Thirty magistrates were present when the Mainz Council met to hear Fust's complaint and Gutenberg's answer. Dr. Humery, Henne Humbrecht and Arnold Gelthuss sat with Gutenberg. Fust's brother, Jacob, and two clerics sat with Fust. Only a small number of other visitors were present.

It was a long session, lasting all morning and afternoon. When Henne returned home, he told Else everything that had happened. Fust had spoken first, he said, then Gutenberg. In the afternoon, each replied to the statements previously made by the other and to questions asked by the Council. The Council's verdict would be given in a fortnight.

Fust had testified that he gave Gutenberg 800 gulden on two occasions, that he had borrowed the money for him against interest and paid the interest himself. This interest totaled 250 gulden on the first 800 gulden, 140 gulden and 36 gulden on the second, making a total of 426 gulden. The interest was figured at six percent annually on each 100 gulden borrowed. Including the principal of 1600 gulden, Gutenberg owed a total of 2026 gulden. Fust stated that Gutenberg had paid none of the principal or interest in five years.

"Uncle explained very clearly the terms of their first agreement," Henne reported, "and how the money had been spent. He said that most of the first 800 gulden was a loan for the shop equipment he would make and which he gave as security for the loan. This equipment was for Uncle's gain, he said. Should he and Fust no longer be in agreement, Uncle would repay the loan and Fust would release his lien on the equipment."

"The first loan was not for the books then," Else said.

"No, it was not," Henne told her. "Uncle made this point also. He said he did not think he was obligated to apply the first 800 gulden to the common work of the books."

Fust hadn't mentioned either, Henne went on, that 300 gulden of this money was for operating expenses for one year. Fust was to pay 300 gulden annually for expenses, and did not. Gutenberg told the Council this, and also that the money had not been paid in full and at once, according to their agreement.

"The biggest surprise," Henne said, "was when Uncle said that although the 1450 written agreement stated he was to pay six percent interest on each 100 gulden, Fust had said he did not wish to collect this interest from him. The magistrate couldn't believe it.''

"But that was true," Else said.

"I know," Henne replied. "Uncle told me."

Gutenberg had offered then to provide a written account of how the second 800 gulden was spent, Henne continued. "The two agreements were not based on a partnership understanding but were a loan agreement and an investment agreement, he said. 'I have no intention of defaulting on the loan or on the investment Fust made in our common work of the Bibles,' Uncle said."

"Well, what did Fust say about that?" Else asked.

"He didn't say anything," Henne replied. "Fust complained again that Gutenberg hadn't shared all the common work with him, referring, it was thought, to the Indulgences and other printing to come, like the Psalters. Gutenberg repeated his statement that only the Bible printing had been undertaken for common or joint profit and that the metal and shop equipment was for his own benefit and did not constitute common work."

In the afternoon session, the Council magistrates had asked questions. How did the shop remain in operation if the expenses for wages and rent had not been paid, they wanted to know. Exactly how had the 1600 gulden been spent?

Gutenberg told them he used his own money and the money he had received from printing the Papal Indulgences and a calendar for two years' expenses. He said that a total of 700 gulden was spent for metal and shop equipment and 900 gulden for three years' operating expenses. The 700 gulden included 500 gulden for the Bible letters and 200 gulden for the new Psalter letters. The 900 gulden for expenses included Fust's investment of 600 gulden in the Bibles themselves.

"Fust wasn't asked about the investment agreement," Henne said. "I think this was a mistake. Only Uncle mentioned it. I also think it strange that Fust, of his own accord, didn't produce receipts for the 426 gulden interest he claims to have paid. Someone asked if he had receipts and Fust was insulted. 'You have my word,' he said, 'that I raised the money among Christians and Jews and have paid the interest and compound interest on it.' ''

"Then he should have receipts," Else said. "He should be made to produce them! I wonder if he really has them."

"I wonder how much money Fust really borrowed," Henne answered. "The money lenders should be asked to testify. But I doubt if any of them would dispute Fust's word before the Council."

An outraged Gutenberg, Dr. Humery and Gelthuss also discussed the hearing. "Fust's word means nothing!" Gutenberg exclaimed. "He told me one thing, now he tells the Council something else. I need not pay the interest, he said. And he knows 1600 gulden was not spent for common work. The equipment was not common work! Only the Bibles!"

"Fust ignored your distinction between loan and investment," Dr. Humery said. "The Council should have asked some questions about that. You are not obligated to return his investment."

"You see, Arnold," Gutenberg told his cousin, "The first 800 gulden was a loan, to buy metal and all the shop equipment and the expenses for one year. It took two years before we could begin printing the Bibles, and I paid a year's expenses myself. Then when we made the second agreement, 200 gulden was also a loan, for metal only, for the Psalter equipment. Fust invested the remaining 600 gulden in printing the Bibles. This money covered two years' expenses, and I paid the expenses again this year myself."

There was no way to prove the terms of the 1452 verbal agreement, however, Dr. Humery said. Gutenberg would give an account, but it was his word against Fust's. Who would the Council believe?

Gelthuss didn't think Fust had borrowed 1600 gulden. "I think the first 800 gulden was Fust's own money," he said. "You gave the equipment as security for your loan from him, but you hadn't made any equipment in 1450! I don't think anyone would loan Fust money on equipment that didn't exist. Or on the Cardinal's request only. Because if you died, Johannes, the creditors stood to lose 800 gulden. The Cardinal lost only the Bibles. Fust would have had to borrow on his own security. But I think he took the risk himself. I don't think Fust has receipts for 250 gulden interest on the first 800 gulden which he says he borrowed and loaned to you."

"Fust may have had other investors or he may have borrowed part of the second 800 gulden," Dr. Humery said, "but I agree, none of the first. The Cardinal and the Archbishop wanted the Bibles printed, and Fust provided the money. He's a very rich man. He didn't need to borrow."

The only reason Fust claimed to have borrowed 1600 gulden, in Dr. Humery's opinion, was so he could include 426 gulden interest on it. "He wants to make the debt as large as possible to insure that Johannes cannot pay. Even Fust might find it difficult to raise 2000 gulden in 90 days."

"And if Fust loaned money at six percent," Gelthuss added, "you know he borrowed it at five!"

It was ironic, Gutenberg thought, that his future, for the second time, should depend on a decision of the Mainz Council. A Council decision 27 years before had changed his life when guild members demanded that patricians also belong to guilds in order to serve. He had opposed the Council then and gone to Strasbourg with his brother, exiled from Mainz, because Friele's eligibility to serve on the Council had been denied. Now Gutenberg was hoping the Council would not oppose him and not deny him the right to keep his printing shop.

Most of the older Council members serving in 1428 had died, and many of those serving now were Gutenberg's contemporaries, men who knew him and his brother. Gutenberg felt he could count on their support. They know I speak the truth, he thought. Being a patrician was not a disadvantage any longer. He was still a guild member. He was still a citizen of Mainz. In five years he had built a large printing office and he had succeeded in printing almost 200 Bibles! This project, so nearly complete, would bring tremendous prestige to the city. Surely the Council would recognize these things.

Fust had friends on the Council too. Some were indebted to him and others were intimidated by him. Gutenberg didn't underestimate Fust's influence. My best support rests with the abbot and Custos Isenburg, he thought. They have influence on earth and in heaven! I shall pray for a just decision.

To members of the Mainz Council, it seemed that Fust wanted to take over ownership of the printing office, but they had to agree with Chairman Bayer that Fust's demand for 2000 gulden in 90 days was unreasonable. Five years was a long time for anyone to wait for repayment of money, Bayer told the Council, but Fust would be repaid when the Bibles were finished and sold. Publication of the Bibles must not be threatened, Bayer said. Master Gutenberg must be given time to finish the work or the Council risked censure itself from the archbishop. Herr Fust had waited this long for his money, surely he could wait a little longer.

The facts of the case were difficult to understand. Fust had implied that 1600 gulden was all for their common work and that the common work included the equipment and the books. But no partnership existed, Gutenberg had said. Gutenberg made it plain that the capital investment in equipment was for his own gain, and the common work was the books only. He had also distinguished between a loan for the equipment and an investment in the work of the books. Fust had not loaned money for the common work, in other words, as Gutenberg defined it.

"If the loan was for equipment and the investment was in the Bibles," Bayer said, "Fust isn't entitled to 1600 gulden. Fust may have borrowed the money at interest, but he cannot claim this interest from Gutenberg if he invested part of the money."

The capital investment for equipment should not be applied to the work of the books, Bayer believed, and should not be confused with an investment in the common work. If Gutenberg gave a written account of how the second 800 gulden was spent, his account and Fust's statement should agree.

"How much did Master Gutenberg borrow then?" one Councilman asked.

"More to the point, how much did Herr Fust borrow?" Bayer replied. "If Fust borrowed 1600 gulden, then he should have receipts for the interest. If Gutenberg borrowed 1600 gulden, why should he share profits with anyone? Everything, equipment and the books, would be for his own gain. But he said this wasn't the case."

"Part of the second 800 gulden must have been Fust's investment," another councilman conceded. "Didn't Fust put any of his own money into the project?"

Whether Fust had borrowed 1600 gulden or whether part of it was from his own funds, they argued, Gutenberg was still obliged to pay the interest. But only on that which constituted a loan, Bayer insisted. An investment, however, could not be proved because the second agreement was not in writing.

Why was the amount of interest different on the two agreements when the principal was the same? No one knew. Should Fust be asked to present receipts for the interest or was his word sufficient? On this critical point the council was divided. Did the Council recognize the common work as printing of the Bibles only? Again there was disagreement. In the end, a compromise was worked out.

"I propose that we allow Master Gutenberg six months to finish the Bibles," Bayer said, "and to repay Fust, if he can, in that time. I will concede that Gutenberg must pay the principal and interest as stated in the 1450 agreement, or 1050 gulden, because it was used primarily for equipment for his own gain. His account of the second agreement in 1452 will show what he spent for the common work or work for joint profit. Printing of the Bibles will be considered that common work, and Gutenberg need not repay what he received for this common work. Whatever Gutenberg received in addition, for his own gain, he must repay."

But if Fust raised the second 800 gulden against interest, it was argued, Gutenberg must pay this interest also, 176 gulden. Bayer thought the Council should demand receipts for the interest, but his motion was defeated. Fust would be given the choice of proving by oath or by reputable information the amount of money he borrowed and the amount of interest paid. Those in favor of the receipted information gave in on this point in exchange for a six month's delay before the oath would be sworn. The date set for Fust's sworn statement was November 6, 1455.

Bayer was not satisfied with the verdict. He was certain that the capital investment for equipment only had been arranged by loan. And even if Fust had loaned Gutenberg money for the common work, why should he charge Gutenberg interest when they would both share in the profits when the Bibles were sold? The books would sell for a lot of money! Fust's share could be twice 1600 gulden. Bayer thought any interest Fust paid on money he may have borrowed for the common work was his responsibility. And sharing profits made Fust an investor, in Bayer's opinion, however he got the money.

"At least by defining the common work as printing the Bibles only, the Council has obligated Gutenberg to repay less than 2026 gulden, and he has been given six months to raise the money," Bayer told one of Gutenberg's friends. "We did what we could. I hope it is enough."

Bayer was not resigned to forgiving Fust the written receipts. For someone known to keep detailed records of revenues received and money spent, and known to be involved in many other financial matters, it was incredible that Fust did not present proof of interest paid when he made his complaint.

Why hadn't a written agreement been made in 1452, Bayer wondered. Why hadn't Gutenberg and Fust become partners? Why had Gutenberg been the only one to mention the word investment? And what had Gutenberg said about the 300 gulden annual expense money? Used for expenses, wages, rent, paper, parchment, ink? Bayer couldn't remember. But surely the cost of paper and vellum could not have been included in 300 gulden. Paper and vellum were not tools and equipment. No doubt these materials came from a monastery, and no one had asked the cost, Bayer decided.

Why did Herr Fust want to ruin Gutenberg? Why should Fust want to own a printing shop? There were still more questions than answers, and Bayer doubted if they would ever be fully resolved. The whole affair was very puzzling and made more complicated by the conflicting testimony.

HOW THE 1600 GULDEN WAS SPENT

1st 800 gulden	2nd 800 gulden
800 principal	200 loan (18 gulden interest
250 interset	600 investment (176 gulden interest
1050 gulden	

Gutenberg's totals:	Council totals:	Fust totals:	
1050	1050	1050	1600 principal
200	200	800 or	426 interest
18	176	176	
1268 gulden	1426 gulden	2026 gulden	2026 gulden

CHAPTER 54

Gutenberg and his friends had mixed reactions to the Council verdict. Six month's grace represented a partial victory, and it was important. But the amount Gutenberg was to repay was still more than it should be.

"I owe Fust 1000 gulden principal and no interest," Gutenberg said. "This is what I borrowed. This was the amount of the two loans. And it does not apply to the work of the books." His account of the second agreement would show 600 gulden spent for the common work, he said, and 200 gulden for equipment.

Dr. Humery did not think Gutenberg could avoid paying the interest, however, on the first agreement, and the Council had said he must pay all the interest on the second agreement, if Fust borrowed the money, and whatever had been spent for his own gain.

"This comes to 1050 gulden, plus 176 gulden, plus 200 gulden, or 1426 gulden," he told Gutenberg.

Gelthuss did not agree. He had analyzed the 176 gulden interest, he said, which represented six percent interest and one percent compound interest on 600 gulden.

"You say 600 gulden was Fust's investment in the common work. I see no reason for you to pay interest on this. At the most, I'd say you should pay 1050 gulden and 200 gulden but only 18 gulden interest on it, or 1268 gulden total."

"And I say," Dr. Humery answered, "of the three sets of figures, Johannes must be prepared to pay the largest amount. If Fust swears he borrowed all the money, and concedes no capital investment for the equipment for your own gain, and no investment by himself in the common work, and declares that the equipment, books, everything was common work, you must raise 2026 gulden. However much Fust borrowed at interest, however it was spent, becomes the amount you must pay."

Gutenberg would mortgage his home, if necessary, he said. He would also contact his friends in Strasbourg for help. The Bibles should have been finished by Corpus Christi, but now Gutenberg wasn't sure if six months was enough time.

"I will send the four Gospels to Strasbourg," Gutenberg said. "I should get orders for complete Bibles on the basis of that sample. And I will reprint the Missal."

Rudi Sogenloch was optimistic. He was sure the books would be printed soon and that from sale of Gutenberg's share, the loan could be repaid and Fust's investment returned. "Whatever Fust swears to, Johannes, you will have the money," Rudi assured him.

Henne Humbrecht doubted that Fust would produce any receipts or change any of the statements he had made at the hearing. "The Council has given Uncle some consideration," he told Else. "The six month's delay before final settlement is an advantage to him, and a disadvantage to Fust. However, I think we must try to raise money ourselves and not depend on selling the Bibles."

Else thought this was wise. "Go to Frankfurt, Henne, and see what you can do," she said. "It is a frightful amount of money."

"I'd like to have seen Fust's face when he heard the verdict," Henne smiled. "He must have been furious!"

Fust never anticipated a postponement, and he and his brother, both, were furious at what they considered betrayal by their friends on the Council.

"Gutenberg doesn't need time to finish the Bibles!" Jacob Fust said. "Schoeffer can finish the Bibles! The books will be printed whether Gutenberg keeps the shop or not!"

"The verdict gives Gutenberg time to raise the money!" Fust retorted. "I can prevent this in Mainz, but Gutenberg might succeed in getting funds elsewhere!"

It wasn't clear to Jacob Fust, however, why his brother was so determined to acquire the printing office. "What difference does it make to you if Gutenberg manages to recover the lien on the printing equipment?" he asked. "The other investors, all of us, will get our money back when the books are sold, from your share of the profits."

"Of course," Fust snapped. "You lose nothing whoever owns the shop. But the equipment is valuable! It's future business I'm thinking of!"

When the three other investors arrived at Fust's home to discuss the verdict, all of them were concerned. They had invested in the Bibles and Psalter, they thought. Would the books be printed? Was Peter Schoeffer going to manage the shop? Fust had explained very little to them at the time the investments were made. Even the lawsuit had come as a surprise, and its outcome remained uncertain.

The Bibles and Psalters were only the first books to be printed for the Church, Fust told them. Mainz was the only city where volume printing was done with metal letters. Suppose Mainz was given a monopoly for all liturgical printing from Rome?

"There is a fortune to be made here," Fust said, "and if I own the shop, we shall prosper for years to come!"

Now Jacob and the others understood why Fust had started proceedings against Gutenberg and why he demanded 2000 gulden in 90 days, before the Bibles could be completed and sold. Gutenberg did not know about the possibility of printing from Rome. Fust, who had closer connections with the papal legate and the archbishop than anyone in Mainz, had kept the printing monopoly a secret, even from his brother.

"It was shrewd of you, Herr Fust, not to mention the word 'investment' in your complaint," one of the men remarked. "We gave you money which you invested for us. You said you borrowed it at interest."

"Do you want to give me receipts for the interest?" Fust laughed. "Nothing was in writing in 1452, remember. And if the Council had asked for an explanation about investment, I would have denied any investment. I was not a partner with Gutenberg. Why should I invest?"

"I thought you were partners," an investor said.

"No," Fust replied, without elaboration.

"What about Peter Schoeffer? He is important to your plans also."

"Yes, he is," Fust acknowledged. "He will manage the shop."

"But not for you, if Master Gutenberg is able to raise 2000 gulden," the investor observed.

There was little chance Gutenberg could get that much money anywhere, Fust assured him. Or that Schoeffer would leave. He was not worried, he said. Fust was angry that the Council had not issued an immediate verdict, but he foresaw no difficulties. Gutenberg's written account of the second agreement? It was worthless!

Privately, Fust's investors had other questions, but did not ask them. Johann Fust did not encourage questions about his motives or methods. Yet the investors wondered who besides themselves had loaned money to Fust, or to Gutenberg. Was Fust acting on his own? Or was someone in the Church conspiring with Fust at Gutenberg's expense? It seemed strange, for one thing, that the Church had not contributed to the Bible project. Paper and vellum were expensive and must have been purchased separately, through a monastery perhaps.

The amount of 2000 gulden was ten to twenty times the yearly salary of most magistrates. One investor had just paid fifteen gulden for a good horse. He could mount a calvary unit of 100 men for 2000 guilden, he said. If Gutenberg could raise half that amount in six months, it would be a miracle.

More than one of the investors found himself sympathetic to Gutenberg and was disturbed by Fust's quick and ruthless attempt to take the printing office away from him. The Master was printing the Bible. after all, and he should be allowed to finish the work. Why hadn't Fust and Gutenberg become partners, they wondered. Fust had let them think a partnership existed in order to secure their investment. Yet why should Fust want to be partners with a goldsmith?

If somehow Gutenberg did raise 2000 gulden, he would keep the printing office. He should keep it, some said. They would not lose their investment whoever published the Bibles. But if other business came from Rome and Fust was not associated with Gutenberg, only the Master would benefit.

Fust had invested their money wisely, partner or not, the investors argued. He was within his right to bring the matter of a 2000 gulden debt to court. If he wanted the shop, he had to act now. After the Bibles were printed would be too late. And the printing office would continue to prosper with Schoeffer in charge.

Fust seemed more concerned about the final verdict, however, than he let on, they thought. He was not as confident as he pretended to be. Yet if Fust wanted something, he got it. All of the investors knew this.

CHAPTER 55

Despite Gutenberg's precautions not to alarm the men in the shop or to distrupt work on the Bibles, they had learned of the hearing and anxiously awaited the result. The work had gone on as usual, but speculation was high about what would happen now that the Council had given its decision. The tremendous sum of 2000 gulden, some said 5000, was more money than any of them ever saw in a lifetime. How could the Master possible raise it? And where did Schoeffer's loyalties lie? Schoeffer was going to marry Fust's daughter. Gutenberg shouldn't trust him!

Gutenberg wanted to put to rest the rumors and anxieties which upset his men, and he spoke to them soon after the verdict had been announced. The shop would not close. The work on the Bibles would not stop, he told them, though there would be some changes in the schedule.

Gutenberg hoped to finish the Bibles inside of six months, he said, but the work must not be rushed or delayed. Above all, he cautioned, they must avoid careless mistakes. The compositors would report to Pannartz and the printers to Kefer. Kefer and Pannartz would continue to work with Fr. Gunther and Schoeffer in Gutenberg's absence.

Gutenberg also wanted to print another edition of the Missal. This could be done rather quickly, he thought, because better than half of the page forms were still intact and stored on the shelf. The sixth press would be used, and Johann and Wenderlin von Speyer were assigned to the work. Gutenberg would order another bale of paper, 5000 folio sheets, for 50 new copies of the book.

"I know I can count on you to help me," Gutenberg told the men.

"We will do our best, Master," they promised.

"And I will do my best to raise the money I need," Gutenberg answered.

Gutenberg's spirit gave the men confidence. They were glad to know that work on the Bibles would continue, and thought that reprinting the Missal was a good idea also. No Master in Mainz was respected more than Gutenberg, and no one respected him more at this moment than Peter Schoeffer.

Peter had known nothing about Fust's plans, and the lawsuit and Council hearing had been terribly upsetting to him, Fust's testimony most of all. The verdict had favored Gutenberg, and Peter was glad of that. But now he found himself in a very awkward and difficult situation: loyal to Gutenberg, disillusioned and angry with Christine's father, and placed in charge of men who were suspicious and distrustful of him.

Peter couldn't blame the men for their feelings. He was suspicious, too, of Fust and his intentions! What would Fust say to him, Peter wondered. Did Fust expect him to manage the shop if Gutenberg lost it? Could this be why he had consented to the marriage?

"It doesn't matter who owns the shop, does it?" Christine asked, annoyed by Peter's preoccupation with Master Gutenberg's problems with her father.

Christine looked forward to their Sunday afternoon walks along the Rheinstrasse, and today Peter had talked only about the printing shop and the lawsuit. Christine knew that Gutenberg owed her father a lot of money, but she was not interested in the lawsuit. She wanted to talk about the wedding.

"Papa has promised us a house, Peter. Isn't that wonderful!" she bubbled.

"The printing shop is important too," Peter said, refusing to change the subject. "What your father is doing is wrong, Christine. Can't you see?"

"But you will work for Papa just like you do for Master Gutenberg," Christine answered. "You may even become a partner. Oh, Peter, you mustn't worry so. You haven't even noticed my new dress!"

It was useless, Peter decided, to discuss his concerns with Christine, and perhaps it was best that he not discuss them with her. He quickly made amends by smiling and giving her the compliment she had been waiting for.

Peter waited in the cloister yard of St. Christoph's for Fr. Gunther to return from evening prayers. He wanted to talk with him about the verdict. It was annoying for Peter to be an observer of the lawsuit, hearing what had happened but not seeing or understanding all that was going on. And he was concerned about what he could do to help Gutenberg. Frustration showed in his face, and Peter spoke abruptly when Fr. Gunther appeared.

"Isn't there anything we can do to help the Master?" Peter demanded. "He must keep the printing shop! I'll resign if he doesn't. I'll go back to Gernsheim and open a printing office there. Herr Fust must not..."

"Peter, Peter," the priest answered. "We are as troubled as you are. But we must not let concern distract us from our responsibilities. We must finish the Bibles! Whether Gutenberg keeps the shop or not. Do you really want to go to Gernsheim? You know Herr Fust will have the marriage annulled if you resign."

Shocked by the blunt statements, Peter was silent.

They could do nothing to change whatever might happen between Fust and Gutenberg, Fr. Gunther went on. But by completing Gutenberg's work, by publishing the Bibles and the Psalter, they were helping the Master as no one else could. And it was possible that Gutenberg would keep the shop.

"Herr Fust is a powerful man, but Master Gutenberg is not powerless against him," the priest said. "You must stay, Peter."

Peter wanted to stay, for Gutenberg's sake and his own, he said, but not to accommodate Herr Fust. "What do you think is going to happen, Father?" he asked.

"I don't know, the priest replied. "Pray and work. And don't let Herr Fust or the men upset you. Keep your own counsel, Peter."

As Peter considered his position more soberly, he knew this was good advice. He thought of what Christine had said, 'work for Papa..may even become a partner.' I could not become a partner with Fust, Peter thought. I hope to become his son-in-law. But I would never be both.

It was strange, he reflected. Until now I have had no personal reason to dislike Herr Fust. The man was autocratic and overbearing, but he could be generous and had shown a genuine interest and respect for Peter's ability. Master Gutenberg could be stubborn and exacting, but he was honest and forthright. He was kind and unassuming. Peter had affection for Gutenberg. Fust did not invite affection from anyone except Christine. The two men were so different, Peter thought. How they became associated in the Bible printing he had wondered many times.

For Fust to bring suit against Gutenberg was contemptible, and they could only wait and see what the outcome would be, Peter realized. My job is to finish the Bibles, he told himself. This I can and will do. God help me!

The fall wedding was postponed. Fust was too occupied with other things, he said, and thought the following spring would be a better time. Christine was very unhappy about the change in plans, but Peter was strangely relieved. He was much too busy and agreed that they should wait until the Bibles were finished, or the lawsuit resolved. "Your father is right," he told her. "We can wait. It's just a few months."

Some of Fust's friends thought postponement of the marriage was unfortunate. Fust was taking Peter's presence at the shop for granted, they said. A son-in-law would be under obligation and now Peter was relieved of such obligation. There was no guarantee that he would remain in Mainz. On the other hand, the friends argued, the promise of marriage was inducement to stay. Peter would not leave Christine, they said.

CHAPTER 56

When Custos Isenburg returned to Mainz shortly after the verdict had been given, he was already fully informed about the hearing and the Council's decision. Furious at Fust's move to gain control of the printing shop, Isenburg had exerted pressures of his own on members of the Council. The verdict was not everything he wanted, but Gutenberg had been given time, enough time, he hoped, to finish the Bibles. Fust's statements about the money he had borrowed and given to Gutenberg, Isenburg knew not to be true, and before the oath was sworn, something must be done. It was unthinkable that Gutenberg should lose his shop now.

Isenburg discussed the lawsuit with Archbishop Erbach. "It was my suggestion that Fust make an investment!" Isenburg said. "I can corroborate Gutenberg's statement about investment. The Council should know this, and about the cardinal's contribution as well. His gift for paper and vellum should be a secret no longer!"

The lawsuit is not our affair, Custos," the archbishop replied sternly. "It is a matter between Gutenberg and Fust. I shall not interfere and counsel you not to interfere."

"But I am sure Fust gave money from his own funds initially," Isenburg argued. "Wasn't this your understanding also?"

"If Fust says he borrowed it, I believe him," Erbach answered. "Who owns the printing office does not concern me. I have more important things that require my attention."

As he left the electoral palace, Isenburg was upset. By keeping silent, Erbach is protecting Fust, he thought bitterly. Why? Unless Erbach himself was one of Fust's investors! That possibility had not occurred to Isenburg before, but if true, it would be to Erbach's advantage for Fust to take over the printing office. The archbishop had denied any interest in the outcome of the lawsuit, but in fact, he could be prejudiced.

Angry now and determined to act, Isenburg decided to write Cardinal Cusanus and ask his permission to testify before the Council. A word from Cusanus would make a difference and force the Council to reconsider the testimony and the verdict.

Taking the abbots of St. James and St. Victor into his confidence, Isenburg told them what he planned to do and asked them to write the cardinal also. It was important that Cusanus received confirmation from more than one source of events in Mainz and possible result if nothing was done.

The Collegiate abbot respected Isenburg for taking the bold step of contacting Cusanus directly, and he was sure the cardinal would intervene. He was equally sure that Fust would swear he had borrowed 1600 gulden unless the cardinal intervened.

"Cardinal Cusanus knows about the lawsuit," the abbot said. "And he did not impress me as a man who will keep silent when that silence damages another. Of course we will write to him."

"The Council must have his statement before the oath is sworn," Isenburg said. "Before November 6. I hope we are not too late."

"The lawsuit is a local affair, however," the St. James abbot cautioned. "Cusanus may think he should allow Erbach to decide whether or not to present evidence repudiating Fust's testimony."

"That would be unwise," Isenburg answered.

"We shall do what we can," the abbot said. "And perhaps Herr Fust can be persuaded to change his mind."

"Fust is lying," Gutenberg said bluntly, when he sat down with Isenburg to discuss the situation. "The first agreement did not apply to the work of the books, and I don't think he borrowed the money. The second aggreement was a loan and investment. He may have borrowed some of this, but I shouldn't have to pay the interest! I owe him 1000 gulden only for the shop equipment.

"Fust wanted to become partners, did I tell you that?" Gutenberg went on. "Before he filed the suit, he said 'cancel what you owe me and we will share in everything.' I said 'Let's wait until the Bibles are published.' I do not want Fust as a partner."

This information came as a surprise to Isenburg. "Now Fust is forcing you to buy out his interest, in other words, and hoping you can't raise 2000 gulden."

"But I must raise at least 1400 gulden before the Bibles are published and sold," Gutenberg said, "excluding Fust's investment."

"You must abide by the Council verdict, yes," Isenburg told him, "as it stands."

"I don't understand why Fust was so anxious to continue our association," Gutenberg said. "We don't get along. We never became friends."

"Herr Fust expects to receive enormous printing revenues from Rome, Master. The Indulgences, he believes, are just the beginning," Isenburg replied.

"Is that true?" Gutenberg asked.

"Perhaps, Master, perhaps."

"Why doesn't Archbishop Erbach tell the Council what happened," Gutenberg asked.

"Why indeed!" Isenburg answered angrily.

"The paper and vellum cost 1600 gulden also, you know," Gutenberg said. "The cardinal and the abbot paid for these materials. Fust did not."

"Yes, I know," Isenburg replied. "We know it, and Fust and Erbach know it, and soon the Council will know it too, Master. Two of the abbots and myself have written the Cardinal. He has been told everything, and, we are sure, will have a statement to make before Fust swears the oath. I have asked his permission to address the Mainz Council."

"Oh, that is good news! Why didn't you tell me this before?" Gutenberg chided.

Isenburg was not offended by the remark. "Nothing must be said to anyone, Master, until I am able to present the Cardinal's statement," he said. "We must wait and hope there are no delays."

Under Schoeffer's guidance, the men worked hard to keep the work on schedule. A second issue of the Papal Indulgence was ordered, 31 lines this time, and printed with fewer problems. Still, it took a month to publish another 1000 copies, and printing of the Missal was delayed. The new Psalter letters had been cast. Schoeffer did not anticipate any serious difficulties with the Bible, except perhaps in the books of Esdras.

There a problem did develop, as Gutenberg feared it might, if all of Esdras was to be 68 pages. The first three books were 39 pages, with Esdras 3 ending on a right page. If Esdras 4 was 28 pages, it too would end on a right page, followed by a blank page. But what if it was 27 pages? There would be two blank pages together at the end!

Esdras 3 ended with a full text page. The next page, on the left, could be blank, Schoeffer reasoned. If Esdras 4 was 27 pages, it would still end on a right page, and the second blank page could follow on the left. The two blank pages would be separated by almost two quires. On the other hand, if Esdras 4 was 28 pages, only the one blank page after Esdras 3 would be necessary.

Schoeffer was undecided whether to go ahead and insert the first blank page and continue printing Quire 31, or stop and wait until all the pages of Esdras 4 had been composed. To do this would take a month and hold up many page forms.

"We have a choice," Schoeffer told Kefer. "One blank page before *or* after Esdras 4, if Esdras 4 is 28 pages. Two blank pages, before *and* after Esdras 4, if it is 27 pages. We can't stop printing. It's taken ten weeks to print Esdras 1-2-3. It will take seven weeks to print Esdras 4. We must insert a blank page now."

"We should wait and let Master Gutenberg decide," Kefer said.

"But we can't wait," Schoeffer insisted. "And we can't risk two blank pages together at the end of Esdras 4 if we start without a blank page at the beginning."

Esdras 1-2-3, including the blank page, was 40 pages, he explained. Esdras 4 could be 27 or 28 pages. If it was 27, another blank page would have to follow at the end. If it was 28 pages, a second blank page would not be necesary.

"It's your responsibility!" Kefer said angrily. "Esdras 4 might be 29 pages! Then we'd have to do all of Quire 31 over again, composing and printing! Think of the time and paper lost, if you're wrong."

Schoeffer was right to put a blank page after Esdras 3 and not to delay printing of Esdras 4, Gutenberg said, when told of the decision. It was the only thing to do. Esdras 4 would not be 29 or 28 pages, he said. It would be 27. So Schoeffer would place the other blank page after Esdras 4 and before Tobias. Gutenberg was positive that all of Esdras would be 66 pages of text, and positive also that Tobias to Psalms was 64 pages, the same length as Psalms.

"Just remember, Esdras ends with a half quire of eight pages, Peter," Gutenberg reminded him. "Don't forget that!"

After almost 500 pages of continuous text, there would be two blank pages in Volume I of the Bible. It was a bitter reality for Gutenberg to accept.

The 68 pages of Esdras and the 68 pages preceding totalled 136 pages or 8-1/2 quires. Tobias through Psalms was 128 pages, or 8 quires. Volume I would have a total of 648 pages, 40-1/2 quires, exactly what Gutenberg had figured.

Peter Schoeffer had learned valuable lessons from the misfortunes in Esdras, and he had gained confidence in his own judgment. Miscounting two pages in Paralipomenon and Oromanasses had caused a change in the number of book pages which fell within each quire. Counting the pages in each book correctly was important, and counting the book pages in each quire was even more important, it seemed. Sometimes adjustments were possible, sometimes they were not.

Peter hoped Volume II of the Bible would not present any major problems. One blank page before the New Testament had been allowed. According to plan, total pages should be 632, or 39-1/2 quires.

CHAPTER 57

In Strasbourg, Count von Ramstein received Gutenberg's letter informing him of the lawsuit and asking for help. The Count was old and not in good health, but he hurried to consult with Nicholas Heilmann at the paper mill and his brother, Fr. Anthony. Gutenberg's friends were tremendously proud of his work on the Bibles, and the news from Mainz shocked and angered all of them.

Another lawsuit was disturbing. They remembered the Dritzehn suit fifteen years before, when Georg and Nicholas Dritzehn had tried to become partners with Gutenberg. The Master had won that case when the court upheld his partnership agreement stating that heirs could not become partners.

Fr. Anthony wondered if Herr Fust had also wanted to become a partner, been refused, and was seeking revenge by trying to take over the printing shop. In 1439, only 100 florin were involved. Now the sum of 2000 gulden was unbelievable.

"Of course we will help Johannes," Nicholas said. "How much money does he need?"

"The 2000 gulden includes 400 gulden interest and Fust's investment of 600 gulden," von Ramstein answered. "We could raise 1000 gulden,

I think, don't you?"

The Count would be able to contribute 500 gulden, he said. Nicholas Heilmann would give 350 gulden. The abbey of St. Arbogast and St. Thomas church would advance 100 gulden each for the Bibles they wanted to purchase, Fr. Anthony said. He was sure the score or more Benedictine, Cisterian, and Dominican houses in Alsace would want Bibles also, when they saw the impressive Gospel pages Gutenberg had sent, but there was no time then to visit these monasteries.

The money could be sent safely, in gold, with the next shipment of paper, Nicholas suggested. His brother, Andreas, and one of the monks would accompany the shipment.

"I shall write Johannes at once," von Ramstein said, "and tell him that we are sending 1050 gulden. I'm sure he can raise the rest in Mainz."

He would advise Gutenberg, moreover, to pay the 400 gulden interest on the loan and to refund Fust's investment of 600 gulden. There was too much at stake, the printing shop and the Bibles, he believed, to think that Fust would settle for anything less than the full amount he demanded.

"The Dritzehns coveted the printing equipment and the books," Fr. Anthony said. "Herr Fust is no better than they. But he is the papal collector of revenues! A man of such position is a much more dangerous adversary. Johannes says he has not told the truth." Von Ramstein and Nicholas agreed.

Dr. Humery traveled to Fulda to see his friend, the Senator, and returned to Mainz with a pledge of 500 gulden. Humery himself, Gelthuss, Henne Humbrecht and Rudi Sorgenloch raised another 450 gulden between them in Frankfurt.

His friends' efforts and generosity touched Gutenberg deeply, especially the unexpectedly large amount of money from Strasbourg and from the Senator. It meant that he did not have to mortgage Hof zum Gutenberg and could reprint the Missal later. It was also encouraging to know that he could look forward to selling many Bibles in Alsace. From his own funds, Gutenberg could raise 200 gulden. November 6 was still a month away, and he had in his hand 1700 gulden. With the Senator's pledge, promised to arrive before Fust swore his oath, he would be able to return Fust's investment and repay 2000 gulden.

Dr. Humery had thought it would be impossible to get all the money. Now he said, they should talk with Chairman Bayer and tell him that

Gutenberg was prepared to meet the terms of the Council verdict. And if Fust acknowledged his investment of 600 gulden and accepted 1426 gulden, then he could keep his half share of the Bibles.

"Fust's share is about 75 Bibles," Gutenberg said, "and his profit from sale will be over 300 gulden. I don't think he will want to cancel this part of the 1452 agreement."

"But he wants the equipment, Johannes," Dr. Humery answered, "so you must pay 2026 gulden. Then, of course, Fust forfeits any share of the Bibles. You are free of all debt to him and all the profits are yours also. From these profits, you can repay us, your good friends in Strasbourg, and still have money to enlarge the printing shop."

"The Psalter profits are what Fust wants," Gutenberg said. "I told him if he wanted to become a partner, he should reinvest in the Psalters. Not just cancel my loan of 1000 gulden. Well, if it costs me 2000 gulden, it's worth it to keep my printing office. We will meet with Herr Bayer and Fust as soon as possible."

Chairman Bayer was a merchant, not a lawyer, but his experience and intuition told him there were still missing pieces in the tangle of testimony of the Fust/Gutenberg case.

Bayer noted that the abbot of St. Stephan's showed interest in the proceedings from the beginning, and he wondered if this meant that the monastery had given the paper and vellum. Perhaps Fust was not the only one to help finance the Bible project.

Fust's insistence that he had borrowed 1600 gulden still seemed strange to Bayer. A wealthy man like Fust might arrange to borrow for, and lend large amounts of money to, someone like the archbishop. Why should he do this for Gutenberg? Fust could afford to lend Gutenberg at least part of the money himself!

Bayer liked Dr. Humery's proposal that Gutenberg and Fust meet with him, and invited Fust and his brother, Jacob, to meet Gutenberg and Dr. Humery in his office. Should he ask another Council member to attend, Bayer wondered, and decided he would not. The hearing would be private, and he would report the result to the Council himself. Perhaps the dispute could be settled and a judgment made by the Council without Fust's oath being sworn.

"Master Gutenberg has here a record of how the second 800 gulden was spent," Bayer began. "The account shows that 200 gulden was spent for shop equipment for his own gain, and 600 gulden for the common work of printing the Bibles. The 600 gulden was spent, specifically, for wages and rent for two years, and constituted Herr Fust's investment in the project. The two of you are to share equally in the Bibles printed and in the sales therefrom. You may have raised this money at interest, Herr Fust, but on the investment portion, Master Gutenberg is not obliged to pay interest."

Fust started to protest, but Bayer continued.

"Master Gutenberg is prepared to repay the money loaned to him as stated in the first 1450 agreement, 800 gulden, plus interest. He will repay the second loan of 200 gulden for equipment and 18 gulden interest on it. He is also prepared to refund the 600 gulden investment, conceding no interest, in which case you relinquish your claim to a share of the Bibles."

"I acknowledge no investment!" Fust answered angrily. "And I do not intend to relinquish my share of the Bibles! My account shows that Master Gutenberg received 1600 gulden from me, all of which I raised against interest and will so swear! How it was spent, for equipment or the books, whether it was a loan and/or investment, as he says, does not matter. Unless Gutenberg repays 2000 gulden, he forfeits his share of the Bibles to me!"

"I think the first 800 gulden was your own money, Herr Fust," Gutenberg said evenly. "It was a loan for equipment only, and three years ago you told me I could forget the interest on it. Now you say you borrowed it against interest. And the second 800 gulden as well. All or part of this you may have borrowed, but I only borrowed 200 gulden of it from you, also for equipment. The equipment was never considered common work, only the Bibles in which you made an investment of 600 gulden."

Bayer and Dr. Humery were astonished by Gutenberg's statement. Fust's expression changed. The concise assessment was not made as an accusation, but Fust appeared to be defensive. His brother was plainly agitated.

"Your sworn statement does not matter, Herr Fust," Gutenberg went on. "Swear as you like. I want my account to be recorded before the Council. It is an accurate account. Interest on the loan is proper. Interest on the investment is not proper, whether or not you borrowed the money. The Council obligated me to repay 1426 gulden. By my account and the terms of the first agreement, I should pay you 1268 gulden. With return of the investment, and conceding no interest, this becomes 1868 gulden. I am prepared, however, to pay the full 2026 gulden. All that you ask."

But none of the books or the equipment will belong to you."

Fust was flabbergasted as Gutenberg placed the gold in neat stacks on the table.

"I have 1700 gulden in gold and a pledge for the rest. Within a month I shall pay you the additional 326 gulden," Gutenberg said.

The room had become very quiet as Gutenberg spoke. No one ever heard him make such a lengthy speech before, and what he said startled everyone. Bayer and Dr. Humery could see by Fust's reaction that he knew Gutenberg spoke the truth.

"You actually have 2000 gulden?" Fust asked.

"I have," Gutenberg told him.

"You could have repaid me long ago, it seems," Fust said with a sneer. "I have never received one gulden from you until today!"

Fust dismissed Gutenberg's statement about the first 800 gulden being his own money. Unless Archbishop Erbach or Cardinal Cusanus corroborated it, Fust would remain silent. Seeing the heap of gold coins was a shock. Fortunately, Gutenberg did not have the full amount.

"A pledge for the remainder will not do," Fust said, confident once again. "Without proof to the contrary, I will swear that my statement at the hearing is correct. Unless you have 2026 gulden before November 6, the equipment and Bibles are mine. After that, Master Gutenberg, I will not accept twice 2000 gulden from anyone. The printing office is not for sale!"

"Gutenberg's pledge is from the Senator at Fulda," Dr. Humery said. "Surely you don't challenge his word, Herr Fust!"

Fust hesitated. The Senator was one of the most respected men in Oberhessen.

"I have it in writing!" Dr. Humery persisted. "you may read it for yourself."

Fust cleared his throat. "I will not accept a pledge from anyone," he said finally. "There is nothing more to discuss. Good day, gentlemen." Fust and his brother left the room.

Bayer looked after them in disbelief. Dr. Humery stood up and pounded the table with his fist, a rare show of emotion for the usually calm man. This was an insult he would never forget. "I will write the Senator immediately," Dr. Humery said, "and urge him to come to Mainz as soon as possible.

"The shop equipment is Fust's by right of lien until the loan is repaid," Dr. Humery explained to Bayer. "If Gutenberg did not pay, then Fust could file for breach of their agreement. He could also attach Gutenberg's share of profits from the Bibles, in addition to holding the equipment. But Johannes has the money!"

"He had also fulfilled his agreement to print the books," Bayer said. "If he failed to do that, there would be no profits for anyone to share!"

Bayer was angry, not only because of what Fust had said, but because he knew Fust would obtain the printing shop, if the Senator did not arrive before the oath was sworn. The date for swearing the oath could not be changed. The Council must abide by the oath, and Gutenberg could not appeal.

Gutenberg clenched the gold coins in his hand. He had raised more money than he actually owed. He had offered Fust all that he asked for. Now at last Fust's intentions were perfectly clear, and Dr. Humery was right. Fust didn't want the money, he wanted the shop. Gutenberg's face was pale and his hand trembled. Deliberately, he swept the stacks of coins on to the floor and watched them roll away.

"Henne," Else said, putting on her hat, "I am going to Eltville to ask Aunt Friele-Else to help Uncle. But don't tell him where I've gone or why. I think Aunt should know that Uncle has raised 1700 gulden."

"Do you want me to go with you?' Henne asked.

"No, I'll be back before dinner. I'll take a carriage."

Else knew that her aunt would be surprised to see her again so soon, as she and Henne had visited Eltville a few weeks before on St. Michael's Day. Friele-Else had known about the lawsuit, but showed little interest. "Johannes has always had money problems," she said, and then changed the subject.

Friele had left his wife a large annuity, and Friele-Else was a wealthy woman. Her husband had an elaborate monument in the churchyard, and she sent a large bequest to St. Odile every year in her childrens' memory. Friele-Else was lonely, but did little to encourage friendships outside the family. She rarely went anywhere and always dressed in black.

Carrying small gifts of candy and soap, Else rapped at the door of her aunt's home. Frau Gensfleisch was in her room, the housekeeper said, and Else went upstairs without waiting to be announced. Friele-Else was startled to see her niece and immediately thought that someone had died.

"Oh, no, Aunt," Else said, "but I am so upset! Uncle would not ask you for help, but he is desperate, Aunt. Will you help him? Please!"

"Sit down and tell me what has happened, Else!" Friele-Else replied.

Else seated herself and quickly related the recent events in the lawsuit and Herr Fust's refusal to accept less than 2000 gulden. Her uncle had raised all but 300 gulden, Else explained, and the Senator at Fulda has promised him 500 gulden.

"If you can give Uncle the money, he will pay you back as soon as the funds arrive," Else said. "It's just a loan until November 6. Please Aunt!"

"Johannes hasn't been to see me in months," Friele-Else answered. "And he knows I can't come to Mainz. Friele was very generous to his brother. I'm afraid I can't be so generous, Else. I can let him have 100 gulden, but not more."

"Uncle needs 326 gulden!" Else pleaded. "He planned to mortgage Hof zum Gutenberg until he got the money from Strasbourg. Now there isn't time!"

"I would have considered loaning Johannes money against the house, Else. But you want a gift, a loan of 300 gulden. I'm sorry. I give money to the Church so all of my dear ones will rest in peace." Friele-Else dabbed at her eyes. "I can't afford to give money for the printing shop too."

"But Uncle has worked so hard! And 100 gulden won't help now. It won't help at all!" Else tried not to scream. "Uncle Friele would be so proud of the Bibles and the shop. He wouldn't want Uncle to lose it!"

"I will purchase one of the Bibles, if you like, for 100 gulden," Friele-Else suggested. "My husband would approve of that."

Else looked down so her aunt couldn't see her face. When she spoke, her voice was calm. "No, thank you, Aunt," Else said. "It is not enough."

"Well, I'm sorry, Else," her aunt replied. "If Johannes loses the shop, I'm sure it's his own fault. He has always been in debt! Now, my dear, stay and have lunch with me."

Else sobbed for an hour as she rode in the carriage back to Mainz. Uncle would give Friele-Else a Bible, if she loaned him the rest of the money! And Uncle Friele would turn in his grave, if he knew she hadn't. I really believed Aunt would help, Else cried to herself. But I was wrong! And I'll never tell Uncle I asked her. Never! At least I had the courage to refuse 100 gulden, Else thought, wiping her eyes. Her husband and her uncles would approve of that!

CHAPTER 58

Peter customarily accompanied Christine to Sunday Vespers, and as he waited for her at her home, he chatted amicably with her mother. A refined, aristocratic woman, Margarete Fust liked Peter and was happy about the forthcoming marriage. She always expressed interest in the Bibles and the progress being made. The lawsuit had never been mentioned and for this Peter was grateful.

When Christine joined them, her father was with her. She was smiling and Fust seemed in good humor also.

"Papa wishes to speak with you," Christine said, exchanging glances with her father. "Mama and I will go now and you can come later."

"We won't be long, my dear," Fust answered. He gave his wife and daughter each a light kiss on the cheek, then turned his attention to Peter.

"Perhaps the wedding can be sooner than planned," Fust began expansively when they were alone. "You see, Peter, soon the printing office will belong to me. Master Gutenberg cannot repay what he owes me. I will own the shop, and I want you to manage it for me. More than that, I would like you to become a partner. I'd like my son-in-law to be my partner. A wedding present for you and Christine."

Peter was more surprised by Fust's announcement of ownership than by another change in the wedding plans. He hesitated before replying.

"I don't understand, Herr Fust," Peter said. "I know the Master owes you money, but how do you know he will not keep the shop? He has said nothing to me. The Bibles aren't finished."

"I will own the shop before the Bibles are finished, Peter," Fust answered. "You admire the Master, I know, but when a man does not pay his debts, this is what happens."

Master Gutenberg was a great inventor, Fust conceded, but he was more interested in experimenting with metal letters than in printing books. "I look beyond Bibles and Psalters, Peter," Fust said. "There will be other important work and I would like my son-in-law in charge of the printing from now on."

Gathering his thoughts, Peter struggled against the anger rising inside him. Fust had not sworn his oath, yet he seemed sure of the outcome of the lawsuit! And it was important to Fust that he manage the shop. The offer of partnership, however, sounded more like a bribe than an opportunity or a wedding present.

His face flushed, Peter replied, "I cannot accept your offer, Herr Fust. I am not ungrateful, but I cannot accept."

Fust frowned. "May I ask why, Peter?"

"I will manage the shop but not as a partner," Peter said evenly. "If Master Gutenberg loses the shop, I don't wish to become partners with the man who took it from him."

Completely taken back, Fust looked sharply at the young man. He never expected such bluntness from Peter Schoeffer. "But you wish to marry my daughter! You are willing to become my son-in-law," Fust said accusingly.

"I love Christine," Peter answered. "But I shall not become your partner in order to marry her, if that's what you mean."

"I mean for her husband to be more than an ordinary printer!" Fust replied. "I can refuse to permit the marriage, Peter!"

"It's important to you that I remain in Mainz, Herr Fust," Peter went on. "I could leave Mainz when the Bibles are completed. I will stay, however, because Gutenberg's work is important to me. Christine is important to me. But I will not become a partner if you take over the printing shop!"

Unaccustomed to opposition and angered by Peter's refusal to be compromised, Fust bade Peter a curt good evening. His threat to forbid the wedding had made no difference in Peter's decision.

Peter left the house and walked home in a daze. The lawsuit should not concern Christine and me, he thought. There should be no connection between their marriage and his management of the shop. Would Herr Fust see that? Or was he too angry? It had been a mistake for Fust to suggest partnership now. And if he cancelled the wedding, would Christine understand her father's reasons, and my decision, Peter wondered unhappily. He had stood up to Fust in this first test of wills. There was satisfaction in that. Fust had not said he no longer wanted Peter to manage the shop. But Peter was miserable. "Christine, Christine," he thought, "what have I done to you? and to us!"

Peter was puzzled also. How could Herr Fust be so certain that Master Gutenberg would lose the shop? And how could he think that he would turn his back on the Master if that happened, before it happened? "I will stay on my own terms," Peter told himself. "I will not be a party to what Fust is doing!"

It seemed to Peter that everything was conspiring against him and Gutenberg just when the Bibles were so nearly complete. How could he ever finish them now!

A light rain had started to fall, and an evening mist rose from the river. The streets were damp, and lights from windows made shimmering yellow patches on the cobblestones. As Peter passed the corner, he saw a light in the printing shop.

CHAPTER 59

Alone in the shop, Gutenberg sat at his desk, absently fingering one of the copper engravings. It was a stork design, like those Wilhelm had used to illustrate the Benedictine's Bible. The edges were rough, and Gutenberg looked around for a file to even them off. Not finding one, he got up and went into the foundry. He was very tired, yet routinely checked the presses as he went by and lingered briefly over the page forms to be printed the next day. The final Missal forms were on the press. The irony of knowing that fifty copies of the Missal had almost been completed, but that sale of these books would no longer help to meet his debt to Fust, added to the bitterness in Gutenberg's heart.

In the foundry, the pots of molten metal were still hot. Gutenberg added some coals to the firepot. On the table nearby were the handcasting instrument, some punches, matrices and new letter casting, scattered where the men had left them. Gutenberg picked up a few castings to examine more closely. Then he threw them into the pot and watched impassively as they melted and sank to the bottom.

Gutenberg hadn't heard Peter come in and barely looked up as he appeared in the doorway.

"Is anything wrong, Master?" Peter asked anxiously. "What are you doing?"

Gutenberg didn't answer and resolutely tossed more letters into the pot.

"No!" Peter protested, and moved to restrain him.

"I made them. I can destroy them," Gutenberg said, pushing Peter's arm to one side. He picked up the casting instrument. "This is mine, too. Everything in this shop belongs to me!"

"Master!" Peter implored, "what has happened?"

Before Gutenberg could reply, there was loud thunder and a crash in the other room. Suddenly a strong gust of wind blew through the shop.

"The storage room!" Peter cried, and ran to investigate.

There, he saw that a window had blown out and rain was coming in through the open casement, dangerously close to a stack of printed sheets on the shelf.

"I'll fix the window!" Peter yelled to Gutenberg, who had hurried after him. "You cover the pages!"

Looking around frantically, Peter saw a ream of new vellum being pressed between boards. He quickly loosened the vise and pulled out a handful of sheets. Then standing on the table, he stuffed them around the casement. Just as quickly, Gutenberg spread the vellum over the printed sheets and on the floor to absorb the puddles. Rain was still seeping in from the window.

"I'll get a bucket" Gutenberg said, and ran back to the foundry.

In the foundry, the only bucket was the large melting pot with metal in it. Without hesitation, Gutenberg tipped the metal onto the floor. Then he dragged the pot into the storage room and placed it under the leak.

"Did any of the prints get wet?" Peter asked.

"No. They're safe," Gutenberg told him. "Thank God!"

Gutenberg leaned exhausted against the table as Peter jumped down. The brief crisis was over.

"Thank God we were here!" Peter said. Then he noticed the steaming pot. The drips of water sizzled as they struck the hot iron.

"I dumped the metal," Gutenberg said. "Forgive me, Peter. We could have lost everything many times before."

"We can always mix more metal," Peter answered. "I'm glad we had the vellum!" He laughed, seeing the expensive calfskin sheets being used like blotting paper. "And I always worried about your pipe starting a fire!"

"The angels protect the books," Gutenberg murmured. He was relieved, but there was emptiness in his voice. Back in the office, Gutenberg slumped in his chair.

"Are you all right, Master?" Peter asked, wiping his hands.

"The angels protect the Bibles," Gutenberg repeated, "but they do not protect me. You will have to finish the books, Peter. Herr Fust has refused my offer to repay 2000 gulden. When he swears his oath on Thursday, I will lose the printing shop."

"What!" Peter exclaimed.

"I have 1700 gulden in gold now," Gutenberg continued, "and the rest is promised within a fortnight. But that will be too late. There's nothing more I can do. I really can't believe he will take my shop from me."

"Master!" Peter cried. "You mean Fust refused payment from you?

If I had known that, I would have resigned. I should have resigned!"

"I don't understand," Gutenberg said.

"Herr Fust invited me just tonight to become a partner with him," Peter answered. "I refused. I said I would not become a partner if he took the shop from you. A wedding present, he said. Now there may not be a wedding."

Sadness and anger turned to pride as Gutenberg listened to Peter relate his conversation with Fust. Fust had underestimated Peter Schoeffer. And so have I, Gutenberg thought. So have I.

Gutenberg stood up and put on his coat. He looked around the room, then picked up the gold initial letter A from his desk and put it in his pocket. "I'll keep this," he said. "My first letter."

Then removing the large ring of keys from his belt, Gutenberg handed them to Peter. "My life's work is here in this shop. I give it to you, my son. Take the keys."

"Oh, you keep them, Master," Peter said gently. "Let's go home."

"The keys are yours, Peter!" Gutenberg insisted. "I'll not give them to Fust!"

Peter took the keys, but as he locked the door his hands were shaking. The two men stood briefly in the front of the shop, then walked down the street together. Neither of them noticed it had stopped raining.

CHAPTER 60

The night before Fust was to swear the oath, he received a message that the abbot of St. Victor wished to see him. The matter was urgent, the abbot wrote. Probably a problem in the transport of revenues, Fust thought irritably. The collegiate abbot habitually made last minute changes in plans. Surely such business could wait until morning! Fust was annoyed at being called away from home so late, though he would see the abbot, of course.

Receiving Fust in his apartment, rather than in the reception hall, and wearing simple black robes, the abbot said nothing until the porter left them alone. Fust was puzzled. This was not an official conversation then.

"You will take your oath tomorrow," the abbot began.

"Yes, Your Grace," Fust answered, frowning. Why was the abbot concerned about that, at this hour, he wondered.

"An oath should not be necessary, Herr Fust," the abbot continued. "I understand Master Gutenberg has offered to meet your demand for 2000 gulden. No, don't interrupt. I also know that you did not borrow all of the money you claim to have borrowed. False witness is a serious sin, Herr Fust. You must swear to the truth. You must not swear to a lie."

Fust was stunned by the abbot's words. Clearly, Bayer and Isenburg had spoken to him. Fust did not answer immediately, to confirm or deny what the abbot had said. No one would dispute the oath once it was sworn, he thought. And he must swear the oath so everyone would believe him!

"Master Gutenberg was given six months grace," Fust said. "His offer to repay was not in full. I am not obliged to accept it. The first agreement was in writing, you know."

"Destroying a man and his life's work is not worthy of a patrician of Mainz," the abbot replied sternly. "I urge you to reconsider, Herr Fust. It is my duty to tell you this."

"Don't preach to me!" Fust answered, becoming defensive and angry at the abbot's interference. "Master Gutenberg and I might have become partners, but he refused me! I refuse to accommodate him! The work has taken five years! Now the Bibles will be published without him. The archbishop has my assurance of this. And I intend to operate a profitable printing office, Father Abbot, not a workshop for costly experiments. Gutenberg is only interested in the letters, always more letters. We shall publish other books in addition to the Bibles and Psalters, I assure you!"

In Fust's attempt to justify himself, he had avoided any mention of the money he borrowed against interest, the abbot noticed. Unfortunately, word from Cardinal Cusanus had not arrived, yet the abbot knew the statement would come and be followed with action, if ignored. The abbot did not threaten Fust with exposure, however. Fust wanted printing revenues in addition to his papal revenues. He also wanted a cardinal's hat for his son. Greed had distorted the man's thinking. Fust was very foolish, the abbot believed, to expect the cardinal would reward him for what he was planning to do.

Without dismissing Fust, the abbot turned and walked to the door, then stopped and looked back. "Again I ask you, Herr Fust, think about what I have said. Avarice is a deadly sin because it leads to greater sins. Swear not at all! Be generous and be truthful."

The abbot departed, leaving Fust alone, and slowly, sadly went to the chapel to pray. He could hear Fust's footsteps gradually fade away as he strode down the corridor and left the abbey.

The abbot knew Fust would not confess his guilt, or change his mind. The oath would be sworn. And Master Gutenberg, who deserved the highest praise from the Church and city he had served so well, would be victimized instead by unscrupulous men and by weak men in civil and church authority.

The abbot crossed himself and knelt before the Crucifix. The man who printed the Bibles and the man who would publish them were both in need of his prayers.

CHAPTER 61

Early Thursday morning, November 6, 1455, Dr. Humery came to Gutenberg's home. He was tired and anxious, thinking the Senator may have left sooner than expected and was on his way to Mainz.

"He might arrive before the oath is sworn," Dr. Humery said, pacing the floor. "We must not give up hope."

"You have done everything you could, Conrad," Gutenberg told him. "We shall wait until noon. If the Senator comes, we shall go to the monastery. If he doesn't, I shall ask Kefer and Fr. Gunther to go in my place. I shall not attend."

"Nor I," Dr. Humery replied.

"I am sure the Senator will come," Gutenberg said, "even if it is too late. I look forward to meeting him and thanking him."

At 11 o'clock, Fust arrived at the refectory of the Barefooted Monks where his oath would be sworn. Traditionally, oaths were sworn under an oak tree, but it was cold and Fust requested that they remain inside.

Fust was accompanied by his brother, Jacob, Peter Schoeffer, and five other friends, Peter Granss, Johann Kist, Johann Kumoff, Johann Yseneck and Johannes Bonne, who would serve as witnesses. Ulrich Helmasperger, a cleric from the diocese of Bamberg serving in Mainz, was the public notary who would record the proceedings.

The group waited impatiently for Gutenberg to appear. At noon, he still had not come. Exasperated by Gutenberg's absence and the delay,

Fust sent a messenger to inquire if there were any persons in the monastery to represent Gutenberg.

Waiting outside were Fr. Gunther of St. Christoph church, and the printers Heinrich Kefer and Bechtolf von Hanau, who now came forward. They been sent, they said, by Master Gutenberg to hear and report to him what transpired.

"At last we can begin!" Fust declared. When everyone was seated, he rose and said he was ready to carry out the terms of the verdict. "First, however, I request that the Council verdict be read, word for word, as well as my complaint and Gutenberg's answer, as transcribed at the Council hearing," he said.

Jacob Fust, representing his brother, read the verdict in a monotone. Then placing his hand on the Scriptures held by notary Helmasperger, Fust swore that everything as read was "perfectly right and true, without falsehood, in accordance with the verdict, so help me God."

"I have another statement to make at this time, Fust added. Holding up a piece of paper, Fust read from it, in a loud voice. "I, Fust, have borrowed 15-1/2 hundred gulden, given to Johannes Gutenberg, and used for our common work. For which sum I have given annually rent, interest and compound interest and still owe part to the present day. I figure for each 100 gulden so borrowed, six gulden annual interest. What Gutenberg has received of said borrowed money that has not been used for our common work, as revealed by the account, I also demand the interest according to the terms of the verdict. All this is true, I am willing to affirm, and is legal."

Helmasperger finished writing the document, naming the witnesses for Fust, the place, date, month, year, city, reign and pontificate. Then he signed it and attached his signet.

"I want you to make one or as many copies as I may need." Fust instructed the notary. "Master Gutenberg will receive a copy."

The whole transaction had lasted less than an hour. Satisfied and anxious to leave, Fust and the others went out of the refectory as the monks came in for their midday meal. Fust was seen to offer the abbot a coin which was declined.

In the hallway outside, an angry Kefer accosted Schoeffer, demanding to know why he had appeared as a witness for Fust. "If you are loyal to the Master, you should have sat with us!" he said.

"Perhaps Peter had no choice," Fr. Gunther told Kefer, noting the pain in Peter's face.

"Herr Fust insisted I come," Peter answered. "And I wanted to hear the oath for myself. I hate what has happened as much as you, Kefer. I'm glad the Master wasn't here."

It seemed strange to Fr. Gunther that Council chairman, Bayer, wasn't there either and that the notary rather than one of the monks had held the Holy Scriptures.

Standing with his friends a few steps away, Fust noticed Peter's conversation and frowned his disapproval.

"Don't keep Herr Fust waiting!" Kefer muttered.

Peter paid no attention to Fust or to Kefer's remark and shook hands with Fr. Gunther. Their eyes met briefly but neither spoke. The priest knew Peter was staying on at the printing office. It was the only good thing to come out of this terrible, heartbreaking business, he thought.

Kefer and von Hanau went immediately to Gutenberg Hof to tell the Master and Dr. Humery what had occurred at the monastery. A little later in the afternoon, Henne arrived, followed by Fr. Gunther and Fr. Cremer. When the printing shop closed for the day, Pannartz, Sweynheym, Ruppel, the Bechtermuntz brothers and the von Speyer brothers came. Arnold Gelthuss, his wife and son called in the evening.

The story of the proceedings and the lawsuit was repeated over and over as each group of visitors came and went. It was like a requiem, Else thought. A requiem for the living instead of the dead. She lost count of the amounts of beer and wine Henne brought up from the cellar and of the cheese, sausage, bread and cake consumed.

Gutenberg drank with everyone but ate little. When the last visitors finally left, long after curfew, Henne helped Gutenberg climb the stairs to bed. It was the first time Else had seen her uncle drunk.

Fust and his friends were relieved that the oath had finally been sworn and that Fust now owned the printing office. Schoeffer would not be a full partner, Fust told them, but he would continue to be in charge of the shop. When would Schoeffer and Christine be married, Fust was asked. Perhaps when the Bibles and Psalter are finished, he replied. In the spring, Fust would take some of the Bibles to Paris. He intended to show them and to sell them as soon as possible. Would not he go to Rome? Of course to Rome, but later, Fust said. Paris was closer! At last all of them could envision a profitable year ahead, Fust boasted, and everyone drank to his success.

Fust sent a message to Cardinal Cusanus stating that Gutenberg's printing office now belonged to him. Fust expected the suit to have been resolved six months earlier, he wrote, and blamed the Mainz Council for the delay. He had been sure of the outcome, which was favorable to both of them, but thought it prudent not to write until the suit was final. The papal legate could be certain the Bibles would be published early the following year. Then other publishing requests from Rome could be honored by the Fust-Schoeffer printing office. Fust enclosed a copy of the Helmasperger record of the hearing, verdict and his oath.

CHAPTER 62

In Rome, Cardinal Cusanus had been very much disturbed by the letters from Isenburg, the Benedictine abbot of St. James and Collegiate abbot of St. Victor, and by the fact he had had no word whatever concerning the lawsuit from Archbishop Erbach or Fust. Answering Isenburg immediately, Cusanus acknowledged that 1500 gulden had been given by himself for paper and vellum and stated his understanding of Fust's cooperation. He instructed the Custos to so testify before the Mainz Council. He told the abbot that he had written Archbishop Erbach demanding that Erbach either refute Fust's statements or prevail upon Fust to reconsider and not proceed with the oath.

The cardinal had not forseen such serious difficulties between Gutenberg and Fust. A conflict of personalities he could understand, and a man was within his rights to collect a debt, but it must be a fair debt. By attempting to take over ownership of the printing office, Fust thinks he is proving his loyalty to me, Cusanus thought, and expects printing revenues from Rome in return.

The cardinal was incensed also because the archbishop was obviously allowing Fust to further his own plans. Justice was not served, the Church was not well served, by weak men or by men who acted with presumption and impunity as Fust had done. Cusanus was keenly aware that many men served the Church who were motivated by personal ambition and greed, but this did not lessen his contempt for such men and their motives. Isenburg had acted with responsibility, he thought, while the archbishop has acted not at all!

When the Cardinal's letters were received in Mainz, however, it was mid-November, too late for Isenburg to testify. Disheartened by their failure to alter the course of events, Isenburg met with the abbots to talk about what had happened.

"The Master raised 1700 gulden! Yet his friends in the Church couldn't help him," the Collegiate abbot said. "You must tell him we tried."

"I did tell him. Now I must tell the cardinal we have failed. There is little consolation for anyone in knowing that help came too late," Isenburg answered. "The Master knows the archbishop could have intervened. I wanted him to invtervene! Erbach could have voided the verdict and the oath! He did nothing, which was what Fust was counting on. And I think I know why!"

"Erbach could have been one of Fust's investors," the abbot of St. James replied quietly. "Oh yes. I have suspected that for some time."

The abbot admired the cardinal's prompt action and support, admitting that once he thought Fust might be allied with Cusanus. The alliance, however, appeared to be between Fust and Erbach. Isenburg agreed. The cardinal was an honorable man, he said, and would not be drawn into such a conspiracy. Nor would Fust have dared to approach the cardinal and mention his intent. But he could rely on Erbach not to thwart his plans.

Isenburg was also angry with himself for not informing the Council of Cusanus' role. The Council assumed that Erbach had ordered the Bibles! The cardinal's money gift had been given privately! And no one could speak for the cardinal without his permission. Isenburg had been obedient to authority but would not be so scrupulous in the future, and vowed to use his own judgment from then on regardless of consequences. By not going before the Council himself, he had not put the archbishop or the cardinal on the spot, as it were, but perhaps he should have!

St. James abbot regretted that Cusanus had given Archbishop Erbach the opportunity to act in Gutenberg's behalf. The cardinal was politically correct, the abbot said, because the Bibles were under Erbach's jurisdiction, even though the request to print them had come from Rome. That the archbishop refused to take further direction from Cusanus showed a stubborn resistance which the abbot found surprising. On the other hand, the cardinal knew there was collusion and had not ignored nor approved of it. Cusanus should have gone over Erbach's head, in the abbot's opinion, and asserted papal authority.

The Collegiate abbot held the Mainz Council in contempt. Surely Bayer and other members of the Council knew that Fust should be made to produce receipts, he said. The testimony was contradictory and incomplete! But they knew enough, even without the cardinal's statement, to reach a different verdict. Fust should never have been allowed to swear an oath!

"The Council was intimidated by Fust!" the abbot said. "If anyone is to blame, they are. Not you, Custos, not the cardinal, nor the archbishop, but the men in Mainz who are Gutenberg's peers. They have condemned a man for a fault and condoned the sin of another."

In the middle of November also, the Senator from Fulda arrived in Mainz with the 500 gulden he had promised to Gutenberg. He had not entrusted so large a sum with a messenger, he explained to Dr. Humery, and his departure had been delayed when his wife became ill. The Senator was furious that Fust had not honored his pledge. "The Council would have accepted it without question!" he said. "I am no stranger here!"

"Fust would have been obliged to accept 2000 gulden before the oath was sworn," Dr. Humery told him. "Now he is only obliged to finish the Bibles!"

"And it seems I have made this trip for nothing," the Senator said. "If only I could have left sooner."

"I am sorry," Dr. Humery answered. "It has been a terrible experience for all of us. Johannes raised 1050 gulden in Strasbourg and 650 in Mainz, including 200 gulden of his own. We only needed 326 gulden from you. Now he will return the money given him."

The Senator would tell Fust to his face, and the Council too, he said, of his presence in Mainz to redeem the pledge. "Fust will not damage my reputation," the Senator said firmly. "And his pledges will never be accepted in Fulda again."

Dr. Humery found it most difficult to see injustice being done and his friend suffer so terribly as a result. "Johannes blames himself," he said. "And time does heal, but it often leaves an ugly, lasting scar."

XV. THE ABYSS
CHAPTER 63

As Christmas drew nearer, Else decided they should go to Frankfurt rather than remain in Mainz for the holy days.

"Uncle has suffered so much," she told Henne. "Christmas and his name day will be happier for all of us if we visit your aunt and family in Frankfurt. I can't bear to attend Mass in Mainz this year."

Henne still wondered why none of the clergy had come forward publicly to support Gutenberg at the hearing, to challenge the verdict, to try and postpone the oath or declare it invalid. "I thought Custos Isenburg would surely say something even if the archbishop did not. The cardinal had sent a letter to Isenburg, Uncle said, but it came too late to do any good."

Fust's oath was a sham, in Henne's opinion. It should have been administered by the prior, for one thing, he said, not by a notary. And without proof of receipts, it should never have been allowed by the Council.

"Uncle is such a good man," Else cried, wiping her tears. "I don't understand why God has let this happen to him!"

"Heaven will have its revenge," Henne answered firmly. "Peter Schoeffer has suffered too."

For the last time and before leaving for Frankfurt, Gutenberg went to the printing office to say goodbye to his men. He knew that now, more than ever, they needed his encouragement and to know that he relied on them to continue working together until the Bibles were finished. Gutenberg also knew that Kefer and others thought Schoeffer had supported Fust. They didn't know Peter's decision to stay was his own or what it might cost him. I must show them that Peter has my deepest respect and trust, Gutenberg thought.

It was an emotional reunion. Gutenberg made a short speech, and then gave each man a gold guilder. His warmth and dignity touched everyone. Several of the men wept as he shook their hands. Embracing Peter last of all, Gutenberg walked to the door and raised his hat. Then someone began to sing "Gaudeamus Igitur!" The others joined in singing this rousing Latin hymn which meant 'Then let us praise him.' It was a tribute Gutenberg would never forget.

Peter had not seen Christine since his argument with her father and his refusal to accept Fust's offer of partnership. It was now nearly Christmas, and Peter was going to Gernsheim to visit his father. Before he left, however, he had to talk to Christine. He must know how she felt about his decision and its possible effect on their future happiness. Not wishing to call at Fust's home, Peter asked Brother Jean-Marie to deliver a note, asking Christine to meet him at the Dom after morning Mass.

Peter waited in the Blessed Sacrament chapel and had lighted two candles when Christine appeared. The joy of seeing one another again made them forget for a moment the troubles that had kept them apart so long.

"Why don't you want to be partners with Papa?" Christine asked as they walked around the wide side aisles of the nave. "He says you are more loyal to Master Gutenberg than you are to me or to him. He might even forbid the wedding!"

"I told your father I would manage the printing shop," Peter answered, "but that I would not become partners with the man who took the shop away from Master Gutenberg. His offer was not just a wedding gift to please you and me, Christine. Your father wants his son-in-law under obligation to him. He needs me here to manage the shop, and is afraid I will leave Mainz because I don't approve of what he did to the Master."

Fust didn't want his daughter married to an ordinary printer, Peter went on, and that unless he became a partner, Fust would not allow the wedding to take place. "I refuse to become a partner in order to marry you," Peter said. "I will stay in Mainz, but not to please your father. I will stay because I want to complete Gutenberg's work. I don't need to be a partner, Christine, and we should be allowed to marry whether I am a partner or not!"

Her father had ruined Master Gutenberg, Peter told her. The master raised most of the money asked for, and it was more than he actually owed. Fust had refused to accept it. If Peter had known that, he would have resigned right then, he said. Peter wanted to resign when Gutenberg told him what happened, but changed his mind.

"Perhaps you can persuade your father to change his mind about us, Christine," Peter said. "I only want to be your husband and a son-in-law. Nothing else."

Christine had not interrupted or protested anything Peter had to say. They walked silently out of the side door of the great church into the Domplatz. It was filled with visitors and shoppers, but they took no notice of them.

"I'm sorry, Christine," Peter said. "This hurts you terribly, I know. I've been sick about it. If your father wants me to stay, he should let us be married as soon as possible! The partnership isn't important. You and Gutenberg's work are important to me!"

"Papa isn't a bad man, Peter," Christine said quietly, "but he always wants his way with people. He wanted the printing shop. He wants my brother to be a cardinal and for Cardinal Cusanus to arrange it. He even tells my mother who she can visit and who she must entertain. I think I'm the only one Papa really loves. He has never forced me to do anything I didn't want to do. Yet he would forbid our marriage because you have opposed him!"

Christine began to cry. "It shouldn't matter that you aren't a partner! It doesn't matter to me! I just thought it would make you happy. I love you, Peter!"

"I love you," Peter said, "and we have waited so long!" He took Christine's hand and squeezed it hard. "I love you so much!"

Before the troubles with the lawsuit began, Fust had said they could be married in the spring. When the Bibles were finished, Christine would ask her father again when they could be married. He had not forbidden them to see each other, she said.

Peter doubted that Fust would relent and permit their marriage, but did not say so. It was enough to know that Christine still loved him and understood. She had not urged him to give in to her father's wishes, and it was possible Fust would change his mind when the Bibles were printed.

Peter planned to be in Gernsheim for a fortnight and would be back when the shop reopened. His family knew about the lawsuit and its outcome, he said, but not about the proposed partnership. His father was looking forward to meeting his new daughter-in-law! Next time he went home, Peter hoped to take Christine with him, he told her, as his wife. Peter put his arms around the girl and held her close. Then he drew Christine behind a wall and kissed her.

On Christmas Eve, Fust called on Archbishop Erbach. It was his first visit since the oath was sworn, and Erbach was piqued by Fust's absence. Erbach still feared censure for ignoring the cardinal's instructions and wanted assurance that his investment would bring dividends. He hoped the Bibles and Psalters would be completed soon, he told Fust. He also expected a share of the profits from the printing revenues Fust would receive, he added pointedly.

Fust dismissed the archbishop's concerns. He had done Cusanus a service by taking charge of the printing office, he said. And of course Erbach would benefit also. The archbishop was getting old, Fust thought, and this needling and apprehension he found annoying. Erbach's support had been useful, but Fust felt confident now of furthering his own and a more profitable relationship with Cardinal Cusanus.

The cardinal received Fust's letter, the letters from Isenburg and the abbot, and a note from Erbach shortly before Christmas. The archbishop said he had been in Aschaffenburg and was not fully informed about the lawsuit or its outcome until he returned to Mainz. A weak excuse! Gutenberg had suffered tragically at the hands of callous, ambitious men. Erbach can accept it with indifference, but I cannot, Cusanus thought. I wanted the Bibles published but not at such cost!

The marvelous printing equipment was the result of Gutenberg's genius, and the Bibles would be recognized as masterpieces of his printing art. The Master had placed the highest priority on the Bibles. He had devoted himself to the work for five years! And printed two issues of the Papal Indulgences. 'It is impossible for me to be insensitive to Gutenberg's great personal loss and to his great contribution to the Church,' the cardinal wrote Erbach. 'Even now, it is possible for you to nullify the Council verdict and Fust's oath.'

Cusanus knew this would not happen and that he could not undo the wrong to Gutenberg. It was within his power, however, to see that Fust did not profit further. Answering Fust's letter briefly, the cardinal said he was saddened to learn of the delay in publishing the Bibles. Copies were anxiously awaited by the Holy Father, he wrote, who was dying.

CHAPTER 64

Resuming work on the Bibles was difficult after the events of the past six months. Less than 100 pages remained, but the men made careless mistakes and composition and printing soon fell behind schedule. "What difference does it make," was the way the men expressed it.

In Volume I, Team 5 had begun at Tobias and expected to finish the last quire, 16 pages of Job, in about a month. Genesis through Esdras and all of Psalms were complete. In Volume II, however, the work had gone more slowly. The letters of St. Paul had begun well enough and Team 4 was ending Philippians. There remained 24 pages of Colossians through Hebrews, 33 pages of the Acts of the Apostles, and 15 pages containing the last four Apostle letters. If the page count estimates were correct, Schoeffer figured 72 pages, or 4-1/2 quires, still had to be completed in Volume II. The work would take 4-1/2 months. Proverbs to Philippians and the Apocalypse had been done.

"The Bibles were supposed to be finished by Christmas. Do you think they can be finished by Easter?" Fust asked Peter sarcastically. "I want the Bibles published before Easter, Peter. Use six presses if you have to!"

"We could perhaps finish the New Testament using two teams instead of one," Peter told him. "That would cut the finishing time in half. But it's not as simple as it sounds."

"Do what you have to!" Fust answered. "Time meant nothing to Gutenberg, but it's important to me!"

Time was important to Peter also. It meant Gutenberg would be able to sell his share of the Bibles sooner, and that the men could be put to work full time on the Psalter. Peter considered where he could best divide the remaining pages of Volume II so two teams could work at the same time. Despite Gutenberg's care in counting the number of pages in each book and the number of books in each quire, they had had a major problem in Esdras. For Peter, the number of epistles coming before the Acts made counting and planning difficult. Perhaps it was too much of a risk to divide the work, he thought. Still, it was the only way the Bibles could be finished before summer.

Studying the situation, Peter found one place where the books and quires could be divided. Quire 36 contained eight pages of Hebrews and eight pages of Acts. Quire 39 was a half quire and came before the Apocalypse. But Quire 36 could also be a half quire, Peter thought, and Quire 39 could be made a full quire. By switching the position of the half quire, the Acts would begin Quire 37, followed by Quire 38 and full Quire 39. Totals were the same, 48 plus 8 pages or 3-1/2 quires.

"You want to start composing and printing at the Acts?" Kefer questioned, when Peter told him of his plan. "Start a new quire before we finish Philippians and Quire 35? How can you take such a chance! This is Fust's idea, I suppose, and you agree with him!"

"Dividing the work was my idea," Schoeffer said, "but I do agree with him that the Bibles should be finished as soon as possible. I've found a way. If the pages in each book are counted correctly, there'll be no problem."

"And if there is a problem, what then?"

"I'll take the responsibility," Schoeffer answered.

"And if you are wrong," Kefer said angrily, "it will look like our fault!"

Pannartz too was surprised at Schoeffer's bold plan but thought it would work. "I'll use three compositors and we'll compose as many pages as we can," he said. "Then we can be fairly sure of where we are before printing begins. We have enough letters for 24 pages to be in work at one time."

"Thank you, Arnold." Peter said. "That was my thought, too. We must be very careful, of course. "I'm counting on both of you, and I'm sure Fr. Gunther will cooperate all he can."

At the scriptorium, Peter outlined his plan to Fr. Gunther. The priest agreed that completing the Bible in smaller sections, with more men, was the thing to do. He understood the risks, and was sure Gutenberg would approve. The monks would be reading more pages than usual to keep ahead of the printers and would read as many pages in sequence as possible, he said. Fr. Gunther also offered to help Peter keep track of the pages and books within each quire. They must not make mistakes now!

DAY	C	P
	1ST WEEK	2ND WEEK
M	1	1-2
T	2	
W	3	
T	4	3-4
F	5	
S		

Peter's plan called for three teams of compositors and printers to work at one time. Team 4 compositor would continue Colossians through Hebrews. Team 5 compositor would complete all of Acts. Team 6 compositor would complete St. James through St. Jude. Team 4 printer would complete Colossians, Quire 34, then the 24 pages of Quire 35 and the half Quire 36 ending Hebrews. Team 5 printer would print Quires 37 and 38, 32 pages of Acts. Team 6 printer would complete the last 16 pages, Acts and the four Apostle letters of Quire 39, but he would not begin until Schoeffer knew exactly how long the Acts would be.

Composition and printing time would be based on Acts because it was the longest section. The 33 pages would take six and a half weeks for the compositor to finish. The printing would require eight weeks. The compositor needed a head start of one week in order to finish the first four or five pages before the printer began. After that composition and printing could proceed concurrently. This meant that the total time required to complete Acts would be nine to ten weeks. Based on these calculations, and if all went well, Peter was confident the Bibles could be finished in April.

The change in schedule and the silent hostility of some of the men who believed like Kefer that he had had a part with Fust in Gutenberg's loss of the shop could make the work much more difficult, Peter realized. Printing the Bibles had never been easy, but the enthusiasm and cooperation between himself and the men had made a big difference. A sense of purpose and pride in workmanship had created a strong bond of mutual respect. Now, personal antagonism could jeopardize efficiency in the final stages of work. He would do his best, Peter told the men, and expected them to do the same.

For his part, Fust thought he could safely tell his friends that publication of the Bibles was in sight. His creditors did not concern themselves that Fust had not recovered any money from Gutenberg or that their investment had not produced dividends in three years. The work had simply taken longer than anyone expected, and all were relieved that Schoeffer was still directing the work.

Despite Schoeffer's careful planning, however, acceleration of the work resulted in mistakes. The first occurred when a page handler discovered that one page of Timothy had been printed on page 16, the last page of Quire 34, instead of where it belonged, on page 14 in Quire 35. Both pages were the left-hand page 4 of a sheet, but the printer had picked up the wrong sheet in the wrong quire. He had not checked the facing page or had misread the quire number. Ten prints had been made before the error was found.

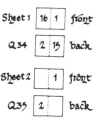

Schoeffer was furious. Why had page 16 in Quire 34 been left blank, he wanted to know. Why had the printer gone ahead and printed most of Quire 35 before completing Quire 34? Colossians was three pages. Two pages should have ended Quire 34 and one begin Quire 35. Instead, two pages of Colossians opened Quire 35, followed by Thessalonians and Timothy. Had the printer counted Colossians as four pages instead of three?

The trouble began, as best Schoeffer was able to determine, when page 16 of Quire 34 had been left blank while the printer waited for corrections to be made on page 2 of Colossians. The printer forgot, and printed pages 2 and 3 of Colossians in Quire 35. Then he printed the page of Timothy on the wrong blank page.

The first thing to be done was to remove the page of Timothy from the midst of Colossians by replacing the ten misprinted sheets in Quire 34, containing pages 1, 2, 15 and 16, composing and printing them again so the total number of sheets would be 185, and including the blank page on page 16.

Quire 35 was more than half printed. Work on it was stopped immediately until Schoeffer determined whether the balance of pages in this quire and in the half Quire 36, yet to be printed, counted out as ten pages or eleven. If the balance of pages was eleven, as expected, all 740 printed sheets of Quire 35 would have to be replaced, composed again and reprinted in order to back up everything one page and absorb the blank page. Fortunately, composition confirmed that there were ten pages remaining. Schoeffer had miscounted Hebrews, but a major problem had been avoided. Unfortunately, Quire 34 still ended with a blank page, conspicuously present within the three-page book of Colossians.

Ruppel suggested that the blank page be transferred. It could be moved to the end of Colossians and before Thessalonians, he said, where it was still a left page but separated the two books. Quire 34 could end with Colossians on page 16, and the last page of Colossians would become the first page of Quire 35, as intended in the first place, followed then by the blank page. To accomplish this meant replacing the 185 paper and vellum sheets 1 in Quire 35. Schoeffer would sacrifice the sheets, he said.

When the gigantic mix-up was at last sorted out and corrected, four pages on sheet 4 in Quire 34 and the first page of Quire 35 were recomposed and reprinted. Colossians was in order, and the page of Timothy was printed in its proper place on page 14, Quire 35. They had not had to compose and print 13 pages of Quire 35 twice, but a month's time had been lost.

"You lost 195 sheets, Peter," Ruppel told him. "You might have lost all of Quire 35, 740 sheets, and 185 sheets in Quire 34, if Hansel had not seen the mistake when he did. If those quires had been printed correctly, you still would have had a blank page at the end of Hebrews."

"There should have been no blank pages," Schoeffer said. "I made a mistake too." And now he was worried whether the Acts and Apostle letters would be 48 pages, or had he miscounted again?

It was not long before Schoeffer knew the answer. Acts was 34 pages, not 33, and the 15 pages of Apostle letters would be one page too many. Finishing the Bible had become a nightmare.

The additional page of Acts meant that the last two pages of Acts, not just one page, would begin Quire 39, leaving only 14 pages for the Apostle letters and no room for the last page of St. Jude. Having one blank page before Thessalonians was bad enough, but having an extra text page and nowhere to put it was a disaster.

The first page of Acts should have ended the half Quire 36, Schoeffer realized. Then the 32 pages in Quires 37 and 38 would have made the 33 pages he estimated, and Quire 39 would have included the 15 pages of Apostle letters and a blank page before the Apocalypse. A blank page here was acceptable. Or, Quire 39 could have included the 34th page of Acts and the Apostle letters, with no blank page at the end.

The problems in Esdras, Colossians and Timothy seemed trivial by comparison. The Apocalypse had already been printed as Quire 40. What could possibly be done to include all of St. Jude!

The division of work and moving the position of the half quire did not cause the series of problems. They were caused by carelessness in printing and errors in counting. Schoeffer was glad the young page handler had had the courage to point out the Timothy error, but Hansel did not feel like a hero. Kefer wanted to resign. The printer had got drunk and didn't come back to the shop for three days.

It was history now, Schoeffer told the men, and affixing blame didn't solve anything. The whole experience had taught them something, he said, and everyone had suffered enough, especially Kefer and the printer. He did not dismiss them.

Addressing himself now to the immediate and crucial problem in Quire 39, Schoeffer knew he must find a way to include the last page of St. Jude in the Bible. Again it was Ruppel who saw the only solution. They must insert another 4-page sheet, he said.

"We must put the sheet around the Apocalypse," Ruppel told Peter. "Two pages in front and two pages following. St. Jude will be on page 1, page 2 will be blank, and pages 3 and 4 will be blank at the very end of the Bible."

It was impossible to bind in a single folio of two pages, Schoeffer knew. It had to be a sheet of two folios, four pages. "Another 185 sheets just to print one page!" he said, but he knew Ruppel had found the answer. A blank page before the Apocalypse, and two blank pages at the end didn't matter at all.

Quire 40 would be 20 pages instead of 16, and Volume II of the Bible would be 636 pages, four pages larger than originally planned.

When Schoeffer told Fust what had happened and that 600 additional sheets had been used to complete the Bibles, surprisingly Fust was unconcerned. After 100 reams of paper and 11,000 vellum sheets, he said, what difference did another few hundred sheets make. Nor did the blank pages concern him. "Don't worry about blank pages, Peter," Fust said. "Finish the books! That's all I'm interested in!"

The blank pages were an abomination to Schoeffer, however, in spite of resolving the most serious problems successfully. Gutenberg had redesigned and recast the letters to get 42 lines in each column of the Bible, for the very purpose of saving paper and vellum. Now there were five blank pages! Two were in Volume I and two were in the 100 pages of Volume II Schoeffer was responsible for. Only the single blank page before the New Testament had been planned from the beginning.

"You must not discredit yourself or the Bibles because of the blank pages," Fr. Gunther told Schoeffer. "Nor must Master Gutenberg. He accepted Esdras, you must accept Colossians and St. Jude. You handled both situations like a master, Peter. The blank folio at the end? Gutenberg has a place to write his name!"

"The printing is not perfect," Peter replied disconsolately.

"There are mistakes in the text too," Fr. Gunther said. "Some mispellings and words left out, despite our best efforts. Not many, but a few. We corrected all those we found by hand in each copy, but there are others we missed, I'm sure. We must remember, Peter, that the Word of God is perfect, though the work of men may be imperfect. I think it's a miracle these Bibles have been printed at all!"

The men in the shop knew the responsibility for errors was not Schoeffer's alone. The delays, confusion and clashes of opinion had also played a part. Schoeffer had done his best, even Kefer acknowledged this, and the men admired his ability and determination to do whatever was necessary to correct the mistakes. Blame and credit, both, must be shared. This was an honest admission, made by proud and conscientious men. No longer would they be resentful or distrusting of Schoeffer's leadership.

In Fr. Gunther's opinion, winning the respect of Gutenberg's men was a lasting benefit, far more important to Schoeffer, the work and the future of the printing shop than blank pages in the Bible and 600 sheets.

CHAPTER 65

Peter had seen little of Christine during these difficult months, and after Easter she had gone to Bingen to visit her aunt. He looked forward to her return. When the Bibles were finished, Peter would ask Fust again when they could be married.

Peter also hoped to give the men a short holiday before beginning the Psalter, but Fust would not consider it. He wanted to move the printing shop, he said, and the men would be needed in Mainz. Fust had no intention of paying rent when he owned another building himself, not far away, he told Peter. He expected the new office to be ready by the end of summer, and wanted the Psalter to be started immediately.

Fust was going to Cologne, he said, and taking Christine with him. He did not ask if Peter had changed his mind about the partnership, and Peter did not inquire about the wedding. Peter would speak with Frau Fust and try to meet Christine secretly before she left. Their romance had begun with letters, it would continue with letters. Her mother would see that the letters were exchanged.

The last page of the Bible to come from the press was the single page of St. Jude, but on that eventful day neither Fust, Isenburg nor Gutenberg witnessed the occasion. Only the abbot of St. James and Fr. Gunther came to the shop to congratulate Peter and the men. The following day, when the last sheets and quires were received at the scriptorium, a Mass of Thanksgiving was offered in the monastery chapel. Archbishop Erbach made no announcement that the first printed Bibles had been published in Mainz. They had been finished before Corpus Christi, but a year later than Gutenberg had planned.

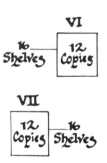

Fr. Cremer was given the remaining quires he needed to complete the paper Bible being illustrated and bound for the archbishop. The other printed quires, 184 copies each, were numbered 1-41, Volume I, and 1-40, Volume II, and rested on shelves in St. James storage room. There the monks gathered them together, counting quire by quire, until each volume was complete. Then the volumes were carefully wrapped in calfskin, sealed, numbered Volume I or Volume II, and labeled Paper or Vellum. It was a laborious task but a very satisfying one for the monks to perform. Never before had so many copies of Sacred Scripture been under one roof.

Including the archbishop's Bible, initial distribution was limited to 21 copies, according to Isenburg's instructions, and this was handled personally by Fr. Gunther and the abbot of St. James. Gutenberg, the Cathedral Chapter, the Dom of St. Martin, and Fust were to have vellum copies. Two vellum Bibles were to be sent to the University of Paris. Six Bibles, three vellum and three paper, were sent to Cardinal Cusanus in Rome and to Brixen in the Tyrol where he had been named bishop in 1450. Paper copies were given to the three abbots of Mainz, and two paper Bibles were sent to Strasbourg. Archbishop Erbach was expected to send three paper copies to the Rhein electors at Trier, Cologne and the Palatinate in Heidelberg. Those receiving and later purchasing a Bible would have their books illustrated and then bound in two volumes.

The remaining 164 Bibles were to be divided equally between Gutenberg and Fust for their own sale and profit, as agreed upon in the 1452 agreement and upheld by the Mainz Council.

Peter took Gutenberg's Bible to him. This first opportunity to talk with the Master about the finished Bibles might be difficult for both of them, Peter thought. He knew Gutenberg has been informed of the problems encountered in Volume II and the decisions that had had to be made. He would offer no apologies or excuses, and hoped Fr. Gunther was right, that even with the additional blank pages, Gutenberg would be pleased with the results.

Peter was surprised to find Gutenberg strangely detached and uninterested in the Bibles. He thanked Peter for coming but showed no enthusiasm in the purpose of his visit. He didn't unwrap either volume. He asked no questions, offered no praise, no disapproval. The blank pages were not mentioned. Instead, Gutenberg asked about the Psalters.

"I hope the initial letters work out well," Gutenberg said. "You printed the Psalms once. The second time should be easier."

"I'll show you the first quire when it is finished," Peter told him. He was using the small letters from the Missal, he said, with the new Psalter capitals.

"You might as well," Gutenberg replied indifferently. "I'm sure they will be fine."

Reproach, even anger, Peter was prepared for. He was not prepared to have Gutenberg ignore the Bibles so completely. The warmth and vigor the Master had always shown were missing, and there was a sadness in his face which made Peter realize that finishing the Bibles was a joy and achievement they could no longer share. Peter felt like a stranger.

"I'm glad the Bible is printed," Peter said lightly. "The Psalter will be easier."

Gutenberg turned to Peter then and spoke kindly. "You finished the Bibles as you promised, Peter," he said. "I want you to have one for yourself."

Peter had not thought of receiving or purchasing one of the Bibles, and he was touched by this generous expression of gratitude. He had wished, he said, that he could give a Bible to the church in Gernsheim.

"Now you can," Gutenberg replied, and changed the subject.

Perhaps another time they could talk about the Bibles and look at the pages together, Peter thought. On the other hand, perhaps this wasn't important anymore and would always be too painful for Gutenberg. The work and the books were things the Master wanted to forget, not remember. Peter didn't mention Fust's plans to move the shop, and Gutenberg had not asked about Christine.

Else was troubled by her uncle's behavior. She proudly displayed the Bible pages for Dr. Humery, Rudi and Arnold Gelthuss to see. Arnold offered to have the two volumes illustrated and bound. There was no hurry about that, Gutenberg told him.

Gutenberg was irritated by all the fuss and attention given to the Bibles. He scarcely looked at the pages, and for days the quires lay covered up on the table where Peter had left them. One day when Else and Henne were away, he put both volumes into a chest and locked it. He refused to give Else the key.

When the Collegiate church in Frankfurt and the abbey St. James in Wurzburg requested that Gutenberg deliver their printed Bibles personally, he would not go. The abbots were more interested in the lawsuit, Gutenberg said bitterly, and he would not discuss it.

When letters arrived praising the Bibles, Gutenberg did not answer them, even those from Strasbourg. A message from Archbishop Erbach saying the Bibles would bring honor to Mainz, he read and tossed aside. He did not keep it.

A letter from Cardinal Cusanus was at once congratulatory and sympathetic. This letter Gutenberg shared with Isenburg. The custos, in turn, shared a letter he had received from the Carmelite abbot whose great manuscript Bible was now eclipsed by publication of the printed Bibles.

In his letter, the abbot said that Gutenberg's Bible was a remarkable volume and that 185 copies would be of great benefit to the Church. He believed that manuscript would always be held in higher esteem, however, and should continue to be used for liturgical books. Printing would not replace manuscript, he said. The abbot sincerely regretted the sad circumstances that had befallen Master Gutenberg "who is an honorable man."

The abbot had not praised the Bible and could not bring himself to write Gutenberg directly. One day he would change his mind about printing, Isenburg predicted. Some Benedictine houses had already said they were interested in the new art.

No words from any source could give solace to Gutenberg, however, and only seemed to deepen his despair. Not even Dr. Humery could bridge the abyss into which Gutenberg's spirits had fallen. The loss of the printing shop meant more than the loss of property and the work of a lifetime, he discovered. It meant the loss of Gutenberg's claim to the Bibles as his own work. Gutenberg was glad Schoeffer had finished them, but his own sense of satisfaction in this accomplishment had been destroyed.

"Schoeffer and I printed the Bibles," Gutenberg told his friend, "but Fust and Schoeffer published the Bibles! The shop is not mine. The books are not mine. I have achieved nothing!"

"The Bibles are undeniably your achievement, Johannes," Dr. Humery insisted. "People know that whoever owns the printing shop, the Bibles are the work of Master Gutenberg, not of Master Schoeffer or Herr Fust."

"My good name has been destroyed!" Gutenberg answered. "I don't pay my debts. The Gensfleisch family is disgraced, dishonored. If the name Gutenberg is remembered at all, it will be because I lost the printing shop, not because I printed Bibles, made the letters and the press! Perhaps it is good I am the last of the family. To die and be forgotten."

Dr. Humery finally understood how completely Gutenberg's spirit had been crushed. He did not argue or try to say that vindication would come in time. He knew also that Gutenberg could be right. The Bibles might be remembered long after the Master was buried and forgotten.

"You are master printer of the Holy Bible in Mainz," Dr. Humery said. "No one living today will allow the name of Gensfleisch or Gutenberg to be dishonored or forgotten. No one in Mainz, in Rome, in Strasbourg, no one throughout the whole monastic world."

Gutenberg was not listening, and Dr. Humery left the house feeling as depressed as his friend. Somehow, he told Else, they must put hope and light into Gutenberg's eyes again.

Soon after the Bibles were published, Schoeffer moved the printing shop to the new location and preparations were made to print the Psalter. Most of the printers remained in Mainz, which pleased Schoeffer, although two of them took this opportunity to leave. Committed only to finishing the Bibles, Albrecht Pfister was going to Bamberg and Heinrich Eggestein to Strasbourg, where they planned to open printing offices of their own. Pfister took a supply of the first Bible letters they had made, a set of punches and matrices, and a casting mold Schoeffer sold to him.

If things had turned out differently, Schoeffer thought, he might be going to Gernsheim with the same desire and plans for the future. His future lay in Mainz, however, with the printing shop and with Christine. He did not regret the choices he had made.

CHAPTER 66

For months following the lawsuit, Gutenberg suffered from bitterness and depression. Anxiety and tension had exhausted him. He couldn't sleep and had no appetite. Increasingly aware of his failing eyesight, Gutenberg was reluctant to leave the house and spent hours each day just sitting in his chair. Else and Henne did everything they could to make life pleasant, but Gutenberg remained withdrawn and unresponsive. They knew that only time, kindness and patience would ease the great loss Gutenberg felt so deeply.

Gutenberg felt old. He could look back upon more years than he could look ahead, and took no interest in the present. Memories flooded his mind. He remembered the day Andreas Dritzehn had spilled the hot casting metal on his foot. He remembered when Johann Hultz had carried home the body of a workman who fell from the spire, then cursed the mason who said the man was drunk ... His mother had understood when he wanted to become a goldsmith. "Make Papa proud," she had said. Gutenberg was glad neither of his parents knew about the Bibles ...

Friele would have found a way for him to keep the printing office! His brother had always stood by him, like the time they were acolytes and accused of stealing candles from the Dom. Friele had said, "I didn't do it, and I know Johannes didn't do it. The sacristan was the only other person here. He must have done it." Friele would not lie, and the sacristan, it turned out, was guilty, Just like Fust was guilty...Peter! Why didn't Peter resign after the Bibles were published, Gutenberg thought angrily. He should have taken Christine to Gernsheim and let Fust print the Psalter by himself!

Nothing made sense to Gutenberg any more. And nothing mattered any more. A lifetime had been spent and to what purpose? The work and the books were gone.

That summer, in June, 1456, an enormous comet appeared in the sky. It had a long luminous tail and was visible for days. Church bells rang. People were terrified and thought they would die. Like eclipses of the sun and moon, the comet was seen as a sign of God's anger, certain to be followed by signs of God's vengeance - war, famine, plague and death. So widespread was fear of the phenomenon that Pope Callistus III issued a papal bull, ordering the Ave Maria to be recited three times daily, with a prayer "Lord, save us from the Devil, the Turk and the Comet!" Gutenberg was sure the comet foretold his own death.

The many prayers that had been said following the Pope's decree were answered, however. On the feast of the Transfiguration of Our Lord on Mount Tabor, August 6, it was announced in Rome that John Hunyady had defeated the Turks near Belgrade. To commemorate this important victory, Pope Callistus ordered the feast day to be observed by the whole Church throughout the Empire.

A week later, Fr. Cremer completed illustration of the Bible for the Archbishop of Mainz. At the end of Psalms and at the top of the blank page which followed the Apocalypse, he recorded the date - Volume II finished on Assumption Day, August 15, and Volume I finished on St. Bartholomew's Day, August 24. He signed his name and added the word "Alleluia!"

The abbot of St. Stephan's urged Gutenberg to see the Bible before it was bound. Gutenberg consented, but declined to add his name, saying that the printing was the work of many men, not just one. He admired the illustrated pages and variety of artistic triangular patterns throughout, but had always thought the full text pages were very beautiful in themselves, without any ornamentation. Seeing them again, at this time and place, gave Gutenberg the first stirrings of pride and the first lessening of despair.

Spending a second Christmas in Frankfurt, Gutenberg was heartened by the bishop's announcement that one of the new printed Bibles from Mainz was being used for the first time on Christmas Eve. And in the familiar story of Christ's birth, he heard another celestial phenomenon described in detail.

"Fear not," the angel told the shepherds, "And suddenly there was with the angel a multitude of the heavenly host praising God and saying, 'Glory to God in the highest, and on earth peace among men of good will'." Gutenberg remembered when the pages of St. Luke had been printed. The words were not merely words on paper, he realized, but words which expressed the power of God to replace darkness with light, despair with hope, and to bring joy and peace into the hearts of men. The bright star over Bethlehem was a sign of life and divine love, not an omen of death and of evil.

The Mass made Gutenberg reflect again on what it meant to be a Franciscan. His old friend, Johann Hultz, had been a true son of St. Francis, aspiring to live according to the Gospel of Christ, the laws of God and the Church. I've not always done that, Gutenberg thought, but I must. I must try. Hultz would have been so pleased to see one of the Bibles on the altar of Notre-Dame in Strasbourg.

The following year, 1457, Peter Schoeffer published the Psalter, a beautiful volume on vellum, using the two-color initial letters designed by Gutenberg. The Master was proud of Schoeffer's achievement, but he deeply resented Fust being able to sell the Psalters. He was particularly vexed that these books carried a small double shield insignia linking the names of Fust and Schoeffer only as the publishers.

Pfister was said to be printing a 36-line Bible in Bamberg. Who had commissioned this work, Gutenberg wondered. It would be larger than the Mainz Bible and require many sheets of paper and vellum for even 100 copies. Pfister would benefit from his experience in Mainz, however, and not repeat the mistakes they had made.

Sadness touched Gutenberg's personal life again when Friele-Else died in Eltville. The big house she had been so proud of had become a tomb. What would become of it now, Gutenberg thought, and all of its elegant furnishings?

Else, Henne, Gelthuss and Gutenberg went to the funeral. There were few other mourners. Remembering the happy times he had spent with Friele and the children was painful for Gutenberg. The years had gone so fast. I was busy and had my own problems, he thought. I was not as attentive to my brother's widow as I should have been. Friele-Else had not been close, but he would miss her.

Friele-Else knew he had lost the printing shop, but Gutenberg had received no word of sympathy from her. His work had never interested his sister-in-law and the lawsuit embarrassed her, he believed. Gutenberg never considered asking Friele-Else for help when he needed money, nor had he expected her to offer help, though he knew his brother would have. His niece was surprisingly bitter about her aunt's lack of concern, Gutenberg noticed. "Aunt Friele-Else could have helped you, Uncle," Else had said. "She should have helped you! If Uncle Friele were alive, everything would have been different!"

In Mainz, a cleric reported that Bertholdus de Steyna had added another note to the archbishop's Bible, saying that on St. George's Day and every Tuesday thereafter, high Mass was celebrated in the Dom to mark the completion of the Bible on Corpus Christi.

On All Saints Day, November 1, it was customary for the children to dress like many of the saints and take part in procession through the streets of Mainz. They assembled at St. Stephan's, walked down the hill to St. Emmeran, then to St. Christoph, St. Quentin, St. Francis, and final-ly to the Dom where they received the archbishop's blessing.

Gutenberg always liked to watch this assembly of little saints, and he and Fr. Gunther stood in St. Christoph's churchyard, trying to identify the youngsters as they passed by. There were several of the Fourteen Holy Helpers-St. Eustace with his hunting cap, bow and arrows; St. George, the soldier, with helmet and sword; St. Denis with his head wrapped in bandages; and St. Giles, the patron of blacksmiths, wearing a leather apron and leading a pony.

There was St. John the Baptist, barefoot with an animal skin over his shoulders. St. Peter and St. Paul were dressed in long robes and drag-ging their chains. St. James and St. John carried fishermen's nets. Twin boys declared they were St. Thomas and his brother. There were many Blessed Mothers, wearing blue shawls, some with chaplets of flowers on their heads, each carrying a doll wrapped in a blanket. Nuns with white veils were as young as four years old. St. Nicholas, St. Boniface and St. Emmeran wore their bishop's miters. St. Gotthard was an abbot. St. Quentin was in a Roman toga. St. Martin wore a beard and old tunic and carried the branch of a tree. St. Francis appeared with a big dog walking by his side.

Two boys stood off by themselves, arguing. Neither was in costume, and the youngest, about five, was in tears.

"What's the trouble?" Fr. Gunther asked them. "Saints mustn't argue, and they mustn't cry."

"He won't let me be in the parade!" the child answered, looking up at the older boy and rubbing his eyes.

"My brother is too little to be a saint," the boy said. "And he can't walk far. He's got a blister on his foot."

"I'm not too little!" the child cried.

"Well, let's see," Father said. "It is a long way. I could bandage your foot. You could be a martyr and ride in a wagon. Would you like that?"

"What's a martyr?" the child asked.

"I know," Gutenberg injected. "You can be St. Christopher," he said to the older boy, "and carry your brother."

"But we don't have a costume," the boy said.

"Take my walking stick," Gutenberg answered. Then scooping the little fellow up in his arms, Gutenberg put him on his brother's shoulders. "There! How's that?"

"Who am I?" the child asked.

"You are the Lord Jesus today," Fr. Gunther told him. He wiped the child's face, then took the Crucifix from his belt, kissed it, and put it in the child's hand. "I'll let you carry this," he said, "but you must promise to hold it very tight. Can you do that?"

"He'll drop it, Father," his brother cautioned.

"No, I won't!" the child answered, his face beaming.

"We'll bring it back, the stick too," the older boy said. "Thank you, Father! Thank you, Master!"

"Hurry up now and join the others," Fr. Gunther told them, and made the sign of the cross over their heads.

As Gutenberg and the priest watched the children leave the churchyard, they saw the little boy clinging to his brother's neck and holding the Crucifix high in his hand. People standing on the street smiled and quietly bowed their heads.

Gutenberg and Fr. Gunther walked across the yard and sat down near the well. The Master seemed worried about something, the priest noticed. What was troubling him, he asked.

Gutenberg had made a loan fifteen years ago with the St. Thomas brotherhood in Strasbourg, he said, for 80 pounds denari. He had paid the interest every year since but had never been able to reduce the principal.

"Every year I am reminded of the money due," Gutenberg said, "because my co-signer, Brechter, is probably dead. But I can't even manage the interest any more."

Fr. Gunther was struck by Gutenberg's faithfulness in paying the interest. "You've done the best you could as long as you could," he said. "Forget it, Master." He suggested that Gutenberg send the St. Thomas chapter one of the Bibles, and ask them to accept it in forgiveness of the debt. A zealous clerk could learn a lesson from this, he thought.

CHAPTER 67

The next spring, Dr. Humery received momentous news from Fulda. The abbot of the Benedictine monastery, the Senator wrote, would purchase a Bible and wanted Master Gutenberg to come and help the monks open a small printing shop of their own. The monastery had been founded by St. Boniface, the great bishop and apostle of Germany. It was 600 years old, and its library was the largest and most valuable in Christendom. An invitation from Fulda was an honor indeed, and to induce Gutenberg to accept it, Dr. Humery and his son Conrad went to Gutenberg with a plan.

"Schoeffer has sold me some casting metal and a supply of letters," Dr. Humery began. "Take my son with you, and show them how the letters and prints are made. You will be guests of the Senator for as long as you wish to stay. Will you go, Johannes?"

Gutenberg was honored by the invitation and pleased that the abbot wanted a printed Bible. That he also wanted his monks to learn printing showed vision and courage.

"Fulda is the first monastery to want to use the new art," Dr. Humery said, "and has great influence throughout the Empire."

"I know," Gutenberg answered, "but I think it would be better if the monks visited Mainz instead. I can demonstrate letter casting and simple page printing, but building a press and book printing involves much more than we can accomplish in a short time."

"Just think, Master," young Conrad interrupted. "The monks have never seen metal letters before. Printing will look like magic to them!" Conrad was 14 years old, a bright, cheerful lad who had been apprenticed in the printing shop for two years. Going to Fulda would be very exciting.

"What do you think, Else?" Gutenberg asked his niece.

"I think you should go, Uncle," Else said firmly. "Conrad will be a good companion."

Gutenberg had never been to Fulda, and it was three days journey at least. Though perhaps they could build a letter press and he could show how the punches and matrices were made. Conrad could do the composing and printing.

Henne offered to go with them as far as Frankfurt, and said that one of his cousins would accompany them the rest of the way. "You'll be safe, Uncle," Henne told him, "and the mountain air will be good for you."

"Perhaps we could go hunting," Conrad ventured hopefully.

"Hunting!" Gutenberg exclaimed, frowning but amused. "You can pray at the tomb of St. Boniface! He was archbishop of Mainz, you know, and is buried at Fulda, I'm told. All right, all right. We'll go to Fulda. To sell a Bible and teach the monks to read backwards. But tell the Senator we'll stay a month only."

Within a week, Gutenberg and Conrad were ready to leave. The carriage was carefully loaded with two wrapped volumes of the Bible, and several bags of letters and metal were hidden in a chest bearing the Isenburg coat of arms. Highwaymen would not risk stealing from the Custos of Mainz, Henne reasoned, and his cousin would be armed. Gutenberg smiled at the precautions. The books are more important than I am, he thought.

As they approached Fulda, they could see the monastery, a large and imposing group of buildings, situated on a wooded slope of the Wasserkuppe overlooking the city. Gutenberg and Conrad received a warm welcome from the Senator and the abbot awaiting them. The monks felt privileged to have the Master himself instruct them and were eager to show him the manuscripts in their scriptorium which they wanted to copy and print.

After a few days rest, Gutenberg and Conrad began work. Gutenberg worked in the foundry casting letters, but it was Conrad who held the monks spellbound as he put the reverse letters together into words and then quickly read the text back to them. Composition was the most difficult task, everyone agreed, but the printing of whole pages of words was magic to see. The days passed quickly and Gutenberg was pleased by the monk's enthusiasm and by how skilled they became despite the inevitable mistakes.

Lent began, and attending Vespers reminded Gutenberg of his days in Strasbourg with the monks at St. Arbogast. The words of the Psalms had special meaning for him now. "Judge Thou, O Lord, them that wrong me." "Forsake me not, O, Lord, my God." "Hear, O Lord, my prayer." "Out of the depths I have cried to Thee."

The abbot could not praise the printed Bible enough, and as Gutenberg looked at the pages with him, it was as if he were seeing them for the first time. He still considered the blank pages a major flaw, but to the abbot, they were completely unimportant.

"Many of our books have blank pages, Master," the abbot told him. "But no two manuscript books are alike. We cannot write identical texts. You must see this Bible as we do, not in terms of perfect printing, but in terms of its perfect and uniform text. You have given us an exemplar printed Bible, Master. I assure you, it will be accepted and used by monasteries everywhere because every copy is exactly the same!"

For the Easter Fair, Conrad printed 100 copies of the Benedictus, the canticle of Zachary which is recited daily from the Gospel of St. Luke. To the great amusement of the monks who had composed the letters, many of their brothers thought the page was manuscript and exceptionally well done.

The monks took Conrad fishing and to hunt for mushrooms. Gutenberg and the Senator went falcon hunting and on leisurely rides through the countryside. The warm spring air, quiet woods and valleys, gave Gutenberg a feeling of contentment he had not experienced in years. His appetite improved on hearty meals of wild boar, hare, partridge and fish from the mountain streams. With the Senator, here at Fulda, Gutenberg found he could talk about the lawsuit and the loss of his printing shop.

Refusing Fust partnership was very wise, in the Senator's opinion. "Either as a partner or as the loser in the lawsuit, Fust would have plagued you. Master," he said. "You should not have lost the shop, but had you managed to keep it, Fust would have challenged your right to ownership, to the Psalter profits, everything."

"I am sure you're right," Gutenberg answered. "But the equipment is mine! And if anything happens to Peter Schoeffer, Fust may have to close the shop and will sell the equipment!"

"You cannot worry about that, Master. You can always cast more letters and go on printing yourself!" the Senator said. "Tell me more about the relief plates."

"I sold the engravings and the relief plates," Gutenberg told him, "because I needed money. My friend Wilhelm, the master engraver from Basel, bought them after the lawsuit. Now his son is using them to print playing cards." This was a new venture, he said, and the young man hoped to make a lot of money. Printing cards was much cheaper and faster than handpainting each one.

The playing card figures were different from the figures Wilhelm and his son had made earlier in Mainz, Gutenberg said. "We made relief plates of those engravings and used them to decorate pages in two Bibles. In other books, however, it is much more important to have the same illustrations in every copy. Not marginal designs only, but pictures important to the text. This can be done using copper relief plates. Text, initial letters, and pictures can be printed at the same time, you see, but it involves much work."

"You mean you can print the words and pictures, everything on a page from metal?" the Senator asked.

"Yes," Gutenberg answered. "It will be done one day, by another printer, I'm sure. But copper is expensive. Everything about printing is expensive! I'm not interested in the relief plates anymore. Young Wilhelm can use them any way he wants."

Gutenberg and Conrad left Fulda in mid-summer with a knight as escort and two monks who would visit St. James scriptorium and the printing shop in Mainz. The visit with the Senator and the work at the monastery had been very satisfying. Gutenberg was glad they had come. He was especially proud of Conrad. The boy had worked hard and was a good teacher as well as a good companion. Conrad had also killed a stag, and the antlers he took home were more cherished than his relic of St. Boniface.

Gutenberg too felt a sense of self-esteem and went home with new hope and interest in the future. Perhaps he and Wilhelm could work together again. Perhaps with the money he received for the Bible, he could visit Strasbourg again and take Else and Henne with him. Gutenberg was in good spirits. He was able to work and make plans again.

Glancing back from the carriage to the hills of Fulda behind them, Gutenberg saw a rainbow in full arc high above the city. He asked the driver to stop and got out to look. All the colors were there, interspersed with fast moving clouds. He lingered to admire the beauty until the colors blew away. The monks said it was a good omen for a safe journey to Mainz.

XVI. THE VISITOR
CHAPTER 68

Else was delighted to see the change in her uncle. Gutenberg had gained weight and did not seem too tired after the long trip to Fulda. When he suggested going to Strasbourg, she knew he was well again.

"How good of you, Uncle," Else told him. "Though you might be too busy, or want to use the money for something else. Dr. Humery is here and he has a surprise for you."

Gutenberg was puzzled when Dr. Humery handed him the key to the room he had used as a printing shop when he first returned to Mainz. It was used now as a storage room.

Henne, Conrad, Nicholas and Heinrich Bechtermuntz, who still worked with Schoeffer, appeared too. Gutenberg wondered why the Bechtermuntz brothers should have come, but they only smiled and said they were glad he was home.

"We thought it was time you began working again, Johannes," Dr. Humery said.

During Gutenberg's absence, and unknown to Fust, Dr. Humery had acquired more letters and printing equipment from Peter Schoeffer, and with the help of the Bechtermuntz brothers, Else and Henne had turned the room into a printing shop once again. Gutenberg could continue printing or go on with his work with the copper relief plates, whatever he chose to do.

"Do open the door, Uncle!" Else urged.

Gutenberg turned the key and stepped inside. There he saw a small letter press, a letter box next to the window, paper, ink, a stool, and worktable. Even his work apron was hung on the wall.

"Are you pleased, Master?" Conrad asked.

Turning around, Gutenberg blinked the tears from his eyes. "It's wonderful, wonderful! Why didn't you tell me, Else!"

"We will help you, Master," Heinrich said.

"And so will I," Conrad injected. "Tell him, Father!"

"There's something else?" Gutenberg asked.

"The mintmaster from Tours is coming to Mainz, Johannes," Dr. Humery said. "Master Nicolaus Jensen is being sent here by command of King Charles of France to see how the new printing is done. When he arrives, you must meet him in your own shop and be able to show him yourself!"

The University of Paris had received copies of the printed Bible from the abbot of St. Victor, Dr. Humery explained. The university abbot had presented one of the Bibles to the king. And the king was so impressed, he had ordered Jensen to establish a royal printing office in Paris.

"Master Jensen will visit the Fust-Schoeffer shop, of course," Dr. Humery said. "But it is you and your Bibles that bring him to Mainz!"

They must drink to the king, Henne said, and invited everyone to sit down and have a glass of wine.

"Where is Tours?" Else wanted to know.

"It's a great city in Anjou, on the Loire river," Henne told her. "Near Chinon, I think."

"And Chinon is where the king met Jeanne d'Arc," Conrad added expansively. "She was the girl soldier whose army defeated the English so Charles could be crowned king. Then she was captured by the English and burned to death, as a witch!"

"And the king's son, Louis, is the dauphin whose mercenary soldiers, the Armagnacs, besieged Strasbourg when I lived there," Gutenberg replied. Everyone agreed that Gutenberg and Master Jensen would have many things to talk about besides printing.

"I shall be honored to meet the Master from Tours," Gutenberg said. "He is a goldsmith so I'm sure he will understand printing from metal. But Peter Schoeffer can teach him how the letters are made as well as I. How much Jensen will learn depends on the man himself and how long he will stay."

Jensen was given an elaborate welcome by the Archbishop Erbach when he arrived in Mainz in the summer of 1458. The abbots, guild and council members, Fust and Schoeffer attended a reception at the episcopal palace. It was reported that Jensen looked more like a courtier than a goldsmith, although his manner seemed gracious and friendly.

Fust personally escorted Jensen through the printing office and showed him the finished Psalter. Jensen was informed that the first pages of a second Psalter for St. James monastery in Mainz would be printed soon, and that he would be able to observe each step in its publication. Schoeffer was directed to make sure the honored guest spent his time profitably. Jensen, who knew Gutenberg no longer owned the printing office, discreetly refrained from asking questions.

Jensen and Schoeffer were close in age, they discovered, both in their 30's, with Schoeffer the younger by only five years. They had both studied in Paris and were excellent calligraphers. Jensen was married, but as a bachelor in Mainz, he greatly enjoyed the social affairs to which Schoeffer and Christine invited him. Their visitor was charming with women, Schoeffer observed, and hoped he was as talented as a goldsmith.

Facinated by what he saw in the printing office, Jensen spent weeks listening and watching as Schoeffer explained the techniques and procedures necessary to produce the metal letters and printed pages. He insisted on doing the casting, composition, and printing himself, and then designed letters from his own handwriting and cut his own punches and matrices. The man had enormous skill, Schoeffer noted with admiration.

"I am an apprentice," Jensen told Schoeffer. "I must become a master!"

"I will introduce you to Master Gutenberg as soon as Fust leaves for Rome," Peter said. "I know you are anxious to meet him. I hope you understand the delay." It had been a difficult time for Gutenberg since the lawsuit, he said.

Gutenberg had written Schoeffer to thank him for providing the equipment they had taken to Fulda and for equipping the workshop in his home. He was especially pleased that Schoeffer had used the two-color initials in the Psalters. But they had seen little of each other since the Bibles were published. Jensen's visit could be an opportunity, Schoeffer hoped, to erase the distance that had developed between them.

Gutenberg was very impressed with Jensen. The Frenchman's intense interest in printing and his application to work, particularly to the designing of punches and casting of letters, won Gutenberg's respect. Together they would construct a hand-casting instrument, Gutenberg told him. He would also teach Jensen how the initials and copper relief plates were made.

After their first meeting, Jensen became a regular visitor to Gutenberg Hof. He enjoyed Gutenberg's stories about the early days at the Sorgenloch mint, how Rudi and Uncle Otto had solved the letter height problem, and hearing about the work in Strasbourg and Basel. He was amused by the Master's candor in answering questions.

Why did he go to Strasbourg? "Because my brother and I were exiles from Mainz!" Gutenberg said. How did the work begin? "It began with the alphabet. But printing with metal letters is not as simple as A-B-C!"

Writing in his journal, Jensen commented on the complexities involved in printing books in volume and the paradoxical simplicity of printing single pages exactly alike. "Printing books is difficult," he wrote, "because of the number of pages. The sheets must be in proper order, in each quire section, or individual pages will be printed in the wrong place. Yet one page, of any text, any statement, can be copied in a few hours and 100 prints made in a single day!"

"Casting letters is simple enough. Composing them into words spelled correctly is difficult," Jensen wrote. "A press can be large or small. One man with a supply of letters, a small letter press, paper and ink, can compose and print pages by himself and carry his workshop on his back! The big printing press in the printing office is a marvelous piece of equipment and what I shall need in Paris. Master Gutenberg and Peter Schoeffer are truly artist craftsmen!"

Jensen also spent considerable time at the St. James scriptorium where the Bible quires were stored. The monks showed him the new Psalter pages they were working on, and counseled Jensen to print no ill books. "You must serve the king, but your work must honor God first of all," he was told.

Jensen hoped he could do both. Interest in printing may be a whim of the king, he thought, but it has become an obsession with me. He might never print a Bible, yet Jensen hoped one day to design letters as fine as Master Gutenberg's, and to print books of the same quality and with the same success as the men in Mainz.

Reluctantly, after almost a year, Jensen announced his departure. He had postponed his return to France several times for various reasons. It had been the most important and unforgetable year of his life, he told Schoeffer. In his trunk were a casting mold, a supply of letters, punches and matrices, and Gutenberg's metal formula for the letter castings. Most treasured among Jensen's possessions were the letters he had cast from gold florins and the prints he had made on Gutenberg's letter press.

Fust gave Jensen two Psalters, one for the king of France and one for the bishop of Tours. Gutenberg gave Jensen a Bible for the bishop and Missal for himself. Schoeffer promised to send him one of the new Psalters as soon as they were completed. The gifts Jensen left behind seemed trivial, he thought, compared to the dream and knowledge he had received.

"Master Jensen has been in Mainz a long time," Dr. Humery observed. "When he gets home, he may find that King Charles has lost all interest in printing."

"Jensen must not rely on the king or the dauphin for anything,"

Gutenberg replied. "The king may have changed his mind about a royal printing office. But somehow I don't think Jensen will change his mind about wanting to become a master printer. He is a brilliant designer of letters."

"Nicolaus is the most exciting man I have ever met," Else told her husband, "except you, of course. It's too bad we won't see him again."

If Jensen was as serious about printing as he was about romance, Henne smiled, he was certain to become the greatest printer in France. He knew Schoeffer agreed with him. Else knew Christine agreed with her.

XVII. THE SIEGE
CHAPTER 69

On May 6, 1459, after an episcopate of 25 years, Archbishop Dietrich von Erbach of Mainz died. His body lay in state before the main altar of the Dom, and everyone in Mainz passed by to offer prayers. Viewing Erbach on his bier, Gutenberg was reminded of Guillaume von Diest, the archbishop of Strasbourg who had died so soon after Johann Hultz completed the cathedral spire. Erecting the spire had been the dream and passion of von Diest, Gutenberg thought. Had printing the Bibles been Erbach's dream, things might have ended differently. Erbach was proud of the Bibles now that they were published, but his own interest and involvement had been dispassionate from the beginning. The archbishop had taken no part in the Fust lawsuit. Whether he later regretted Fust's action or his own inaction, Gutenberg never knew.

Six weeks after the funeral, Chancellor Diether von Isenburg was proclaimed Erbach's successor. With the exception of Johann Fust, who lost his appointment as collector of papal revenues, and some others, the people of Mainz were happy about Isenburg's ascension to the princely throne. He was a popular prelate, but had taken the throne without the blessing of Pope Pius II.

Under the terms of the Concordat of Vienna, which Cardinal Cusanus had helped to conclude, the Pope could depose a hostile German archbishop-elector if he chose to do so. Isenburg was not hostile to Rome, but Rome was still hostile to him because of his old alliance with Duke Sigismund. His presumption to the see of Mainz was not pleasing to the pontiff, although Cusanus favored Isenburg.

The abbots of Mainz hoped that Cusanus, who was now a member of the Curia and general vicar in Rome, could persuade the Pope to accept Isenburg rather than depose him. Two years later, however, on August 21, 1461, Adolf von Nassau was named Archbishop of Mainz. This announcement resulted in preparation for war - Isenburg to defend his title, and Nassau to claim his. The city of Mainz could become a battleground.

Peter Schoeffer published Isenburg's call to arms. He published Nassau's notice of attack unless Isenburg withdrew and the Mainz Council surrendered the city peaceably. The Council's reply was delayed, and three weeks before Christmas, on December 2, Nassau's men stormed the city gates.

For the next ten months the citizens of Mainz rallied to Isenburg and withstood the siege. Arming themselves, they turned back countless forays, but Nassau's forces did not retreat. Fust and his wife and daughter went to live in Eltville. Schoeffer and his men remained in Mainz to complete the new 48-line Bibles, and planned to take them to Eltville or Eberbach for safekeeping, if necessary. Some of Gutenberg's Bibles had already been removed to other monasteries.

On the night of October 28, 1462, Archbishop Nassau himself arrived at Mainz with a large army. Church bells rang the alarm, and the walls of the city were breached. Henne Humbrecht was with the militia, and waiting anxiously at Hof Gutenberg, Else and Gutenberg prayed for his safe return. The noise of fighting could be heard everywhere.

Henne appeared in the morning with Arnold Gelthuss who had been injured. Dr. Humery and his family were safe, Henne said. He had not seen Schoeffer, but the printing office was barricaded and had not been broken into. Fust's son was said to have fled the city. Over 150 homes had been set afire, and 400 men lay dead in the streets. The convents and churches were crowded with wounded. Lost and frightened children hid in the rubble, waiting to be found.

At noon Nassau entered Mainz triumphant. Commanding citizens to assemble in the market square, the archbishop denied their pleas for mercy and banished 800 men from the city. Only bakers, butchers, those needed to care for the sick and bury the dead, clergy and old people were allowed to stay. Isenburg had escaped to Trier; and as punishment to the guilds that had supported him, Nassau deprived Mainz of its charter and its many privileges as a free city of the Empire.

In the week following that terrible night of fighting, Hof zum Gutenberg was confiscated for use by Nassau's men. Because of his age, Gutenberg could have remained in Mainz, but chose to go to Frankfurt with Else and Henne. Gelthuss and his family went to Bishofsheim, where they had relatives.

In March of 1463, after a cold and difficult winter, the exiled citizens were allowed to return, but only 300 were permitted to stay. Henne was among them, and he, Else and Gutenberg moved into a small house near St. Christoph's.

Nassau ordered the printing office closed, but allowed Schoeffer to reopen after the Easter octave. Many of the printers had fled to other cities, however, and would not be returning to Mainz. Pfister and Eggestein had left following the lawsuit. Now, Rusch and Mentelin were in Strasbourg.

Ruppel and von Hanau were in Basel. Kefer had gone to Nuremburg and Zell to Cologne. Johann and Wenderlin von Speyer had returned to Speyer. Sweynheym and Pannartz were on their way to Subiaco, near Rome, to begin printing at the Benedictine abbey of Santa Scholastica. Only the Bechtermuntz brothers remained in the Rheingau, at Eltville.

Fust returned to Mainz, anxious to be of service to Nassau and to resume printing operations. But with the most experienced men gone, what could they do, Schoeffer asked. Hire and teach new men, Fust told him. He would never close the shop. What books would they print? Fust would go to Rome again, he said. Cardinal Cusanus had promised printing from the church, but so far they had received nothing! Extremely angry at this, Fust was determined to get Cusanus' support and prepared to travel to Brixen, if necessary. He would return in the fall.

Taking his rightful seat by force and exacting harsh retribution from the people of Mainz, Nassau now turned his attention to rebuilding the city and relieving hardship. Prolonged discontent among the clergy, guild and council members would not serve him, the Pope or Germany well, and Nassau saw his duty to bring peace and prosperity to Mainz once again.

From the abbots, Nassau learned of the circumstances surrounding the Fust-Gutenberg lawsuit and the important roles Isenburg and Cardinal Cusanus had played in publication of the Bibles. At the Dom the Gospel was read from a printed Bible. Monks sang the Office from a Psalter printed by Fust and Schoeffer. The Benedictines at St. James had read and corrected the text of the Psalters, Nassau was told.

The aging abbot of St. James, Adrian Brielis, made a personal appeal on behalf of Gutenberg. The Master was still alive, he said, but had never received proper honor for his great work. "A great injustice was done," Brielis said. "It will be ten years since the Bibles were printed. Master Gutenberg is old. He is almost blind. He lost his printing office and he lost his home. He deserves recognition by the Church for printing the magnificent Bibles of Mainz!"

"What do you suggest, Father Abbot?" Nassau asked.

"Restore his home to him, Your Grace," the abbot answered, "and I'm sure he needs money, even though many of the Bibles have been sold."

It seemed strange to Nassau that the abbot should be pleading Gutenberg's cause, yet Brielis was not alone in his praise of Master Gutenberg and desirous of righting a wrong done to him. The Master had earned the respect of abbots throughout the see of Mainz, and so must I, Nassau thought. These powerful men could be helpful allies or obstinate

opponents, and their good will was worth a gesture to Gutenberg.
He would consider the abbot's suggestion, Nassau said.

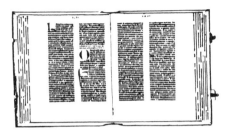

XVIII. THE REWARD
CHAPTER 70

Bright sunshine ushered in the first day of the new year, 1465. Else had baked the traditional New Year's cake to serve when visitors came, and Gutenberg sat near the window, carefully polishing the silver head of his new walking stick. It had been a gift from Else and Henne on his name day, December 27, the feast of St. John the Apostle.

Gutenberg smiled as he stroked the metal and rough-carved hickory. "Now I can walk to Mass by myself," he said. "It is beautiful and it's useful. I like that!"

The house on Schustergasse was comfortable and though smaller than Hof zum Gutenberg, it had a well and garden of its own. Else was pleased that her uncle seemed content. He never complained, was cheerful, and in good health, except for his eyesight. His hands were thinner and his hair whiter, but his voice was still strong. Else read aloud to him every afternoon until he dozed off for a nap. In good weather they went for walks together.

Gutenberg was not lonely. He had outlived most of his comtemporaries but still saw Dr. Humery at the Weinstube every week, and cousins Rudi and Arnold came frequently for a game of cards. Former apprentices, printers and abbots wrote to him. Nicholas and Heinrich Bechtermuntz continued to work on the copper relief plates and came into Mainz regularly to show Gutenberg what they had done. With an unerring sense of touch, the Master could tell if the edges were sharp enough to print clearly. The plates were improving, he told them.

Gutenberg missed seeing Peter Schoeffer most of all. Their father-son relationship, once on a daily basis, had been strained following publication of the Bibles. Gutenberg had been too angry and hurt then to be interested in the Bibles or the printing office. He would always be grateful for the equipment Peter had sold to Dr. Humery, and Jensen's visit had been pleasant, but that was seven years ago. Peter had never sought his advice or shared any problem.

After the lawsuit, a number of volumes had been published, including two issues of the Psalter in 1457 and in 1459, and in 1462, the beautiful 48-line Bible with engraved calligraphic ornaments and new letters Peter had designed himself. Since the siege of Mainz, however, only one Papal Bull had been issued. Getting new men and training them had undoubtedly taken much of Peter's time. Gutenberg hadn't seen him in almost a year.

Fust was still in France or Italy, and rarely in Mainz anymore. Peter had not become a partner of Fust, although the double shield representing both their names still hung above the door of the printing shop. But Peter and Christine had not married. The lawsuit had cast long, long shadows over many lives, Gutenberg thought sadly.

Looking up from her work, Else was surprised to see a messenger turn in at the gate. She was expecting her husband but this man was in uniform.

"We have company, Uncle," Else said. "I don't know who it is."

A knock came at the door, and Else opened it to a young man wearing the insignia of the Archbishop of Mainz. Politely he asked to see Master Gutenberg.

"My uncle is at home," Else told him. "Please come in."

"I have a message from His Eminence Adolf von Nassau," the officer announced to Gutenberg and presented him with a sealed paper.

"Will you read it, my dear," Gutenberg asked Else. "Please sit down," Gutenberg said, as the messenger continued to stand at attention.

"No, thank you," he replied, bowing slightly as he spoke. "It is an honor to meet you, Master."

Else opened the seal and read aloud. "Master Johannes Gensfleisch zum Gutenberg, patrician of Mainz, is requested to be present at the episcopal palace of Archbishop-Elector Adolf von Nassau on the 17th day of January, year of our Lord 1465, one hour before noon, at which time and place he will be honored for his work as the first printer of the Holy Bible."

"Oh, my goodness," Else cried. "It says this recognition is given on behalf of the diocese and city of Mainz, the electors of the Palatinate and other German Sees, and the Holy Father in Rome! Do you hear, Uncle!"

"Yes, yes," Gutenberg answered.

"There's more," Else said. "You are to be made a noble of the archbishop's court and receive a pension for as long as you live."

Else handed the paper back to her uncle. Quite overcome by this news she began to cry.

Gutenberg studied the paper closely. "It must be true," he said. "It is signed 'Adolf'. I can read the name."

"Oh, isn't it wonderful, Uncle!" Else exclaimed. "I wish Henne were here!"

"May I tell His Eminence that you will attend, Master?" the messenger asked.

Gutenberg rose to respond. "Yes, I shall attend. Please say that I thank the archbishop most sincerely, and am most grateful for this honor to me."

"Will you have some cake?" Else asked the young officer. "You are our first visitor in the new year. And you bring us such wonderful news!"

Word of the forthcoming event spread quickly as copies of the achbishop's message were delivered to the monastery abbots, Council members, and masters of the craft guilds. January 17 was only two weeks away!

The intervening days were filled with activity as Else shopped hurriedly to order new clothes for her husband and uncle and to have a new dress made for herself.

"Your dress should be blue velvet, my dear," Gutenberg told his niece. "Blue was your mother's favorite color, and you are so like her. Blue velvet with silk ribbon. Don't you agree, Henne?"

Henne smiled his assent. He was always agreeable and as attentive to Gutenberg's needs as his wife.

"A grey coat for you, Henne," Gutenberg went on, "with a fur collar. And I want new boots, Else. Soft, brown leather boots, and a new hat." All of them must look their best, he said.

The matter of escorts, however, presented a problem. Dr. Humery was Gutenberg's oldest friend, but he had hurt his foot and could not walk without pain. Rudi, Arnold and Henne were relatives, but Gutenberg did not wish to favor one over the other. It was appropriate, perhaps, for one of the abbots to have the honor. If only his brother, Friele, or Johann Hultz could be here, Gutenberg thought. In the end he chose young Conrad Humery. The boy who had gone to Fulda with him was now a young man and a journeyman in Schoeffer's shop. Conrad was proud to represent his father.

The evening before the ceremony, Schoeffer left the printing office, carrying a large package wrapped in a blanket. He made his way carefully through the snow to Hof zum Humbrecht. Mainz was beautiful in winter too, Peter thought. It was quiet, and only his footsteps could be heard crunching the snow as he walked.

Nassau's special attention to Gutenberg had served two purposes,

Schoeffer was sure. The honors, however long overdue, would cheer Gutenberg immensely, and they would also benefit the archbishop by giving him an opportunity to show magnaminity which would reflect well on himself.

Fust had had no success in Rome where the Cardinal was too ill to see him. In his absence, Schoeffer had received an important printing order from Frankfurt, and Johann and Wenderlin von Speyer came back to Mainz to help train the apprentices. Satisfied with their progress, Fust had returned to France. He always sold several Bibles and Psalters there, and did not interfere with the work in Mainz. I am my own master, Schoeffer thought with satisfaction, even though I am not a partner!

In the past ten years, Schoeffer had cast thousands of new letters in different sizes and styles, and he was sure that now, with well-trained letter casters, compositors and printers, the business would prosper more than ever before. He had made some changes in operation, but had not changed the Master's methods of casting or scheduling the flow of work. It was a very efficient system.

I wanted to succeed on my own, and I have, Schoeffer thought, but I should have discussed more of the work with the Master. And I should have been more attentive to Christine and her mother since their return to Mainz.

Schoeffer had had little time for a personal life, however. For months he had worked day and night. Had I been married, he thought, with family responsibilities, the work and Christine would have suffered. Now he would be able to see her and the Master more often.

"It's Peter, Uncle!" Else announced, as she opened the door. "How good of you to come!"

Stomping the snow from his boots, Peter removed his hat and came into the room where Gutenberg was sitting. "Good evening, Master," Peter said. "I came to wish you well tomorrow."

Surprise and pleasure showed in Gutenberg's face when he heard Peter's voice. "Thank you, Peter," he answered. "Come here where I can see you."

Peter put down the package he was carrying and shook Gutenberg's hand. "It's good to see you, Master." he said.

Gutenberg looked well, Schoeffer thought. His face was flushed from the excitement or from the wine sitting by his hand. His hair and beard were white and he seemed a little thinner. But his handclasp was firm.

Peter seemed heavier and older than Gutenberg remembered. His hair was grey at the temples now. How old was Peter, he wondered.

"I am very happy to see you," Gutenberg said. "Sit down, Peter. Sit down. Will you have a glass of wine?"

"Of course he will," Else answered. How was Christine, she asked.

Christine was fine and was coming with him to the palace tomorrow, Peter said. "I've brought you a present, Master," he went on. "It's not finished, but when it is, I'll have a copy bound for you."

Peter unwrapped the blanket and laid several quires on the table. "It's Cicero's "De Officiis," Peter said, "and has several Greek phrases in it. I've cast those letters in Greek."

Gutenberg held the quartos close to his face, looking intently at the Latin and Greek words on the page. He rubbed the pages between his fingers. They were vellum, he noted.

"May I see too, Uncle," Else asked. "Oh, how beautiful! I wish I could read it."

"Cicero would be pleased as I am, Peter," Gutenberg said. "It must have taken months of work. When will you publish the book?"

"This year," Peter told him.

"More than one edition, I hope," Gutenberg replied. How many pages was it? How many copies would be printed? Which monastery had requested the book? Peter smiled at the Master's desire to know.

Gutenberg asked about the men at the shop and wondered if any of those who had printed the 42-line Bible with him would be in Mainz for the ceremonies. From Strasbourg and Cologne, surely, Peter thought. The Speyer brothers were still here, he said, but would be going on to Venice soon. Sweynheym and Pannartz were doing well in Subiaco, where they were printing Lactantius' "Opera."

Gutenberg had heard that Mentelin published a Bible in Strasbourg, but felt that Peter's 48-line Bible must be superior. The new letters were very readable, he said, and fewer pages, one volume, was easier to handle.

No word had been received from Nicolaus Jensen in over two years. Perhaps because there was a new king in France, Schoeffer thought. Since Louis Dauphin became King Louis XI, Jensen might not be favored by the court. The new pope, Paul II, was reported to be interested in printing, however.

Cardinal Cusanus was dead, Gutenberg said. He had died in August, in Italy, the abbot told him, and every Benedictine house in the Empire sang a requiem for him. "The cardinal left instructions that if he died south of the Alps, he was to be buried in Rome, and if he died north of the Alps, he wanted to be buried at Kues. So his body is in Rome, but his heart will be buried in the place where he was born."

Earlier, in 1458, Gutenberg related, the cardinal had established a hospice in Kues for 33 old and needy men. The number represented the years of Christ's lifetime on earth, and was to include six men from the clergy and six noblemen. The hospice was named St. Nicholas for the holy bishop, and had cost 10,000 gulden.

"It was Cardinal Cusanus who wanted the Bibles printed, you know," Gutenberg went on. "He gave the money for the paper and vellum. And he knew Fust's oath was a lie."

Peter had not known this before. Gutenberg had never told him! It explained a lot of things, he thought. Fust's son had never become a cardinal because Cusanus had never made the appointment!

"I met the cardinal only once," Gutenberg said, "and will always remember his face. I so wish that he, Isenburg, my brother and sister could share the day tomorrow."

"They all will be here in spirit, Uncle," Else told him.

"The shop will be closed so all the printers can come," Peter said.

Lost momentarily in his own thoughts, Gutenberg stood up and seemed to reach a decision about something he wanted to say. "I asked Dr. Humery's son to be my escort," Gutenberg said. "I should prefer that you be my escort, Peter. Will you?"

"Oh, that is a splendid idea, Uncle," Else injected. "Will you do it, Peter? I'm sure Conrad and Christine will understand."

Surprised and touched by Gutenberg's words, Peter hesitated briefly before replying. "Perhaps Conrad would escort Christine," he said. "Her mother will not come, of course. I will be honored to be your escort, Master."

Deep satisfaction showed in Gutenberg's face. "I shall ask Dr. Humery and Conrad to invite Christine," he answered. "Thank you, Peter. Thank you!"

They must be ready to leave before 11 o'clock, Gutenberg added. They must not be late!

"Else hugged her Uncle and kissed Peter on the cheek. "Oh, this is as it should be," she cried. "I know Christine will think so too!"

That night as Else put out the candles and went to bed, she remembered another evening long ago, when her mother had wished Grandfather was alive to see Uncle's first prints from Strasbourg. She remembered when her uncle had left Mainz, promising to send silk ribbon for her hair. She remembered how happy they had been when he came back to Mainz to stay.

"If only Orte...or Uncle had had a son, Henne," Else told her husband. "He is the last Gensfleisch to bear the name."

"And the first Gutenberg to be honored by an archbishop," Henne answered. "Your uncle is the first goldsmith-printer, Else. He is the first to cast letters from metal and the first to print books. He is the first man to print the Bible! I am glad he has lived long enough to be honored for his work."

The heartaches of ten years ago could not be forgotten, either, Else reflected, but neither would the wonderful day tomorrow be forgotten. Did they have enough wine, she asked Henne, to serve the guests she had invited to Hof Humbrecht after the ceremony.

CHAPTER 71

At exactly 11 o'clock, January 17, the carriage containing Gutenberg and Schoeffer, Else and Henne, stopped in front of the archbishop's residence. The day was chilly with a grey, overcast sky, and snow from the night before had laid a thin white carpet on the cobblestones. At the door the abbots and pastors of St. Francis, St. Christoph, St. Stephan, St. James, and St. Victor were waiting. Friars, monks and curates from the Dom stood silent and smiling near the steps.

Else and Henne alighted first, then Schoeffer, who held out his hand for Gutenberg. Stepping down firmly and carrying his walking stick, Gutenberg bowed to the clergy and then followed behind them through the massive oak doors.

Inside, the audience room was brightly lighted and Gutenberg could see guild and council members standing on either side of the aisle, as the procession passed by. Gutenberg and Peter took their places in the front row.

A bell sounded, signalling the arrival of the archbishop who entered from the right, escorted by four acolytes and two monsignori. Nassau took his seat on a raised platform at the front. His scarlet cape trimmed with ermine, his face stern under his white miter, Nassau was an impressive figure. On each lectern on either side of the platform was a volume of the printed Bible.

The crowd applauded the archbishop and then hushed as one of the monsignors took a rolled document from Nassau's hand and faced the assembly.

"This marks the tenth year since the publication of the first printed Bible in Mainz by Master Johannes Gutenberg," he began.

Else's eyes were on her uncle. He looked handsome, she thought. His black coat fit him well and he stood straight and unaided, listening to each word.

"We, Adolf," the monsignor continued, "do make known and publish by this certificate, by reason of the grateful and willing services rendered, and that may still be rendered in the future, to us and our See by our dear and faithful Johannes Gutenberg..."

Else noticed that Herr Bayer, chairman of the Mainz Council, and Master Schmitt, head of the goldsmith guild, were present. She recognized friends from Frankfurt, Eltville and Wiesbaden. She saw shoulder patches from Heidelberg, Fulda, Cologne, Trier, even Strasbourg! Could the two young men standing with the Franciscans be the sons of Uncle's old friends there, Else wondered.

"Moreover, we shall not deprive him of such services as long as he lives; and in order that he may benefit all the more from such services, we shall each and every year when we clothe our ordinary courtiers, clothe him at the same time like one of our noblemen, and have our court clothing given to him."

Else's thoughts went back to the day Gutenberg had returned to Strasbourg after her grandmother died. His hair and mustache were red then. She had knitted him a scarf. Her little cousins, Orte and Odilgen, had sung Wiedersehn as the barge left the Fischtor. How proud they would have been of their uncle today! Else wiped her eyes.

"And each and every year 20 malder of grain and two fieder of wine for the use of his household, yet so that he neither sell it or give it away, let it enter free of tax, duty and toll into our city of Mainz; and also exempt him graciously, as long as he lives and will be and remain our servant, from watch duty, military service, taxation and sundries which we have already imposed and shall hereafter impose upon our citizens and residents of said city of Mainz."

Else smiled at this. Age had freed Gutenberg from some responsibilities and their store of wine had never diminished except during the siege. Now, her uncle would say that the wine tasted better, without tax or toll added! No mention was made, however, of restoring Hof zum Gutenberg to his possession. Uncle would like that better than anything else, Else thought.

Still, the archbishop had been generous.

"In witness thereof, we have attached our seal to this document which is issued at Eltville, on Thursday, the day of St. Anthony, January 17, 1465."

The monsignor bowed to the archbishop, then stepped down and presented the document to Gutenberg. He also attached ribbons of the episcopal colors to Gutenberg's shoulder, indicating that Gutenberg was now a member of Nassau's court.

Gutenberg gripped Schoeffer's arm. Isenburg should be here, he thought suddenly. Nassau is a stranger! Yet he is lauding me because I printed the Bible. I lost my home because of him. Now I prosper because of him.

The audience applauded again as the abbot of St. Victor left his seat and rose to speak. The abbot was a friend of Isenburg. What would he have to say? Gutenberg wondered. And the abbot reminded him of someone. Who was it? Then he remembered the Cisterian monk who had preached so long ago at St. Odile.

"If you abide by my word, you shall be my disciples indeed, and you shall know the truth and the truth shall make you free." Words taken from the Holy Gospel of St. John," the abbot began.

"God is truth," the abbot said. "This book we call the Holy Bible, here before us, contains the Word and Acts of God, recorded by men, inspired by God, to bring His Truth to the world. It is the history of a chosen people, and of a promise made to them. It is the witness also of an adopted people to the promise fulfilled for all mankind by Jesus Christ, the Son of God.

"St. Paul tells us in his second letter to Timothy, 'All scripture is inspired by God, and useful for teaching, for reproving, for correcting, for instruction in justice, that the man of God be perfect, equipped for every good work.' The Holy Scriptures have but one purpose - to lead all men to God. And this purpose is the Will of God. God revealed Himself to Abraham as the one and true God of heaven and earth; He gave His law to Moses; but He gave His only begotten Son to us."

The archbishop and the clergy listened with attention. The abbot's knowledge of scripture, the content and tone of his address, were different from anything they had heard before or expected to hear that day.

"Now," the abbot went on, "we are children of God and heirs in Christ to life everlasting in the kingdom of heaven. 'For this is the Will of my Father who sent me, that whoever beholds the Son and believes in Him, shall have everlasting life, and I will raise him up on the last day,' promises the Lord in the Gospel of St. John.

"The establishment of Christ's church upon earth occurred less than sixty days after the Resurrection, at Pentecost, when, according to the Book of Acts, the disciples 'were all filled with the Holy Spirit and began to speak in foreign tongues.' And the church 'continued steadfastly in the teaching of the apostles and in the communion of the breaking of the bread and in the prayers.'

"It is an interesting fact that the written Word of God, like the Word Incarnate, was also born in Bethlehem. It was in a cell next to the grotto of the Nativity where St. Jerome wrote the first complete and authoritive Bible in Latin.

"In the year 405 this Latin Vulgate text was established by the Holy Father as the one, universal Bible of the universal, catholic and apostolic Christian Church. Who can measure the love and labor of centuries as men of God copied these Sacred Scriptures! Who but God can know and measure the new victories in the quest for souls because of the printed Word of God!

"Before 1455 it took one monk one year to make one manuscript copy of the Bible. Master Gutenberg and his men printed 185 Bibles in three years! And it is with God's help that the Vulgate text, intact and unchanged for 1000 years, is the same text found in the printed Bible you see here before you.

"Yes, we enter now a new era in Sacred Writings!" The abbot looked briefly at Gutenberg.

"St. Matthew says, 'By their fruits you will know them.' We know Master Gutenberg by the fruits of his life, and we thank him for his generous heart and his beautiful gifts to the honor and glory of Almighty God."

The abbot paused, then went on. "To the world, the art of printing means new books and new knowledge undreamed of. It means a new craft, a new business. To the Church, it means a new and wonderful era of apostleship for God. Within a few years we will have thousands of dedicated religious, free to leave the monasteries where they copied the Gospels, and free to go into the world as missionaries preaching the Gospel! What men could be better equipped for this holy work, and what an opportunity to fulfill our Lord's command!

"One day, I believe, the printed Bible will be used throughout the Empire, and printed in many languages. One day every Christian may be able to read the Holy Scriptures for himself.

"Truly we in Mainz are 'humbled under the mighty hand of God' who has used one of our own to help fulfill His desire and plan for mankind: that all men come to know Him, to love Him, and to serve Him in this world and to be happy with Him forever in the next.

"Master Gutenberg's works will live on! He has found a way for all to know God's words of truth as revealed by the Holy Spirit. 'That we might be', as St. James says, 'the first-fruits of His creatures.' "

The abbot returned to his seat amid loud applause. Then the archbishop rose, was handed his crosier, and prepared to bless the assembly.

"I have received permission to grant everyone present this day the papal blessing of His Holiness Pope Paul II," Nassau announced.

The audience knelt as the archbishop intoned the blessing. Then rising to their feet, people cheered and began to chant "Ad multos annos!" As Nassau left the platform and moved to speak a few words with Gutenberg and the abbot, the acclaim was deafening.

CHAPTER 72

The pension brought several changes to Gutenberg's life. He didn't travel much anymore, but was able to live more comfortably and entertained frequent visitors to Hof zum Humbrecht. Sharing reminiscences, talking about the work other printers were doing, was always stimulating to Gutenberg, who never lost his enthusiasm and his interest in the metal letters. He never discussed the lawsuit, however, or the loss of his shop. "Those days are gone," he would say. "I forget them."

Johann Hultz' son and von Ramstein's son, whose Alsacian hats Else had seen at the pension ceremony, went back to Strasbourg and reported that Master Gutenberg was in good health and spirits. As a result, Fr. Anthony Heilmann and his brothers, Nicholas and Andreas, came for a visit later that summer and stayed a month in Mainz. It was a joyous reunion between old friends.

Johann Fust did not receive the coveted printing contract from Rome, but because of his papal connections was able to sell many Bibles and Psalters among the lords and clergy in Germany and in France. On one of his regular trips to Paris, Fust died. The letter his family received stated that death came on October 30, 1466 from plague then raging through the city.

GUTENBERG - THE MASTER PRINTER

Schoeffer and Christine Fust were married the following spring. After so many years, the couple was finally united and everyone was happy for them. The same year also Fust's widow, Margarete, was married to Conrad Henly who became Schoeffer's partner. With Schoeffer and Henly to manage their affairs, both Christine and her mother would benefit from the success of the printing office. Schoeffer was at last master of the shop in is own right, and the double shield printer's mark of Fust and Schoeffer was changed to the mark of Schoeffer only.

Schoeffer made plans now to publish the Summa Theologica of St. Thomas Aquinas. This was a mammoth project, fully as ambitious and difficult as printing the Bibles had been, and he consulted Gutenberg about the work. The Master appreciated their closer relationship, and even consented to visit the printing office.

There, Gutenberg found the presses, letter cases and foundry as he remembered them. Few things had been moved, though furniture had been added. There was more storage space for paper and printed sheets, and all of the presses had been repaired. Nailed to the first printing press built in Mainz was a silver casting of the Gensfleisch coat of arms.

The young apprentices and journeymen who had attended the archbishop's ceremony but not met Master Gutenberg personally were proud to speak with him. These were the printers who could carry on his work in Mainz, and Gutenberg was proud to know them.

It was an emotional visit and Schoeffer hoped that Gutenberg would come more often now to see the work in progress.

On Candlemas Day, February 2, 1468, Schoeffer took the first finished pages of the Summa to show Gutenberg. When he arrived at the house, Else looked worried and told him her uncle was in bed.

"He hasn't felt good, you know," she said. "But he will be happy to see you, Peter."

Shoeffer was concerned to find Gutenberg much thinner and paler. Sitting up in bed but breathing heavily, Gutenberg brightened when Peter came into the room.

"I've brought you the Summa," Peter said.

"Oh, yes," Gutenberg answered, "I want to see that." His voice was weak, and talking seemed to be an effort.

Peter sat down and placed the pages on the edge of the bed. Gutenberg touched them lightly with his finger tips but his hands shook when he tried to pick them up.

"I know they are beautiful, Peter," he said. "I'll study them tomorrow."

"Don't tire yourself, Master," Peter replied gently.

"You will print many fine books," Gutenberg said. "I printed three and the Bible. As beautiful as Hultz' spire in Strasbourg, that's what I wanted it to be."

"And I've tried to print books as beautiful as your Bible," Peter answered. Such reflection saddened Peter, and he changed the subject. "I've brought you something else," he said, taking a small package from his pocket. "Today is Candlemas, and these are blessed candle from the Dom. Tomorrow is the feast of St. Blaise. You must ask Fr. Gunther to bless your throat!"

"I'll do that," Gutenberg smiled. "Thank you, Peter."

When Peter left the house, he knew the Master was dying. Else too sensed the end was near. Death did not distress her uncle, however. "I'm in God's hands," he had told her. "There is nothing to fear."

Else looked in on Gutenberg after Peter had gone. He appeared to be asleep but opened his eyes when he heard her footsteps.

"Is there anything you want, Uncle?" Else asked.

"Yes," Gutenberg said. "I forgot something. My gold letter A. I want Peter to have it. And the letters Dr. Humery gave me. I want Claus and Heine Bechtermuntz to have them. Tell Dr. Humery he must give the archbishop a receipt."

"I'll tell him," Else replied. She leaned over and smoothed Gutenberg's hair and kissed his forehead. "I love you so," she said.

"I love you, my dear," Gutenberg told her, "my dear little Else."

The next day, Wednesday, Dr. Humery, Rudi and Arnold came to see Gutenberg. In early evening, with his niece, Henne and Fr. Gunther at his bedside, Gutenberg died. The angel of death came quietly as they prayed the Angelus together.

Many who attended the pension ceremony were present again for the requiem in the church of St. Francis. Three abbots, the pastor, Fr. Gunther and Fr. Cremer offered the Mass of the Dead. The eulogy was given by Fr. Leonhard Mengoss of the St. Victor chapter of St. Francis brotherhood.

Gutenberg was buried in the brown robe of a Franciscan tertiary and laid to rest in the floor of the church beside his parents and grandparents. The grave was covered with simple pine branches and holly as the friars sang the De Profundis, "Eternal rest grant to him, O Lord, and let perpetual light shine upon him."

Words from Estras 4, Peter remembered, where they had had their first problems with blank pages. Standing with Christine and the other mourners, and holding their infant son, Gratian, in his arms, Peter pondered the great legacy he had received from Gutenberg and from Fust. Yes, the printing will continue, he promised again, with me and my son, for the honor and glory of God and of Mainz!

When Else and Henne returned to the church on Sunday to offer prayers, they found two wreaths from Archbishop von Nassau and Diether von Isenburg, still residing in Trier. Later they ordered a black marble slab put on the grave. The epitaph engraved upon it in Latin read:

JOHANNES
GENSFLEISCH
ZUR LADEN
ZUM GUTENBERG
MASTER GOLDSMITH
MASTER PRINTER
OF THE HOLY BIBLE
MAINZ
BORN 1398
DIED 3 FEB. 1468
FOREVER
REST IN PEACE

XIX. THE LEGACY
CHAPTER 73

In July, 1468, Schoeffer went to Paris in an attempt to recover the books Fust had taken with him. These had been confiscated, however, by the French crown as property of a deceased alien, and Schoeffer was never able to get them back. He had a Mass said for his father-in-law at St. Victor Abbey near the University of Paris. The following year, three printers were summoned from Mainz by King Louis XI and established the first printing office in France.

At home, Schoeffer published his first book list of 21 titles. These included the Summa, two Psalters, Canon of the Missal, Durandus "Rationale," the "Constitutiones" of Pope Clement V, the first book of canon law, two editions of Cicero's "De Officiis," and the 48-line Bible. He also began a monumental folio edition of the "Epistolae," the letters of St. Jerome, on vellum.

Over the years, Schoeffer achieved great success as a printer and publisher, issuing no less than 130 different volumes in theology, liturgy, law and philosophy. The majority of these books were in Latin, and only eighteen titles were in German. None were scientific books. He employed book salesmen, and in addition to court bishops and members of the nobility, his customers included professors, lawyers, students and teachers at monastery schools and universities. Schoeffer also published over 100 different single sheets -papal bulls, briefs, and indulgences, and governmental decrees concerning wars, coronations and taxes. He was never a formal printer, however, for the Church or for the Empire and modestly signed his bills "bookbinder."

Much respected by his peers, Schoeffer served as a secular judge in Mainz in his later years. Four sons were born to him and Christine - Gratian, Johannes, Peter and Ludwig. Two of them became printers. Peter Schoeffer died in 1502 at age 77.

Else and Henne Humbrecht sold their home in Mainz to Schoeffer in 1470 and moved to Frankfurt. Else died there in 1475 and her husband two years later. Gutenberg's Bible, and copies of the Missal, Donatus, World Judgment, first prints of the Pater Noster and all personal mementoes were bequeathed to the child of Gutenberg's half-sister, Patze Blashof, and to Arnold Gelthuss, whose son, Adam, inherited them.

In a book published in Mainz in 1499, Adam Gelthuss wrote the following tribute, "To the inventor of the art of printing, Johann Gensfleisch, who highly deserved of every people and every language...this volume stands as a monument for the eternal remembrance of his name."

Archbishop Adolf von Nassau died on September 6, 1475. Diether von Isenburg was chosen as his successor by Pope Sixtus IV. The man once forced to give up the episcopal throne was now confirmed Archbishop of Mainz and served successfully until his death in 1482.

Printers who had learned the art from Gutenberg went on to work in other cities. Conrad Sweynheym and Arnold Pannartz moved their printing shop from Subiaco to Rome and in 1469 published Pliny's "Historia Naturalis." In Venice, Johann and Wenderlin von Speyer, or "da Spira" as they were known in Italy, cast a beautiful set of Roman capital letters, and in 1470 published "De Civitate Dei" of St. Augustine. Nicolaus Jensen, who fled the French court of King Louis XI, also went to Venice where he established his own printing office. In 1470 he published Eusebius' "De Evangelica Preparatorie." His Roman small letters, complementing the da Spira capitals, were acclaimed the finest ever cut, and were destined to establish the style of all Roman type to come. Jensen became, as Gutenberg had foretold, the first master designer of metal letters.

The first generation of printers after Gutenberg could be found in every major city of the Empire. Anton Koberger was at Nuremburg; Johannes Balbus, Genoa; Jacob Sabon, Lyons; Gering and Garamond, Paris; and William Caxton, London. Printing offices were in Augsburg, Prague, Warsaw, Vienna, Berlin, Copenhagen, and as far away as Lisbon, Valencia and Barcelona.

Books printed before 1490 included Euclid's "Elementa Geometriae" by Erhard Ratdolt, Venice. 1482. The first pocket size books (half octavo) were printed in Venice by Aldus Manutis. Also, a Treatise on the Theory of Music, Naples, 1480; "De Consolatione Philosophiae," Ghent, 1485, by de Keysere; Breydenbach's "Pilgrimage," Mainz, printed by Reuwich, 1486; and "The Golden Legend" by de Varagine, printed by Caxton at Westminster, 1483. Dante's "La Divina Comedia," printed in Florence, 1481, by Nicholas Laurentii, was the earliest book using copper engravings.

Other Latin Bibles were the work of Jensen, 1476, who used Gothic letters and quarto size pages; Adolf Rusch in Strasbourg, who published a four-volume Bible in 1479, folio size, using Gothic letters. The Bible printed by Johann Froben in Basel, 1491, had Gothic letters and octavo size pages. A Bible history, written by Peter Comestor, was printed in Augsburg by Gunther Zainer, 1473, who used Roman letters.

Gutenberg's printed Bible was always recognized as authoritative by the Church, and it was copied and recopied in complete confidence by printers after him, who knew the text to be an approved and perfect edition of Sacred Scripture. Abbots and monastery monks continued to read liturgical books for accuracy and to give their approval to the printed Latin texts. The bishop of Terano served Ulrich Hahn's printing office in this capacity as the Benedictine monks had done at Subiaco.

By the year 1500, there were 1000 printers in 200 cities throughout the Empire. Thirteen printing towns along the Rhein and in Germany produced one-third of all printed work in Europe. By the end of the century, America had been discovered and the first printing press appeared in New Spain, Mexico, in 1539, by order of the Franciscan bishop.

Just as the name Gutenberg became obscure in the centuries after the advent of printing, because many men later claimed the honor of being the first printer in Europe, so too did Gutenberg's Bibles disappear into the obscurity and security of monastic and episcopal libraries. The Bibles rarely changed hands until the 18th and 19th centuries. In 1763, an original printed Bible was discovered in the library of Cardinal Mazarin in Paris. Soon after, another was reported by the librarian of St. Blasius, a Benedictine abbey in the Black Forest.

It was not until 1900 that German scholars undertook serious study of Gutenberg and the Bibles known to be in existence. Books by Paul Schwenke, Seymour deRicci and Karl Schorbach appeared. Significant studies were made by Karl Dziatzko, Otto Hupp and Gottfried Zedler. Then Aloys Ruppel, Ferdinand Geldner, Heinrich Schneider and Rudolf Blum published their findings, which resolved many of the controversies surrounding Gutenberg's life and work. The *Gutenberg Jahrbuch* has been published since 1926 by the Gutenberg-Gesellschaft in Mainz, and contains articles by international scholars on specific aspects of Gutenberg's work.

Since 1940 in the United States, Otto Fuhrmann, Hellmut Lehmann-Haupt and Curt Buhler have written about the Strasbourg documents, Peter Schoeffer, Gutenberg's work with copper relief plates, and the dating of the Constance Missal. Their studies have contributed greatly to the present day knowledge about Gutenberg in English. Max Plaut's survey of the literature concerning the Helmasperger Document was submitted as a master's thesis to the University of Chicago in 1970.

The latest complete census of the Gutenberg Bibles was made by Josef Stummvoll in 1971, and updated by Otto Mazal to include the three sales in the United States, 1978-9. These changes in ownership are listed in the Kommentarband of the Berlin facsimile Bible.

EPILOGUE

Of the 185 Bibles printed by Gutenberg, only 49 are known to be in existence today: 11 are in the United States and 37 in Europe, and one in Japan. There are 12 copies on vellum and 37 on paper. Sixteen of the paper copies and only four vellum copies are perfect and complete. These four Exemplar and most valuable Bibles are owned by the Universitatsbibliothek, Gottingen; the Bibliothèque Nationale, Paris; the British Museum, London; and the United States Library of Congress in Washington, D.C.

The four-volume Paris Exemplar was originally owned by the Benedictine Abbey of St. James in Mainz. The other Bibliothèque Nationale copy, on paper, is the only Bible to bear the illustrator's name, any name, in fact, and any date. It is the Bible illustrated by Fr. Heinrich Cremer of St. Stephan's church in Mainz, 1456. Unfortunately, many pages are now missing, including most of the illustrated opening book pages. Fr. Cremer's handwritten note in red ink appears at the end of Psalms, Volume I, and at the top of folio 318 recto in Volume II after the Apocalypse. Beneath it are the deSteyna note of 1457 and a third dated 1467 stating that Fischer Berthold celebrated Mass in the Dom for the diocese.

Prints of illustrations made from copper relief plates appear in only one printed Bible, the Scheide Library copy at Princeton, New Jersey, and in the Great manuscript Bible published in Mainz, 1453, now owned by the Library of Congress.

The extant Gutenberg Bibles are located in the following libraries. The most recent discovery was made in 1975 at Immenhausen, Germany.

Germany

MAINZ	Gutenberg Museum (2)
ASCHAFFENBURG	Hofbibliothek
BERLIN	Staatsbibliothek
FRANKFURT	Stadt und Universitatsbibliothk
FULDA	Landesbibliothek
GOTTINGEN	Niedersachsische Staats und Universitatsbibliothek
IMMENHAUSEN	(KASSEL) Morhardshe Bibliothek
LEIPZIG	Karl Marx Universitatsbibliothek
MUNICH	Bayerische Staatsbibliothek

Germany (continued)
SCHWEINFURT — Stadtbibliothek
STUTTGART — Stadtbibliothek
TRIER — Stadtbibliothek

Austria
VIENNA — Oesterreichische National-bibliothek

Belgium
MONS — Bibliothèque Publique

Denmark
COPENHAGEN — Konelige Bibliotek

England
CAMBRIDGE — University Library
ETON — Eton College Library
LONDON — British Museum (2)
Archepiscopal Library, Lambeth Palace
MANCHESTER — John Rylands Library
OXFORD — Bodleian Library

France
PARIS — Bibliothèque Nationale (2)
Bibliothèque Mazarin
ST. OMER — Bibliothèque Publique

Italy
ROME — Biblioteca Apostolica Vaticana (2)

Japan
TOKYO — Maruzen Co., Ltd.

Liechtenstein
VADUZ — Stadtbibliothek*

Poland
PELPLIN — Biblioteka Seminarium Duchewnego

Portugal
    LISBON   Biblioteca Nacional

Scotland
    EDINBURGH   National Library of Scotland

Spain
    BURGOS   Biblioteca Provincial
    SEVILLE   Biblioteca Universitaria y Provincial

Switzerland
    COLONY/GENEVA   Private Library of Dr. Martin Bodmer

U.S.S.R.
    LOCATION UNKNOWN   Two copies believed to be in Russia

United States
    CONNECTICUT   Yale University Library, New Haven
    INDIANA   Indiana University, Lilly Library,
                           Bloomington*
    MASSACHUSETTS   Harvard University Widener
                           Memorial Library, Cambridge
    NEW JERSEY   Scheide Library, Princeton
    NEW YORK   New York Public Library, New York
                           Pierpont Morgan Library (3)
                           New York
    TEXAS   University of Texas, Austin
    WASHINGTON, D.C.   Library of Congress

*Both are listed in the Kommentar as No. 46, and are parts of the same Bible.

    An original Gutenberg Bible continues to be an investment which appreciates in value year by year. In 1979, the Carl H. Pforzheimer copy was sold to the University of Texas for $2,400,000. The year before, the New York General Theological Seminary Bible was sold to the Stadtsbibliothek in Stuttgart for $2,000,000. In the same year, the H. P. Kraus "Shuckburgh" copy, formerly owned by Arthur Houghton, Jr., was purchased by the Gutenberg Museum, Mainz, for $1,800,000. The sale in 1987 of the Doheny Bible in California, Volume I only, to the Maruzen Co.,

Tokyo, for $5,390,000 is the highest price ever paid.

Only a few of the present owners can trace the history of their Bibles to the 15th century directly. Three of the stories concerning history of ownership are particularly interesting.

The Library of Congress Bible was acquired first in 1457-8 from Paris by the Benedictine monks of St. Blasius Abbey in the Black Forest. The monks had it in their possession more than 450 years, carrying it to Einseideln, Switzerland, during the Napoleonic wars and then to the Abbey of St. Paul in Carinthia, Austria, where it remained over a century. After World War I, the Benedictines were forced to sell "the most precious jewel of their archives.. as an exchange for bread." In 1926, the Bible was purchased by Dr. Otto Vollbehr for $300,000, with the intent and promise that it would be given to the United States Library of Congress. In 1930, by Act of Congress, the Bible and a collection of 15th century books were purchased from Dr. Vollbehr for $1,500,000. Today the Bible alone is priceless. It is a flawless copy on vellum, with simple red and blue initials and page headings, and the only one bound in three volumes.

The Stadtbibliothek at Trier acquired a two-volume Gutenberg Bible in 1828 after its discovery in a peasant's hut at Olewig. Some leaves had been used as covers for children's school books and many others were missing. The Bible is believed to have belonged to a Benedictine monastery near Trier before 1803. The Trier library still owns Volume I but sold Volume II at auction in 1927 to Arthur Houghton, Jr. of New York. He sold it to Charles Scribner publishing house in 1953. The New Testament, lacking 12 leaves, was purchased by George Poole of Chicago, who sold it in 1959 to Indiana University, its present owner. Part of the Old Testament is owned by the Stadtbibliothek in Liechtenstein. Other leaves of the Old Testament portion were sold individually by Scribner's, each in a handsome folder with an essay titled "A Noble Fragment." This is the only Bible to be so divided. Leaves 1 and 317 helped improve the "Shuckburgh" copy, and the person owning leaf 111 gave it to the General Theological Seminary, the only Bible to be restored to completeness with the acquisition of a single missing leaf.

The paper Bible illustrated by Father Cremer and owned by the Archbishop of Mainz was given by him to the church at Ostheim (today Grossostheim) near his residence at Aschaffenburg. When the Archbishop returned to Mainz, he presumably took the Bible with him. It was found 300 years later, 1789, in the Electoral Library of Mainz by Dom Maugerard. He saw the Cremer signature and date and knew the Bible to be one printed

by Gutenberg. Placing the volumes in two leather cases with royal wrapp-
ings, he took them to Metz and in the same year to the Royal Library in
Paris where they have remained to this day. When and by whom the illuminated pages were removed is not known.

Each Gutenberg Bible or portion thereof has an intrinsic value of its
own. Each Bible is unique because, while the text is identical in each volume,
the page decoration is different in each volume. Some Bibles have glorious
multicolored initial letters and scrollwork on the 93 illustrated pages; others
have simple initials and no elaborate ornamentation. It is this individuality
of illustration and the uniformity of the strikingly beautiful black text
throughout which make these Bibles true works of art.

The Bibles are not letter perfect. There are typographical mistakes,
and 17 pages in Genesis and Kings have 40 and 41-line columns while all
the rest are 42 lines.

When the Seminary Bible was purchased by the Stuttgart library in
1978, a duplicate page was discovered. It is the only duplication known
to exist and is a printer's error. Folio 279b (p. 558) in Timothy is printed
in its proper place and again as folio 272b (p.544) in Colossians. In every
other copy of the Gutenberg Bible, the page after Colossians is blank.
How the duplication may have occurred and the mistake corrected have
been explained in this story.

There are five blank pages in the Bible and only one was planned,
before the opening of the New Testament. The others - before and after
Esdras 4, after Colossians, and before the Apocalypse - undoubtedly
resulted from miscalculations in counting and, as also explained in the
story, were deliberately placed where they are.

The Lisbon Bible has a collating error for which the binder is responsible. It too is the only such error known to exist and is of major importance to researchers. In this Bible, the 16-page Apocalypse follows Hebrews
instead of St. Jude. It comes before Acts and the last four Apostle letters
instead of after them. In Gutenberg's time, Acts was positioned after
Hebrews. At a later date in history, the sequence was made chronological
and the Acts placed before Romans and the other letters of St. Paul.

This collating error proves that the Apocalypse was printed by itself
as a separate and complete quire. It confirms that Hebrews ended as a
half quire of eight pages and that Acts began a quire. Otherwise, transfer
of the Apocalypse to where it is in the Lisbon Bible would have been
impossible.

Because in all Bibles, a blank page precedes the Apocalypse, the collating error also indicates that folio 309 (pp. 617-18) and folio 318 (pp. 635-36) make up an additional four-page sheet which "wraps around" the Apocalypse (one text, three blank pages); that the last quire has 20 pages instead of 16; and that Volume II has 636 pages instead of the 632 originally planned.

The last text page of St. Jude, folio 309a (p. 617), is followed by the blank page, folio 309b. The Apocalypse begins on folio 310 and ends on folio 317b (p. 634). It should be followed by two blank pages, folio 318.

Does the Lisbon Bible contain the second text page and blank page ending St. Jude, folio 309, and blank folio 318 at the end? This sheet may have been lost when the Apocalypse was transferred. The Lisbon Bible may be incomplete and should be reexamined for answers to these questions.

The four-page wrap-around insert of folios 309 and 318 in Volume II has been verified by examination of the last pages and binding of the original paper Bible illustrated by Fr. Heinrich Cremer, at the Bibliothèque Nationale in Paris. The evidence is conclusive.

It is possible to "forge" or fake a Gutenberg Bible? No, because the type, paper and ink cannot be duplicated. It is possible to photograph original pages and to print them in color or black and white. This has been done with a number of individual pages and even for full folio size reproductions of the entire Bible.

Because of the expense involved, only four such reproductions or facsimile editions have been published to date. Each is beautifully illustrated in color and gold leaf and printed in limited, numbered, two-volume editions. They are the Insel Verlag facsimile of the Berlin-Fulda Bibles, Leipzig, 1913; the Pageant Press edition of the Leipzig facsimile, Paterson, New Jersey, 1961; the Idion Verlag facsimile of the Berlin Bible only, Munich, 1979; and the Dodu-Picot reproduction of the Mazarin Bible, Paris, 1986.

Like prints of fine paintings or tapestries, or replicas of sculpture, these reproductions of the Gutenberg Bibles are, in themselves, treasured volumes of great esthetic and practical value. They are extremely useful to libraries who cannot obtain an original Bible, and give any individual the opportunity to leaf through the pages at leisure, for research or pleasure, without fear of damaging an irreplaceable work of art.

Some Bibles have been microfilmed, and it is hoped that soon every owner will microfilm the pages of their Gutenberg Bible so that this film record may be available for comparative study by other owners, printing, incunabula, Latin and Bible scholars, and the results shared by all. From the style of illustration, it would be possible to match up single volumes that belong together as one Bible.

The pages of the Gutenberg Bible are not fragile. The paper, ink and colors used 500 years ago are, in most copies, as perfect as the day the Bibles were printed. Some pages show signs of daily use, mishandling, or exposure to the weather and other hardships. Some volumes have the original bindings which are still in good condition. But the original Bibles are too precious to be handled freely, and are displayed publicly under guard and under glass, because like the Mona Lisa, each copy is "one of a kind." They have been transported in armored cars and carried by hand in unmarked suitcases. They cannot be insured.

Whether in two volumes complete, one volume only, in perfect or imperfect condition, single leaves, on paper or on vellum - the Gutenberg Bibles continue to be the most beautiful and most highly prized printed books in the world. And whether as spoils of war or as long forgotten buried treasure, other Gutenbergs will surely come to light.

"Caelum, et terra transibunt, verba autem mea non praeteribunt."
"Heaven and earth will pass away, but my words will not pass away."

These spoken words of Jesus Christ are recorded in the gospel of St. Matthew, written first in Aramaic, then Greek, then in Vulgate Latin, the language of the Gutenberg Bibles. It is the message all Bibles contain, however, both in the New and Old Testaments, which is the real pearl of great price.

Before 1455, this message appeared in perhaps a dozen languages. Today, it is printed in over 1600 languages, with more than 50 million copies of the Bible published annually. The Holy Bible will always be the most sought after, most quoted, most widely read, and most cherished book in the world. It is the world's best seller because it contains the message of love, hope, and salvation which all men seek.

Religion, it has been said, is the key to history. If this is true, the first printed Bibles, the Gutenberg Bibles, are part of that key.

AMEN!
ALLELUIA!

BIBLIOGRAPHY

Primary Sources

Chronological Order

Constance Missal. Mainz: Johannes Gutenberg, 1449-50.
Tresors, Haus der Kulturinstitute, Munich.

Bible of 42 Lines, Mainz: Johannes Gutenberg, 1452-55, 2v, paper,
Bibliothèque Nationale, Paris.

Bible of 42 Lines. Mainz: Johannes Gutenberg, 1452-55. 3v. vellum
Exemplar, Library of Congress, Washington, D.C.

Bible of 42 Lines. Mainz: Johannes Gutenberg, 1452-55. lv. paper,
Gutenberg Museum, Mainz.

Bible of 42 Lines. Mainz: Johannes Gutenberg, 1452-55. 2v. paper.
Gutenberg Museum, Mainz.

Bible of 42 Lines. Folio Ruth. Mainz: Johannes Gutenberg,
1452-55. Newberry Library, Chicago.

Bible of 42 Lines. Folio Daniel. Mainz: Johannes Gutenberg,
1452-55. Newberry Library.

Bible of 42 Lines. Folio Numbers. Mainz: Johannes Gutenberg,
1452-55. University of California Library, Berkeley.

Great Bible. Manuscript. Mainz: 1453. 2v. Library of Congress.

Bible of 36 Lines. Single folio. Mainz. Fust and Schoeffer,
1457-58. Newberry Library.

Lantantius. *Opera.* Subiaco: Sweynhelm and Pannartz, 1465.
Newberry Library.

Cicero. *De Officiis.* 2nd ed. Mainz: Fust and Schoeffer, 1466.
Newberry Library and Library of Congress.

Lactantius. *Opera*. Rome: Sweynhelm and Pannartz, 1468.
Library of Congress.

Pliny. *Encyclopedia of Natural Science*. Rome: Sweynhelm and Pannartz,
1469. Library of Congress.

Augustine. *De Civitate Dei*. Venice: Johannes daSpira, 1470.
Library of Congress.

Biblia Pauperum. Block book. Netherlands: 1470. Library of Congress.

Eusebius. *De Preparatione Evangelica*. Venice: Nicolaus Jensen, 1470.
Newberry Library and Library of Congress.

Hieronymus. *Epistolae*. Mainz: Peter Schoeffer, 1470. Library of Congress.

Clemens V, Pope. *Constitutiones*. Mainz: Peter Schoeffer, 1471.
Library of Congress.

Boccaccio, Giovanni. *La Fiammetta*. Padua: 1472. Newberry Library.

Comestor, Petrus. *Historiae Biblicae*. Augsburg: Gunther Zainer, 1473.
Chicago Bible Society.

Calendarium. Venice: Erhard Ratdolt, 1476. Library of Congress.

Sacre Biblia Latina. 1st ed. Venice: Nicolaus Jensen, 1476.
Chicago Bible Society.

Biblia Latina Cum Glossa Strabonis. Strassburg: Adolf Rusch for Anton
Koberger, 1479-81. 4v. Chicago Bible Society.

Treatis on Theory of Music. Naples: 1480. Library of Congress.

Dante. *La Commedia*. Florence: Nicholaus Laurentii, 1481. Library
of Congress.

Euclid. *Elementa Geometriae*. Venice: Erhard Ratdolt, 1482. Library
of Congress.

deVaragine. *The Golden Legend*. Westminster: William Caxton, 1483. Library of Congress.

De Consolatione Philosophiae. Ghent: deKeysere, 1485. Library of Congress.

von Breydenbach, Bernhard. *Pilgrimage*. Mainz: Reuwich, 1486. Library of Congress.

Biblia Integra. Basel: Johann Froben, 1491. Chicago Bible Society.

Aesop. *Vitae et Fabulae*. Basel: c. 1492. Library of Congress.

Hartmann, Schedel. *Liber Chronicarum*. Nuremburg: Anton Koberger, 1493. Library of Congress.

Boccaccio, Giovanni. English translation by John Lydgate. *The Fall of Princes*. London: Pynson, 1494. Library of Congress.

Liber Horae. Manscript. Late fifteenth century. Chicago Bible Society.

Colonna. *The Strife of Love in a Dream*. Venice: Aldus Manutius, 1499. Library of Congress.

Cantos. Venice: Petrucci, 1504. Library of Congress.

Ptolemy, Claudius. *Geographia*. Rome: 1507. Newberry Library.

Ptolemy, Claudius. *Geographia*. Strasbourg: Johann Rusch, 1508. Library of Congress.

Origen. *Opera Omnia*. Paris: Jododuc Badius, 1512. Library of Congress.

Erasmus. *Novum Testamentum Omne*. 3rd ed. Rotterdam: 1522. Chicago Bible Society.

Bible. Luther German translation. 2nd ed. Wittemberg: Hans Lufft, 1535. Chicago Bible Society.

Biblia. Cloverdale English translation. Zurich: Christopher Froschover, 1535. Chicago Bible Society.

Copernicus. *The Evolution of Heavenly Bodies.* Nuremburg: Johannes Petreius, 1543. Library of Congress.

Ordenzas y Compilacion de Leyes. Mexico City: Juan Pablos, 1548. San Francisco California State Library.

Book of Common Prayer. London: 1549. Newberry Library.

Great Bible. Cranmer English translation. Rouen: Richard Carmarden, 1566. Chicago Bible Society.

Bishop's Bible. 1st ed. London: R. Jugge, 1568. Chicago Bible Society.

Catholic New Testament. English edition. Rhemes: John Fogny, 1582. Chicago Bible Society.

Euridice. Florence: Jacobo Peri, 1600. Newberry Library.

Catholic Old Testament. English edition. Doway: Lavrence Kellam, 1609-10. Chicago Bible Society.

King James Bible. 1st ed. London: Robert Barker, 1611. Chicago Bible Society.

Bible. John Eliot Algonquin Indian translation. Cambridge, N.E.: Samuel Green, 1685. Newberry Library and Chicago Bible Society

Books

Allen, Agnes. *The Story of the Book.* London: Faber & Faber, 1952.

Ames, Joseph and T. F. Dibden. *Typographical Antiquities.* Vol. I. London: W. Faden, 1810.

Ashley, Frederick M. *The Vollbehr Incunabula and the Book of Books.* Washington, D.C.: U. S. Government Printing Office, 1932.

Bauer, Konrad F. *Eine Gedenkschrift zu Seinem Siebzigsten Geburtstag am 1973*, Mainz: Kleiner Druck der Gutenberg-Gesellschaft Nr. 96, 1973.

Bible. *The Holy Bible.* Confraternity edition. Edited by Rev. John P. O'Connell. Chicago: The Catholic Press, Inc., 1959.

Bible of 42 Lines. Berlin-Fulda Facsimile. Leipzig: Insel Verlag, 1913. 2v.

Bible of 42 Lines. New edition of the Leipzig Facsimile. Paterson, N.J.: Pageant Books, Inc., 1960. 2v.

Bible of 42 Lines. Berlin Facsimile. Munich: Idion Verlag, 1976. 2v.

Blum, Rudolph. *Der Prozess Fust gegen Gutenberg.* Weisbaden: O. Harrassowitz, 1954.

Brown, Horatio F. *The Venetian Printing Press.* London: John C. Nimmo, 1891.

Buhler, Curt F. *Another View on the Dating of the Constance Missal.* London: The Biographical Society, 1959.

Buhler, Curt. F. *The Fifteenth Century Book—The Scribes, The Printers, The Decorators.* Philadelphia: University of Pennsylvania Press, 1960.

The Cambridge Medieval History, Vol. VIII: *The Close of the Middle Ages.* New York: The Macmillan Company, 1936.

Carter, Thomas F. *The Invention of Printing in China and Its Spread Westward.* New York: Columbia University Press, 1931.

Cary, Melbert B. *The Missing Gutenberg Wood Blocks.* New York: Press of the Woolly Whale, 1940.

The Catholic Encyclopedia. New York: The Encyclopedia Press, Inc., 1913. 15v.

Chartier, Jean. *Grandes Chroniques Roi Charles VII.* Vol. III. Nouvelle edition edited by Vallet de Viriville. Paris: P. Jannet, Libraire, 1858.

Chartier, Jean. *Histoire de Charles VII Roy de France.* Edited by Denys Godefroy. Paris: de l'Imprimerie Royale, 1661.

Clair, Colin. *A Chronology of Printing.* New York: Frederick A. Praeger, Inc., 1969.

Daley, Rev. Charles M., O.P. *Dominican Incunabula in the Library of Congress.* Reprinted from Historical Records and Studies, Vol. XXII, October, 1932.

Daniel-Rops, Henri. *What is the Bible?* New York: Hawthorn Books, 1958.

Davies, Hugh William. *Devices of the Early Printers.* London: Grafton & Co., 1935.

DeVilliers, P. *The Signature of Gutenberg.* London: Kerby and Endean, 1878.

Diringer, David. *Hand Produced Book.* New York: Philosophical Library, 1953.

Dollinger, Phillippe. *Histoire de l'Alsace.* Toulouse: Edouard Privat, Ed., 1970.

Dougherty, Rev. John J. *Searching the Scriptures.* Garden City, N.Y.: Hanover House, 1959.

Duff, E. Gordon. *Early Printed Books.* London: Kegan Paul, Trench, Trubner & Co., Ltd., 1893.

Edwards, George Wharton. *Alsace-Lorraine.* Philadelphia: The Penn Publishing Co., 1918.

Emerson, Edwin. *Incunabulum Incunabulorum.* New York: Tudor Press, 1928.

The Encyclopaedia Britannica. Chicago: William Benton, 1973. 24v.

Farrell, Rev. Walter, O.P. and Martin J. Healy. *My Way of Life: Saint Thomas.* Brooklyn, N.Y.: Confraternity of the Precious Blood, 1952.

Farrow, John. *Pageant of the Popes.* St. Paul, Minn.: Catechetical Guild Educational Society, 1955.

Fontana, John M. *Mankind's Greatest Invention and the Story of the First Printed Bible.* Brooklyn, N.Y., 1964.

Ford, Franklin L. *Strasbourg in Transition.* Cambridge: Harvard University Press, 1958.

Forkert, Otto M. *From Gutenberg to the Cuneo Press.* Chicago: The Cuneo Press, Inc., 1933.

Fournier, Edouard. *Gutenberg: A Drama in Five Acts and in Verse.* Paris: E. Dentu, 1869.

Fuhrmann, Otto W. *Gutenberg and the Strasbourg Documents.* New York: Press of the Woolly Whale, 1940.

Gabriel, Astrick L. *The Educational Ideas of Vincent of Beauvais.* Notre Dame, Ind.: The University of Notre Dame Press, 1962.

Gabriel, Astrick L. *Student Life in Ave Maria College, Mediaeval Paris.* Notre Dame, Ind.: University of Notre Dame Press, 1955.

Gams, P. Pius Bonifacius, O.S.B. (ed.). *Series Episcoporum Ecclesiae Catholicae.* Ratisbonae: Georgii Josephi Manz, 1873.

Geck, Elisabeth. *Johannes Gutenberg 1468-1968.* Bad Godesberg: Inter Nationes, 1968.

General Theological Seminary. *Pages from the Gutenberg Bible of 42 Lines.* New York: The H. W. Wilson Company, 1940.

Goff, Frederick R., *The Permanence of Johann Gutenberg.* Austin: University of Texas Press, 1970.

Greenhood, David and Helen Gentry. *Chronology of Books and Printing.* New York: The Macmillan Company, 1936.

Guppy, Henry. *Stepping Stones to the Art of Typography.* Manchester, Vt.: The University Press, 1928.

Gutenberg Jahrbuch. Mainz: Gutenberg-Gesellschaft, 1983.

Hatt, Jacques. *Une Ville du XVe Siecle.* Strasbourg: Collection Historique de la Vie en Alsace, 1929.

Harris, Brayton. *Johannes Gutenberg and the Invention of Printing.* New York: Franklin Watts, Inc. 1972.

Hayes, Carlton J.H., Marshall W. Baldwin and Charles W. Cole. *History of Europe.* New York: The Macmillan Company, 1949.

Hessels, Jan Hendrik. *Gutenberg: Was He the Inventor of Printing?* London: B. Quaritch, 1882.

Hetzenauer, P. Michael. *Biblia Sacra Vulgatae Editionis.* Ratisbone et Rome, Neo Eboraci et Cincinnati: Apud Friderici Pustet & Co., 1914.

Hunter, Dard. *Papermaking.* New York: Alfred A. Knopf, 1947.

Jennett, Sean. *The Making of Books.* London: Faber & Faber Limited, 1964.

Johnson, Joh. *Typographia.* Vols. I, II. London: J. Johnson, 1824.

Kaemmerer, Walter (hist.) *Neue Deutsche Bibliographie.* Berlin: Dritter Band Burklein-Ditmar, Duncher & Humblot, 1957.

Kapr, Albert. *Johannes Gutenberg.* Leipzig: Tatsachen und Thesen, 1977.

Kendall, Paul. *Louis XI—The Universal Spider.* New York: W. W. Norton, 1970.

Kommentarband. Johannes Gutenberg Zweiundvierzigzeilige Bibel. München: Idion Verlag, 1979.

Koster, Kurt. *Gutenberg in Strassburg.* Mainz: Kleiner Druck der Gutenberg-Gesellschaft, Nr. 93, 1973.

LeClerc, Eloi. *Wisdom of the Poverello.* Chicago: Franciscan Herald Press, 1961.

Lehmann-Haupt, Hellmut. *Gutenberg and the Master of Playing Cards.* New Haven: Yale University Press, 1966.

Lehmann-Haupt, Hellmut. *Peter Schoeffer of Gernsheim and Mainz.* Rochester: The Leo Hart Co., Inc., 1950.

Lenhart, Rev. John M., O.M.Cap. *Pre-Reformation Printed Books.* New York: Joseph F. Wagner, Inc., 1935.

Mallaber, Kenneth A. *A Printer of Bibliography.* London: Associates of Assistant Librarians, 1954.

Middleton, J. Henry. *Illuminated Manuscripts in Classical and Medieval Times.* Cambridge: Cambridge University Press, 1892.

McLuhan, Marshall. *The Gutenberg Galaxy.* Toronto: University of Toronto Press, 1962.

McMurtrie, Douglas C. *Some Facts Concerning the Invention of Printing.* Chicago: Chicago Club of Printing House Craftsmen, 1939.

McMurtrie, Douglas, C. *Wings for Words.* Chicago: Rand McNally & Company, 1940.

McMurtrie, Douglas C. *The Gutenberg Documents.* New York: Oxford University Press, 1941.

McMurtrie, Douglas C. *The Book—Story of Printing and Bookmaking.* New York: Oxford University Press, 1943.

The New Larned History. Springfield, Mass.: C. A. Nichols Publishing Company, 1924. 12v.

Newton, A. Edward. *A Noble Fragment—Being a Leaf from the Gutenberg Bible.* New York: Gabriel Wells, 1921,

Norman, Don Cleveland. *The 500th Anniversary Pictorial Census of the Gutenberg Bible.* Chicago: The Cloverdale Press, 1961.

Ogg, Oscar. *The 26 Letters.* New York: Thomas Y. Crowell Company, 1948.

Orcutt, Wm. Dana. *The Magic of the Book.* Boston: Little Brown & Company, 1930.

Pastor, Ludwig. *The History of the Popes.* Vol. II. London: John Hodges, 1891.

Pottinger, David. *Printers and Printing.* Cambridge, Mass.: Harvard University Press, 1941.

Presser, Helmut. *Johannes Gutenberg.* Reinbek bei Hamburg: Rowohlt Taschenbuch Verlag GmbH, 1967.

Reade, Charles. *The Cloister and the Hearth.* New York: The Heritage Press, 1932.

Rhodes, Dennis E. (ed.) *Fifty Essays in 15th and 16th Century Bibliography.* Amsterdam: M. Hertzberger & Co., 1966.

Ritter, Francois. *Histoire de l'Imprimerie Alsacienne aux XVe et XVIe Siecles.* Strasbourg-Paris: Editions F. -X. LeRoux, 1955.

Ruppel, Aloys. *Johannes Gutenberg, sein Leben und sein Werk.* Berlin: Verlag Gebruder Mann, 1947. 3rd ed. Nieuwkoop: B. DeGraaf, 1967.

Scholderer, Victor. *Johann Gutenberg, the Inventor of Printing.* London: The Trustees of the British Museum, 1963. 2nd Ed. (rev.) London: British Museum, 1970.

Smith, Adele. *Printing and Printing Materials*. Philadelphia: Adele Smith, 1901.

Stefferud, Alfred (ed.). *The Wonderful World of Books*. New York: Houghton-Mifflin Co., 1953.

Steinberg, S.H. *500 Years of Printing*. Edinburgh: Penguin Books, R. & R. Clark Ltd., 1955.

Steinmueller, Rev. John E. *A Companion to Scripture Studies*. Vol. I. New York: Joseph F. Wagner, Inc., 1941.

Stillwell, Margaret Bingham. *Gutenberg and the Catholicon of 1460*. New York: The Brick Row Book Shop, Inc., 1936.

Sutton, Albert A. *Design and Makeup of the Newspaper*. New York: Prentice-Hall, Inc., 1948.

This is Our Heritage: Faith and Freedom. Washington, D.C.: Catholic University of America Press, 1943.

Tomlinson, Laurence E. *Gutenberg and the Invention of Printing—An Anniversary Review*. Washington, D.C.: Judd & Detweiler, Inc., 1938.

Treasures from the Pierpont Morgan Library—50th Anniversary Exhibition. New York: Pierpont Morgan Library, 1957.

Updike, Daniel Berkeley. *Printing Types—Their History, Forms and Use*. Vol. I. Cambridge Mass.: Harvard University Press, 1937.

Vawter, Rev. Bruce, C.M. *The Bible in the Church*. New York: Sheed and Ward, Inc., 1959.

Winship, George Parker. *Gutenberg to Plantin*. Cambridge, Mass.: Harvard University Press, 1930.

Wroth, Lawrence (ed.). *A History of the Printed Book, No. 3 of the Dolphin*. New York: Limited Editions Club, 1938.

Articles and Pamphlets

Bayer, Robert John. "Humble Genius," *Franciscan Herald,* XVIII (May, 1930), 203-4.

"Beginnings of Printing," *The St. Bona Venture,* March 8, 1940, p. 4.

Bulletin de la Société des Amis de la Cathédrale de Strasbourg—Le Jubilé du Demi-Millenaire de la Flèche 1439-1939. 2e Serie, No. 5. Strasbourg: Imprimerie Alsacienne, 1939.

"Franciscans' Aid Important in Printing Art," *The St. Bona Venture,* March 8, 1940, p. 4.

Gekler, Mary E. *Johannes Gutenberg: Father of Printing.* Chicago: Franciscan Herald Press, 1968.

"Gutenberg's Great Gift," *Tips,* (December, 1961). Distributed by Knowlton Printing Company, Chicago.

Herscher, Rev. Irenaeus, O.F.M. "History of Printing Traced from Origin," *The St.Bona Venture,* March 8, 1940, p. 1.

von Kuehnett-Leddihn, Erik. "The Middle Ages in Focus," *Extension,* LIV (February, 1960), 22.

Kunzog, John C. "Religious Significance of Printing Terms," *The St. Bona Venture,* March 8, 1940, p. 3.

Lehmann-Haupt, Hellmut. "Gutenberg's Grand Design: New Facts and a Hypothesis," *Publishers' Weekly,* CLXXXIII (December 24, 1962), 19-21.

Little, Evelyn Steele. "Twenty-Six Lead Soldiers," *The St. Bona Venture,* March 8, 1940, p. 13.

Mainz on the Rhine. Mainz: Druckhaus Schmidt & Co., n.d.

Mainz on the Rhine. Mainz: Verkehrsverein Mainz e. V., n.d.

Mainz Stadt und Dom. Bayreuth: Hans Schwarz, n.d.

Plan de Strasbourg. Von Poellnitz. Strasbourg: Druck und Verlag von R. Schulz und Cie., 1877.

Plaut, Max L. "The Helmaspergersche Notariatsinstrument of 1455 in Gutenberg Scholarship, a Survey of the Literature." Unpublished Master's thesis, Graduate Library School, The University of Chicago, 1970.

"A Predecessor of the Gutenberg Bible," *Life,* XXVI (March 1, 1954), 80.

Printing — Its Form and Designations. (How to Plan Printing To Promote Business, No. 8.) Boston: S. D. Warren Company, n. d.

Printing—Papers and Their Uses. (How to Plan Printing to Promote Business, No. 7.) Boston: S. D. Warren Company, n.d.

Printing—Types and Typography. (How to Plan Printing to Promote Business, No. 6.) Boston: S. D. Warren Company, n.d.

Printing—The Processes of Reproduction. (How To Plan Printing to Promote Business, No. 5.) Boston: S. D. Warren Company, n.d.

Rieger, Theodore. *The Cathedral of Strasbourg.* Strasbourg: Imprimerie des Dernières Nouvelles, 1971.

Risley, Marius. "Gutenberg's Invention One of the World's Greatest," *The St. Bona Venture,* March 8, 1940, p. 1.

Ruppel, Aloys. *Das Werdende Weltmuseum der Druckkunst und Die Internationale Gutenberg-Gesellschaft.* Mainz: Gutenberg-Gesellschaft, 1960.

Stevenson, Allan. *Observations on Paper as Evidence.* Lawrence: The University of Kansas Libraries, 1961.

Valentry, Duane. "The Worst of Halley's Comet," *Modern Maturity,* (April-May 1982), 69-71.

Werner, Dietrich. "He Changed the World," *Scala International.* (March, 1963), 21-25.

Williams, J. Emlyn. "Mainz: City of the Ages," *Christian Science Monitor,* (Boston), August 1, 1962.

Audio-Visual Materials

Gutenberg. Grafelfing bei Munchen: Diehl-Film, 1963. Sound. B&W. 5-1/2 min.

Homann, Joh. Bapt. *S.R.I. Circulus Rhenanas Superior.* Nurnberg: Urbes Imperiales, 1664-1724. Colored map 95x81 cm.

de L'Isle, G. *The Seat of War on the Rhine being a New Map of the Course of That River from Strasbourg to Bonne with the Adjacent Countries.* Printed for Tho. Bowles next to the Chapter House in St. Paul's Church Yard & I. Bowles at ye Black Horse in Cornhill, 1680-1740. Black and white map, 92x152 cm.

Interviews
Chronological Order

Fuchs, F. J., Archiviste de la Ville de Strasbourg, Municipal Archives. Interview, Strasbourg, France, September 15, 1964; May 2, 3, 4, 1972; October 4, 1983.

Geck, Elisabeth, Professor, Gutenberg-Museum. Interview, Mainz, Germany, September 17, 1964; April 24, 1972.

Ruppel, Aloys, Professor-Dr., Johannes Gutenberg University; President Emeritus, Gutenberg Gesellschaft; Director Emeritus, Gutenberg-Museum. Interview, Mainz, Germany, September 17, 18, 21, 1964; Chicago, Ill., May 15-18, 1968; Mainz, April 23, 25, 29, 1972.

Heist, Walter, Director, City of Mainz, Public Relations Office. Interview, Mainz, Germany, September 21, 1964.

Geldner, Ferdinand, Dr., Bayerische Staatsbibliothek. By telephone, Munich, Germany, Sept. 25, 1964.

Dachs, Dr., and Dr. Middendorf, Bayerische Staatsbibliothek. Interview, Munich, Germany, Sept. 25, 1964.

Battelli, Guilio, Archivist, Vatican Library. Interview, Rome, Italy, October 6, 1964.

Donati, Lamberto, Professor. Vatican Library. Interview, Rome, Italy, October 6, 1964.

Buhl, Bruno, retired teacher, Mittelheim. Interview, Mittelheim, Germany, April 24, 27, 1972.

Rosensprung, H., former teacher at Eltville, local historian. Interview, Mittelheim, Germany, April 27, 1972.

Widmann, Hans, Professor, Johannes Gutenberg University. Interview, Mainz, Germany, April 25, 1972.

Oberle, G., Service d'Architecture de l'Oeuvre Notre-Dame. Interview, Strasbourg, France, May 4, 1972; October 5, 1983.

Haeusser, J. R., Architecte de l'Oeuvre Notre-Dame. Interview, Strasbourg, France, October 4, 1983.

Gehrmann, Heinz, Geschaftsfuhrer der Gutenberg-Gesellschaft. Interview, Mainz, Germany, October 6, 1983.

Diop, Abdoulaye, Maitre Imprimeur, Nouadhibou, Mauritanie. Interview, Mainz, Germany, October 7, 1983.

CREDITS

Gutenberg's punch, matrix, mold and type casting instrument. *A History of the Printed Book, No. 3 of the Dolphin.* Edited by Lawrence C. Wroth. The Limited Editions Club, New York, 1938. Illustrations from Das Moderne Buch (Graphische Kunste der Gegenwart III)

Donatus page. Ibid. From Bogeng, Geschichte der Buchdruckerkunst.

Page set in individual, movable metal letters. *Scala International,* No. 2, Feb. 1968. English Edition. Frankfurter Societäts-Druckerei GmbH, Frankfurt.

Fragment of the Weltgericht. *Johannes Gutenberg: Sein Leben und Sein Werk.* Aloys Ruppel, DeGraaf, Nieuwkoop, Holland, 1967.

Gutenberg's font of letters for the 42-line Bible. Ibid.

Letter of Indulgence. Ibid.

Mirror for Aachen Pilgrimage. *Gutenburg in Strassburg,* Kurt Koster. Gutenberg-Gessellschaft, Mainz, 1973.

Constance Missal page. Photographed from the original volume owned by the Pierpont Morgan Library, New York. Reproduced with permission of the Trustees of the Library.

Mainz Psalter, 1459. Ibid.

leben wil niulze do dien do got orcn ron·
gebē Sie gene mit ſchrechē dobien Die
got nye erkante noch forchte en Niema
mag ſich ôbergē nicht Dor ď gotlichē
angeſiecht Criſtus wil do urtel ſprechen·
Dū wil alle boſzheit rechen Die nie ge=
dacē ten willē iin Den wil er gebē ewige
pin Dū wil ten gutē gebē Svym freuw
oñ ewig lebē Siſt die werlt oñ alle ding
Die in ď werlt geſchaffē ſint Czu gene
oñ werdē auch zu nicht Als man wol

Fragment of the
"Weltgericht" or
World Judgment,
printed in German
for the Dominican
Fathers. Believed
to be Gutenberg's
first printed work,
1440-1445.

Page from the Constance Missal showing Introit and part of the Mass for Trinity Sunday. Printed by Gutenberg in Mainz, 1449-1450.

Page for the Donatus Latin grammars. Several editions of these schoolbooks were printed by Gutenberg between 1440 and 1450.

Vniuersis Christifidelibus presentes litteras inspecturis **Paulinus** Chappe Consiliari Ambasiator z procurator generalis Sereinissimi Regis Cypri Iohannes pro Sanctissimo in Christo Salutem in domino...

...

Forma plenissime absolutionis et remissionis in vita

Misereatur tui &c. Dominus noster Iesus Christus per sua sanctissima et piissima misericordia te absoluat Et auctoritate ipsius Beatorum petri et pauli apostolorum ac auctoritate apostolica michi commissa et tibi concessa Ego te absoluo ab omnibus peccatis tuis...

Forma plenarie remissionis in mortis articulo

Misereatur tui &c. Dominus noster ut supra Ego te absoluo ab omnibus peccatis tuis contritis confessis et oblitis restituendo te vnitati fidelium et sacramentis ecclesie...

Beatus
vir ā Seruite dño. Euouae.
qui nō abiit in cōsilio im=
pioꝝ: ꝝ in via peccatoꝝ nō
stetit: et in cathedra pestilē
tie nō sedit. Sed in lege
dñi volūtas eius: ꝝ in lege ei⁹ meditabit̃ die
ac nocte. Et erit tanꝗ̃ lignū qđ plantatū est
secus decursus aꝗꝝ: qđ fruchū suū dabit in
tꝝe suo. Et foliū ei⁹ nō defluet: ꝝ oīa queꝗq̃
t psperabūt̃. Non sic impij nō sic: sed
ꝝ pulnis quē proicit ventus a facie terre.
o nō resurgūt impij in iudicio: neꝗ̃ peccō=
ꝝ cōsilio iustoꝝ. Qm̃ nouit dñs via iu=
i: et iter impioꝝ pibit. Gloria ptĩ. Of dđ
Quare fremuerūt gētes: ꝝ ipsi meditati
sūt inania. Astiterūt reges tre et prin=
conuenerūt in vnū: aduersus dñm ꝝ aduersus
ei⁹. Dirūpam⁹ vincla eoꝝ: ꝝ piciam⁹
bis iugū ipoꝝ. Qui habitat in celis irri=
eos: et dñs subsannabit eos. Tūc lo=

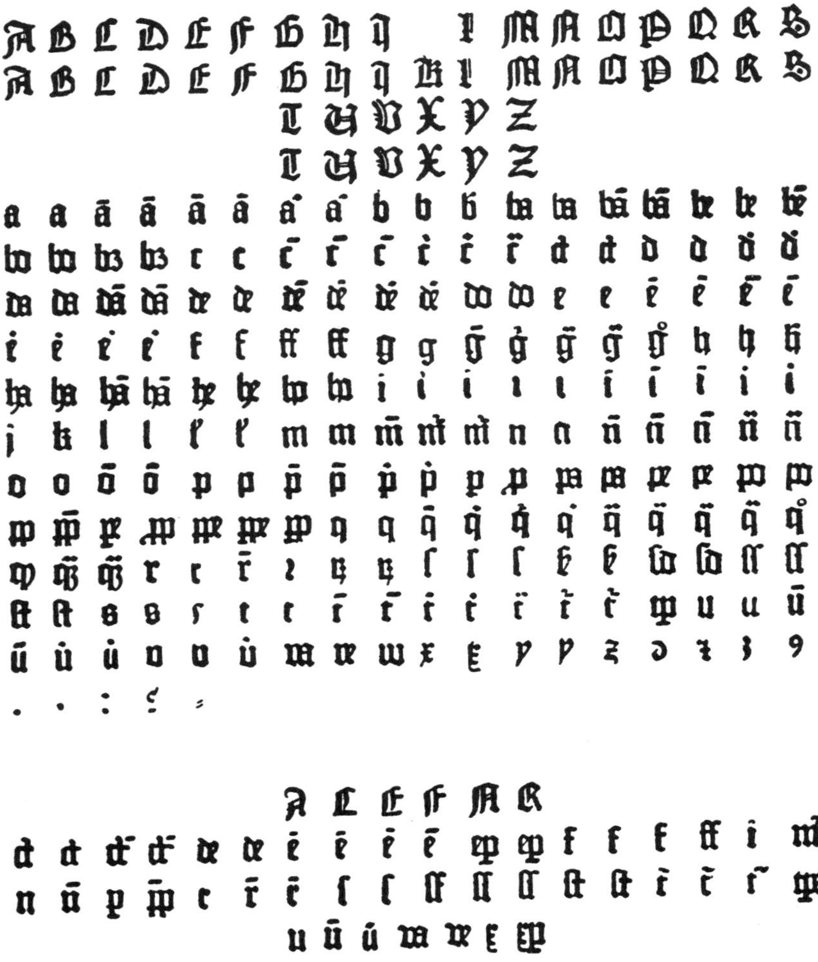

Gutenberg's font of letters for the 42-line Gutenberg Bible.

The core of Gutenberg's invention—letterpress printing from individual, movable metal type.